BLACKSTONE LAW LIBRARY

6727
341.242R

BASIC COMMUNITY LAWS

G 2001

D0120859

BPP Law School

000777

BASIC COMMUNITY LAWS

SEVENTH EDITION

edited by

BERNARD RUDDEN FBA

Professor of Comparative Law, University of Oxford,
Fellow of Brasenose College, Oxford

and

DERRICK WYATT QC

Professor of Law, University of Oxford,
Fellow of St Edmund Hall, Oxford

OXFORD
UNIVERSITY PRESS

OXFORD

UNIVERSITY PRESS

Great Clarendon Street, Oxford OX2 6DP

Oxford University Press is a department of the University of Oxford.
It furthers the University's objective of excellence in research, scholarship,
and education by publishing worldwide in

Oxford New York

Athens Auckland Bangkok Bogotá Buenos Aires Calcutta
Cape Town Chennai Dar es Salaam Delhi Florence Hong Kong Istanbul
Karachi Kuala Lumpur Madrid Melbourne Mexico City Mumbai
Nairobi Paris São Paulo Singapore Taipei Tokyo Toronto Warsaw

and associated companies in Berlin Ibadan

Oxford is a registered trade mark of Oxford University Press
in the UK and in certain other countries

Published in the United States
by Oxford University Press Inc., New York

© Bernard Rudden and Derrick Wyatt 1999

The moral rights of the author have been asserted
Database right Oxford University Press (maker)

First published 1999

All rights reserved. No part of this publication may be reproduced,
stored in a retrieval system, or transmitted, in any form or by any means,
without the prior permission in writing of Oxford University Press,
or as expressly permitted by law, or under terms agreed with the appropriate
reprographics rights organizations. Enquiries concerning reproduction
outside the scope of the above should be sent to the Rights Department,
Oxford University Press, at the address above

You must not circulate this book in any other binding or cover
and you must impose this same condition on any acquirer

British Library Cataloguing in Publication Data

Data available

Library of Congress Cataloging in Publication Data

Data available

ISBN 0-19-876554-1

1 3 5 7 9 10 8 6 4 2

Typeset by Hope Services (Abingdon) Ltd.
Printed in Great Britain
on acid-free paper by
Bookcraft Ltd.,
Midsomer Norton, Somerset

Preface to the Seventh Edition

Our original aim, some 20 years ago, was to make available at a modest price, and in a convenient format, a handbook of the basic primary and secondary legislative sources of Community law. We tried to be slender. Over the years this ambition has been sorely tested by the dozen or so Treaty amendments, and by the thousands of regulations, directives, and decisions. Our hearts sank on first seeing the 1997 Treaty of Amsterdam with its turgid prose, its thirteen Protocols, and its fifty-odd Declarations.

On closer inspection, however, it emerged that one achievement of this instrument is to provide a consolidated version of the Treaties establishing the European Community and the European Union. This is bad news in that it changes the numbers of many key articles, but good news in so far that it provides a much more streamlined text. It has enabled us to reduce Part I, and we have also taken the opportunity to rethink the material included in Part II. This aims to give the reader access to the main secondary legislation on those fields studied by every Community lawyer: freedom of goods and services, of workers and the self-employed; the concomitant provisions on social policy; competition; consumer protection; and the environment. As before, Part III contains the key United Kingdom provisions necessitated by membership of the European Union.

BR
DW
Oxford
1 May 1999

Contents

PART III. UNITED KINGDOM SOURCES

Significant Dates and Developments

This table aims to give a swift, if superficial, overview, without detail or punctilious dating. References to 1E, 2E etc. indicate where relevant documents will be found in those earlier editions of this work.

1945 End of War in Europe

1949 Council of Europe created with consultative Assembly, and Committee of Ministers. UK joins.

1950 Declaration of Robert Schuman (French Foreign Minister): Franco–German coal and steel to be under a common 'higher authority'.

1952 ECSC established by Treaty of Paris, signed by the Six: France, Germany, Italy, Belgium, Netherlands, Luxembourg. Has Assembly, High Authority, Council, and Court. UK declines to join.

1953 Council of Europe's European Convention on Human Rights (ECHR) comes into force, with Commission on Human Rights.

1954 The Six fail to set up a European Defence Community.

1955 Intergovernmental Conference of the Six to prepare for the EEC. UK sends observers but declines to participate.

1958 EEC and Euratom Treaties come into force (signed 25/3/57). They share Assembly ('Parliament') and Court with ECSC.

1959 European Court of Human Rights (established under 1950 ECHR) comes into operation.

1960 European Free Trade Area (EFTA) set up.

1961 Negotiations begin on UK membership of EC.

1962 Start of Common Agricultural Policy.

1963 UK's application to EC fails.

1964 First Yaoundé Convention associates 17 African States with EEC.

1965 Merger Treaty: ECSC and EEC share High Authority/Commission and Council (1E/111).
  Deadlock on CAP and majority voting. France boycotts Council.

1966 Luxembourg Accords break political deadlock (1E/71, 2E/79).

1967 UK, Ireland, Denmark, Norway apply for membership of EC.

1970 Council Decision on Own Resources (1E/120).

1971 Start of Common Fisheries Policy.
  Second Yaoundé Convention in force.

1972 UK, Ireland, Denmark, Norway sign Accession Treaty. Norway (by referendum) rejects ratification.

1973 UK, Ireland, Denmark members of EC (2E/153).
  Judgments Convention in force for Six.

1974 EC gains observer status at UNO.

1975 Budget Treaty. Joint Declaration on Conciliation Procedure (1E/124, 2E/131).

UK referendum on continued membership.

1976 First Lomé Convention (EEC and 46 African, Caribbean, Pacific countries). Direct Elections decision (1E/126, 2E/133).

1977 Fishery limits extended to 200 miles.

Joint Declaration on Fundamental Rights (1E/131, 2E/138, 3E/158)

1978 European Monetary System (EMS) and exchange rate mechanism (ERM) set up by Council Resolution.

1979 First Direct Elections to EC Parliament.

1981 Greece joins EC (2E/163).

Second Lomé Convention in force.

1984 Second direct elections to European Parliament.

1985 Greenland leaves EC, remains associated territory (2E/172). Second Council Decision on Own Resources (2E/142).

1986 Spain and Portugal join EC (2E/175).

Third Lomé Convention in force.

1987 Single European Act in force (2E/147).

Turkey applies to join EC.

1988 EC Court of First Instance established.

1989 Third direct elections to European Parliament.

Austria applies to join EC.

1990 Germany united. UK joins ERM.

Fourth Lomé Convention in force.

Cyprus and Malta apply to join EC.

1991 Intergovernmental Conferences on Economic and Monetary Union and on Political Union: Maastricht accords.

Agreement on European Economic Area signed by EEC and EFTA ; ECJ holds it incompatible with community law.

Rome Convention (1980) on the law applicable to contractual obligations enters into force.

Soviet Union dies. Sweden applies to join EC.

1992 TEU signed. Denmark (by June referendum) rejects ratification; European Council December Decision on Denmark. Finland and Switzerland apply to join EC. Amended Agreement on European Economic Area signed by EEC and EFTA (Austria, Finland, Iceland, Liechtenstein, Norway, Sweden, Switzerland); ECJ holds it compatible with community law; Switzerland (by December referendum) rejects accession. UK and Italy leave ERM..

1993 Deadline for internal market. Second Danish referendum approves TEU ratification. TEU then enters into force on 1 November. European Economic Area Agreement (amended to exclude Switzerland) enters into force.

1994 Second stage for achieving economic and monetary union began on 1 January. Third Own Resources Decision. Fourth direct elections to European Parliament. EMI established. Parliament appoints Ombudsman (6E/260).

1996 Austria, Finland, and Sweden accede to EC and EU.

1997 Treaty of Amsterdam signed by the 15 Member States.

1999 Monetary union for all MS except Denmark, Greece, Sweden, UK. On 15 March, the entire Commission resigns (but continues in post until replaced). On 1 May, Treaty of Amsterdam enters into force. Fifth direct elections to European Parliament.

2002 On 1 July, national currencies of EMU MS to cease as legal tender. On 23 July, ECSC Treaty expires.

200? Czech Republic, Cyprus, Estonia, Hungary, Poland, Slovenia may accede to EU.

Old and New Treaty Numbers

Tables of Equivalences referred to in Article 12 of the Treaty of Amsterdam

A. TREATY ON EUROPEAN UNION

Previous numbering	New numbering	Previous numbering	New numbering
Title I	Title I	Article J.16	Article 26
Article A	Article 1	Article J.17	Article 27
Article B	Article 2	Article J.18	Article 28
Article C	Article 3		
Article D	Article 4	Title VI(b)	Title VI
Article E	Article 5	Article K.1	Article 29
Article F	Article 6	Article K.2	Article 30
Article F.1(a)	Article 7	Article K.3	Article 31
		Article K.4	Article 32
Title II	Title II	Article K.5	Article 33
Article G	Article 8	Article K.6	Article 34
		Article K.7	Article 35
Title III	Title III	Article K.8	Article 36
Article H	Article 9	Article K.9	Article 37
		Article K.10	Article 38
Title IV	Title IV	Article K.11	Article 39
Article I	Article 10	Article K.12	Article 40
		Article K.13	Article 41
Title V(b)	Title V	Article K.14	Article 42
Article J.1	Article 11		
Article J.2	Article 12	Title VIa(c)	Title VII
Article J.3	Article 13	Article K.15(a)	Article 43
Article J.4	Article 14	Article K.16(a)	Article 44
Article J.5	Article 15	Article K.17(a)	Article 45
Article J.6	Article 16		
Article J.7	Article 17	Title VII	Title VIII
Article J.8	Article 18	Article L	Article 46
Article J.9	Article 19	Article M	Article 47
Article J.10	Article 20	Article N	Article 48
Article J.11	Article 21	Article O	Article 49
Article J.12	Article 22	Article P	Article 50
Article J.13	Article 23	Article Q	Article 51
Article J.14	Article 24	Article R	Article 52
Article J.15	Article 25	Article S	Article 53

(a) New Article introduced by the Treaty of Amsterdam.
(b) Title restructured by the Treaty of Amsterdam.
(c) New Title introduced by the Treaty of Amsterdam.
(d) Chapter 1 restructured by the Treaty of Amsterdam.

B. Treaty Establishing the European Community

Previous numbering	New numbering	Previous numbering	New numbering
Part One	*Part One*	Article 21 (repealed)	—
Article 1	Article 1	Article 22 (repealed)	—
Article 2	Article 2	Article 23 (repealed)	—
Article 3	Article 3	Article 24 (repealed)	—
Article 3a	Article 4	Article 25 (repealed)	—
Article 3b	Article 5	Article 26 (repealed)	—
Article 3c[(a)]	Article 6	Article 27 (repealed)	—
Article 4	Article 7	Article 28	Article 26
Article 4a	Article 8	Article 29	Article 27
Article 4b	Article 9		
Article 5	Article 10	*Chapter 2*	*Chapter 2*
Article 5a[(a)]	Article 11	Article 30	Article 28
Article 6	Article 12	Article 31 (repealed)	—
Article 6a[(a)]	Article 13	Article 32 (repealed)	—
Article 7 (repealed)	—	Article 33 (repealed)	—
Article 7a	Article 14	Article 34	Article 29
Article 7b (repealed)	—	Article 35 (repealed)	—
Article 7c	Article 15	Article 36	Article 30
Article 7d[(a)]	Article 16	Article 37	Article 31
Part Two	*Part Two*	*Title II*	*Title II*
Article 8	Article 17	Article 38	Article 32
Article 8a	Article 18	Article 39	Article 33
Article 8b	Article 19	Article 40	Article 34
Article 8c	Article 20	Article 41	Article 35
Article 8d	Article 21	Article 42	Article 36
Article 8e	Article 22	Article 43	Article 37
		Article 44 (repealed)	—
Part Three	*Part Three*	Article 45 (repealed)	—
Title I	*Title I*	Article 46	Article 38
Article 9	Article 23	Article 47 (repealed)	—
Article 10	Article 24		
Article 11 (repealed)	—	*Title III*	*Title III*
		Chapter 1	*Chapter 1*
Chapter 1	*Chapter 1*	Article 48	Article 39
Section 1 (deleted)	—	Article 49	Article 40
Article 12	Article 25	Article 50	Article 41
Article 13 (repealed)	—	Article 51	Article 42
Article 14 (repealed)	—		
Article 15 (repealed)	—	*Chapter 2*	*Chapter 2*
Article 16 (repealed)	—	Article 52	Article 43
Article 17 (repealed)	—	Article 53 (repealed)	—
		Article 54	Article 44
Section 2 (*deleted*)	—	Article 55	Article 45
Article 18 (repealed)	—	Article 56	Article 46
Article 19 (repealed)	—	Article 57	Article 47
Article 20 (repealed)	—	Article 58	Article 48

Previous numbering	New numbering	Previous numbering	New numbering
Chapter 3	*Chapter 3*	Article 84	Article 80
Article 59	Article 49	*Title V*	*Title VI*
Article 60	Article 50	*Chapter 1*	*Chapter 1*
Article 61	Article 52	*Section 1*	*Section 1*
Article 62 (repealed)	—	Article 85	Article 81
Article 63	Article 52	Article 86	Article 82
Article 64	Article 53	Article 87	Article 83
Article 65	Article 54	Article 88	Article 84
Article 66	Article 55	Article 89	Article 85
Chapter 4	*Chapter 4*	Article 90	Article 86
Article 67 (repealed)	—	*Section 2 (deleted)*	—
Article 68 (repealed)	—	Article 91 (repealed)	—
Article 69 (repealed)	—	*Section 3*	*Section 2*
Article 70 (repealed)	—	Article 92	Article 87
Article 71 (repealed)	—	Article 93	Article 88
Article 72 (repealed)	—	Article 94	Article 89
Article 73 (repealed)	—	*Chapter 2*	*Chapter 2*
Article 73a (repealed)	—	Article 95	Article 90
Article 73b	Article 56	Article 96	Article 91
Article 73c	Article 57	Article 97 (repealed)	—
Article 73d	Article 58	Article 98	Article 92
Article 73e (repealed)	—	Article 99	Article 93
Article 73f	Article 59	*Chapter 3*	*Chapter 3*
Article 73g	Article 60	Article 100	Article 94
Article 73h (repealed)	—	Article 100a	Article 95
Title IIIa[c]	*Title IV*	Article 100b (repealed)	—
Article 73i[a]	Article 61	Article 100c (repealed)	—
Article 73j[a]	Article 62	Article 100d (repealed)	—
Article 73k[a]	Article 63	Article 101	Article 96
Article 73l[a]	Article 64	Article 102	Article 97
Article 73m[a]	Article 65	*Title VI*	*Title VII*
Article 73n[a]	Article 66	*Chapter 1*	*Chapter 1*
Article 73o[a]	Article 67	Article 102a	Article 98
Article 73p[a]	Article 68	Article 103	Article 99
Article 73q[a]	Article 69	Article 103a	Article 100
Title IV	*Title V*	Article 104	Article 101
Article 74	Article 70	Article 104a	Article 102
Article 75	Article 71	Article 104b	Article 103
Article 76	Article 72	Article 104c	Article 104
Article 77	Article 73	*Chapter 2*	*Chapter 2*
Article 78	Article 74	Article 105	Article 105
Article 79	Article 75	Article 105a	Article 106
Article 80	Article 76	Article 106	Article 107
Article 81	Article 77		
Article 82	Article 78		
Article 83	Article 79		

Previous numbering	New numbering	Previous numbering	New numbering
Article 107	Article 108	Article 119a	Article 142
Article 108	Article 109	Article 120	Article 143
Article 108a	Article 110	Article 121	Article 144
Article 109	Article 111	Article 122	Article 145
Chapter 3	*Chapter 3*	*Chapter 2*	*Chapter 2*
Article 109a	Article 112	Article 123	Article 146
Article 109a	Article 113	Article 124	Article 147
Article 109c	Article 114	Article 125	Article 148
Article 109d	Article 115	*Chapter 3*	*Chapter 3*
Chapter 4	*Chapter 4*	Article 126	Article 149
Article 109e	Article 116	Article 127	Article 150
Article 109f	Article 117	*Title IX*	*Title XII*
Article 109g	Article 118	Article 128	Article 151
Article 109h	Article 119		
Article 109i	Article 120	*Title X*	*Title XIII*
Article 109j	Article 121	Article 129	Article 152
Article 109k	Article 122	*Title XI*	*Title XIV*
Article 109l	Article 123	Article 129a	Article 153
Article 109m	Article 124		
Title VIa[c]	*Title VIII*	*Title XII*	*Title XV*
Article 109n[a]	Article 125	Article 129b	Article 154
Article 109o[a]	Article 126	Article 129c	Article 155
Article 109p[a]	Article 127	Article 129d	Article 156
Article 109q[a]	Article 128	*Title XIII*	*Title XVI*
Article 109r[a]	Article 129	Article 130	Article 157
Article 109s[a]	Article 130		
Title VII	*Title IX*	*Title XIV*	*Title XVII*
Article 110	Article 131	Article 130a	Article 158
Article 111 (repealed)	—	Article 130b	Article 159
Article 112	Article 132	Article 130c	Article 160
Article 113	Article 133	Article 130d	Article 161
Article 114 (repealed)	—	Article 130e	Article 162
Article 115	Article 134		
Title VIIa[c]	*Title X*	*Title XV*	*Title XVIII*
Article 116[a]	Article 135	Article 130f	Article 163
Title VIII	*Title XI*	Article 130g	Article 164
Chapter 1[d]	*Chapter 1*	Article 130h	Article 165
Article 117	Article 136	Article 130i	Article 166
Article 118	Article 137	Article 130j	Article 167
Article 118a	Article 138	Article 130k	Article 168
Article 118b	Article 139	Article 130l	Article 169
Article 118c	Article 140	Article 130m	Article 170
Article 119	Article 141	Article 130n	Article 171
		Article 130o	Article 172
		Article 130p	Article 173

Previous numbering	New numbering	Previous numbering	New numbering
Article 130q (repealed)	—	Article 151	Article 207
		Article 152	Article 208
Title XVI	*Title XIX*	Article 153	Article 209
Article 130r	Article 174	Article 154	Article 210
Article 130s	Article 175		
Article 130t	Article 176	*Section 3*	*Section 3*
		Article 155	Article 211
Title XVII	*Title XX*	Article 156	Article 212
Article 130u	Article 177	Article 157	Article 213
Article 130v	Article 178	Article 158	Article 214
Article 130w	Article 179	Article 159	Article 215
Article 130x	Article 180	Article 160	Article 216
Article 130y	Article 181	Article 161	Article 217
		Article 162	Article 218
Part Four	*Part Four*	Article 163	Article 219
Article 131	Article 182		
Article 132	Article 183	*Section 4*	*Section 4*
Article 133	Article 184	Article 164	Article 220
Article 134	Article 185	Article 165	Article 221
Article 135	Article 186	Article 166	Article 222
Article 136	Article 187	Article 167	Article 223
Article 136a	Article 188	Article 168	Article 224
		Article 168a	Article 225
Part Five	*Part Five*	Article 169	Article 226
Title I	*Title I*	Article 170	Article 227
Chapter 1	*Chapter 1*	Article 171	Article 228
Section 1	*Section 1*	Article 172	Article 229
Article 137	Article 189	Article 173	Article 230
Article 138	Article 190	Article 174	Article 231
Article 138a	Article 191	Article 175	Article 232
Article 138b	Article 192	Article 176	Article 233
Article 138c	Article 193	Article 177	Article 234
Article 138d	Article 194	Article 178	Article 235
Article 138e	Article 195	Article 179	Article 236
Article 139	Article 196	Article 180	Article 237
Article 140	Article 197	Article 181	Article 238
Article 141	Article 198	Article 182	Article 239
Article 142	Article 199	Article 183	Article 240
Article 143	Article 200	Article 184	Article 241
Article 144	Article 201	Article 185	Article 242
		Article 186	Article 243
Section 2	*Section 2*	Article 187	Article 244
Article 145	Article 202	Article 188	Article 245
Article 146	Article 203		
Article 147	Article 204	*Section 5*	*Section 5*
Article 148	Article 205	Article 188a	Article 246
Article 149 (repealed)	—	Article 188b	Article 247
Article 150	Article 206	Article 188c	Article 248

Previous numbering	New numbering	Previous numbering	New numbering
Chapter 2	*Chapter 2*	*Part Six*	*Part Six*
Article 189	Article 249	Article 210	Article 281
Article 189a	Article 250	Article 211	Article 282
Article 189b	Article 251	Article 212[a]	Article 283
Article 189c	Article 252	Article 213	Article 284
Article 190	Article 253	Article 213a[a]	Article 285
Article 191	Article 254	Article 213b[a]	Article 286
Article 191a[a]	Article 255	Article 214	Article 287
Article 192	Article 256	Article 215	Article 288
		Article 216	Article 289
Chapter 3	*Chapter 3*	Article 217	Article 290
Article 193	Article 257	Article 218[a]	Article 291
Article 194	Article 258	Article 219	Article 292
Article 195	Article 259	Article 220	Article 293
Article 196	Article 260	Article 221	Article 294
Article 197	Article 261	Article 222	Article 295
Article 198	Article 262	Article 223	Article 296
		Article 224	Article 297
Chapter 4	*Chapter 4*	Article 225	Article 298
Article 198a	Article 263	Article 226 (repealed)	—
Article 198b	Article 264	Article 227	Article 299
Article 198c	Article 265	Article 228	Article 300
		Article 228a	Article 301
Chapter 5	*Chapter 5*	Article 229	Article 302
Article 198d	Article 266	Article 230	Article 303
Article 198e	Article 267	Article 231	Article 304
		Article 232	Article 305
Title II	*Title II*	Article 233	Article 306
Article 199	Article 268	Article 234	Article 307
Article 200 (repealed)	—	Article 235	Article 308
Article 201	Article 269	Article 236[a]	Article 309
Article 201a	Article 270	Article 237 (repealed)	—
Article 202	Article 271	Article 238	Article 310
Article 203	Article 272	Article 239	Article 311
Article 204	Article 273	Article 240	Article 312
Article 205	Article 274	Article 241 (repealed)	—
Article 205a	Article 275	Article 242 (repealed)	—
Article 206	Article 276	Article 243 (repealed)	—
Article 206a (repealed)	—	Article 244 (repealed)	—
Article 207	Article 277	Article 245 (repealed)	—
Article 208	Article 278	Article 246 (repealed)	—
Article 209	Article 279		
Article 209a	Article 280	*Final Provisions*	*Final Provisions*
		Article 247	Article 313
		Article 248	Article 314

PART I

THE TREATIES AND RELATED ACTS

Treaties

Treaty Establishing the European Community
(Consolidated Version)

HIS MAJESTY THE KING OF THE BELGIANS, THE PRESIDENT OF THE FEDERAL REPUBLIC OF GERMANY, THE PRESIDENT OF THE FRENCH REPUBLIC, THE PRESIDENT OF THE ITALIAN REPUBLIC, HER ROYAL HIGHNESS THE GRAND DUCHESS OF LUXEMBOURG, HER MAJESTY THE QUEEN OF THE NETHERLANDS,[1]

DETERMINED to lay the foundations of an ever closer union among the peoples of Europe,

RESOLVED to ensure the economic and social progress of their countries by common action to eliminate the barriers which divide Europe,

AFFIRMING as the essential objective of their efforts the constant improvements of the living and working conditions of their peoples,

RECOGNISING that the removal of existing obstacles calls for concerted action in order to guarantee steady expansion, balanced trade and fair competition,

ANXIOUS to strengthen the unity of their economies and to ensure their harmonious development by reducing the differences existing between the various regions and the backwardness of the less-favoured regions,

DESIRING to contribute, by means of a common commercial policy, to the progressive abolition of restrictions on international trade,

INTENDING to confirm the solidarity which binds Europe and the overseas countries and desiring to ensure the development of their prosperity, in accordance with the principles of the Charter of the United Nations,

RESOLVED by thus pooling their resources to preserve and strengthen peace and liberty, and calling upon the other peoples of Europe who share their ideal to join in their efforts,

DETERMINED to promote the development of the highest possible level of knowledge for their peoples through a wide access to education and through its continuous updating,

HAVE DECIDED to create a EUROPEAN COMMUNITY and to this end have designated as their Plenipotentiaries:

His Majesty the King of the Belgians: Mr Paul Henri SPAAK, Minister for Foreign Affairs, Baron J. Ch. Snoy et d'Oppuers, Secretary-General of the Ministry of Economic Affairs, Head of the Belgian Delegation to the Intergovernmental Conference;

The President of the Federal Republic of Germany: Dr. Konrad Adenauer, Federal Chancellor, Professor Dr. Walter Hallstein, State Secretary of the Federal Foreign Office;

---

[1] The Kingdom of Denmark, the Hellenic Republic, the Kingdom of Spain, Ireland, the Republic of Austria, the Portuguese Republic, the Republic of Finland, the Kingdom of Sweden and the United Kingdom of Great Britain and Northern Ireland have since become members of the European Community.

The President of the French Republic: Mr Christian Pineau, Minister for Foreign Affairs, Mr Maurice Faure, Under-Secretary of State for Foreign Affairs;

The President of the Italian Republic: Mr Antonio Segni, President of the Council of Ministers, Professor Gaetano Martino, Minister for Foreign Affairs;

Her Royal Highness the Grand Duchess of Luxembourg: Mr Joseph Bech, President of the Government, Minister for Foreign Affairs, Mr Lambert Schaus, Ambassador, Head of the Luxembourg Delegation to the Intergovernmental Conference;

Her Majesty the Queen of the Netherlands: Mr Joseph Luns, Minister for Foreign Affairs, Mr J. Linthorst Homan, Head of the Netherlands Delegation to the Intergovernmental Conference;

WHO, having exchanged their full powers, found in good and due form, have agreed as follows.

PART ONE: PRINCIPLES

Article 1 (ex Article 1)   By this Treaty, the HIGH CONTRACTING PARTIES establish among themselves a EUROPEAN COMMUNITY.

Article 2 (ex Article 2)   The Community shall have as its task, by establishing a common market and an economic and monetary union and by implementing common policies or activities referred to in Articles 3 and 4, to promote throughout the Community a harmonious, balanced and sustainable development of economic activities, a high level of employment and of social protection, equality between men and women, sustainable and non-inflationary growth, a high degree of competitiveness and convergence of economic performance, a high level of protection and improvement of the quality of the environment, the raising of the standard of living and quality of life, and economic and social cohesion and solidarity among Member States.

Article 3 (ex Article 3)   1. For the purposes set out in Article 2, the activities of the Community shall include, as provided in this Treaty and in accordance with the timetable set out therein:
 (a) the prohibition, as between Member States, of customs duties and quantitative restrictions on the import and export of goods, and of all other measures having equivalent effect;
 (b) a common commercial policy;
 (c) an internal market characterised by the abolition, as between Member States, of obstacles to the free movement of goods, persons, services and capital;
 (d) measures concerning the entry and movement of persons as provided for in Title IV;
 (e) a common policy in the sphere of agriculture and fisheries;
 (f) a common policy in the sphere of transport;
 (g) a system ensuring that competition in the internal market is not distorted;
 (h) the approximation of the laws of Member States to the extent required for the functioning of the common market;
 (i) the promotion of coordination between employment policies of the Member States with a view to enhancing their effectiveness by developing a coordinated strategy for employment;

(j) a policy in the social sphere comprising a European Social Fund;
(k) the strengthening of economic and social cohesion;
(l) a policy in the sphere of the environment;
(m) the strengthening of the competitiveness of Community industry;
(n) the promotion of research and technological development;
(o) encouragement for the establishment and development of trans-European networks;
(p) a contribution to the attainment of a high level of health protection;
(q) a contribution to education and training of quality and to the flowering of the cultures of the Member States;
(r) a policy in the sphere of development cooperation;
(s) the association of the overseas countries and territories in order to increase trade and promote jointly economic and social development;
(t) a contribution to the strengthening of consumer protection;
(u) measures in the spheres of energy, civil protection and tourism.

2. In all the activities referred to in this Article, the Community shall aim to eliminate inequalities, and to promote equality, between men and women.

Article 4 (ex Article 3a)   1. For the purposes set out in Article 2, the activities of the Member States and the Community shall include, as provided in this Treaty and in accordance with the timetable set out therein, the adoption of an economic policy which is based on the close coordination of Member States' economic policies, on the internal market and on the definition of common objectives, and conducted in accordance with the principle of an open market economy with free competition.

2. Concurrently with the foregoing, and as provided in this Treaty and in accordance with the timetable and the procedures set out therein, these activities shall include the irrevocable fixing of exchange rates leading to the introduction of a single currency, the ECU, and the definition and conduct of a single monetary policy and exchange-rate policy the primary objective of both of which shall be to maintain price stability and, without prejudice to this objective, to support the general economic policies in the Community, in accordance with the principle of an open market economy with free competition.

3. These activities of the Member States and the Community shall entail compliance with the following guiding principles: stable prices, sound public finances and monetary conditions and a sustainable balance of payments.

Article 5 (ex Article 3b)   The Community shall act within the limits of the powers conferred upon it by this Treaty and of the objectives assigned to it therein.
   In areas which do not fall within its exclusive competence, the Community shall take action, in accordance with the principle of subsidiarity, only if and insofar as the objectives of the proposed action cannot be sufficiently achieved by the Member States and can therefore, by reason of the scale or effects of the proposed action, be better achieved by the Community.
   Any action by the Community shall not go beyond what is necessary to achieve the objectives of this Treaty.

Article 6 (ex Article 3c)   Environmental protection requirements must be integrated into the definition and implementation of the Community policies and activities referred to in Article 3, in particular with a view to promoting sustainable development.

Article 7 (ex Article 4)   1. The tasks entrusted to the Community shall be carried out by the following institutions:

— a EUROPEAN PARLIAMENT,
— a COUNCIL,
— a COMMISSION,
— a COURT OF JUSTICE,
— a COURT OF AUDITORS.

Each institution shall act within the limits of the powers conferred upon it by this Treaty.

2. The Council and the Commission shall be assisted by an Economic and Social Committee and a Committee of the Regions acting in an advisory capacity.

Article 8 (ex Article 4a)   A European System of Central Banks (hereinafter referred to as 'ESCB') and a European Central Bank (hereinafter referred to as 'ECB') shall be established in accordance with the procedures laid down in this Treaty; they shall act within the limits of the powers conferred upon them by this Treaty and by the Statute of the ESCB and of the ECB (hereinafter referred to as 'Statute of the ESCB') annexed thereto.

Article 9 (ex Article 4b)   A European Investment Bank is hereby established, which shall act within the limits of the powers conferred upon it by this Treaty and the Statute annexed thereto.

Article 10 (ex Article 5)   Member States shall take all appropriate measures, whether general or particular, to ensure fulfilment of the obligations arising out of this Treaty or resulting from action taken by the institutions of the Community. They shall facilitate the achievement of the Community's tasks.

They shall abstain from any measure which could jeopardise the attainment of the objectives of this Treaty.

Article 11 (ex Article 5a)   1. Member States which intend to establish closer cooperation between themselves may be authorised, subject to Articles 43 and 44 of the Treaty on European Union, to make use of the institutions, procedures and mechanisms laid down by this Treaty, provided that the cooperation proposed:

(a) does not concern areas which fall within the exclusive competence of the Community;
(b) does not affect Community policies, actions or programmes;
(c) does not concern the citizenship of the Union or discriminate between nationals of Member States;
(d) remains within the limits of the powers conferred upon the Community by this Treaty; and
(e) does not constitute a discrimination or a restriction of trade between Member States and does not distort the conditions of competition between the latter.

2. The authorisation referred to in paragraph 1 shall be granted by the Council, acting by a qualified majority on a proposal from the Commission and after consulting the European Parliament.

If a member of the Council declares that, for important and stated reasons of national policy, it intends to oppose the granting of an authorisation by qualified majority, a vote shall not be taken. The Council may, acting by a qualified majority, request that the matter be referred to the Council, meeting in the composition of the Heads of State or Government, for decision by unanimity.

Member States which intend to establish closer cooperation as referred to in paragraph 1 may address a request to the Commission, which may submit a proposal to the Council to that effect. In the event of the Commission not submitting a proposal, it shall inform the Member States concerned of the reasons for not doing so.

3. Any Member State which wishes to become a party to cooperation set up in accordance with this Article shall notify its intention to the Council and to the Commission, which shall give an opinion to the Council within three months of receipt of that notification. Within four months of the date of that notification, the Commission shall decide on it and on such specific arrangements as it may deem necessary.

4. The acts and decisions necessary for the implementation of cooperation activities shall be subject to all the relevant provisions of this Treaty, save as otherwise provided for in this Article and in Articles 43 and 44 of the Treaty on European Union.

5. This Article is without prejudice to the provisions of the Protocol integrating the Schengen acquis into the framework of the European Union.

Article 12 (ex Article 6) Within the scope of application of this Treaty, and without prejudice to any special provisions contained therein, any discrimination on grounds of nationality shall be prohibited.

The Council, acting in accordance with the procedure referred to in Article 251, may adopt rules designed to prohibit such discrimination.

Article 13 (ex Article 6a) Without prejudice to the other provisions of this Treaty and within the limits of the powers conferred by it upon the Community, the Council, acting unanimously on a proposal from the Commission and after consulting the European Parliament, may take appropriate action to combat discrimination based on sex, racial or ethnic origin, religion or belief, disability, age or sexual orientation.

Article 14 (ex Article 7a) 1. The Community shall adopt measures with the aim of progressively establishing the internal market over a period expiring on 31 December 1992, in accordance with the provisions of this Article and of Articles 15, 26, 47(2), 49, 80, 93 and 95 and without prejudice to the other provisions of this Treaty.

2. The internal market shall comprise an area without internal frontiers in which the free movement of goods, persons, services and capital is ensured in accordance with the provisions of this Treaty.

3. The Council, acting by a qualified majority on a proposal from the Commission, shall determine the guidelines and conditions necessary to ensure balanced progress in all the sectors concerned.

Article 15 (ex Article 7c) When drawing up its proposals with a view to achieving the objectives set out in Article 14, the Commission shall take into account the extent of the effort that certain economies showing differences in development will have to sustain during the period of establishment of the internal market and it may propose appropriate provisions.

If these provisions take the form of derogations, they must be of a temporary nature and must cause the least possible disturbance to the functioning of the common market.

Article 16 (ex Article 7d)   Without prejudice to Articles 73, 86 and 87, and given the place occupied by services of general economic interest in the shared values of the Union as well as their role in promoting social and territorial cohesion, the Community and the Member States, each within their respective powers and within the scope of application of this Treaty, shall take care that such services operate on the basis of principles and conditions which enable them to fulfil their missions.

PART TWO: CITIZENSHIP OF THE UNION

Article 17 (ex Article 8)   1. Citizenship of the Union is hereby established. Every person holding the nationality of a Member State shall be a citizen of the Union. Citizenship of the Union shall complement and not replace national citizenship.

2. Citizens of the Union shall enjoy the rights conferred by this Treaty and shall be subject to the duties imposed thereby.

Article 18 (ex Article 8a)   1. Every citizen of the Union shall have the right to move and reside freely within the territory of the Member States, subject to the limitations and conditions laid down in this Treaty and by the measures adopted to give it effect.

2. The Council may adopt provisions with a view to facilitating the exercise of the rights referred to in paragraph 1; save as otherwise provided in this Treaty, the Council shall act in accordance with the procedure referred to in Article 251. The Council shall act unanimously throughout this procedure.

Article 19 (ex Article 8b)   1. Every citizen of the Union residing in a Member State of which he is not a national shall have the right to vote and to stand as a candidate at municipal elections in the Member State in which he resides, under the same conditions as nationals of that State. This right shall be exercised subject to detailed arrangements adopted by the Council, acting unanimously on a proposal from the Commission and after consulting the European Parliament; these arrangements may provide for derogations where warranted by problems specific to a Member State.

2. Without prejudice to Article 190(4) and to the provisions adopted for its implementation, every citizen of the Union residing in a Member State of which he is not a national shall have the right to vote and to stand as a candidate in elections to the European Parliament in the Member State in which he resides, under the same conditions as nationals of that State. This right shall be exercised subject to detailed arrangements adopted by the Council, acting unanimously on a proposal from the Commission and after consulting the European Parliament; these arrangements may provide for derogations where warranted by problems specific to a Member State.

Article 20 (ex Article 8c)   Every citizen of the Union shall, in the territory of a third country in which the Member State of which he is a national is not represented, be entitled to protection by the diplomatic or consular authorities of any Member State, on the same conditions as the nationals of that State. Member States shall establish the necessary rules among themselves and start the international negotiations required to secure this protection.

Article 21 (ex Article 8d)   Every citizen of the Union shall have the right to petition the European Parliament in accordance with Article 194.

Every citizen of the Union may apply to the Ombudsman established in accordance with Article 195.

Every citizen of the Union may write to any of the institutions or bodies referred to in this Article or in Article 7 in one of the languages mentioned in Article 314 and have an answer in the same language.

Article 22 (ex Article 8e)   The Commission shall report to the European Parliament, to the Council and to the Economic and Social Committee every three years on the application of the provisions of this Part. This report shall take account of the development of the Union.

On this basis, and without prejudice to the other provisions of this Treaty, the Council, acting unanimously on a proposal from the Commission and after consulting the European Parliament, may adopt provisions to strengthen or to add to the rights laid down in this Part, which it shall recommend to the Member States for adoption in accordance with their respective constitutional requirements.

PART THREE: COMMUNITY POLICIES

TITLE I. FREE MOVEMENT OF GOODS

Article 23 (ex Article 9)   1. The Community shall be based upon a customs union which shall cover all trade in goods and which shall involve the prohibition between Member States of customs duties on imports and exports and of all charges having equivalent effect, and the adoption of a common customs tariff in their relations with third countries.

2. The provisions of Article 25 and of Chapter 2 of this Title shall apply to products originating in Member States and to products coming from third countries which are in free circulation in Member States.

Article 24 (ex Article 10)   Products coming from a third country shall be considered to be in free circulation in a Member State if the import formalities have been complied with and any customs duties or charges having equivalent effect which are payable have been levied in that Member State, and if they have not benefited from a total or partial drawback of such duties or charges.

Chapter 1: The Customs Union

Article 25 (ex Article 12)   Customs duties on imports and exports and charges having equivalent effect shall be prohibited between Member States. This prohibition shall also apply to customs duties of a fiscal nature.

Article 26 (ex Article 28) Common Customs Tariff duties shall be fixed by the Council acting by a qualified majority on a proposal from the Commission.

Article 27 (ex Article 29) In carrying out the tasks entrusted to it under this Chapter the Commission shall be guided by:
(a) the need to promote trade between Member States and third countries;
(b) developments in conditions of competition within the Community insofar as they lead to an improvement in the competitive capacity of undertakings;
(c) the requirements of the Community as regards the supply of raw materials and semi-finished goods; in this connection the Commission shall take care to avoid distorting conditions of competition between Member States in respect of finished goods;
(d) the need to avoid serious disturbances in the economies of Member States and to ensure rational development of production and an expansion of consumption within the Community.

Chapter 2: Prohibition of Quantitative Restrictions between Member States

Article 28 (ex Article 30) Quantitative restrictions on imports and all measures having equivalent effect shall be prohibited between Member States.

Article 29 (ex Article 34) Quantitative restrictions on exports, and all measures having equivalent effect, shall be prohibited between Member States.

Article 30 (ex Article 36) The provisions of Articles 28 and 29 shall not preclude prohibitions or restrictions on imports, exports or goods in transit justified on grounds of public morality, public policy or public security; the protection of health and life of humans, animals or plants; the protection of national treasures possessing artistic, historic or archaeological value; or the protection of industrial and commercial property. Such prohibitions or restrictions shall not, however, constitute a means of arbitrary discrimination or a disguised restriction on trade between Member States.

Article 31 (ex Article 37) 1. Member States shall adjust any State monopolies of a commercial character so as to ensure that no discrimination regarding the conditions under which goods are procured and marketed exists between nationals of Member States.
  The provisions of this Article shall apply to any body through which a Member State, in law or in fact, either directly or indirectly supervises, determines or appreciably influences imports or exports between Member States. These provisions shall likewise apply to monopolies delegated by the State to others.

2. Member States shall refrain from introducing any new measure which is contrary to the principles laid down in paragraph 1 or which restricts the scope of the Articles dealing with the prohibition of customs duties and quantitative restrictions between Member States.

3. If a State monopoly of a commercial character has rules which are designed to make it easier to dispose of agricultural products or obtain for them the best return, steps should be taken in applying the rules contained in this Article to ensure equivalent safeguards for the employment and standard of living of the producers concerned.

TITLE II. AGRICULTURE

Article 32 (ex Article 38) 1. The common market shall extend to agriculture and trade in agricultural products. 'Agricultural products' means the products of the soil, of stockfarming and of fisheries and products of first-stage processing directly related to these products.

2. Save as otherwise provided in Articles 33 to 38, the rules laid down for the establishment of the common market shall apply to agricultural products.

3. The products subject to the provisions of Articles 33 to 38 are listed in Annex I to this Treaty.

4. The operation and development of the common market for agricultural products must be accompanied by the establishment of a common agricultural policy.

Article 33 (ex Article 39) 1. The objectives of the common agricultural policy shall be:
(a) to increase agricultural productivity by promoting technical progress and by ensuring the rational development of agricultural production and the optimum utilisation of the factors of production, in particular labour;
(b) thus to ensure a fair standard of living for the agricultural community, in particular by increasing the individual earnings of persons engaged in agriculture;
(c) to stabilise markets;
(d) to assure the availability of supplies;
(e) to ensure that supplies reach consumers at reasonable prices.

2. In working out the common agricultural policy and the special methods for its application, account shall be taken of:
(a) the particular nature of agricultural activity, which results from the social structure of agriculture and from structural and natural disparities between the various agricultural regions;
(b) the need to effect the appropriate adjustments by degrees;
(c) the fact that in the Member States agriculture constitutes a sector closely linked with the economy as a whole.

Article 34 (ex Article 40) 1. In order to attain the objectives set out in Article 33, a common organisation of agricultural markets shall be established.

This organisation shall take one of the following forms, depending on the product concerned:
(a) common rules on competition;
(b) compulsory coordination of the various national market organisations;
(c) a European market organisation.

2. The common organisation established in accordance with paragraph 1 may include all measures required to attain the objectives set out in Article 33, in particular regulation of prices, aids for the production and marketing of the various products, storage and carryover arrangements and common machinery for stabilising imports or exports.

The common organisation shall be limited to pursuit of the objectives set out in Article 33 and shall exclude any discrimination between producers or consumers within the Community.

Any common price policy shall be based on common criteria and uniform methods of calculation.

3. In order to enable the common organisation referred to in paragraph 1 to attain its objectives, one or more agricultural guidance and guarantee funds may be set up.

Article 35 (ex Article 41)   To enable the objectives set out in Article 33 to be attained, provision may be made within the framework of the common agricultural policy for measures such as:
(a) an effective coordination of efforts in the spheres of vocational training, of research and of the dissemination of agricultural knowledge; this may include joint financing of projects or institutions;
(b) joint measures to promote consumption of certain products.

Article 36 (ex Article 42)   The provisions of the Chapter relating to rules on competition shall apply to production of and trade in agricultural products only to the extent determined by the Council within the framework of Article 37(2) and (3) and in accordance with the procedure laid down therein, account being taken of the objectives set out in Article 33.
   The Council may, in particular, authorise the granting of aid:
(a) for the protection of enterprises handicapped by structural or natural conditions;
(b) within the framework of economic development programmes.

Article 37 (ex Article 43)   1. In order to evolve the broad lines of a common agricultural policy, the Commission shall, immediately this Treaty enters into force, convene a conference of the Member States with a view to making a comparison of their agricultural policies, in particular by producing a statement of their resources and needs.

2. Having taken into account the work of the Conference provided for in paragraph 1, after consulting the Economic and Social Committee and within two years of the entry into force of this Treaty, the Commission shall submit proposals for working out and implementing the common agricultural policy, including the replacement of the national organisations by one of the forms of common organisation provided for in Article 34(1), and for implementing the measures specified in this Title.
   These proposals shall take account of the interdependence of the agricultural matters mentioned in this Title.
   The Council shall, on a proposal from the Commission and after consulting the European Parliament, acting by a qualified majority, make regulations, issue directives, or take decisions, without prejudice to any recommendations it may also make.

3. The Council may, acting by a qualified majority and in accordance with paragraph 2, replace the national market organisations by the common organisation provided for in Article 34(1) if:
(a) the common organisation offers Member States which are opposed to this measure and which have an organisation of their own for the production in question equivalent safeguards for the employment and standard of living of the producers concerned, account being taken of the adjustments that will be possible and the specialisation that will be needed with the passage of time;
(b) such an organisation ensures conditions for trade within the Community similar to those existing in a national market.

4. If a common organisation for certain raw materials is established before a common organisation exists for the corresponding processed products, such raw materials as are used for processed products intended for export to third countries may be imported from outside the Community.

Article 38 (ex Article 46) Where in a Member State a product is subject to a national market organisation or to internal rules having equivalent effect which affect the competitive position of similar production in another Member State, a countervailing charge shall be applied by Member States to imports of this product coming from the Member State where such organisation or rules exist, unless that State applies a countervailing charge on export.

The Commission shall fix the amount of these charges at the level required to redress the balance; it may also authorise other measures, the conditions and details of which it shall determine.

TITLE III. FREE MOVEMENT OF PERSONS, SERVICES AND CAPITAL

Chapter 1: Workers

Article 39 (ex Article 48) 1. Freedom of movement for workers shall be secured within the Community.

2. Such freedom of movement shall entail the abolition of any discrimination based on nationality between workers of the Member States as regards employment, remuneration and other conditions of work and employment.

3. It shall entail the right, subject to limitations justified on grounds of public policy, public security or public health:
(a) to accept offers of employment actually made;
(b) to move freely within the territory of Member States for this purpose;
(c) to stay in a Member State for the purpose of employment in accordance with the provisions governing the employment of nationals of that State laid down by law, regulation or administrative action;
(d) to remain in the territory of a Member State after having been employed in that State, subject to conditions which shall be embodied in implementing regulations to be drawn up by the Commission.

4. The provisions of this Article shall not apply to employment in the public service.

Article 40 (ex Article 49) The Council shall, acting in accordance with the procedure referred to in Article 251 and after consulting the Economic and Social Committee, issue directives or make regulations setting out the measures required to bring about freedom of movement for workers, as defined in Article 39, in particular:
(a) by ensuring close cooperation between national employment services;
(b) by abolishing those administrative procedures and practices and those qualifying periods in respect of eligibility for available employment, whether resulting from national legislation or from agreements previously concluded between Member States, the maintenance of which would form an obstacle to liberalisation of the movement of workers;

(c) by abolishing all such qualifying periods and other restrictions provided for either under national legislation or under agreements previously concluded between Member States as imposed on workers of other Member States conditions regarding the free choice of employment other than those imposed on workers of the State concerned;

(d) by setting up appropriate machinery to bring offers of employment into touch with applications for employment and to facilitate the achievement of a balance between supply and demand in the employment market in such a way as to avoid serious threats to the standard of living and level of employment in the various regions and industries.

Article 41 (ex Article 50)   Member States shall, within the framework of a joint programme, encourage the exchange of young workers.

Article 42 (ex Article 51)   The Council shall, acting in accordance with the procedure referred to in Article 251, adopt such measures in the field of social security as are necessary to provide freedom of movement for workers; to this end, it shall make arrangements to secure for migrant workers and their dependants:

(a) aggregation, for the purpose of acquiring and retaining the right to benefit and of calculating the amount of benefit, of all periods taken into account under the laws of the several countries;

(b) payment of benefits to persons resident in the territories of Member States.

The Council shall act unanimously throughout the procedure referred to in Article 251.

Chapter 2: Right of Establishment

Article 43 (ex Article 52)   Within the framework of the provisions set out below, restrictions on the freedom of establishment of nationals of a Member State in the territory of another Member State shall be prohibited. Such prohibition shall also apply to restrictions on the setting-up of agencies, branches or subsidiaries by nationals of any Member State established in the territory of any Member State.

Freedom of establishment shall include the right to take up and pursue activities as self-employed persons and to set up and manage undertakings, in particular companies or firms within the meaning of the second paragraph of Article 48, under the conditions laid down for its own nationals by the law of the country where such establishment is effected, subject to the provisions of the Chapter relating to capital.

Article 44 (ex Article 54)   1. In order to attain freedom of establishment as regards a particular activity, the Council, acting in accordance with the procedure referred to in Article 251 and after consulting the Economic and Social Committee, shall act by means of directives.

2. The Council and the Commission shall carry out the duties devolving upon them under the preceding provisions, in particular:

(a) by according, as a general rule, priority treatment to activities where freedom of establishment makes a particularly valuable contribution to the development of production and trade;

(b) by ensuring close cooperation between the competent authorities in the Member States in order to ascertain the particular situation within the Community of the various activities concerned;

(c) by abolishing those administrative procedures and practices, whether resulting from national legislation or from agreements previously concluded between Member States, the maintenance of which would form an obstacle to freedom of establishment;

(d) by ensuring that workers of one Member State employed in the territory of another Member State may remain in that territory for the purpose of taking up activities therein as self-employed persons, where they satisfy the conditions which they would be required to satisfy if they were entering that State at the time when they intended to take up such activities;

(e) by enabling a national of one Member State to acquire and use land and buildings situated in the territory of another Member State, insofar as this does not conflict with the principles laid down in Article 33(2);

(f) by effecting the progressive abolition of restrictions on freedom of establishment in every branch of activity under consideration, both as regards the conditions for setting up agencies, branches or subsidiaries in the territory of a Member State and as regards the subsidiaries in the territory of a Member State and as regards the conditions governing the entry of personnel belonging to the main establishment into managerial or supervisory posts in such agencies, branches or subsidiaries;

(g) by coordinating to the necessary extent the safeguards which, for the protection of the interests of members and other, are required by Member States of companies or firms within the meaning of the second paragraph of Article 48 with a view to making such safeguards equivalent throughout the Community;

(h) by satisfying themselves that the conditions of establishment are not distorted by aids granted by Member States.

Article 45 (ex Article 55)   The provisions of this Chapter shall not apply, so far as any given Member State is concerned, to activities which in that State are connected, even occasionally, with the exercise of official authority.

The Council may, acting by a qualified majority on a proposal from the Commission, rule that the provisions of this Chapter shall not apply to certain activities.

Article 46 (ex Article 56)   1. The provisions of this Chapter and measures taken in pursuance thereof shall not prejudice the applicability of provisions laid down by law, regulation or administrative action providing for special treatment for foreign nationals on grounds of public policy, public security or public health.

2. The Council shall, acting in accordance with the procedure referred to in Article 251, issue directives for the coordination of the abovementioned provisions.

Article 47 (ex Article 57)   1. In order to make it easier for persons to take up and pursue activities as self-employed persons, the Council shall, acting in accordance with the procedure referred to in Article 251, issue directives for the mutual recognition of diplomas, certificates and other evidence of formal qualifications.

2. For the same purpose, the Council shall, acting in accordance with the procedure referred to in Article 251, issue directives for the coordination of the provisions laid down by law, regulation or administrative action in Member States concerning the taking-up and pursuit of activities as self-employed persons. The Council, acting

unanimously throughout the procedure referred to in Article 251, shall decide on directives the implementation of which involves in at least one Member State amendment of the existing principles laid down by law governing the professions with respect to training and conditions of access for natural persons. In other cases the Council shall act by qualified majority.

3. In the case of the medical and allied and pharmaceutical professions, the progressive abolition of restrictions shall be dependent upon coordination of the conditions for their exercise in the various Member States.

Article 48 (ex Article 58)   Companies or firms formed in accordance with the law of a Member State and having their registered office, central administration or principal place of business within the Community shall, for the purposes of this Chapter, be treated in the same way as natural persons who are nationals of Member States.

'Companies or firms' means companies or firms constituted under civil or commercial law, including cooperative societies, and other legal persons governed by public or private law, save for those which are non-profit-making.

Chapter 3: Services

Article 49 (ex Article 59)   Within the framework of the provisions set out below, restrictions on freedom to provide services within the Community shall be prohibited in respect of nationals of Member States who are established in a State of the Community other than that of the person for whom the services are intended.

The Council may, acting by a qualified majority on a proposal from the Commission, extend the provisions of the Chapter to nationals of a third country who provide services and who are established within the Community.

Article 50 (ex Article 60)   Services shall be considered to be 'services' within the meaning of this Treaty where they are normally provided for remuneration, insofar as they are not governed by the provisions relating to freedom of movement for goods, capital and persons.

'Services' shall in particular include:
(a) activities of an industrial character;
(b) activities of a commercial character;
(c) activities of craftsmen;
(d) activities of the professions.

Without prejudice to the provisions of the Chapter relating to the right of establishment, the person providing a service may, in order to do so, temporarily pursue his activity in the State where the service is provided, under the same conditions as are imposed by that State on its own nationals.

Article 51 (ex Article 61)   1. Freedom to provide services in the field of transport shall be governed by the provisions of the Title relating to transport.

2. The liberalisation of banking and insurance services connected with movements of capital shall be effected in step with the liberalisation of movement of capital.

Article 52 (ex Article 63)   1. In order to achieve the liberalisation of a specific service, the Council shall, on a proposal from the Commission and after consulting the

Economic and Social Committee and the European Parliament, issue directives acting by a qualified majority.

2. As regards the directives referred to in paragraph 1, priority shall as a general rule be given to those services which directly affect production costs or the liberalisation of which helps to promote trade in goods.

Article 53 (ex Article 64) The Member States declare their readiness to undertake the liberalisation of services beyond the extent required by the directives issued pursuant to Article 52(1), if their general economic situation and the situation of the economic sector concerned so permit.

To this end, the Commission shall make recommendations to the Member States concerned.

Article 54 (ex Article 65) As long as restrictions on freedom to provide services have not been abolished, each Member State shall apply such restrictions without distinction on grounds of nationality or residence to all persons providing services within the meaning of the first paragraph of Article 49.

Article 55 (ex Article 66) The provisions of Articles 45 to 48 shall apply to the matters covered by this Chapter.

The Council, acting unanimously after consulting the European Parliament, shall take a decision with a view to providing for all or parts of the areas covered by this Title to be governed by the procedure referred to in Article 251 and adapting the provisions relating to the powers of the Court of Justice.

Chapter 4: Capital and Payments

Article 56 (ex Article 73b) 1. Within the framework of the provisions set out in this Chapter, all restrictions on the movement of capital between Member States and between Member States and third countries shall be prohibited.

2. Within the framework of the provisions set out in this Chapter, all restrictions on payments between Member States and between Member States and third countries shall be prohibited.

Article 57 (ex Article 73c) 1. The provisions of Article 56 shall be without prejudice to the application to third countries of any restrictions which exist on 31 December 1993 under national or Community law adopted in respect of the movement of capital to or from third countries involving direct investment— including in real estate—establishment, the provision of financial services or the admission of securities to capital markets.

2. Whilst endeavouring to achieve the objective of free movement of capital between Member States and third countries to the greatest extent possible and without prejudice to the other Chapters of this Treaty, the Council may, acting by a qualified majority on a proposal from the Commission, adopt measures on the movement of capital to or from third countries involving direct investment— including investment in real estate—establishment, the provision of financial services or the admission of securities to capital markets. Unanimity shall be required for measures under this paragraph which constitute a step back in Community law as regards the liberalisation of the movement of capital to or from third countries.

Article 58 (ex Article 73d)   1. The provisions of Article 56 shall be without prejudice to the right of Member States:

(a) to apply the relevant provisions of their tax law which distinguish between tax-payers who are not in the same situation with regard to their place of residence or with regard to the place where their capital is invested;

(b) to take all requisite measures to prevent infringements of national law and regulations, in particular in the field of taxation and the prudential supervision of financial institutions, or to lay down procedures for the declaration of capital movements for purposes of administrative or statistical information, or to take measures which are justified on grounds of public policy or public security.

2. The provisions of this Chapter shall be without prejudice to the applicability of restrictions on the right of establishment which are compatible with this Treaty.

3. The measures and procedures referred to in paragraphs 1 and 2 shall not constitute a means of arbitrary discrimination or a disguised restriction on the free movement of capital and payments as defined in Article 56.

Article 59 (ex Article 73f)   Where, in exceptional circumstances, movements of capital to or from third countries cause, or threaten to cause, serious difficulties for the operation of economic and monetary union, the Council, acting by a qualified majority on a proposal from the Commission and after consulting the ECB, may take safeguard measures with regard to third countries for a period not exceeding six months if such measures are strictly necessary.

Article 60 (ex Article 73g)   1. If, in the cases envisaged in Article 301, action by the Community is deemed necessary, the Council may, in accordance with the procedure provided for in Article 301, take the necessary urgent measures on the movement of capital and on payments as regards the third countries concerned.

2. Without prejudice to Article 297 and as long as the Council has not taken measures pursuant to paragraph 1, a Member State may, for serious political reasons and on grounds of urgency, take unilateral measures against a third country with regard to capital movements and payments. The Commission and the other Member States shall be informed of such measures by the date of their entry into force at the latest.

   The Council may, acting by a qualified majority on a proposal from the Commission, decide that the Member State concerned shall amend or abolish such measures. The President of the Council shall inform the European Parliament of any such decision taken by the Council.

TITLE IV. (EX TITLE IIIA) VISAS, ASYLUM, IMMIGRATION AND OTHER POLICIES RELATED TO FREE MOVEMENT OF PERSONS

Article 61 (ex Article 73i)   In order to establish progressively an area of freedom, security and justice, the Council shall adopt:

(a) within a period of five years after the entry into force of the Treaty of Amsterdam, measures aimed at ensuring the free movement of persons in accordance with Article 14, in conjunction with directly related flanking measures with respect to external border controls, asylum and immigration, in accordance with the provisions of Article 62(2) and (3) and Article 63(1)(a) and (2)(a), and measures to prevent and combat crime in accordance with the provisions of Article 31(e) of the Treaty on European Union;

(b) other measures in the fields of asylum, immigration and safeguarding the rights of nationals of third countries, in accordance with the provisions of Article 63;

(c) measures in the field of judicial cooperation in civil matters as provided for in Article 65;

(d) appropriate measures to encourage and strengthen administrative cooperation, as provided for in Article 66;

(e) measures in the field of police and judicial cooperation in criminal matters aimed at a high level of security by preventing and combating crime within the Union in accordance with the provisions of the Treaty on European Union.

Article 62 (ex Article 73j)   The Council, acting in accordance with the procedure referred to in Article 67, shall, within a period of five years after the entry into force of the Treaty of Amsterdam, adopt:

(1) measures with a view to ensuring, in compliance with Article 14, the absence of any controls on persons, be they citizens of the Union or nationals of third countries, when crossing internal borders;

(2) measures on the crossing of the external borders of the Member States which shall establish:

(a) standards and procedures to be followed by Member States in carrying out checks on persons at such borders;

(b) rules on visas for intended stays of no more than three months, including:

(i) the list of third countries whose nationals must be in possession of visas when crossing the external borders and those whose nationals are exempt from that requirement;

(ii) the procedures and conditions for issuing visas by Member States;

(iii) a uniform format for visas;

(iv) rules on a uniform visa;

(3) measures setting out the conditions under which nationals of third countries shall have the freedom to travel within the territory of the Member States during a period of no more than three months.

Article 63 (ex Article 73k)   The Council, acting in accordance with the procedure referred to in Article 67, shall, within a period of five years after the entry into force of the Treaty of Amsterdam, adopt:

(1) measures on asylum, in accordance with the Geneva Convention of 28 July 1951 and the Protocol of 31 January 1967 relating to the status of refugees and other relevant treaties, within the following areas:

(a) criteria and mechanisms for determining which Member State is responsible for considering an application for asylum submitted by a national of a third country in one of the Member States;

(b) minimum standards on the reception of asylum seekers in Member States;

(c) minimum standards with respect to the qualification of nationals of third countries as refugees;

    (d) minimum standards on procedures in Member States for granting or with-
        drawing refugee status;

(2) measures on refugees and displaced persons within the following areas:
    (a) minimum standards for giving temporary protection to displaced persons
        from third countries who cannot return to their country of origin and for
        persons who otherwise need international protection;
    (b) promoting a balance of effort between Member States in receiving and bear-
        ing the consequences of receiving refugees and displaced persons;

(3) measures on immigration policy within the following areas:
    (a) conditions of entry and residence, and standards on procedures for the issue
        by Member States of long term visas and residence permits, including those
        for the purpose of family reunion;
    (b) illegal immigration and illegal residence, including repatriation of illegal
        residents;

(4) measures defining the rights and conditions under which nationals of third
    countries who are legally resident in a Member State may reside in other
    Member States.

  Measures adopted by the Council pursuant to points 3 and 4 shall not prevent any
Member State from maintaining or introducing in the areas concerned national
provisions which are compatible with this Treaty and with international agreements.

  Measures to be adopted pursuant to points 2(b), 3(a) and 4 shall not be subject to
the five year period referred to above.

Article 64 (ex Article 73l)   1. This Title shall not affect the exercise of the responsibilities incumbent upon Member States with regard to the maintenance of law and
order and the safeguarding of internal security.

2. In the event of one or more Member States being confronted with an emergency
situation characterised by a sudden inflow of nationals of third countries and without prejudice to paragraph 1, the Council may, acting by qualified majority on a
proposal from the Commission, adopt provisional measures of a duration not
exceeding six months for the benefit of the Member States concerned.

Article 65 (ex Article 73m)   Measures in the field of judicial cooperation in civil matters
having cross-border implications, to be taken in accordance with Article 67 and
insofar as necessary for the proper functioning of the internal market, shall i
nclude:

(a) improving and simplifying:

    — the system for cross-border service of judicial and extrajudicial documents;
    — cooperation in the taking of evidence;
    — the recognition and enforcement of decisions in civil and commercial cases,
       including decisions in extrajudicial cases;

(b) promoting the compatibility of the rules applicable in the Member States con-
    cerning the conflict of laws and of jurisdiction;
(c) eliminating obstacles to the good functioning of civil proceedings, if necessary
    by promoting the compatibility of the rules on civil procedure applicable in the
    Member States.

Article 66 (ex Article 73n) The Council, acting in accordance with the procedure referred to in Article 67, shall take measures to ensure cooperation between the relevant departments of the administrations of the Member States in the areas covered by this Title, as well as between those departments and the Commission.

Article 67 (ex Article 73o) 1. During a transitional period of five years following the entry into force of the Treaty of Amsterdam, the Council shall act unanimously on a proposal from the Commission or on the initiative of a Member State and after consulting the European Parliament.

2. After this period of five years:

— the Council shall act on proposals from the Commission; the Commission shall examine any request made by a Member State that it submit a proposal to the Council;
— the Council, acting unanimously after consulting the European Parliament, shall take a decision with a view to providing for all or parts of the areas covered by this Title to be governed by the procedure referred to in Article 251 and adapting the provisions relating to the powers of the Court of Justice.

3. By derogation from paragraphs 1 and 2:

— measures referred to in Article 62(2)(b) (i) and (iii) shall, from the entry into force of the Treaty of Amsterdam, be adopted by the Council acting by a qualified majority on a proposal from the Commission and after consulting the European Parliament;
— measures referred to in Article 62(2)(b) (ii) and (iv) shall, after a period of five years following the entry into force of the Treaty of Amsterdam, be adopted by the Council acting in accordance with the procedure referred to in Article 251.

Article 68 (ex Article 73p) 1. Article 234 shall apply to this Title under the following circumstances and conditions: where a question on the interpretation of this Title or on the validity or interpretation of acts of the institutions of the Community based on this Title is raised in a case pending before a court or a tribunal of a Member State against whose decisions there is no judicial remedy under national law, that court or tribunal shall, if it considers that a decision on the question is necessary to enable it to give judgment, request the Court of Justice to give a ruling thereon.

2. In any event, the Court of Justice shall not have jurisdiction to rule on any measure or decision taken pursuant to Article 62(1) relating to the maintenance of law and order and the safeguarding of internal security.

3. The Council, the Commission or a Member State may request the Court of Justice to give a ruling on a question of interpretation of this Title or of acts of the institutions of the Community based on this Title. The ruling given by the Court of Justice in response to such a request shall not apply to judgments of courts or tribunals of the Member States which have become res judicata.

Article 69 (ex Article 73q) The application of this Title shall be subject to the provisions of the Protocol on the position of the United Kingdom and Ireland and to the Protocol on the position of Denmark and without prejudice to the Protocol on the application of certain aspects of Article 14 of the Treaty establishing the European Community to the United Kingdom and to Ireland.

TITLE V. (EX TITLE IV) TRANSPORT

Article 70 (ex Article 74)   The objectives of this Treaty shall, in matters governed by this Title, be pursued by Member States within the framework of a common transport policy.

Article 71 (ex Article 75)   1. For the purpose of implementing Article 70, and taking into account the distinctive features of transport, the Council shall, acting in accordance with the procedure referred to in Article 251 and after consulting the Economic and Social Committee and the Committee of the Regions, lay down:
(a) common rules applicable to international transport to or from the territory of a Member State or passing across the territory of one or more Member States;
(b) the conditions under which non-resident carriers may operate transport services within a Member State;
(c) measures to improve transport safety;
(d) any other appropriate provisions.

2. By way of derogation from the procedure provided for in paragraph 1, where the application of provisions concerning the principles of the regulatory system for transport would be liable to have a serious effect on the standard of living and on employment in certain areas and on the operation of transport facilities, they shall be laid down by the Council acting unanimously on a proposal from the Commission, after consulting the European Parliament and the Economic and Social Committee. In so doing, the Council shall take into account the need for adaptation to the economic development which will result from establishing the common market.

Article 72 (ex Article 76)   Until the provisions referred to in Article 71(1) have been laid down, no Member State may, without the unanimous approval of the Council, make the various provisions governing the subject on 1 January 1958 or, for acceding States, the date of their accession less favourable in their direct or indirect effect on carriers of other Member States as compared with carriers who are nationals of that State.

Article 73 (ex Article 77)   Aids shall be compatible with this Treaty if they meet the needs of coordination of transport or if they represent reimbursement for the discharge of certain obligations inherent in the concept of a public service.

Article 74 (ex Article 78)   Any measures taken within the framework of this Treaty in respect of transport rates and conditions shall take account of the economic circumstances of carriers.

Article 75 (ex Article 79)   1. In the case of transport within the Community, discrimination which takes the form of carriers charging different rates and imposing different conditions for the carriage of the same goods over the same transport links on grounds of the country of origin or of destination of the goods in question shall be abolished.

2. Paragraph 1 shall not prevent the Council from adopting other measures in pursuance of Article 71(1).

3. The Council shall, acting by a qualified majority on a proposal from the Commission and after consulting the Economic and Social Committee, lay down rules for implementing the provisions of paragraph 1.

The Council may in particular lay down the provisions needed to enable the institutions of the Community to secure compliance with the rule laid down in paragraph 1 and to ensure that users benefit from it to the full.

4. The Commission shall, acting on its own initiative or on application by a Member State, investigate any cases of discrimination falling within paragraph 1 and, after consulting any Member State concerned, shall take the necessary decisions within the framework of the rules laid down in accordance with the provisions of paragraph 3.

Article 76 (ex Article 80)   1. The imposition by a Member State, in respect of transport operations carried out within the Community, of rates and conditions involving any element of support or protection in the interest of one or more particular undertakings or industries shall be prohibited, unless authorised by the Commission.

2. The Commission shall, acting on its own initiative or on application by a Member State, examine the rates and conditions referred to in paragraph 1, taking account in particular of the requirements of an appropriate regional economic policy, the needs of underdeveloped areas and the problems of areas seriously affected by political circumstances on the one hand, and of the effects of such rates and conditions on competition between the different modes of transport on the other.

After consulting each Member State concerned, the Commission shall take the necessary decisions.

3. The prohibition provided for in paragraph 1 shall not apply to tariffs fixed to meet competition.

Article 77 (ex Article 81)   Charges or dues in respect of the crossing of frontiers which are charged by a carrier in addition to the transport rates shall not exceed a reasonable level after taking the costs actually incurred thereby into account.

Member States shall endeavour to reduce these costs progressively.

The Commission may make recommendations to Member States for the application of this Article.

Article 78 (ex Article 82)   The provisions of this Title shall not form an obstacle to the application of measures taken in the Federal Republic of Germany to the extent that such measures are required in order to compensate for the economic disadvantages caused by the division of Germany to the economy of certain areas of the Federal Republic affected by that division.

Article 79 (ex Article 83)   An Advisory Committee consisting of experts designated by the governments of Member States shall be attached to the Commission. The Commission, whenever it considers it desirable, shall consult the Committee on transport matters without prejudice to the powers of the Economic and Social Committee.

Article 80 (ex Article 84)   1. The provisions of this Title shall apply to transport by rail, road and inland waterway.

2. The Council may, acting by a qualified majority, decide whether, to what extent and by what procedure appropriate provisions may be laid down for sea and air transport.

The procedural provisions of Article 71 shall apply.

TITLE VI. (EX TITLE V) COMMON RULES ON COMPETITION, TAXATION AND
APPROXIMATION OF LAWS

Chapter 1: Rules on Competition

SECTION 1: RULES APPLYING TO UNDERTAKINGS

Article 81 (ex Article 85)   1. The following shall be prohibited as incompatible with
the common market: all agreements between undertakings, decisions by associations of undertakings and concerted practices which may affect trade between
Member States and which have as their object or effect the prevention, restriction
or distortion of competition within the common market, and in particular those
which:
(a) directly or indirectly fix purchase or selling prices or any other trading conditions;
(b) limit or control production, markets, technical development, or investment;
(c) share markets or sources of supply;
(d) apply dissimilar conditions to equivalent transactions with other trading par-
    ties, thereby placing them at a competitive disadvantage;
(e) make the conclusion of contracts subject to acceptance by the other parties of
    supplementary obligations which, by their nature or according to commercial
    usage, have no connection with the subject of such contracts.

2. Any agreements or decisions prohibited pursuant to this Article shall be automatically void.

3. The provisions of paragraph 1 may, however, be declared inapplicable in the
case of:
— any agreement or category of agreements between undertakings;
— any decision or category of decisions by associations of undertakings;
— any concerted practice or category of concerted practices,

which contributes to improving the production or distribution of goods or to promoting technical or economic progress, while allowing consumers a fair share of
the resulting benefit, and which does not:
(a) impose on the undertakings concerned restrictions which are not indispensable
    to the attainment of these objectives;
(b) afford such undertakings the possibility of eliminating competition in respect
    of a substantial part of the products in question.

Article 82 (ex Article 86)   Any abuse by one or more undertakings of a dominant position within the common market or in a substantial part of it shall be prohibited as
incompatible with the common market insofar as it may affect trade between
Member States.
   Such abuse may, in particular, consist in:
(a) directly or indirectly imposing unfair purchase or selling prices or other unfair
    trading conditions;
(b) limiting production, markets or technical development to the prejudice of con-
    sumers;
(c) applying dissimilar conditions to equivalent transactions with other trading
    parties, thereby placing them at a competitive disadvantage;
(d) making the conclusion of contracts subject to acceptance by the other parties of

supplementary obligations which, by their nature or according to commercial usage, have no connection with the subject of such contracts.

Article 83 (ex Article 87)   1. The appropriate regulations or directives to give effect to the principles set out in Articles 81 and 82 shall be laid down by the Council, acting by a qualified majority on a proposal from the Commission and after consulting the European Parliament.

2. The regulations or directives referred to in paragraph 1 shall be designed in particular:
(a) to ensure compliance with the prohibitions laid down in Article 81(1) and in Article 82 by making provision for fines and periodic penalty payments;
(b) to lay down detailed rules for the application of Article 81(3), taking into account the need to ensure effective supervision on the one hand, and to simplify administration to the greatest possible extent on the other;
(c) to define, if need be, in the various branches of the economy, the scope of the provisions of Articles 81 and 82;
(d) to define the respective functions of the Commission and of the Court of Justice in applying the provisions laid down in this paragraph;
(e) to determine the relationship between national laws and the provisions contained in this Section or adopted pursuant to this Article.

Article 84 (ex Article 88)   Until the entry into force of the provisions adopted in pursuance of Article 83, the authorities in Member States shall rule on the admissibility of agreements, decisions and concerted practices and on abuse of a dominant position in the common market in accordance with the law of their country and with the provisions of Article 81, in particular paragraph 3, and of Article 82.

Article 85 (ex Article 89)   1. Without prejudice to Article 84, the Commission shall ensure the application of the principles laid down in Articles 81 and 82. On application by a Member State or on its own initiative, and in cooperation with the competent authorities in the Member States, who shall give it their assistance, the Commission shall investigate cases of suspected infringement of these principles. If it finds that there has been an infringement, it shall propose appropriate measures to bring it to an end.

2. If the infringement is not brought to an end, the Commission shall record such infringement of the principles in a reasoned decision. The Commission may publish its decision and authorise Member States to take the measures, the conditions and details of which it shall determine, needed to remedy the situation.

Article 86 (ex Article 90)   1. In the case of public undertakings and undertakings to which Member States grant special or exclusive rights, Member States shall neither enact nor maintain in force any measure contrary to the rules contained in this Treaty, in particular to those rules provided for in Article 12 and Articles 81 to 89.

2. Undertakings entrusted with the operation of services of general economic interest or having the character of a revenue-producing monopoly shall be subject to the rules contained in this Treaty, in particular to the rules on competition, insofar as the application of such rules does not obstruct the performance, in law or in fact, of the particular tasks assigned to them. The development of trade must not be affected to such an extent as would be contrary to the interests of the Community.

3. The Commission shall ensure the application of the provisions of this Article and shall, where necessary, address appropriate directives or decisions to Member States.

SECTION 2: AIDS GRANTED BY STATES

Article 87 (ex Article 92)   1. Save as otherwise provided in this Treaty, any aid granted by a Member State or through State resources in any form whatsoever which distorts or threatens to distort competition by favouring certain undertakings or the production of certain goods shall, insofar as it affects trade between Member States, be incompatible with the common market.

2. The following shall be compatible with the common market:
(a) aid having a social character, granted to individual consumers, provided that such aid is granted without discrimination related to the origin of the products concerned;
(b) aid to make good the damage caused by natural disasters or exceptional occurrences;
(c) aid granted to the economy of certain areas of the Federal Republic of Germany affected by the division of Germany, insofar as such aid is required in order to compensate for the economic disadvantages caused by that division.

3. The following may be considered to be compatible with the common market:
(a) aid to promote the economic development of areas where the standard of living is abnormally low or where there is serious underemployment;
(b) aid to promote the execution of an important project of common European interest or to remedy a serious disturbance in the economy of a Member State;
(c) aid to facilitate the development of certain economic activities or of certain economic areas, where such aid does not adversely affect trading conditions to an extent contrary to the common interest;
(d) aid to promote culture and heritage conservation where such aid does not affect trading conditions and competition in the Community to an extent that is contrary to the common interest;
(e) such other categories of aid as may be specified by decision of the Council acting by a qualified majority on a proposal from the Commission.

Article 88 (ex Article 93)   1. The Commission shall, in cooperation with Member States, keep under constant review all systems of aid existing in those States. It shall propose to the latter any appropriate measures required by the progressive development or by the functioning of the common market.

2. If, after giving notice to the parties concerned to submit their comments, the Commission finds that aid granted by a State or through State resources is not compatible with the common market having regard to Article 87, or that such aid is being misused, it shall decide that the State concerned shall abolish or alter such aid within a period of time to be determined by the Commission.

If the State concerned does not comply with this decision within the prescribed time, the Commission or any other interested State may, in derogation from the provisions of Articles 226 and 227, refer the matter to the Court of Justice direct.

On application by a Member State, the Council may, acting unanimously, decide that aid which that State is granting or intends to grant shall be considered to be compatible with the common market, in derogation from the provisions of Article 87 or from the regulations provided for in Article 89, if such a decision is justified by exceptional circumstances. If, as regards the aid in question, the Commission has already initiated the procedure provided for in the first subparagraph of this paragraph, the fact that the State concerned has made its application to the Council shall have the effect of suspending that procedure until the Council has made its attitude known.

If, however, the Council has not made its attitude known within three months of the said application being made, the Commission shall give its decision on the case.

3. The Commission shall be informed, in sufficient time to enable it to submit its comments, of any plans to grant or alter aid. If it considers that any such plan is not compatible with the common market having regard to Article 87, it shall without delay initiate the procedure provided for in paragraph 2. The Member State concerned shall not put its proposed measures into effect until this procedure has resulted in a final decision.

Article 89 (ex Article 94)   The Council, acting by a qualified majority on a proposal from the Commission and after consulting the European Parliament, may make any appropriate regulations for the application of Articles 87 and 88 and may in particular determine the conditions in which Article 88(3) shall apply and the categories of aid exempted from this procedure.

Chapter 2: Tax Provisions

Article 90 (ex Article 95)   No Member State shall impose, directly or indirectly, on the products of other Member States any internal taxation of any kind in excess of that imposed directly or indirectly on similar domestic products.

Furthermore, no Member State shall impose on the products of other Member States any internal taxation of such a nature as to afford indirect protection to other products.

Article 91 (ex Article 96)   Where products are exported to the territory of any Member State, any repayment of internal taxation shall not exceed the internal taxation imposed on them whether directly or indirectly.

Article 92 (ex Article 98)   In the case of charges other than turnover taxes, excise duties and other forms of indirect taxation, remissions and repayments in respect of exports to other Member States may not be granted and countervailing charges in respect of imports from Member States may not be imposed unless the measures contemplated have been previously approved for a limited period by the Council acting by a qualified majority on a proposal from the Commission.

Article 93 (ex Article 99)   The Council shall, acting unanimously on a proposal from the Commission and after consulting the European Parliament and the Economic and Social Committee, adopt provisions for the harmonisation of legislation concerning turnover taxes, excise duties and other forms of indirect taxation to the extent that such harmonisation is necessary to ensure the establishment and the functioning of the internal market within the time-limit laid down in Article 14.

Chapter 3: Approximation of Laws

Article 94 (ex Article 100)   The Council shall, acting unanimously on a proposal from the Commission and after consulting the European Parliament and the Economic and Social Committee, issue directives for the approximation of such laws, regulations or administrative provisions of the Member States as directly affect the establishment or functioning of the common market.

Article 95 (ex Article 100a)   1. By way of derogation from Article 94 and save where otherwise provided in this Treaty, the following provisions shall apply for the achievement of the objectives set out in Article 14. The Council shall, acting in accordance with the procedure referred to in Article 251 and after consulting the Economic and Social Committee, adopt the measures for the approximation of the provisions laid down by law, regulation or administrative action in Member States which have as their object the establishment and functioning of the internal market.

2. Paragraph 1 shall not apply to fiscal provisions, to those relating to the free movement of persons nor to those relating to the rights and interests of employed persons.

3. The Commission, in its proposals envisaged in paragraph 1 concerning health, safety, environmental protection and consumer protection, will take as a base a high level of protection, taking account in particular of any new development based on scientific facts. Within their respective powers, the European Parliament and the Council will also seek to achieve this objective.

4. If, after the adoption by the Council or by the Commission of a harmonisation measure, a Member State deems it necessary to maintain national provisions on grounds of major needs referred to in Article 30, or relating to the protection of the environment or the working environment, it shall notify the Commission of these provisions as well as the grounds for maintaining them.

5. Moreover, without prejudice to paragraph 4, if, after the adoption by the Council or by the Commission of a harmonisation measure, a Member State deems it necessary to introduce national provisions based on new scientific evidence relating to the protection of the environment or the working environment on grounds of a problem specific to that Member State arising after the adoption of the harmonisation measure, it shall notify the Commission of the envisaged provisions as well as the grounds for introducing them.

6. The Commission shall, within six months of the notifications as referred to in paragraphs 4 and 5, approve or reject the national provisions involved after having verified whether or not they are a means of arbitrary discrimination or a disguised restriction on trade between Member States and whether or not they shall constitute an obstacle to the functioning of the internal market.

In the absence of a decision by the Commission within this period the national provisions referred to in paragraphs 4 and 5 shall be deemed to have been approved.

When justified by the complexity of the matter and in the absence of danger for human health, the Commission may notify the Member State concerned that the period referred to in this paragraph may be extended for a further period of up to six months.

7. When, pursuant to paragraph 6, a Member State is authorised to maintain or introduce national provisions derogating from a harmonisation measure, the Commission shall immediately examine whether to propose an adaptation to that measure.

8. When a Member State raises a specific problem on public health in a field which has been the subject of prior harmonisation measures, it shall bring it to the attention of the Commission which shall immediately examine whether to propose appropriate measures to the Council.

9. By way of derogation from the procedure laid down in Articles 226 and 227, the Commission and any Member State may bring the matter directly before the Court of Justice if it considers that another Member State is making improper use of the powers provided for in this Article.

10. The harmonisation measures referred to above shall, in appropriate cases, include a safeguard clause authorising the Member States to take, for one or more of the non-economic reasons referred to in Article 30, provisional measures subject to a Community control procedure.

Article 96 (ex Article 101)   Where the Commission finds that a difference between the provisions laid down by law, regulation or administrative action in Member States is distorting the conditions of competition in the common market and that the resultant distortion needs to be eliminated, it shall consult the Member States concerned.

If such consultation does not result in an agreement eliminating the distortion in question, the Council shall, on a proposal from the Commission, acting by a qualified majority, issue the necessary directives. The Commission and the Council may take any other appropriate measures provided for in this Treaty.

Article 97 (ex Article 102)   1. Where there is a reason to fear that the adoption or amendment of a provision laid down by law, regulation or administrative action may cause distortion within the meaning of Article 96, a Member State desiring to proceed therewith shall consult the Commission. After consulting the Member States, the Commission shall recommend to the States concerned such measures as may be appropriate to avoid the distortion in question.

2. If a State desiring to introduce or amend its own provisions does not comply with the recommendation addressed to it by the Commission, other Member States shall not be required, in pursuance of Article 96, to amend their own provisions in order to eliminate such distortion. If the Member State which has ignored the recommendation of the Commission causes distortion detrimental only to itself, the provisions of Article 96 shall not apply.

TITLE VII. (EX TITLE VI) ECONOMIC AND MONETARY POLICY

Chapter 1: Economic Policy

Article 98 (ex Article 102a)   Member States shall conduct their economic policies with a view to contributing to the achievement of the objectives of the Community, as defined in Article 2, and in the context of the broad guidelines referred to in Article 99(2). The Member States and the Community shall act in accordance with the principle of an open market economy with free competition, favouring an efficient allocation of resources, and in compliance with the principles set out in Article 4.

Article 99 (ex Article 103)   1. Member States shall regard their economic policies as a matter of common concern and shall coordinate them within the Council, in accordance with the provisions of Article 98.

2. The Council shall, acting by a qualified majority on a recommendation from the Commission, formulate a draft for the broad guidelines of the economic policies of the Member States and of the Community, and shall report its findings to the European Council.

The European Council shall, acting on the basis of the report from the Council, discuss a conclusion on the broad guidelines of the economic policies of the Member States and of the Community.

On the basis of this conclusion, the Council shall, acting by a qualified majority, adopt a recommendation setting out these broad guidelines. The Council shall inform the European Parliament of its recommendation.

3. In order to ensure closer coordination of economic policies and sustained convergence of the economic performances of the Member States, the Council shall, on the basis of reports submitted by the Commission, monitor economic developments in each of the Member States and in the Community as well as the consistency of economic policies with the broad guidelines referred to in paragraph 2, and regularly carry out an overall assessment.

For the purpose of this multilateral surveillance, Member States shall forward information to the Commission about important measures taken by them in the field of their economic policy and such other information as they deem necessary.

4. Where it is established, under the procedure referred to in paragraph 3, that the economic policies of a Member State are not consistent with the broad guidelines referred to in paragraph 2 or that they risk jeopardising the proper functioning of economic and monetary union, the Council may, acting by a qualified majority on a recommendation from the Commission, make the necessary recommendations to the Member State concerned. The Council may, acting by a qualified majority on a proposal from the Commission, decide to make its recommendations public.

The President of the Council and the Commission shall report to the European Parliament on the results of multilateral surveillance. The President of the Council may be invited to appear before the competent committee of the European Parliament if the Council has made its recommendations public.

5. The Council, acting in accordance with the procedure referred to in Article 252, may adopt detailed rules for the multilateral surveillance procedure referred to in paragraphs 3 and 4 of this Article.

Article 100 (ex Article 103a)   1. Without prejudice to any other procedures provided for in this Treaty, the Council may, acting unanimously on a proposal from the Commission, decide upon the measures appropriate to the economic situation, in particular if severe difficulties arise in the supply of certain products.

2. Where a Member State is in difficulties or is seriously threatened with severe difficulties caused by exceptional occurrences beyond its control, the Council may, acting unanimously on a proposal from the Commission, grant, under certain con-

ditions, Community financial assistance to the Member State concerned. Where the severe difficulties are caused by natural disasters, the Council shall act by qualified majority. The President of the Council shall inform the European Parliament of the decision taken.

Article 101 (ex Article 104)   1. Overdraft facilities or any other type of credit facility with the ECB or with the central banks of the Member States (hereinafter referred to as 'national central banks') in favour of Community institutions or bodies, central governments, regional, local or other public authorities, other bodies governed by public law, or public undertakings of Member States shall be prohibited, as shall the purchase directly from them by the ECB or national central banks of debt instruments.

2. Paragraph 1 shall not apply to publicly owned credit institutions which, in the context of the supply of reserves by central banks, shall be given the same treatment by national central banks and the ECB as private credit institutions.

Article 102 (ex Article 104a)   1. Any measure, not based on prudential considerations, establishing privileged access by Community institutions or bodies, central governments, regional, local or other public authorities, other bodies governed by public law, or public undertakings of Member States to financial institutions, shall be prohibited.

2. The Council, acting in accordance with the procedure referred to in Article 252, shall, before 1 January 1994, specify definitions for the application of the prohibition referred to in paragraph 1.

Article 103 (ex Article 104b)   1. The Community shall not be liable for or assume the commitments of central governments, regional, local or other public authorities, other bodies governed by public law, or public undertakings of any Member State, without prejudice to mutual financial guarantees for the joint execution of a specific project. A Member State shall not be liable for or assume the commitments of central governments, regional, local or other public authorities, other bodies governed by public law, or public undertakings of another Member State, without prejudice to mutual financial guarantees for the joint execution of a specific project.

2. If necessary, the Council, acting in accordance with the procedure referred to in Article 252, may specify definitions for the application of the prohibition referred to in Article 101 and in this Article.

Article 104 (ex Article 104c)   1. Member States shall avoid excessive government deficits.

2. The Commission shall monitor the development of the budgetary situation and of the stock of government debt in the Member States with a view to identifying gross errors. In particular it shall examine compliance with budgetary discipline on the basis of the following two criteria:
(a) whether the ratio of the planned or actual government deficit to gross domestic product exceeds a reference value, unless:
  — either the ratio has declined substantially and continuously and reached a level that comes close to the reference value;
  — or, alternatively, the excess over the reference value is only exceptional and temporary and the ratio remains close to the reference value;

(b) whether the ratio of government debt to gross domestic product exceeds a reference value, unless the ratio is sufficiently diminishing and approaching the reference value at a satisfactory pace.
    The reference values are specified in the Protocol on the excessive deficit procedure annexed to this Treaty.

3. If a Member State does not fulfil the requirements under one or both of these criteria, the Commission shall prepare a report. The report of the Commission shall also take into account whether the government deficit exceeds government investment expenditure and take into account all other relevant factors, including the medium-term economic and budgetary position of the Member State.
    The Commission may also prepare a report if, notwithstanding the fulfilment of the requirements under the criteria, it is of the opinion that there is a risk of an excessive deficit in a Member State.

4. The Committee provided for in Article 114 shall formulate an opinion on the report of the Commission.

5. If the Commission considers that an excessive deficit in a Member State exists or may occur, the Commission shall address an opinion to the Council.

6. The Council shall, acting by a qualified majority on a recommendation from the Commission, and having considered any observations which the Member State concerned may wish to make, decide after an overall assessment whether an excessive deficit exists.

7. Where the existence of an excessive deficit is decided according to paragraph 6, the Council shall make recommendations to the Member State concerned with a view to bringing that situation to an end within a given period. Subject to the provisions of paragraph 8, these recommendations shall not be made public.

8. Where it establishes that there has been no effective action in response to its recommendations within the period laid down, the Council may make its recommendations public.

9. If a Member State persists in failing to put into practice the recommendations of the Council, the Council may decide to give notice to the Member State to take, within a specified time-limit, measures for the deficit reduction which is judged necessary by the Council in order to remedy the situation.
    In such a case, the Council may request the Member State concerned to submit reports in accordance with a specific timetable in order to examine the adjustment efforts of that Member State.

10. The rights to bring actions provided for in Articles 226 and 227 may not be exercised within the framework of paragraphs 1 to 9 of this Article.

11. As long as a Member State fails to comply with a decision taken in accordance with paragraph 9, the Council may decide to apply or, as the case may be, intensify one or more of the following measures:

— to require the Member State concerned to publish additional information, to be specified by the Council, before issuing bonds and securities;
— to invite the European Investment Bank to reconsider its lending policy towards the Member State concerned;
— to require the Member State concerned to make a non-interest-bearing deposit

of an appropriate size with the Community until the excessive deficit has, in the view of the Council, been corrected;

— to impose fines of an appropriate size.

   The President of the Council shall inform the European Parliament of the decisions taken.

12. The Council shall abrogate some or all of its decisions referred to in paragraphs 6 to 9 and 11 to the extent that the excessive deficit in the Member State concerned has, in the view of the Council, been corrected. If the Council has previously made public recommendations, it shall, as soon as the decision under paragraph 8 has been abrogated, make a public statement that an excessive deficit in the Member State concerned no longer exists.

13. When taking the decisions referred to in paragraphs 7 to 9, 11 and 12, the Council shall act on a recommendation from the Commission by a majority of two-thirds of the votes of its members weighted in accordance with Article 205(2), excluding the votes of the representative of the Member State concerned.

14. Further provisions relating to the implementation of the procedure described in this Article are set out in the Protocol on the excessive deficit procedure annexed to this Treaty.

   The Council shall, acting unanimously on a proposal from the Commission and after consulting the European Parliament and the ECB, adopt the appropriate provisions which shall then replace the said Protocol.

   Subject to the other provisions of this paragraph, the Council shall, before 1 January 1994, acting by a qualified majority on a proposal from the Commission and after consulting the European Parliament, lay down detailed rules and definitions for the application of the provisions of the said Protocol.

Chapter 2: Monetary Policy

Article 105 (ex Article 105)   1. The primary objective of the ESCB shall be to maintain price stability. Without prejudice to the objective of price stability, the ESCB shall support the general economic policies in the Community with a view to contributing to the achievement of the objectives of the Community as laid down in Article 2. The ESCB shall act in accordance with the principle of an open market economy with free competition, favouring an efficient allocation of resources, and in compliance with the principles set out in Article 4.

2. The basic tasks to be carried out through the ESCB shall be:

— to define and implement the monetary policy of the Community;
— to conduct foreign exchange operations consistent with the provisions of Article 111;
— to hold and manage the official foreign reserves of the Member States;
— to promote the smooth operation of payment systems.

3. The third indent of paragraph 2 shall be without prejudice to the holding and management by the governments of Member States of foreign-exchange working balances.

4. The ECB shall be consulted:

— on any proposed Community act in its fields of competence;

— by national authorities regarding any draft legislative provision in its fields of competence, but within the limits and under the conditions set out by the Council in accordance with the procedure laid down in Article 107(6).

The ECB may submit opinions to the appropriate Community institutions or bodies or to national authorities on matters in its fields of competence.

5. The ESCB shall contribute to the smooth conduct of policies pursued by the competent authorities relating to the prudential supervision of credit institutions and the stability of the financial system.

6. The Council may, acting unanimously on a proposal from the Commission and after consulting the ECB and after receiving the assent of the European Parliament, confer upon the ECB specific tasks concerning policies relating to the prudential supervision of credit institutions and other financial institutions with the exception of insurance undertakings.

Article 106 (ex Article 105a)   1. The ECB shall have the exclusive right to authorise the issue of banknotes within the Community. The ECB and the national central banks may issue such notes. The banknotes issued by the ECB and the national central banks shall be the only such notes to have the status of legal tender within the Community.

2. Member States may issue coins subject to approval by the ECB of the volume of the issue. The Council may, acting in accordance with the procedure referred to in Article 252 and after consulting the ECB, adopt measures to harmonise the denominations and technical specifications of all coins intended for circulation to the extent necessary to permit their smooth circulation within the Community.

Article 107 (ex Article 106)   1. The ESCB shall be composed of the ECB and of the national central banks.

2. The ECB shall have legal personality.

3. The ESCB shall be governed by the decision-making bodies of the ECB which shall be the Governing Council and the Executive Board.

4. The Statute of the ESCB is laid down in a Protocol annexed to this Treaty.

5. Articles 5.1, 5.2, 5.3, 17, 18, 19.1, 22, 23, 24, 26, 32.2, 32.3, 32.4, 32.6, 33.1(a) and 36 of the Statute of the ESCB may be amended by the Council, acting either by a qualified majority on a recommendation from the ECB and after consulting the Commission or unanimously on a proposal from the Commission and after consulting the ECB. In either case, the assent of the European Parliament shall be required.

6. The Council, acting by a qualified majority either on a proposal from the Commission and after consulting the European Parliament and the ECB or on a recommendation from the ECB and after consulting the European Parliament and the Commission, shall adopt the provisions referred to in Articles 4, 5.4, 19.2, 20, 28.1, 29.2, 30.4 and 34.3 of the Statute of the ESCB.

Article 108 (ex Article 107)   When exercising the powers and carrying out the tasks and duties conferred upon them by this Treaty and the Statute of the ESCB, neither the ECB, nor a national central bank, nor any member of their decision-making bodies shall seek or take instructions from Community institutions or bodies, from any government of a Member State or from any other body. The Community institutions and bodies and the governments of the Member States undertake to respect this principle and not to seek to influence the members of the decision-making bodies of the ECB or of the national central banks in the performance of their tasks.

Article 109 (ex Article 108) Each Member State shall ensure, at the latest at the date of the establishment of the ESCB, that its national legislation including the statutes of its national central bank is compatible with this Treaty and the Statute of the ESCB.

Article 110 (ex Article 108a) 1. In order to carry out the tasks entrusted to the ESCB, the ECB shall, in accordance with the provisions of this Treaty and under the conditions laid down in the Statute of the ESCB:

— make regulations to the extent necessary to implement the tasks defined in Article 3.1, first indent, Articles 19.1, 22 and 25.2 of the Statute of the ESCB and in cases which shall be laid down in the acts of the Council referred to in Article 107(6);
— take decisions necessary for carrying out the tasks entrusted to the ESCB under this Treaty and the Statute of the ESCB;
— make recommendations and deliver opinions.

2. A regulation shall have general application. It shall be binding in its entirety and directly applicable in all Member States.
Recommendations and opinions shall have no binding force.
A decision shall be binding in its entirety upon those to whom it is addressed.
Articles 253 to 256 shall apply to regulations and decisions adopted by the ECB.
The ECB may decide to publish its decisions, recommendations and opinions.

3. Within the limits and under the conditions adopted by the Council under the procedure laid down in Article 107(6), the ECB shall be entitled to impose fines or periodic penalty payments on undertakings for failure to comply with obligations under its regulations and decisions.

Article 111 (Article 109) 1. By way of derogation from Article 300, the Council may, acting unanimously on a recommendation from the ECB or from the Commission, and after consulting the ECB in an endeavour to reach a consensus consistent with the objective of price stability, after consulting the European Parliament, in accordance with the procedure in paragraph 3 for determining the arrangements, conclude formal agreements on an exchange-rate system for the ECU in relation to non-Community currencies. The Council may, acting by a qualified majority on a recommendation from the ECB or from the Commission, and after consulting the ECB in an endeavour to reach a consensus consistent with the objective of price stability, adopt, adjust or abandon the central rates of the ECU within the exchange-rate system. The President of the Council shall inform the European Parliament of the adoption, adjustment or abandonment of the ECU central rates.

2. In the absence of an exchange-rate system in relation to one or more non-Community currencies as referred to in paragraph 1, the Council, acting by a qualified majority either on a recommendation from the Commission and after consulting the ECB or on a recommendation from the ECB, may formulate general

orientations for exchange-rate policy in relation to these currencies. These general orientations shall be without prejudice to the primary objective of the ESCB to maintain price stability.

3. By way of derogation from Article 300, where agreements concerning monetary or foreign exchange regime matters need to be negotiated by the Community with one or more States or international organisations, the Council, acting by a qualified majority on a recommendation from the Commission and after consulting the ECB, shall decide the arrangements for the negotiation and for the conclusion of such agreements. These arrangements shall ensure that the Community expresses a single position. The Commission shall be fully associated with the negotiations.

   Agreements concluded in accordance with this paragraph shall be binding on the institutions of the Community, on the ECB and on Member States.

4. Subject to paragraph 1, the Council shall, on a proposal from the Commission and after consulting the ECB, acting by a qualified majority decide on the position of the Community at international level as regards issues of particular relevance to economic and monetary union and, acting unanimously, decide its representation in compliance with the allocation of powers laid down in Articles 99 and 105.

5. Without prejudice to Community competence and Community agreements as regards economic and monetary union, Member States may negotiate in international bodies and conclude international agreements.

Chapter 3: Institutional Provisions

Article 112 (ex Article 109a)   1. The Governing Council of the ECB shall comprise the members of the Executive Board of the ECB and the Governors of the national central banks.

2. (a) The Executive Board shall comprise the President, the Vice-President and four other members.
   (b) The President, the Vice-President and the other members of the Executive Board shall be appointed from among persons of recognised standing and professional experience in monetary or banking matters by common accord of the governments of the Member States at the level of Heads of State or Government, on a recommendation from the Council, after it has consulted the European Parliament and the Governing Council of the ECB.
       Their term of office shall be eight years and shall not be renewable.
   Only nationals of Member States may be members of the Executive Board.

Article 113 (ex Article 109b)   1. The President of the Council and a member of the Commission may participate, without having the right to vote, in meetings of the Governing Council of the ECB.

   The President of the Council may submit a motion for deliberation to the Governing Council of the ECB.

2. The President of the ECB shall be invited to participate in Council meetings when the Council is discussing matters relating to the objectives and tasks of the ESCB.

3. The ECB shall address an annual report on the activities of the ESCB and on the monetary policy of both the previous and current year to the European Parliament, the Council and the Commission, and also to the European Council. The President

of the ECB shall present this report to the Council and to the European Parliament, which may hold a general debate on that basis.

The President of the ECB and the other members of the Executive Board may, at the request of the European Parliament or on their own initiative, be heard by the competent committees of the European Parliament.

Article 114 (ex Article 109c)   1. In order to promote coordination of the policies of Member States to the full extent needed for the functioning of the internal market, a Monetary Committee with advisory status is hereby set up.
It shall have the following tasks:

— to keep under review the monetary and financial situation of the Member States and of the Community and the general payments system of the Member States and to report regularly thereon to the Council and to the Commission;
— to deliver opinions at the request of the Council or of the Commission, or on its own initiative for submission to those institutions;
— without prejudice to Article 207, to contribute to the preparation of the work of the Council referred to in Articles 59, 60, 99(2), (3), (4) and (5), 100, 102, 103, 104, 116(2), 117(6), 119, 120, 121(2) and 122(1);
— to examine, at least once a year, the situation regarding the movement of capital and the freedom of payments, as they result from the application of this Treaty and of measures adopted by the Council; the examination shall cover all measures relating to capital movements and payments; the Committee shall report to the Commission and to the Council on the outcome of this examination.

The Member States and the Commission shall each appoint two members of the Monetary Committee.

2. At the start of the third stage, an Economic and Financial Committee shall be set up. The Monetary Committee provided for in paragraph 1 shall be dissolved.

The Economic and Financial Committee shall have the following tasks:

— to deliver opinions at the request of the Council or of the Commission, or on its own initiative for submission to those institutions;
— to keep under review the economic and financial situation of the Member States and of the Community and to report regularly thereon to the Council and to the Commission, in particular on financial relations with third countries and international institutions;
— without prejudice to Article 207, to contribute to the preparation of the work of the Council referred to in Articles 59, 60, 99(2), (3), (4) and (5), 100, 102, 103, 104, 105(6), 106(2), 107(5) and (6), 111, 119, 120(2) and (3), 122(2), 123(4) and (5), and to carry out other advisory and preparatory tasks assigned to it by the Council;
— to examine, at least once a year, the situation regarding the movement of capital and the freedom of payments, as they result from the application of this Treaty and of measures adopted by the Council; the examination shall cover all measures relating to capital movements and payments; the Committee shall report to the Commission and to the Council on the outcome of this examination.

The Member States, the Commission and the ECB shall each appoint no more than two members of the Committee.

3. The Council shall, acting by a qualified majority on a proposal from the Commission and after consulting the ECB and the Committee referred to in this Article, lay down detailed provisions concerning the composition of the Economic and Financial Committee. The President of the Council shall inform the European Parliament of such a decision.

4. In addition to the tasks set out in paragraph 2, if and as long as there are Member States with a derogation as referred to in Articles 122 and 123, the Committee shall keep under review the monetary and financial situation and the general payments system of those Member States and report regularly thereon to the Council and to the Commission.

Article 115 (ex Article 109d)   For matters within the scope of Articles 99(4), 104 with the exception of paragraph 14, 111, 121, 122 and 123(4) and (5), the Council or a Member State may request the Commission to make a recommendation or a proposal, as appropriate. The Commission shall examine this request and submit its conclusions to the Council without delay.

Chapter 4: Transitional Provisions

Article 116 (ex Article 109e)   1. The second stage for achieving economic and monetary union shall begin on 1 January 1994.

2. Before that date:
(a) each Member State shall:
  —   adopt, where necessary, appropriate measures to comply with the prohibitions laid down in Article 56 and in Articles 101 and 102(1);
  —   adopt, if necessary, with a view to permitting the assessment provided for in subparagraph (b), multiannual programmes intended to ensure the lasting convergence necessary for the achievement of economic and monetary union, in particular with regard to price stability and sound public finances;
(b) the Council shall, on the basis of a report from the Commission, assess the progress made with regard to economic and monetary convergence, in particular with regard to price stability and sound public finances, and the progress made with the implementation of Community law concerning the internal market.

3. The provisions of Articles 101, 102(1), 103(1) and 104 with the exception of paragraphs 1, 9, 11 and 14 shall apply from the beginning of the second stage.
   The provisions of Articles 100(2), 104(1), (9) and (11), 105, 106, 108, 111, 112, 113 and 114(2) and (4) shall apply from the beginning of the third stage.

4. In the second stage, Member States shall endeavour to avoid excessive government deficits.

5. During the second stage, each Member State shall, as appropriate, start the process leading to the independence of its central bank, in accordance with Article 109.

Article 117 (ex Article 109f)   1. At the start of the second stage, a European Monetary Institute (hereinafter referred to as 'EMI') shall be established and take up its duties; it shall have legal personality and be directed and managed by a Council, consisting of a President and the Governors of the national central banks, one of whom shall be Vice-President.

The President shall be appointed by common accord of the governments of the Member States at the level of Heads of State or Government, on a recommendation from the Council of the EMI, and after consulting the European Parliament and the Council. The President shall be selected from among persons of recognised standing and professional experience in monetary or banking matters. Only nationals of Member States may be President of the EMI. The Council of the EMI shall appoint the Vice-President.

The Statute of the EMI is laid down in a Protocol annexed to this Treaty.

2. The EMI shall:

— strengthen cooperation between the national central banks;
— strengthen the coordination of the monetary policies of the Member States, with the aim of ensuring price stability;
— monitor the functioning of the European Monetary System;
— hold consultations concerning issues falling within the competence of the national central banks and affecting the stability of financial institutions and markets;
— take over the tasks of the European Monetary Cooperation Fund, which shall be dissolved; the modalities of dissolution are laid down in the Statute of the EMI;
— facilitate the use of the ECU and oversee its development, including the smooth functioning of the ECU clearing system.

3. For the preparation of the third stage, the EMI shall:

— prepare the instruments and the procedures necessary for carrying out a single monetary policy in the third stage;
— promote the harmonisation, where necessary, of the rules and practices governing the collection, compilation and distribution of statistics in the areas within its field of competence;
— prepare the rules for operations to be undertaken by the national central banks within the framework of the ESCB;
  promote the efficiency of cross-border payments;
— supervise the technical preparation of ECU banknotes.

At the latest by 31 December 1996, the EMI shall specify the regulatory, organisational and logistical framework necessary for the ESCB to perform its tasks in the third stage. This framework shall be submitted for decision to the ECB at the date of its establishment.

4. The EMI, acting by a majority of two thirds of the members of its Council, may:

— formulate opinions or recommendations on the overall orientation of monetary policy and exchange-rate policy as well as on related measures introduced in each Member State;
— submit opinions or recommendations to governments and to the Council on policies which might affect the internal or external monetary situation in the Community and, in particular, the functioning of the European Monetary System;
— make recommendations to the monetary authorities of the Member States concerning the conduct of their monetary policy.

5. The EMI, acting unanimously, may decide to publish its opinions and its recommendations.

6. The EMI shall be consulted by the Council regarding any proposed Community act within its field of competence.

Within the limits and under the conditions set out by the Council, acting by a qualified majority on a proposal from the Commission and after consulting the European Parliament and the EMI, the EMI shall be consulted by the authorities of the Member States on any draft legislative provision within its field of competence.

7. The Council may, acting unanimously on a proposal from the Commission and after consulting the European Parliament and the EMI, confer upon the EMI other tasks for the preparation of the third stage.

8. Where this Treaty provides for a consultative role for the ECB, references to the ECB shall be read as referring to the EMI before the establishment of the ECB.

9. During the second stage, the term 'ECB' used in Articles 230, 232, 233, 234, 237 and 288 shall be read as referring to the EMI.

Article 118 (ex Article 109g)   The currency composition of the ECU basket shall not be changed.

From the start of the third stage, the value of the ECU shall be irrevocably fixed in accordance with Article 123(4).

Article 119 (ex Article 109h)   1. Where a Member State is in difficulties or is seriously threatened with difficulties as regards its balance of payments either as a result of an overall disequilibrium in its balance of payments, or as a result of the type of currency at its disposal, and where such difficulties are liable in particular to jeopardise the functioning of the common market or the progressive implementation of the common commercial policy, the Commission shall immediately investigate the position of the State in question and the action which, making use of all the means at its disposal, that State has taken or may take in accordance with the provisions of this Treaty. The Commission shall state what measures it recommends the State concerned to take.

If the action taken by a Member State and the measures suggested by the Commission do not prove sufficient to overcome the difficulties which have arisen or which threaten, the Commission shall, after consulting the Committee referred to in Article 114, recommend to the Council the granting of mutual assistance and appropriate methods therefor.

The Commission shall keep the Council regularly informed of the situation and of how it is developing.

2. The Council, acting by a qualified majority, shall grant such mutual assistance; it shall adopt directives or decisions laying down the conditions and details of such assistance, which may take such forms as:
(a) a concerted approach to or within any other international organisations to which Member States may have recourse;
(b) measures needed to avoid deflection of trade where the State which is in difficulties maintains or reintroduces quantitative restrictions against third countries;
(c) the granting of limited credits by other Member States, subject to their agreement.

3. If the mutual assistance recommended by the Commission is not granted by the Council or if the mutual assistance granted and the measures taken are insufficient, the Commission shall authorise the State which is in difficulties to take protective measures, the conditions and details of which the Commission shall determine.

Such authorisation may be revoked and such conditions and details may be changed by the Council acting by a qualified majority.

4. Subject to Article 122(6), this Article shall cease to apply from the beginning of the third stage.

Article 120 (ex Article 109i)   1. Where a sudden crisis in the balance of payments occurs and a decision within the meaning of Article 119(2) is not immediately taken, the Member State concerned may, as a precaution, take the necessary protective measures. Such measures must cause the least possible disturbance in the functioning of the common market and must not be wider in scope than is strictly necessary to remedy the sudden difficulties which have arisen.

2. The Commission and the other Member States shall be informed of such protective measures not later than when they enter into force. The Commission may recommend to the Council the granting of mutual assistance under Article 119.

3. After the Commission has delivered an opinion and the Committee referred to in Article 114 has been consulted, the Council may, acting by a qualified majority, decide that the State concerned shall amend, suspend or abolish the protective measures referred to above.

4. Subject to Article 122(6), this Article shall cease to apply from the beginning of the third stage.

Article 121 (ex Article 109j)   1. The Commission and the EMI shall report to the Council on the progress made in the fulfilment by the Member States of their obligations regarding the achievement of economic and monetary union. These reports shall include an examination of the compatibility between each Member State's national legislation, including the statutes of its national central bank, and Articles 108 and 109 of this Treaty and the Statute of the ESCB. The reports shall also examine the achievement of a high degree of sustainable convergence by reference to the fulfilment by each Member State of the following criteria:

—   the achievement of a high degree of price stability; this will be apparent from a rate of inflation which is close to that of, at most, the three best performing Member States in terms of price stability;

—   the sustainability of the government financial position; this will be apparent from having achieved a government budgetary position without a deficit that is excessive as determined in accordance with Article 104(6);

—   the observance of the normal fluctuation margins provided for by the exchange-rate mechanism of the European Monetary System, for at least two years, without devaluing against the currency of any other Member State;

—   the durability of convergence achieved by the Member State and of its participation in the exchange-rate mechanism of the European Monetary System being reflected in the long-term interest-rate levels.

The four criteria mentioned in this paragraph and the relevant periods over which they are to be respected are developed further in a Protocol annexed to this

Treaty. The reports of the Commission and the EMI shall also take account of the development of the ECU, the results of the integration of markets, the situation and development of the balances of payments on current account and an examination of the development of unit labour costs and other price indices.

2. On the basis of these reports, the Council, acting by a qualified majority on a recommendation from the Commission, shall assess:

— for each Member State, whether it fulfils the necessary conditions for the adoption of a single currency;
— whether a majority of the Member States fulfil the necessary conditions for the adoption of a single currency,

and recommend its findings to the Council, meeting in the composition of the Heads of State or Government. The European Parliament shall be consulted and forward its opinion to the Council, meeting in the composition of the Heads of State or Government.

3. Taking due account of the reports referred to in paragraph 1 and the opinion of the European Parliament referred to in paragraph 2, the Council, meeting in the composition of the Heads of State or Government, shall, acting by a qualified majority, not later than 31 December 1996:

— decide, on the basis of the recommendations of the Council referred to in paragraph 2, whether a majority of the Member States fulfil the necessary conditions for the adoption of a single currency;
— decide whether it is appropriate for the Community to enter the third stage,

and if so:

— set the date for the beginning of the third stage.

4. If by the end of 1997 the date for the beginning of the third stage has not been set, the third stage shall start on 1 January 1999. Before 1 July 1998, the Council, meeting in the composition of the Heads of State or Government, after a repetition of the procedure provided for in paragraphs 1 and 2, with the exception of the second indent of paragraph 2, taking into account the reports referred to in paragraph 1 and the opinion of the European Parliament, shall, acting by a qualified majority and on the basis of the recommendations of the Council referred to in paragraph 2, confirm which Member States fulfil the necessary conditions for the adoption of a single currency.

Article 122 (ex Article 109k)   1. If the decision has been taken to set the date in accordance with Article 121(3), the Council shall, on the basis of its recommendations referred to in Article 121(2), acting by a qualified majority on a recommendation from the Commission, decide whether any, and if so which, Member States shall have a derogation as defined in paragraph 3 of this Article. Such Member States shall in this Treaty be referred to as 'Member States with a derogation'.

   If the Council has confirmed which Member States fulfil the necessary conditions for the adoption of a single currency, in accordance with Article 121(4), those Member States which do not fulfil the conditions shall have a derogation as defined in paragraph 3 of this Article. Such Member States shall in this Treaty be referred to as 'Member States with a derogation'.

2. At least once every two years, or at the request of a Member State with a derogation, the Commission and the ECB shall report to the Council in accordance with

the procedure laid down in Article 121(1). After consulting the European Parliament and after discussion in the Council, meeting in the composition of the Heads of State or Government, the Council shall, acting by a qualified majority on a proposal from the Commission, decide which Member States with a derogation fulfil the necessary conditions on the basis of the criteria set out in Article 121(1), and abrogate the derogations of the Member States concerned.

3. A derogation referred to in paragraph 1 shall entail that the following Articles do not apply to the Member State concerned: Articles 104(9) and (11), 105(1), (2), (3) and (5), 106, 110, 111, and 112(2)(b). The exclusion of such a Member State and its national central bank from rights and obligations within the ESCB is laid down in Chapter IX of the Statute of the ESCB.

4. In Articles 105(1), (2) and (3), 106, 110, 111 and 112(2)(b), 'Member States' shall be read as 'Member States without a derogation'.

5. The voting rights of Member States with a derogation shall be suspended for the Council decisions referred to in the Articles of this Treaty mentioned in paragraph 3. In that case, by way of derogation from Articles 205 and 250(1), a qualified majority shall be defined as two-thirds of the votes of the representatives of the Member States without a derogation weighted in accordance with Article 205(2), and unanimity of those Member States shall be required for an act requiring unanimity.

6. Articles 119 and 120 shall continue to apply to a Member State with a derogation.

Article 123 (ex Article 109l) 1. Immediately after the decision on the date for the beginning of the third stage has been taken in accordance with Article 121(3), or, as the case may be, immediately after 1 July 1998:

— the Council shall adopt the provisions referred to in Article 107(6);
— the governments of the Member States without a derogation shall appoint, in accordance with the procedure set out in Article 50 of the Statute of the ESCB, the President, the Vice-President and the other members of the Executive Board of the ECB. If there are Member States with a derogation, the number of members of the Executive Board may be smaller than provided for in Article 11.1 of the Statute of the ESCB, but in no circumstances shall it be less than four.

As soon as the Executive Board is appointed, the ESCB and the ECB shall be established and shall prepare for their full operation as described in this Treaty and the Statute of the ESCB. The full exercise of their powers shall start from the first day of the third stage.

2. As soon as the ECB is established, it shall, if necessary, take over tasks of the EMI. The EMI shall go into liquidation upon the establishment of the ECB; the modalities of liquidation are laid down in the Statute of the EMI.

3. If and as long as there are Member States with a derogation, and without prejudice to Article 107(3) of this Treaty, the General Council of the ECB referred to in Article 45 of the Statute of the ESCB shall be constituted as a third decision-making body of the ECB.

4. At the starting date of the third stage, the Council shall, acting with the unanimity of the Member States without a derogation, on a proposal from the

Commission and after consulting the ECB, adopt the conversion rates at which their currencies shall be irrevocably fixed and at which irrevocably fixed rate the ECU shall be substituted for these currencies, and the ECU will become a currency in its own right. This measure shall by itself not modify the external value of the ECU. The Council shall, acting according to the same procedure, also take the other measures necessary for the rapid introduction of the ECU as the single currency of those Member States.

5. If it is decided, according to the procedure set out in Article 122(2), to abrogate a derogation, the Council shall, acting with the unanimity of the Member States without a derogation and the Member State concerned, on a proposal from the Commission and after consulting the ECB, adopt the rate at which the ECU shall be substituted for the currency of the Member State concerned, and take the other measures necessary for the introduction of the ECU as the single currency in the Member State concerned.

Article 124 (ex Article 109m)   1. Until the beginning of the third stage, each Member State shall treat its exchange-rate policy as a matter of common interest. In so doing, Member States shall take account of the experience acquired in cooperation within the framework of the European Monetary System (EMS) and in developing the ECU, and shall respect existing powers in this field.

2. From the beginning of the third stage and for as long as a Member State has a derogation, paragraph 1 shall apply by analogy to the exchange-rate policy of that Member State.

TITLE VIII. (ex TITLE VIa) EMPLOYMENT

Article 125 (ex Article 109n)   Member States and the Community shall, in accordance with this Title, work towards developing a coordinated strategy for employment and particularly for promoting a skilled, trained and adaptable workforce and labour markets responsive to economic change with a view to achieving the objectives defined in Article 2 of the Treaty on European Union and in Article 2 of this Treaty.

Article 126 (ex Article 109o)   1. Member States, through their employment policies, shall contribute to the achievement of the objectives referred to in Article 125 in a way consistent with the broad guidelines of the economic policies of the Member States and of the Community adopted pursuant to Article 99(2).

2. Member States, having regard to national practices related to the responsibilities of management and labour, shall regard promoting employment as a matter of common concern and shall coordinate their action in this respect within the Council, in accordance with the provisions of Article 128.

Article 127 (ex Article 109p)   1. The Community shall contribute to a high level of employment by encouraging cooperation between Member States and by supporting and, if necessary, complementing their action. In doing so, the competences of the Member States shall be respected.

2. The objective of a high level of employment shall be taken into consideration in the formulation and implementation of Community policies and activities.

Article 128 (ex Article 109q) 1. The European Council shall each year consider the employment situation in the Community and adopt conclusions thereon, on the basis of a joint annual report by the Council and the Commission.

2. On the basis of the conclusions of the European Council, the Council, acting by a qualified majority on a proposal from the Commission and after consulting the European Parliament, the Economic and Social Committee, the Committee of the Regions and the Employment Committee referred to in Article 130, shall each year draw up guidelines which the Member States shall take into account in their employment policies. These guidelines shall be consistent with the broad guidelines adopted pursuant to Article 99(2).

3. Each Member State shall provide the Council and the Commission with an annual report on the principal measures taken to implement its employment policy in the light of the guidelines for employment as referred to in paragraph 2.

4. The Council, on the basis of the reports referred to in paragraph 3 and having received the views of the Employment Committee, shall each year carry out an examination of the implementation of the employment policies of the Member States in the light of the guidelines for employment. The Council, acting by a qualified majority on a recommendation from the Commission, may, if it considers it appropriate in the light of that examination, make recommendations to Member States.

5. On the basis of the results of that examination, the Council and the Commission shall make a joint annual report to the European Council on the employment situation in the Community and on the implementation of the guidelines for employment.

Article 129 (ex Article 109r) The Council, acting in accordance with the procedure referred to in Article 251 and after consulting the Economic and Social Committee and the Committee of the Regions, may adopt incentive measures designed to encourage cooperation between Member States and to support their action in the field of employment through initiatives aimed at developing exchanges of information and best practices, providing comparative analysis and advice as well as promoting innovative approaches and evaluating experiences, in particular by recourse to pilot projects.

Those measures shall not include harmonisation of the laws and regulations of the Member States.

Article 130 (ex Article 109s) The Council, after consulting the European Parliament, shall establish an Employment Committee with advisory status to promote coordination between Member States on employment and labour market policies. The tasks of the Committee shall be:

— to monitor the employment situation and employment policies in the Member States and the Community;
— without prejudice to Article 207, to formulate opinions at the request of either the Council or the Commission or on its own initiative, and to contribute to the preparation of the Council proceedings referred to in Article 128.

In fulfilling its mandate, the Committee shall consult management and labour.

Each Member State and the Commission shall appoint two members of the Committee.

TITLE IX. (EX TITLE VII) COMMON COMMERCIAL POLICY

Article 131 (ex Article 110)   By establishing a customs union between themselves Member States aim to contribute, in the common interest, to the harmonious development of world trade, the progressive abolition of restrictions on international trade and the lowering of customs barriers.

The common commercial policy shall take into account the favourable effect which the abolition of customs duties between Member States may have on the increase in the competitive strength of undertakings in those States.

Article 132 (ex Article 112)   1. Without prejudice to obligations undertaken by them within the framework of other international organisations, Member States shall progressively harmonise the systems whereby they grant aid for exports to third countries, to the extent necessary to ensure that competition between undertakings of the Community is not distorted.

On a proposal from the Commission, the Council shall, acting by a qualified majority, issue any directives needed for this purpose.

2. The preceding provisions shall not apply to such a drawback of customs duties or charges having equivalent effect nor to such a repayment of indirect taxation including turnover taxes, excise duties and other indirect taxes as is allowed when goods are exported from a Member State to a third country, insofar as such a drawback or repayment does not exceed the amount imposed, directly or indirectly, on the products exported.

Article 133 (ex Article 113)   1. The common commercial policy shall be based on uniform principles, particularly in regard to changes in tariff rates, the conclusion of tariff and trade agreements, the achievement of uniformity in measures of liberalisation, export policy and measures to protect trade such as those to be taken in the event of dumping or subsidies.

2. The Commission shall submit proposals to the Council for implementing the common commercial policy.

3. Where agreements with one or more States or international organisations need to be negotiated, the Commission shall make recommendations to the Council, which shall authorise the Commission to open the necessary negotiations.

The Commission shall conduct these negotiations in consultation with a special committee appointed by the Council to assist the Commission in this task and within the framework of such directives as the Council may issue to it.

The relevant provisions of Article 300 shall apply.

4. In exercising the powers conferred upon it by this Article, the Council shall act by a qualified majority.

5. The Council, acting unanimously on a proposal from the Commission and after consulting the European Parliament, may extend the application of paragraphs 1 to 4 to international negotiations and agreements on services and intellectual property insofar as they are not covered by these paragraphs.

Article 134 (ex Article 115)   In order to ensure that the execution of measures of commercial policy taken in accordance with this Treaty by any Member State is not obstructed by deflection of trade, or where differences between such measures lead to economic difficulties in one or more Member States, the Commission shall recommend the methods for the requisite cooperation between Member States. Failing this, the Commission may authorise Member States to take the necessary protective measures, the conditions and details of which it shall determine.

In case of urgency, Member States shall request authorisation to take the necessary measures themselves from the Commission, which shall take a decision as soon as possible; the Member States concerned shall then notify the measures to the other Member States. The Commission may decide at any time that the Member States concerned shall amend or abolish the measures in question.

In the selection of such measures, priority shall be given to those which cause the least disturbance of the functioning of the common market.

TITLE X. (EX TITLE VIIA) CUSTOMS COOPERATION

Article 135 (ex Article 116)   Within the scope of application of this Treaty, the Council, acting in accordance with the procedure referred to in Article 251, shall take measures in order to strengthen customs cooperation between Member States and between the latter and the Commission. These measures shall not concern the application of national criminal law or the national administration of justice.

TITLE XI. (EX TITLE VIII) SOCIAL POLICY, EDUCATION, VOCATIONAL TRAINING AND YOUTH

Chapter 1: Social Provisions

Article 136 (ex Article 117)   The Community and the Member States, having in mind fundamental social rights such as those set out in the European Social Charter signed at Turin on 18 October 1961 and in the 1989 Community Charter of the Fundamental Social Rights of Workers, shall have as their objectives the promotion of employment, improved living and working conditions, so as to make possible their harmonisation while the improvement is being maintained, proper social protection, dialogue between management and labour, the development of human resources with a view to lasting high employment and the combating of exclusion.

To this end the Community and the Member States shall implement measures which take account of the diverse forms of national practices, in particular in the field of contractual relations, and the need to maintain the competitiveness of the Community economy.

They believe that such a development will ensue not only from the functioning of the common market, which will favour the harmonisation of social systems, but also from the procedures provided for in this Treaty and from the approximation of provisions laid down by law, regulation or administrative action.

Article 137 (ex Article 118)   1. With a view to achieving the objectives of Article 136, the Community shall support and complement the activities of the Member States in the following fields:

— improvement in particular of the working environment to protect workers' health and safety;
— working conditions;
— the information and consultation of workers;

— the integration of persons excluded from the labour market, without prejudice to Article 150;

— equality between men and women with regard to labour market opportunities and treatment at work.

2. To this end, the Council may adopt, by means of directives, minimum requirements for gradual implementation, having regard to the conditions and technical rules obtaining in each of the Member States. Such directives shall avoid imposing administrative, financial and legal constraints in a way which would hold back the creation and development of small and medium-sized undertakings.

The Council shall act in accordance with the procedure referred to in Article 251 after consulting the Economic and Social Committee and the Committee of the Regions.

The Council, acting in accordance with the same procedure, may adopt measures designed to encourage cooperation between Member States through initiatives aimed at improving knowledge, developing exchanges of information and best practices, promoting innovative approaches and evaluating experiences in order to combat social exclusion.

3. However, the Council shall act unanimously on a proposal from the Commission, after consulting the European Parliament, the Economic and Social Committee and the Committee of the Regions in the following areas:

— social security and social protection of workers;

— protection of workers where their employment contract is terminated;

— representation and collective defence of the interests of workers and employers, including co-determination, subject to paragraph 6;

— conditions of employment for third-country nationals legally residing in Community territory;

— financial contributions for promotion of employment and job-creation, without prejudice to the provisions relating to the Social Fund.

4. A Member State may entrust management and labour, at their joint request, with the implementation of directives adopted pursuant to paragraphs 2 and 3.

In this case, it shall ensure that, no later than the date on which a directive must be transposed in accordance with Article 249, management and labour have introduced the necessary measures by agreement, the Member State concerned being required to take any necessary measure enabling it at any time to be in a position to guarantee the results imposed by that directive.

5. The provisions adopted pursuant to this Article shall not prevent any Member State from maintaining or introducing more stringent protective measures compatible with this Treaty.

6. The provisions of this Article shall not apply to pay, the right of association, the right to strike or the right to impose lock-outs.

Article 138 (ex Article 118a)   1. The Commission shall have the task of promoting the consultation of management and labour at Community level and shall take any relevant measure to facilitate their dialogue by ensuring balanced support for the parties.

2. To this end, before submitting proposals in the social policy field, the Commission shall consult management and labour on the possible direction of Community action.

3. If, after such consultation, the Commission considers Community action advisable, it shall consult management and labour on the content of the envisaged proposal. Management and labour shall forward to the Commission an opinion or, where appropriate, a recommendation.

4. On the occasion of such consultation, management and labour may inform the Commission of their wish to initiate the process provided for in Article 139. The duration of the procedure shall not exceed nine months, unless the management and labour concerned and the Commission decide jointly to extend it.

Article 139 (ex Article 118b)   1. Should management and labour so desire, the dialogue between them at Community level may lead to contractual relations, including agreements.

2. Agreements concluded at Community level shall be implemented either in accordance with the procedures and practices specific to management and labour and the Member States or, in matters covered by Article 137, at the joint request of the signatory parties, by a Council decision on a proposal from the Commission.

The Council shall act by qualified majority, except where the agreement in question contains one or more provisions relating to one of the areas referred to in Article 137(3), in which case it shall act unanimously.

Article 140 (ex Article 118c)   With a view to achieving the objectives of Article 136 and without prejudice to the other provisions of this Treaty, the Commission shall encourage cooperation between the Member States and facilitate the coordination of their action in all social policy fields under this chapter, particularly in matters relating to:

— employment;
— labour law and working conditions;
— basic and advanced vocational training;
— social security;
— prevention of occupational accidents and diseases;
— occupational hygiene;
— the right of association and collective bargaining between employers and workers.

To this end, the Commission shall act in close contact with Member States by making studies, delivering opinions and arranging consultations both on problems arising at national level and on those of concern to international organisations.

Before delivering the opinions provided for in this Article, the Commission shall consult the Economic and Social Committee.

Article 141 (ex Article 119)   1. Each Member State shall ensure that the principle of equal pay for male and female workers for equal work or work of equal value is applied.

2. For the purpose of this Article, 'pay' means the ordinary basic or minimum wage or salary and any other consideration, whether in cash or in kind, which the worker receives directly or indirectly, in respect of his employment, from his employer.
Equal pay without discrimination based on sex means:
(a) that pay for the same work at piece rates shall be calculated on the basis of the same unit of measurement;
(b) that pay for work at time rates shall be the same for the same job.

3. The Council, acting in accordance with the procedure referred to in Article 251, and after consulting the Economic and Social Committee, shall adopt measures to ensure the application of the principle of equal opportunities and equal treatment of men and women in matters of employment and occupation, including the principle of equal pay for equal work or work of equal value.

4. With a view to ensuring full equality in practice between men and women in working life, the principle of equal treatment shall not prevent any Member State from maintaining or adopting measures providing for specific advantages in order to make it easier for the under-represented sex to pursue a vocational activity or to prevent or compensate for disadvantages in professional careers.

Article 142 (ex Article 119a)   Member States shall endeavour to maintain the existing equivalence between paid holiday schemes.

Article 143 (ex Article 120)   The Commission shall draw up a report each year on progress in achieving the objectives of Article 136, including the demographic situation in the Community. It shall forward the report to the European Parliament, the Council and the Economic and Social Committee.

The European Parliament may invite the Commission to draw up reports on particular problems concerning the social situation.

Article 144 (ex Article 121)   The Council may, acting unanimously and after consulting the Economic and Social Committee, assign to the Commission tasks in connection with the implementation of common measures, particularly as regards social security for the migrant workers referred to in Articles 39 to 42.

Article 145 (ex Article 122)   The Commission shall include a separate chapter on social developments within the Community in its annual report to the European Parliament.

The European Parliament may invite the Commission to draw up reports on any particular problems concerning social conditions.

Chapter 2. The European Social Fund

Article 146 (ex Article 123)   In order to improve employment opportunities for workers in the internal market and to contribute thereby to raising the standard of living, a European Social Fund is hereby established in accordance with the provisions set out below; it shall aim to render the employment of workers easier and to increase their geographical and occupational mobility within the Community, and to facilitate their adaptation to industrial changes and to changes in production systems, in particular through vocational training and retraining.

Article 147 (ex Article 124)   The Fund shall be administered by the Commission.

The Commission shall be assisted in this task by a Committee presided over by a Member of the Commission and composed of representatives of governments, trade unions and employers' organisations.

Article 148 (ex Article 125)   The Council, acting in accordance with the procedure referred to in Article 251 and after consulting the Economic and Social Committee and the Committee of the Regions, shall adopt implementing decisions relating to the European Social Fund.

Chapter 3. Education, Vocational Training and Youth

Article 149 (ex Article 126)   1. The Community shall contribute to the development of quality education by encouraging cooperation between Member States and, if necessary, by supporting and supplementing their action, while fully respecting the responsibility of the Member States for the content of teaching and the organisation of education systems and their cultural and linguistic diversity.

2. Community action shall be aimed at:

— developing the European dimension in education, particularly through the teaching and dissemination of the languages of the Member States;
— encouraging mobility of students and teachers, inter alia by encouraging the academic recognition of diplomas and periods of study;
— promoting cooperation between educational establishments;
— developing exchanges of information and experience on issues common to the education systems of the Member States;
— encouraging the development of youth exchanges and of exchanges of socio-educational instructors;
— encouraging the development of distance education.

3. The Community and the Member States shall foster cooperation with third countries and the competent international organisations in the field of education, in particular the Council of Europe.

4. In order to contribute to the achievement of the objectives referred to in this Article, the Council:

— acting in accordance with the procedure referred to in Article 251, after consulting the Economic and Social Committee and the Committee of the Regions, shall adopt incentive measures, excluding any harmonisation of the laws and regulations of the Member States;
— acting by a qualified majority on a proposal from the Commission, shall adopt recommendations.

Article 150 (ex Article 127)   1. The Community shall implement a vocational training policy which shall support and supplement the action of the Member States, while fully respecting the responsibility of the Member States for the content and organisation of vocational training.

2. Community action shall aim to:

— facilitate adaptation to industrial changes, in particular through vocational training and retraining;
— improve initial and continuing vocational training in order to facilitate vocational integration and reintegration into the labour market;
— facilitate access to vocational training and encourage mobility of instructors and trainees and particularly young people;
— stimulate cooperation on training between educational or training establishments and firms;
— develop exchanges of information and experience on issues common to the training systems of the Member States.

3. The Community and the Member States shall foster cooperation with third countries and the competent international organisations in the sphere of vocational training.

4. The Council, acting in accordance with the procedure referred to in Article 251 and after consulting the Economic and Social Committee and the Committee of the Regions, shall adopt measures to contribute to the achievement of the objectives referred to in this Article, excluding any harmonisation of the laws and regulations of the Member States.

Title XII. (ex Title IX) Culture

Article 151 (ex Article 128)   1. The Community shall contribute to the flowering of the cultures of the Member States, while respecting their national and regional diversity and at the same time bringing the common cultural heritage to the fore.

2. Action by the Community shall be aimed at encouraging cooperation between Member States and, if necessary, supporting and supplementing their action in the following areas:
— improvement of the knowledge and dissemination of the culture and history of the European peoples;
— conservation and safeguarding of cultural heritage of European significance;
— non-commercial cultural exchanges;
— artistic and literary creation, including in the audiovisual sector.

3. The Community and the Member States shall foster cooperation with third countries and the competent international organisations in the sphere of culture, in particular the Council of Europe.

4. The Community shall take cultural aspects into account in its action under other provisions of this Treaty, in particular in order to respect and to promote the diversity of its cultures.

5. In order to contribute to the achievement of the objectives referred to in this Article, the Council:
— acting in accordance with the procedure referred to in Article 251 and after consulting the Committee of the Regions, shall adopt incentive measures, excluding any harmonisation of the laws and regulations of the Member States. The Council shall act unanimously throughout the procedure referred to in Article 251;
— acting unanimously on a proposal from the Commission, shall adopt recommendations.

Title XIII. (ex Title X) Public Health

Article 152 (ex Article 129)   1. A high level of human health protection shall be ensured in the definition and implementation of all Community policies and activities.

  Community action, which shall complement national policies, shall be directed towards improving public health, preventing human illness and diseases, and obviating sources of danger to human health. Such action shall cover the fight against the major health scourges, by promoting research into their causes, their transmission and their prevention, as well as health information and education.

The Community shall complement the Member States' action in reducing drugs-related health damage, including information and prevention.

2. The Community shall encourage cooperation between the Member States in the areas referred to in this Article and, if necessary, lend support to their action.

Member States shall, in liaison with the Commission, coordinate among themselves their policies and programmes in the areas referred to in paragraph 1. The Commission may, in close contact with the Member States, take any useful initiative to promote such coordination.

3. The Community and the Member States shall foster cooperation with third countries and the competent international organisations in the sphere of public health.

4. The Council, acting in accordance with the procedure referred to in Article 251 and after consulting the Economic and Social Committee and the Committee of the Regions, shall contribute to the achievement of the objectives referred to in this Article through adopting:

(a) measures setting high standards of quality and safety of organs and substances of human origin, blood and blood derivatives; these measures shall not prevent any Member State from maintaining or introducing more stringent protective measures;

(b) by way of derogation from Article 37, measures in the veterinary and phytosanitary fields which have as their direct objective the protection of public health;

(c) incentive measures designed to protect and improve human health, excluding any harmonisation of the laws and regulations of the Member States.

The Council, acting by a qualified majority on a proposal from the Commission, may also adopt recommendations for the purposes set out in this Article.

5. Community action in the field of public health shall fully respect the responsibilities of the Member States for the organisation and delivery of health services and medical care. In particular, measures referred to in paragraph 4(a) shall not affect national provisions on the donation or medical use of organs and blood.

TITLE XIV. (EX TITLE XI) CONSUMER PROTECTION

Article 153 (ex Article 129a) 1. In order to promote the interests of consumers and to ensure a high level of consumer protection, the Community shall contribute to protecting the health, safety and economic interests of consumers, as well as to promoting their right to information, education and to organise themselves in order to safeguard their interests.

2. Consumer protection requirements shall be taken into account in defining and implementing other Community policies and activities.

3. The Community shall contribute to the attainment of the objectives referred to in paragraph 1 through:

(a) measures adopted pursuant to Article 95 in the context of the completion of the internal market;

(b) measures which support, supplement and monitor the policy pursued by the Member States.

4. The Council, acting in accordance with the procedure referred to in Article 251 and after consulting the Economic and Social Committee, shall adopt the measures referred to in paragraph 3(b).

5. Measures adopted pursuant to paragraph 4 shall not prevent any Member State from maintaining or introducing more stringent protective measures. Such measures must be compatible with this Treaty. The Commission shall be notified of them.

TITLE XV. (EX TITLE XII) TRANS-EUROPEAN NETWORKS

Article 154 (ex Article 129b)   1. To help achieve the objectives referred to in Articles 14 and 158 and to enable citizens of the Union, economic operators and regional and local communities to derive full benefit from the setting-up of an area without internal frontiers, the Community shall contribute to the establishment and development of trans-European networks in the areas of transport, telecommunications and energy infrastructures.

2. Within the framework of a system of open and competitive markets, action by the Community shall aim at promoting the interconnection and interoperability of national networks as well as access to such networks. It shall take account in particular of the need to link island, landlocked and peripheral regions with the central regions of the Community.

Article 155 (ex Article 129c)   1. In order to achieve the objectives referred to in Article 154, the Community:

— shall establish a series of guidelines covering the objectives, priorities and broad lines of measures envisaged in the sphere of trans-European networks; these guidelines shall identify projects of common interest;
— shall implement any measures that may prove necessary to ensure the interoperability of the networks, in particular in the field of technical standardisation;
— may support projects of common interest supported by Member States, which are identified in the framework of the guidelines referred to in the first indent, particularly through feasibility studies, loan guarantees or interest-rate subsidies; the Community may also contribute, through the Cohesion Fund set up pursuant to Article 161, to the financing of specific projects in Member States in the area of transport infrastructure.

   The Community's activities shall take into account the potential economic viability of the projects.

2. Member States shall, in liaison with the Commission, coordinate among themselves the policies pursued at national level which may have a significant impact on the achievement of the objectives referred to in Article 154. The Commission may, in close cooperation with the Member State, take any useful initiative to promote such coordination.

3. The Community may decide to cooperate with third countries to promote projects of mutual interest and to ensure the interoperability of networks.

Article 156 (ex Article 129d)   The guidelines and other measures referred to in Article 155(1) shall be adopted by the Council, acting in accordance with the procedure referred to in Article 251 and after consulting the Economic and Social Committee and the Committee of the Regions.

Guidelines and projects of common interest which relate to the territory of a Member State shall require the approval of the Member State concerned.

TITLE XVI. (EX TITLE XIII) INDUSTRY

Article 157 (ex Article 130)   1. The Community and the Member States shall ensure that the conditions necessary for the competitiveness of the Community's industry exist.

For that purpose, in accordance with a system of open and competitive markets, their action shall be aimed at:

— speeding up the adjustment of industry to structural changes;
— encouraging an environment favourable to initiative and to the development of undertakings throughout the Community, particularly small and medium-sized undertakings;
— encouraging an environment favourable to cooperation between undertakings;
— fostering better exploitation of the industrial potential of policies of innovation, research and technological development.

2. The Member States shall consult each other in liaison with the Commission and, where necessary, shall coordinate their action. The Commission may take any useful initiative to promote such coordination.

3. The Community shall contribute to the achievement of the objectives set out in paragraph 1 through the policies and activities it pursues under other provisions of this Treaty. The Council, acting unanimously on a proposal from the Commission, after consulting the European Parliament and the Economic and Social Committee, may decide on specific measures in support of action taken in the Member States to achieve the objectives set out in paragraph 1.

This Title shall not provide a basis for the introduction by the Community of any measure which could lead to a distortion of competition.

TITLE XVII. (EX TITLE XIV) ECONOMIC AND SOCIAL COHESION

Article 158 (ex Article 130a)   In order to promote its overall harmonious development, the Community shall develop and pursue its actions leading to the strengthening of its economic and social cohesion.

In particular, the Community shall aim at reducing disparities between the levels of development of the various regions and the backwardness of the least favoured regions or islands, including rural areas.

Article 159 (ex Article 130b)   Member States shall conduct their economic policies and shall coordinate them in such a way as, in addition, to attain the objectives set out in Article 158. The formulation and implementation of the Community's policies and actions and the implementation of the internal market shall take into account the objectives set out in Article 158 and shall contribute to their achievement. The Community shall also support the achievement of these objectives by the action it takes through the Structural Funds (European Agricultural Guidance and Guarantee Fund, Guidance Section; European Social Fund; European Regional Development Fund), the European Investment Bank and the other existing financial instruments.

The Commission shall submit a report to the European Parliament, the Council, the Economic and Social Committee and the Committee of the Regions every three years on the progress made towards achieving economic and social cohesion and on the manner in which the various means provided for in this Article have contributed to it. This report shall, if necessary, be accompanied by appropriate proposals.

If specific actions prove necessary outside the Funds and without prejudice to the measures decided upon within the framework of the other Community policies, such actions may be adopted by the Council acting unanimously on a proposal from the Commission and after consulting the European Parliament, the Economic and Social Committee and the Committee of the Regions.

Article 160 (ex Article 130c)   The European Regional Development Fund is intended to help to redress the main regional imbalances in the Community through participation in the development and structural adjustment of regions whose development is lagging behind and in the conversion of declining industrial regions.

Article 161 (ex Article 130d)   Without prejudice to Article 162, the Council, acting unanimously on a proposal from the Commission and after obtaining the assent of the European Parliament and consulting the Economic and Social Committee and the Committee of the Regions, shall define the tasks, priority objectives and the organisation of the Structural Funds, which may involve grouping the Funds. The Council, acting by the same procedure, shall also define the general rules applicable to them and the provisions necessary to ensure their effectiveness and the co-ordination of the Funds with one another and with the other existing financial instruments.

A Cohesion Fund set up by the Council in accordance with the same procedure shall provide a financial contribution to projects in the fields of environment and trans-European networks in the area of transport infrastructure.

Article 162 (ex Article 130e)   Implementing decisions relating to the European Regional Development Fund shall be taken by the Council, acting in accordance with the procedure referred to in Article 251 and after consulting the Economic and Social Committee and the Committee of the Regions.

With regard to the European Agricultural Guidance and Guarantee Fund, Guidance Section, and the European Social Fund, Articles 37 and 148 respectively shall continue to apply.

TITLE XVIII. (EX TITLE XV) RESEARCH AND TECHNOLOGICAL DEVELOPMENT

Article 163 (ex Article 130f)   1. The Community shall have the objective of strengthening the scientific and technological bases of Community industry and encouraging it to become more competitive at international level, while promoting all the research activities deemed necessary by virtue of other Chapters of this Treaty.

2. For this purpose the Community shall, throughout the Community, encourage undertakings, including small and medium-sized undertakings, research centres and universities in their research and technological development activities of high quality; it shall support their efforts to cooperate with one another, aiming, notably, at enabling undertakings to exploit the internal market potential to the full, in particular through the opening-up of national public contracts, the

definition of common standards and the removal of legal and fiscal obstacles to that cooperation.

3. All Community activities under this Treaty in the area of research and technological development, including demonstration projects, shall be decided on and implemented in accordance with the provisions of this Title.

Article 164 (ex Article 130g)   In pursuing these objectives, the Community shall carry out the following activities, complementing the activities carried out in the Member States:
(a) implementation of research, technological development and demonstration programmes, by promoting cooperation with and between undertakings, research centres and universities;
(b) promotion of cooperation in the field of Community research, technological development and demonstration with third countries and international organisations;
(c) dissemination and optimisation of the results of activities in Community research, technological development and demonstration;
(d) stimulation of the training and mobility of researchers in the Community.

Article 165 (ex Article 130h)   1. The Community and the Member States shall coordinate their research and technological development activities so as to ensure that national policies and Community policy are mutually consistent.

2. In close cooperation with the Member State, the Commission may take any useful initiative to promote the coordination referred to in paragraph 1.

Article 166 (ex Article 130i)   1. A multiannual framework programme, setting out all the activities of the Community, shall be adopted by the Council, acting in accordance with the procedure referred to in Article 251 after consulting the Economic and Social Committee.
   The framework programme shall:
— establish the scientific and technological objectives to be achieved by the activities provided for in Article 164 and fix the relevant priorities;
— indicate the broad lines of such activities;
— fix the maximum overall amount and the detailed rules for Community financial participation in the framework programme and the respective shares in each of the activities provided for.

2. The framework programme shall be adapted or supplemented as the situation changes.

3. The framework programme shall be implemented through specific programmes developed within each activity. Each specific programme shall define the detailed rules for implementing it, fix its duration and provide for the means deemed necessary. The sum of the amounts deemed necessary, fixed in the specific programmes, may not exceed the overall maximum amount fixed for the framework programme and each activity.

4. The Council, acting by a qualified majority on a proposal from the Commission and after consulting the European Parliament and the Economic and Social Committee, shall adopt the specific programmes.

Article 167 (ex Article 130j) For the implementation of the multiannual framework programme the Council shall:

— determine the rules for the participation of undertakings, research centres and universities;
— lay down the rules governing the dissemination of research results.

Article 168 (ex Article 130k) In implementing the multiannual framework programme, supplementary programmes may be decided on involving the participation of certain Member States only, which shall finance them subject to possible Community participation.

The Council shall adopt the rules applicable to supplementary programmes, particularly as regards the dissemination of knowledge and access by other Member States.

Article 169 (ex Article 130l) In implementing the multiannual framework programme the Community may make provision, in agreement with the Member States concerned, for participation in research and development programmes undertaken by several Member States, including participation in the structures created for the execution of those programmes.

Article 170 (ex Article 130m) In implementing the multiannual framework programme the Community may make provision for cooperation in Community research, technological development and demonstration with third countries or international organisations.

The detailed arrangements for such cooperation may be the subject of agreements between the Community and the third parties concerned, which shall be negotiated and concluded in accordance with Article 300.

Article 171 (ex Article 130n) The Community may set up joint undertakings or any other structure necessary for the efficient execution of Community research, technological development and demonstration programmes.

Article 172 (ex Article 130o) The Council, acting by qualified majority on a proposal from the Commission and after consulting the European Parliament and the Economic and Social Committee, shall adopt the provisions referred to in Article 171.

The Council, acting in accordance with the procedure referred to in Article 251 and after consulting the Economic and Social Committee, shall adopt the provisions referred to in Articles 167, 168 and 169. Adoption of the supplementary programmes shall require the agreement of the Member States concerned.

Article 173 (ex Article 130p) At the beginning of each year the Commission shall send a report to the European Parliament and the Council. The report shall include information on research and technological development activities and the dissemination of results during the previous year, and the work programme for the current year.

TITLE XIX. (EX TITLE XVI) ENVIRONMENT

Article 174 (ex Article 130r) 1. Community policy on the environment shall contribute to pursuit of the following objectives:

— preserving, protecting and improving the quality of the environment;
— protecting human health;
— prudent and rational utilisation of natural resources;
— promoting measures at international level to deal with regional or worldwide environmental problems.

2. Community policy on the environment shall aim at a high level of protection taking into account the diversity of situations in the various regions of the Community. It shall be based on the precautionary principle and on the principles that preventive action should be taken, that environmental damage should as a priority be rectified at source and that the polluter should pay.

In this context, harmonisation measures answering environmental protection requirements shall include, where appropriate, a safeguard clause allowing Member States to take provisional measures, for non-economic environmental reasons, subject to a Community inspection procedure.

3. In preparing its policy on the environment, the Community shall take account of:

— available scientific and technical data;
— environmental conditions in the various regions of the Community;
— the potential benefits and costs of action or lack of action;
— the economic and social development of the Community as a whole and the balanced development of its regions.

4. Within their respective spheres of competence, the Community and the Member States shall cooperate with third countries and with the competent international organisations. The arrangements for Community cooperation may be the subject of agreements between the Community and the third parties concerned, which shall be negotiated and concluded in accordance with Article 300.

The previous subparagraph shall be without prejudice to Member States' competence to negotiate in international bodies and to conclude international agreements.

Article 175 (ex Article 130s)   1. The Council, acting in accordance with the procedure referred to in Article 251 and after consulting the Economic and Social Committee and the Committee of the Regions, shall decide what action is to be taken by the Community in order to achieve the objectives referred to in Article 174.

2. By way of derogation from the decision-making procedure provided for in paragraph 1 and without prejudice to Article 95, the Council, acting unanimously on a proposal from the Commission and after consulting the European Parliament, the Economic and Social Committee and the Committee of the Regions, shall adopt:

— provisions primarily of a fiscal nature;
— measures concerning town and country planning, land use with the exception of waste management and measures of a general nature, and management of water resources;
— measures significantly affecting a Member State's choice between different energy sources and the general structure of its energy supply.

The Council may, under the conditions laid down in the preceding subparagraph, define those matters referred to in this paragraph on which decisions are to be taken by a qualified majority.

3. In other areas, general action programmes setting out priority objectives to be attained shall be adopted by the Council, acting in accordance with the procedure referred to in Article 251 and after consulting the Economic and Social Committee and the Committee of the Regions.

The Council, acting under the terms of paragraph 1 or paragraph 2 according to the case, shall adopt the measures necessary for the implementation of these programmes.

4. Without prejudice to certain measures of a Community nature, the Member States shall finance and implement the environment policy.

5. Without prejudice to the principle that the polluter should pay, if a measure based on the provisions of paragraph 1 involves costs deemed disproportionate for the public authorities of a Member State, the Council shall, in the act adopting that measure, lay down appropriate provisions in the form of:

— temporary derogations, and/or
— financial support from the Cohesion Fund set up pursuant to Article 161.

Article 176 (ex Article 130t)   The protective measures adopted pursuant to Article 175 shall not prevent any Member State from maintaining or introducing more stringent protective measures. Such measures must be compatible with this Treaty. They shall be notified to the Commission.

Title XX. (ex Title XVII) Development Cooperation

Article 177 (ex Article 130u)   1. Community policy in the sphere of development cooperation, which shall be complementary to the policies pursued by the Member States, shall foster:

— the sustainable economic and social development of the developing countries, and more particularly the most disadvantaged among them;
— the smooth and gradual integration of the developing countries into the world economy;
— the campaign against poverty in the developing countries.

2. Community policy in this area shall contribute to the general objective of developing and consolidating democracy and the rule of law, and to that of respecting human rights and fundamental freedoms.

3. The Community and the Member States shall comply with the commitments and take account of the objectives they have approved in the context of the United Nations and other competent international organisations.

Article 178 (ex Article 130v)   The Community shall take account of the objectives referred to in Article 177 in the policies that it implements which are likely to affect developing countries.

Article 179 (ex Article 130w)   1. Without prejudice to the other provisions of this Treaty, the Council, acting in accordance with the procedure referred to in Article 251, shall adopt the measures necessary to further the objectives referred to in Article 177. Such measures may take the form of multiannual programmes.

2. The European Investment Bank shall contribute, under the terms laid down in its Statute, to the implementation of the measures referred to in paragraph 1.

3. The provisions of this Article shall not affect cooperation with the African, Caribbean and Pacific countries in the framework of the ACP-EC Convention.

Article 180 (ex Article 130x) 1. The Community and the Member States shall coordinate their policies on development cooperation and shall consult each other on their aid programmes, including in international organisations and during international conferences. They may undertake joint action. Member States shall contribute if necessary to the implementation of Community aid programmes.

2. The Commission may take any useful initiative to promote the coordination referred to in paragraph 1.

Article 181 (ex Article 130y) Within their respective spheres of competence, the Community and the Member States shall cooperate with third countries and with the competent international organisations. The arrangements for Community cooperation may be the subject of agreements between the Community and the third parties concerned, which shall be negotiated and concluded in accordance with Article 300.

  The previous paragraph shall be without prejudice to Member States' competence to negotiate in international bodies and to conclude international agreements.

PART FOUR: ASSOCIATION OF THE OVERSEAS COUNTRIES AND TERRITORIES

Article 182 (ex Article 131) The Member States agree to associate with the Community the non-European countries and territories which have special relations with Denmark, France, the Netherlands and the United Kingdom. These countries and territories (hereinafter called the 'countries and territories') are listed in Annex II to this Treaty.

  The purpose of association shall be to promote the economic and social development of the countries and territories and to establish close economic relations between them and the Community as a whole.

  In accordance with the principles set out in the Preamble to this Treaty, association shall serve primarily to further the interests and prosperity of the inhabitants of these countries and territories in order to lead them to the economic, social and cultural development to which they aspire.

Article 183 (ex Article 132) Association shall have the following objectives.

(1) Member States shall apply to their trade with the countries and territories the same treatment as they accord each other pursuant to this Treaty.
(2) Each country or territory shall apply to its trade with Member States and with the other countries and territories the same treatment as that which it applies to the European State with which is has special relations.
(3) The Member States shall contribute to the investments required for the progressive development of these countries and territories.
(4) For investments financed by the Community, participation in tenders and supplies shall be open on equal terms to all natural and legal persons who are nationals of a Member State or of one of the countries and territories.

(5) In relations between Member States and the countries and territories the right of establishment of nationals and companies or firms shall be regulated in accordance with the provisions and procedures laid down in the Chapter relating to the right of establishment and on a non-discriminatory basis, subject to any special provisions laid down pursuant to Article 187.

Article 184 (ex Article 133) 1. Customs duties on imports into the Member States of goods originating in the countries and territories shall be prohibited in conformity with the prohibition of customs duties between Member States in accordance with the provisions of this Treaty.

2. Customs duties on imports into each country or territory from Member States or from the other countries or territories shall be prohibited in accordance with the provisions of Article 25.

3. The countries and territories may, however, levy customs duties which meet the needs of their development and industrialisation or produce revenue for their budgets.

The duties referred to in the preceding subparagraph may not exceed the level of those imposed on imports of products from the Member State with which each country or territory has special relations.

4. Paragraph 2 shall not apply to countries and territories which, by reason of the particular international obligations by which they are bound, already apply a non-discriminatory customs tariff.

5. The introduction of or any change in customs duties imposed on goods imported into the countries and territories shall not, either in law or in fact, give rise to any direct or indirect discrimination between imports from the various Member States.

Article 185 (ex Article 134)   If the level of the duties applicable to goods from a third country on entry into a country or territory is liable, when the provisions of Article 184(1) have been applied, to cause deflections of trade to the detriment of any Member State, the latter may request the Commission to propose to the other Member States the measures needed to remedy the situation.

Article 186 (ex Article 135)   Subject to the provisions relating to public health, public security or public policy, freedom of movement within Member States for workers from the countries and territories, and within the countries and territories for workers from Member States, shall be governed by agreements to be concluded subsequently with the unanimous approval of Member States.

Article 187 (ex Article 136)   The Council, acting unanimously, shall, on the basis of the experience acquired under the association of the countries and territories with the Community and of the principles set out in this Treaty, lay down provisions as regards the detailed rules and the procedure for the association of the countries and territories with the Community.

Article 188 (ex Article 136a)   The provisions of Articles 182 to 187 shall apply to Greenland, subject to the specific provisions for Greenland set out in the Protocol on special arrangements for Greenland, annexed to this Treaty.

PART FIVE: INSTITUTIONS OF THE COMMUNITY

TITLE I. PROVISIONS GOVERNING THE INSTITUTIONS

Chapter 1: The Institutions

SECTION 1: THE EUROPEAN PARLIAMENT

Article 189 (ex Article 137)   The European Parliament, which shall consist of representatives of the peoples of the States brought together in the Community, shall exercise the powers conferred upon it by this Treaty.

The number of Members of the European Parliament shall not exceed seven hundred.

Article 190 (ex Article 138)   1. The representatives in the European Parliament of the peoples of the States brought together in the Community shall be elected by direct universal suffrage.

2. The number of representatives elected in each Member State shall be as follows:

Belgium	25
Denmark	16
Germany	99
Greece	25
Spain	64
France	87
Ireland	15
Italy	87
Luxembourg	6
Netherlands	31
Austria	21
Portugal	25
Finland	16
Sweden	22
United Kingdom	87

In the event of amendments to this paragraph, the number of representatives elected in each Member State must ensure appropriate representation of the peoples of the States brought together in the Community.

3. Representatives shall be elected for a term of five years.

4. The European Parliament shall draw up a proposal for elections by direct universal suffrage in accordance with a uniform procedure in all Member States or in accordance with principles common to all Member States.

The Council shall, acting unanimously after obtaining the assent of the European Parliament, which shall act by a majority of its component members, lay down the appropriate provisions, which it shall recommend to Member States for adoption in accordance with their respective constitutional requirements.

5. The European Parliament shall, after seeking an opinion from the Commission and with the approval of the Council acting unanimously, lay down the regulations and general conditions governing the performance of the duties of its Members.

Article 191 (ex Article 138a)   Political parties at European level are important as a factor for integration within the Union. They contribute to forming a European awareness and to expressing the political will of the citizens of the Union.

Article 192 (ex Article 138b)   Insofar as provided in this Treaty, the European Parliament shall participate in the process leading up to the adoption of Community acts by exercising its powers under the procedures laid down in Articles 251 and 252 and by giving its assent or delivering advisory opinions.

The European Parliament may, acting by a majority of its Members, request the Commission to submit any appropriate proposal on matters on which it considers that a Community act is required for the purpose of implementing this Treaty.

Article 193 (ex Article 138c)   In the course of its duties, the European Parliament may, at the request of a quarter of its Members, set up a temporary Committee of Inquiry to investigate, without prejudice to the powers conferred by this Treaty on other institutions or bodies, alleged contraventions or maladministration in the implementation of Community law, except where the alleged facts are being examined before a court and while the case is still subject to legal proceedings.

The temporary Committee of Inquiry shall cease to exist on the submission of its report.

The detailed provisions governing the exercise of the right of inquiry shall be determined by common accord of the European Parliament, the Council and the Commission.

Article 194 (ex Article 138d)   Any citizen of the Union, and any natural or legal person residing or having its registered office in a Member State, shall have the right to address, individually or in association with other citizens or persons, a petition to the European Parliament on a matter which comes within the Community's fields of activity and which affects him, her or it directly.

Article 195 (ex Article 138e)   1. The European Parliament shall appoint an Ombudsman empowered to receive complaints from any citizen of the Union or any natural or legal person residing or having its registered office in a Member State concerning instances of maladministration in the activities of the Community institutions or bodies, with the exception of the Court of Justice and the Court of First Instance acting in their judicial role.

In accordance with his duties, the Ombudsman shall conduct inquiries for which he finds grounds, either on his own initiative or on the basis of complaints submitted to him direct or through a Member of the European Parliament, except where the alleged facts are or have been the subject of legal proceedings. Where the Ombudsman establishes an instance of maladministration, he shall refer the matter to the institution concerned, which shall have a period of three months in which to inform him of its views. The Ombudsman shall then forward a report to the European Parliament and the institution concerned. The person lodging the complaint shall be informed of the outcome of such inquiries.

The Ombudsman shall submit an annual report to the European Parliament on the outcome of his inquiries.

2. The Ombudsman shall be appointed after each election of the European Parliament for the duration of its term of office. The Ombudsman shall be eligible for reappointment.

The Ombudsman may be dismissed by the Court of Justice at the request of the European Parliament if he no longer fulfils the conditions required for the performance of his duties or if he is guilty of serious misconduct.

3. The Ombudsman shall be completely independent in the performance of his duties. In the performance of those duties he shall neither seek nor take instructions from any body. The Ombudsman may not, during his term of office, engage in any other occupation, whether gainful or not.

4. The European Parliament shall, after seeking an opinion from the Commission and with the approval of the Council acting by a qualified majority, lay down the regulations and general conditions governing the performance of the Ombudsman's duties.

Article 196 (ex Article 139) The European Parliament shall hold an annual session. It shall meet, without requiring to be convened, on the second Tuesday in March.

The European Parliament may meet in extraordinary session at the request of a majority of its Members or at the request of the Council or of the Commission.

Article 197 (ex Article 140) The European Parliament shall elect its President and its officers from among its Members.

Members of the Commission may attend all meetings and shall, at their request, be heard on behalf of the Commission.

The Commission shall reply orally or in writing to questions put to it by the European Parliament or by its Members.

The Council shall be heard by the European Parliament in accordance with the conditions laid down by the Council in its Rules of Procedure.

Article 198 (ex Article 141) Save as otherwise provided in this Treaty, the European Parliament shall act by an absolute majority of the votes cast.

The Rules of Procedure shall determine the quorum.

Article 199 (ex Article 142) The European Parliament shall adopt its Rules of Procedure, acting by a majority of its Members.

The proceedings of the European Parliament shall be published in the manner laid down in its Rules of Procedure.

Article 200 (ex Article 143) The European Parliament shall discuss in open session the annual general report submitted to it by the Commission.

Article 201 (ex Article 144) If a motion of censure on the activities of the Commission is tabled before it, the European Parliament shall not vote thereon until at least three days after the motion has been tabled and only by open vote.

If the motion of censure is carried by a two-thirds majority of the votes cast, representing a majority of the Members of the European Parliament, the Members of the Commission shall resign as a body. They shall continue to deal with current business until they are replaced in accordance with Article 214. In this case, the term of office of the Members of the Commission appointed to replace them shall expire on the date on which the term of office of the Members of the Commission obliged to resign as a body would have expired.

SECTION 2: THE COUNCIL

Article 202 (ex Article 145)   To ensure that the objectives set out in this Treaty are attained the Council shall, in accordance with the provisions of this Treaty:
— ensure coordination of the general economic policies of the Member States;
— have power to take decisions;
— confer on the Commission, in the acts which the Council adopts, powers for the implementation of the rules which the Council lays down. The Council may impose certain requirements in respect of the exercise of these powers. The Council may also reserve the right, in specific cases, to exercise directly implementing powers itself. The procedures referred to above must be consonant with principles and rules to be laid down in advance by the Council, acting unanimously on a proposal from the Commission and after obtaining the Opinion of the European Parliament.

Article 203 (ex Article 146)   The Council shall consist of a representative of each Member State at ministerial level, authorised to commit the government of that Member State.

The office of President shall be held in turn by each Member State in the Council for a term of six months in the order decided by the Council acting unanimously.

Article 204 (ex Article 147)   The Council shall meet when convened by its President on his own initiative or at the request of one of its members or of the Commission.

Article 205 (ex Article 148)   1. Save as otherwise provided in this Treaty, the Council shall act by a majority of its members.

2. Where the Council is required to act by a qualified majority, the votes of its members shall be weighted as follows:

Belgium	5
Denmark	3
Germany	10
Greece	5
Spain	8
France	10
Ireland	3
Italy	10
Luxembourg	2
Netherlands	5
Austria	4
Portugal	5
Finland	3
Sweden	4
United Kingdom	10

For their adoption, acts of the Council shall require at least:
— 62 votes in favour where this Treaty requires them to be adopted on a proposal from the Commission,

— 62 votes in favour, cast by at least 10 members, in other cases.

3. Abstentions by members present in person or represented shall not prevent the adoption by the Council of acts which require unanimity.

Article 206 (ex Article 150)   Where a vote is taken, any member of the Council may also act on behalf of not more than one other member.

Article 207 (ex Article 151)   1. A committee consisting of the Permanent Representatives of the Member States shall be responsible for preparing the work of the Council and for carrying out the tasks assigned to it by the Council. The Committee may adopt procedural decisions in cases provided for in the Council's Rules of Procedure.

2. The Council shall be assisted by a General Secretariat, under the responsibility of a Secretary-General, High Representative for the common foreign and security policy, who shall be assisted by a Deputy Secretary-General responsible for the running of the General Secretariat. The Secretary-General and the Deputy Secretary-General shall be appointed by the Council acting unanimously.
   The Council shall decide on the organisation of the General Secretariat.

3. The Council shall adopt its Rules of Procedure.
   For the purpose of applying Article 255(3), the Council shall elaborate in these Rules the conditions under which the public shall have access to Council documents. For the purpose of this paragraph, the Council shall define the cases in which it is to be regarded as acting in its legislative capacity, with a view to allowing greater access to documents in those cases, while at the same time preserving the effectiveness of its decision-making process. In any event, when the Council acts in its legislative capacity, the results of votes and explanations of vote as well as statements in the minutes shall be made public.

Article 208 (ex Article 152)   The Council may request the Commission to undertake any studies the Council considers desirable for the attainment of the common objectives, and to submit to it any appropriate proposals.

Article 209 (ex Article 153)   The Council shall, after receiving an opinion from the Commission, determine the rules governing the committees provided for in this Treaty.

Article 210 (ex Article 154)   The Council shall, acting by a qualified majority, determine the salaries, allowances and pensions of the President and Members of the Commission, and of the President, Judges, Advocates-General and Registrar of the Court of Justice. It shall also, again by a qualified majority, determine any payment to be made instead of remuneration.

SECTION 3: THE COMMISSION

Article 211 (ex Article 155)   In order to ensure the proper functioning and development of the common market, the Commission shall:
— ensure that the provisions of this Treaty and the measures taken by the institutions pursuant thereto are applied;
— formulate recommendations or deliver opinions on matters dealt with in this Treaty, if it expressly so provides or if the Commission considers it necessary;

— have its own power of decision and participate in the shaping of measures taken by the Council and by the European Parliament in the manner provided for in this Treaty;

— exercise the powers conferred on it by the Council for the implementation of the rules laid down by the latter.

Article 212 (ex Article 156)   The Commission shall publish annually, not later than one month before the opening of the session of the European Parliament, a general report on the activities of the Community.

Article 213 (ex Article 157)   1. The Commission shall consist of 20 Members, who shall be chosen on the grounds of their general competence and whose independence is beyond doubt.

The number of Members of the Commission may be altered by the Council, acting unanimously.

Only nationals of Member States may be Members of the Commission.

The Commission must include at least one national of each of the Member States, but may not include more than two Members having the nationality of the same State.

2. The Members of the Commission shall, in the general interest of the Community, be completely independent in the performance of their duties.

In the performance of these duties, they shall neither seek nor take instructions from any government or from any other body. They shall refrain from any action incompatible with their duties. Each Member State undertakes to respect this principle and not to seek to influence the Members of the Commission in the performance of their tasks.

The Members of the Commission may not, during their term of office, engage in any other occupation, whether gainful or not. When entering upon their duties they shall give a solemn undertaking that, both during and after their term of office, they will respect the obligations arising therefrom and in particular their duty to behave with integrity and discretion as regards the acceptance, after they have ceased to hold office, of certain appointments or benefits. In the event of any breach of these obligations, the Court of Justice may, on application by the Council or the Commission, rule that the Member concerned be, according to the circumstances, either compulsorily retired in accordance with Article 216 or deprived of his right to a pension or other benefits in its stead.

Article 214 (ex Article 158)   1. The Members of the Commission shall be appointed, in accordance with the procedure referred to in paragraph 2, for a period of five years, subject, if need be, to Article 201.

Their term of office shall be renewable.

2. The governments of the Member States shall nominate by common accord the person they intend to appoint as President of the Commission; the nomination shall be approved by the European Parliament.

The governments of the Member States shall, by common accord with the nominee for President, nominate the other persons whom they intend to appoint as Members of the Commission.

The President and the other Members of the Commission thus nominated shall be subject as a body to a vote of approval by the European Parliament. After approval by the European Parliament, the President and the other Members of the Commission shall be appointed by common accord of the governments of the Member States.

Article 215 (ex Article 159)   Apart from normal replacement, or death, the duties of a Member of the Commission shall end when he resigns or is compulsorily retired.

The vacancy thus caused shall be filled for the remainder of the Member's term of office by a new Member appointed by common accord of the governments of the Member States. The Council may, acting unanimously, decide that such a vacancy need not be filled.

In the event of resignation, compulsory retirement or death, the President shall be replaced for the remainder of his term of office. The procedure laid down in Article 214(2) shall be applicable for the replacement of the President.

Save in the case of compulsory retirement under Article 216, Members of the Commission shall remain in office until they have been replaced.

Article 216 (ex Article 160)   If any Member of the Commission no longer fulfils the conditions required for the performance of his duties or if he has been guilty of serious misconduct, the Court of Justice may, on application by the Council or the Commission, compulsorily retire him.

Article 217 (ex Article 161)   The Commission may appoint a Vice-President or two Vice-Presidents from among its Members.

Article 218 (ex Article 162)   1. The Council and the Commission shall consult each other and shall settle by common accord their methods of cooperation.

2. The Commission shall adopt its Rules of Procedure so as to ensure that both it and its departments operate in accordance with the provisions of this Treaty. It shall ensure that these rules are published.

Article 219 (ex Article 163)   The Commission shall work under the political guidance of its President.

The Commission shall act by a majority of the number of Members provided for in Article 213.

A meeting of the Commission shall be valid only if the number of Members laid down in its Rules of Procedure is present.

SECTION 4: THE COURT OF JUSTICE

Article 220 (ex Article 164)   The Court of Justice shall ensure that in the interpretation and application of this Treaty the law is observed.

Article 221 (ex Article 165)   The Court of Justice shall consist of 15 Judges.

The Court of Justice shall sit in plenary session. It may, however, form chambers, each consisting of three, five or seven Judges, either to undertake certain preparatory inquiries or to adjudicate on particular categories of cases in accordance with rules laid down for these purposes.

The Court of Justice shall sit in plenary session when a Member State or a Community institution that is a party to the proceedings so requests.

Should the Court of Justice so request, the Council may, acting unanimously, increase the number of Judges and make the necessary adjustments to the second and third paragraphs of this Article and to the second paragraph of Article 223.

Article 222 (ex Article 166)   The Court of Justice shall be assisted by eight Advocates-General. However, a ninth Advocate-General shall be appointed as from 1 January 1995 until 6 October 2000.

It shall be the duty of the Advocate-General, acting with complete impartiality and independence, to make, in open court, reasoned submissions on cases brought before the Court of Justice, in order to assist the Court in the performance of the task assigned to it in Article 220.

Should the Court of Justice so request, the Council may, acting unanimously, increase the number of Advocates-General and make the necessary adjustments to the third paragraph of Article 223.

Article 223 (ex Article 167)   The Judges and Advocates-General shall be chosen from persons whose independence is beyond doubt and who possess the qualifications required for appointment to the highest judicial offices in their respective countries or who are jurisconsults of recognised competence; they shall be appointed by common accord of the governments of the Member States for a term of six years.

Every three years there shall be a partial replacement of the Judges. Eight and seven Judges shall be replaced alternately.

Every three years there shall be a partial replacement of the Advocates-General. Four Advocates-General shall be replaced on each occasion.

Retiring Judges and Advocates-General shall be eligible for reappointment.

The Judges shall elect the President of the Court of Justice from among their number for a term of three years. He may be re-elected.

Article 224 (ex Article 168)   The Court of Justice shall appoint its Registrar and lay down the rules governing his service.

Article 225 (ex Article 168a)   1. A Court of First Instance shall be attached to the Court of Justice with jurisdiction to hear and determine at first instance, subject to a right of appeal to the Court of Justice on points of law only and in accordance with the conditions laid down by the Statute, certain classes of action or proceeding defined in accordance with the conditions laid down in paragraph 2. The Court of First Instance shall not be competent to hear and determine questions referred for a preliminary ruling under Article 234.

2. At the request of the Court of Justice and after consulting the European Parliament and the Commission, the Council, acting unanimously, shall determine the classes of action or proceeding referred to in paragraph 1 and the composition of the Court of First Instance and shall adopt the necessary adjustments and additional provisions to the Statute of the Court of Justice. Unless the Council decides otherwise, the provisions of this Treaty relating to the Court of Justice, in particular the provisions of the Protocol on the Statute of the Court of Justice, shall apply to the Court of First Instance.

3. The members of the Court of First Instance shall be chosen from persons whose independence is beyond doubt and who possess the ability required for appointment to judicial office; they shall be appointed by common accord of the governments of the Member States for a term of six years. The membership shall be par-

tially renewed every three years. Retiring members shall be eligible for reappointment.

4. The Court of First Instance shall establish its Rules of Procedure in agreement with the Court of Justice. Those rules shall require the unanimous approval of the Council.

Article 226 (ex Article 169) If the Commission considers that a Member State has failed to fulfil an obligation under this Treaty, it shall deliver a reasoned opinion on the matter after giving the State concerned the opportunity to submit its observations.

If the State concerned does not comply with the opinion within the period laid down by the Commission, the latter may bring the matter before the Court of Justice.

Article 227 (ex Article 170) A Member State which considers that another Member State has failed to fulfil an obligation under this Treaty may bring the matter before the Court of Justice.

Before a Member State brings an action against another Member State for an alleged infringement of an obligation under this Treaty, it shall bring the matter before the Commission.

The Commission shall deliver a reasoned opinion after each of the States concerned has been given the opportunity to submit its own case and its observations on the other party's case both orally and in writing.

If the Commission has not delivered an opinion within three months of the date on which the matter was brought before it, the absence of such opinion shall not prevent the matter from being brought before the Court of Justice.

Article 228 (ex Article 171) 1. If the Court of Justice finds that a Member State has failed to fulfil an obligation under this Treaty, the State shall be required to take the necessary measures to comply with the judgment of the Court of Justice.

2. If the Commission considers that the Member State concerned has not taken such measures it shall, after giving that State the opportunity to submit its observations, issue a reasoned opinion specifying the points on which the Member State concerned has not complied with the judgment of the Court of Justice.

If the Member State concerned fails to take the necessary measures to comply with the Court's judgment within the time-limit laid down by the Commission, the latter may bring the case before the Court of Justice. In so doing it shall specify the amount of the lump sum or penalty payment to be paid by the Member State concerned which it considers appropriate in the circumstances.

If the Court of Justice finds that the Member State concerned has not complied with its judgment it may impose a lump sum or penalty payment on it.

This procedure shall be without prejudice to Article 227.

Article 229 (ex Article 172) Regulations adopted jointly by the European Parliament and the Council, and by the Council, pursuant to the provisions of this Treaty, may give the Court of Justice unlimited jurisdiction with regard to the penalties provided for in such regulations.

Article 230 (ex Article 173) The Court of Justice shall review the legality of acts adopted jointly by the European Parliament and the Council, of acts of the Council, of the

Commission and of the ECB, other than recommendations and opinions, and of acts of the European Parliament intended to produce legal effects vis-à-vis third parties.

It shall for this purpose have jurisdiction in actions brought by a Member State, the Council or the Commission on grounds of lack of competence, infringement of an essential procedural requirement, infringement of this Treaty or of any rule of law relating to its application, or misuse of powers.

The Court of Justice shall have jurisdiction under the same conditions in actions brought by the European Parliament, by the Court of Auditors and by the ECB for the purpose of protecting their prerogatives.

Any natural or legal person may, under the same conditions, institute proceedings against a decision addressed to that person or against a decision which, although in the form of a regulation or a decision addressed to another person, is of direct and individual concern to the former.

The proceedings provided for in this Article shall be instituted within two months of the publication of the measure, or of its notification to the plaintiff, or, in the absence thereof, of the day on which it came to the knowledge of the latter, as the case may be.

Article 231 (ex Article 174)   If the action is well founded, the Court of Justice shall declare the act concerned to be void.

In the case of a regulation, however, the Court of Justice shall, if it considers this necessary, state which of the effects of the regulation which it has declared void shall be considered as definitive.

Article 232 (ex Article 175)   Should the European Parliament, the Council or the Commission, in infringement of this Treaty, fail to act, the Member States and the other institutions of the Community may bring an action before the Court of Justice to have the infringement established.

The action shall be admissible only if the institution concerned has first been called upon to act. If, within two months of being so called upon, the institution concerned has not defined its position, the action may be brought within a further period of two months.

Any natural or legal person may, under the conditions laid down in the preceding paragraphs, complain to the Court of Justice that an institution of the Community has failed to address to that person any act other than a recommendation or an opinion.

The Court of Justice shall have jurisdiction, under the same conditions, in actions or proceedings brought by the ECB in the areas falling within the latter's field of competence and in actions or proceedings brought against the latter.

Article 233 (ex Article 176)   The institution or institutions whose act has been declared void or whose failure to act has been declared contrary to this Treaty shall be required to take the necessary measures to comply with the judgment of the Court of Justice.

This obligation shall not affect any obligation which may result from the application of the second paragraph of Article 288.

This Article shall also apply to the ECB.

Article 234 (ex Article 177)   The Court of Justice shall have jurisdiction to give preliminary rulings concerning:

(a) the interpretation of this Treaty;
(b) the validity and interpretation of acts of the institutions of the Community and of the ECB;
(c) the interpretation of the statutes of bodies established by an act of the Council, where those statutes so provide.

Where such a question is raised before any court or tribunal of a Member State, that court or tribunal may, if it considers that a decision on the question is necessary to enable it to give judgment, request the Court of Justice to give a ruling thereon.

Where any such question is raised in a case pending before a court or tribunal of a Member State against whose decisions there is no judicial remedy under national law, that court or tribunal shall bring the matter before the Court of Justice.

Article 235 (ex Article 178)   The Court of Justice shall have jurisdiction in disputes relating to compensation for damage provided for in the second paragraph of Article 288.

Article 236 (ex Article 179)   The Court of Justice shall have jurisdiction in any dispute between the Community and its servants within the limits and under the conditions laid down in the Staff Regulations or the Conditions of Employment.

Article 237 (ex Article 180)   The Court of Justice shall, within the limits hereinafter laid down, have jurisdiction in disputes concerning:
(a) the fulfilment by Member States of obligations under the Statute of the European Investment Bank. In this connection, the Board of Directors of the Bank shall enjoy the powers conferred upon the Commission by Article 226;
(b) measures adopted by the Board of Governors of the European Investment Bank. In this connection, any Member State, the Commission or the Board of Directors of the Bank may institute proceedings under the conditions laid down in Article 230;
(c) measures adopted by the Board of Directors of the European Investment Bank. Proceedings against such measures may be instituted only by Member States or by the Commission, under the conditions laid down in Article 230, and solely on the grounds of non-compliance with the procedure provided for in Article 21(2), (5), (6) and (7) of the Statute of the Bank;
(d) the fulfilment by national central banks of obligations under this Treaty and the Statute of the ESCB. In this connection the powers of the Council of the ECB in respect of national central banks shall be the same as those conferred upon the Commission in respect of Member States by Article 226. If the Court of Justice finds that a national central bank has failed to fulfil an obligation under this Treaty, that bank shall be required to take the necessary measures to comply with the judgment of the Court of Justice.

Article 238 (ex Article 181)   The Court of Justice shall have jurisdiction to give judgment pursuant to any arbitration clause contained in a contract concluded by or on behalf of the Community, whether that contract be governed by public or private law.

Article 239 (ex Article 182)   The Court of Justice shall have jurisdiction in any dispute between Member States which relates to the subject matter of this Treaty if the dispute is submitted to it under a special agreement between the parties.

Article 240 (ex Article 183) Save where jurisdiction is conferred on the Court of Justice by this Treaty, disputes to which the Community is a party shall not on that ground be excluded from the jurisdiction of the courts or tribunals of the Member States.

Article 241 (ex Article 184) Notwithstanding the expiry of the period laid down in the fifth paragraph of Article 230, any party may, in proceedings in which a regulation adopted jointly by the European Parliament and the Council, or a regulation of the Council, of the Commission, or of the ECB is at issue, plead the grounds specified in the second paragraph of Article 230 in order to invoke before the Court of Justice the inapplicability of that regulation.

Article 242 (ex Article 185) Actions brought before the Court of Justice shall not have suspensory effect. The Court of Justice may, however, if it considers that circumstances so require, order that application of the contested act be suspended.

Article 243 (ex Article 186) The Court of Justice may in any cases before it prescribe any necessary interim measures.

Article 244 (ex Article 187) The judgments of the Court of Justice shall be enforceable under the conditions laid down in Article 256.

Article 245 (ex Article 188) The Statute of the Court of Justice is laid down in a separate Protocol.

The Council may, acting unanimously at the request of the Court of Justice and after consulting the Commission and the European Parliament, amend the provisions of Title III of the Statute.

The Court of Justice shall adopt its Rules of Procedure. These shall require the unanimous approval of the Council.

SECTION 5: THE COURT OF AUDITORS

Article 246 (ex Article 188a) The Court of Auditors shall carry out the audit.

Article 247 (ex Article 188b) 1. The Court of Auditors shall consist of 15 Members.

2. The Members of the Court of Auditors shall be chosen from among persons who belong or have belonged in their respective countries to external audit bodies or who are especially qualified for this office. Their independence must be beyond doubt.

3. The Members of the Court of Auditors shall be appointed for a term of six years by the Council, acting unanimously after consulting the European Parliament.

The Members of the Court of Auditors shall be eligible for reappointment.

They shall elect the President of the Court of Auditors from among their number for a term of three years. The President may be re-elected.

4. The Members of the Court of Auditors shall, in the general interest of the Community, be completely independent in the performance of their duties.

In the performance of these duties, they shall neither seek nor take instructions from any government or from any other body. They shall refrain from any action incompatible with their duties.

5. The Members of the Court of Auditors may not, during their term of office, engage in any other occupation, whether gainful or not. When entering upon their

duties they shall give a solemn undertaking that, both during and after their term of office, they will respect the obligations arising therefrom and in particular their duty to behave with integrity and discretion as regards the acceptance, after they have ceased to hold office, of certain appointments or benefits.

6. Apart from normal replacement, or death, the duties of a Member of the Court of Auditors shall end when he resigns, or is compulsorily retired by a ruling of the Court of Justice pursuant to paragraph 7.

The vacancy thus caused shall be filled for the remainder of the Member's term of office.

Save in the case of compulsory retirement, Members of the Court of Auditors shall remain in office until they have been replaced.

7. A Member of the Court of Auditors may be deprived of his office or of his right to a pension or other benefits in its stead only if the Court of Justice, at the request of the Court of Auditors, finds that he no longer fulfils the requisite conditions or meets the obligations arising from his office.

8. The Council, acting by a qualified majority, shall determine the conditions of employment of the President and the Members of the Court of Auditors and in particular their salaries, allowances and pensions. It shall also, by the same majority, determine any payment to be made instead of remuneration.

9. The provisions of the Protocol on the privileges and immunities of the European Communities applicable to the Judges of the Court of Justice shall also apply to the Members of the Court of Auditors.

Article 248 (ex Article 188c) 1. The Court of Auditors shall examine the accounts of all revenue and expenditure of the Community. It shall also examine the accounts of all revenue and expenditure of all bodies set up by the Community insofar as the relevant constituent instrument does not preclude such examination.

The Court of Auditors shall provide the European Parliament and the Council with a statement of assurance as to the reliability of the accounts and the legality and regularity of the underlying transactions which shall be published in the *Official Journal of the European Communities*.

2. The Court of Auditors shall examine whether all revenue has been received and all expenditure incurred in a lawful and regular manner and whether the financial management has been sound. In doing so, it shall report in particular on any cases of irregularity.

The audit of revenue shall be carried out on the basis both of the amounts established as due and the amounts actually paid to the Community.

The audit of expenditure shall be carried out on the basis both of commitments undertaken and payments made.

These audits may be carried out before the closure of accounts for the financial year in question.

3. The audit shall be based on records and, if necessary, performed on the spot in the other institutions of the Community, on the premises of any body which manages revenue or expenditure on behalf of the Community and in the Member States, including on the premises of any natural or legal person in receipt of payments from the budget. In the Member States the audit shall be carried out in liaison with national audit bodies or, if these do not have the necessary powers, with

the competent national departments. The Court of Auditors and the national audit bodies of the Member States shall cooperate in a spirit of trust while maintaining their independence. These bodies or departments shall inform the Court of Auditors whether they intend to take part in the audit.

The other institutions of the Community, any bodies managing revenue or expenditure on behalf of the Community, any natural or legal person in receipt of payments from the budget, and the national audit bodies or, if these do not have the necessary powers, the competent national departments, shall forward to the Court of Auditors, at its request, any document or information necessary to carry out its task.

In respect of the European Investment Bank's activity in managing Community expenditure and revenue, the Court's rights of access to information held by the Bank shall be governed by an agreement between the Court, the Bank and the Commission. In the absence of an agreement, the Court shall nevertheless have access to information necessary for the audit of Community expenditure and revenue managed by the Bank.

4. The Court of Auditors shall draw up an annual report after the close of each financial year. It shall be forwarded to the other institutions of the Community and shall be published, together with the replies of these institutions to the observations of the Court of Auditors, in the *Official Journal of the European Communities*.

The Court of Auditors may also, at any time, submit observations, particularly in the form of special reports, on specific questions and deliver opinions at the request of one of the other institutions of the Community.

It shall adopt its annual reports, special reports or opinions by a majority of its Members.

It shall assist the European Parliament and the Council in exercising their powers of control over the implementation of the budget.

Chapter 2: Provisions Common to Several Institutions

Article 249 (ex Article 189)   In order to carry out their task and in accordance with the provisions of this Treaty, the European Parliament acting jointly with the Council, the Council and the Commission shall make regulations and issue directives, take decisions, make recommendations or deliver opinions.

A regulation shall have general application. It shall be binding in its entirety and directly applicable in all Member States.

A directive shall be binding, as to the result to be achieved, upon each Member State to which it is addressed, but shall leave to the national authorities the choice of form and methods.

A decision shall be binding in its entirety upon those to whom it is addressed.

Recommendations and opinions shall have no binding force.

Article 250 (ex Article 189a)   1. Where, in pursuance of this Treaty, the Council acts on a proposal from the Commission, unanimity shall be required for an act constituting an amendment to that proposal, subject to Article 251(4) and (5).

2. As long as the Council has not acted, the Commission may alter its proposal at any time during the procedures leading to the adoption of a Community act.

Article 251 (ex Article 189b) 1. Where reference is made in this Treaty to this Article for the adoption of an act, the following procedure shall apply.

2. The Commission shall submit a proposal to the European Parliament and the Council.

The Council, acting by a qualified majority after obtaining the opinion of the European Parliament,

— if it approves all the amendments contained in the European Parliament's opinion, may adopt the proposed act thus amended;
— if the European Parliament does not propose any amendments, may adopt the proposed act;
— shall otherwise adopt a common position and communicate it to the European Parliament. The Council shall inform the European Parliament fully of the reasons which led it to adopt its common position. The Commission shall inform the European Parliament fully of its position.

If, within three months of such communication, the European Parliament:
(a) approves the common position or has not taken a decision, the act in question shall be deemed to have been adopted in accordance with that common position;
(b) rejects, by an absolute majority of its component members, the common position, the proposed act shall be deemed not to have been adopted;
(c) proposes amendments to the common position by an absolute majority of its component members, the amended text shall be forwarded to the Council and to the Commission, which shall deliver an opinion on those amendments.

3. If, within three months of the matter being referred to it, the Council, acting by a qualified majority, approves all the amendments of the European Parliament, the act in question shall be deemed to have been adopted in the form of the common position thus amended; however, the Council shall act unanimously on the amendments on which the Commission has delivered a negative opinion. If the Council does not approve all the amendments, the President of the Council, in agreement with the President of the European Parliament, shall within six weeks convene a meeting of the Conciliation Committee.

4. The Conciliation Committee, which shall be composed of the members of the Council or their representatives and an equal number of representatives of the European Parliament, shall have the task of reaching agreement on a joint text, by a qualified majority of the members of the Council or their representatives and by a majority of the representatives of the European Parliament. The Commission shall take part in the Conciliation Committee's proceedings and shall take all the necessary initiatives with a view to reconciling the positions of the European Parliament and the Council. In fulfilling this task, the Conciliation Committee shall address the common position on the basis of the amendments proposed by the European Parliament.

5. If, within six weeks of its being convened, the Conciliation Committee approves a joint text, the European Parliament, acting by an absolute majority of the votes cast, and the Council, acting by a qualified majority, shall each have a period of six weeks from that approval in which to adopt the act in question in accordance with the joint text. If either of the two institutions fails to approve the proposed act within that period, it shall be deemed not to have been adopted.

6. Where the Conciliation Committee does not approve a joint text, the proposed act shall be deemed not to have been adopted.

7. The periods of three months and six weeks referred to in this Article shall be extended by a maximum of one month and two weeks respectively at the initiative of the European Parliament or the Council.

Article 252 (ex Article 189c)   Where reference is made in this Treaty to this Article for the adoption of an act, the following procedure shall apply:

(a) The Council, acting by a qualified majority on a proposal from the Commission and after obtaining the opinion of the European Parliament, shall adopt a common position.

(b) The Council's common position shall be communicated to the European Parliament. The Council and the Commission shall inform the European Parliament fully of the reasons which led the Council to adopt its common position and also of the Commission's position.

   If, within three months of such communication, the European Parliament approves this common position or has not taken a decision within that period, the Council shall definitively adopt the act in question in accordance with the common position.

(c) The European Parliament may, within the period of three months referred to in point (b), by an absolute majority of its component Members, propose amendments to the Council's common position. The European Parliament may also, by the same majority, reject the Council's common position. The result of the proceedings shall be transmitted to the Council and the Commission.

   If the European Parliament has rejected the Council's common position, unanimity shall be required for the Council to act on a second reading.

(d) The Commission shall, within a period of one month, re-examine the proposal on the basis of which the Council adopted its common position, by taking into account the amendments proposed by the European Parliament.

   The Commission shall forward to the Council, at the same time as its re-examined proposal, the amendments of the European Parliament which it has not accepted, and shall express its opinion on them. The Council may adopt these amendments unanimously.

(e) The Council, acting by a qualified majority, shall adopt the proposal as re-examined by the Commission.

   Unanimity shall be required for the Council to amend the proposal as re-examined by the Commission.

(f) In the cases referred to in points (c), (d) and (e), the Council shall be required to act within a period of three months. If no decision is taken within this period, the Commission proposal shall be deemed not to have been adopted.

(g) The periods referred to in points (b) and (f) may be extended by a maximum of one month by common accord between the Council and the European Parliament.

Article 253 (ex Article 190)   Regulations, directives and decisions adopted jointly by the European Parliament and the Council, and such acts adopted by the Council or the Commission, shall state the reasons on which they are based and shall refer to any proposals or opinions which were required to be obtained pursuant to this Treaty.

Article 254 (ex Article 191) 1. Regulations, directives and decisions adopted in accordance with the procedure referred to in Article 251 shall be signed by the President of the European Parliament and by the President of the Council and published in the *Official Journal of the European Communities*. They shall enter into force on the date specified in them or, in the absence thereof, on the twentieth day following that of their publication.

2. Regulations of the Council and of the Commission, as well as directives of those institutions which are addressed to all Member States, shall be published in the *Official Journal of the European Communities*. They shall enter into force on the date specified in them or, in the absence thereof, on the twentieth day following that of their publication.

3. Other directives, and decisions, shall be notified to those to whom they are addressed and shall take effect upon such notification.

Article 255 (ex Article 191a) 1. Any citizen of the Union, and any natural or legal person residing or having its registered office in a Member State, shall have a right of access to European Parliament, Council and Commission documents, subject to the principles and the conditions to be defined in accordance with paragraphs 2 and 3.

2. General principles and limits on grounds of public or private interest governing this right of access to documents shall be determined by the Council, acting in accordance with the procedure referred to in Article 251 within two years of the entry into force of the Treaty of Amsterdam.

3. Each institution referred to above shall elaborate in its own Rules of Procedure specific provisions regarding access to its documents.

Article 256 (ex Article 192) Decisions of the Council or of the Commission which impose a pecuniary obligation on persons other than States, shall be enforceable.

Enforcement shall be governed by the rules of civil procedure in force in the State in the territory of which it is carried out. The order for its enforcement shall be appended to the decision, without other formality than verification of the authenticity of the decision, by the national authority which the government of each Member State shall designate for this purpose and shall make known to the Commission and to the Court of Justice.

When these formalities have been completed on application by the party concerned, the latter may proceed to enforcement in accordance with the national law, by bringing the matter directly before the competent authority.

Enforcement may be suspended only by a decision of the Court of Justice. However, the courts of the country concerned shall have jurisdiction over complaints that enforcement is being carried out in an irregular manner.

Chapter 3: The Economic and Social Committee

Article 257 (ex Article 193) An Economic and Social Committee is hereby established. It shall have advisory status.

The Committee shall consist of representatives of the various categories of economic and social activity, in particular, representatives of producers, farmers, carriers, workers, dealers, craftsmen, professional occupations and representatives of the general public.

Article 258 (ex Article 194)   The number of members of the Economic and Social Committee shall be as follows:

Belgium	12
Denmark	9
Germany	24
Greece	12
Spain	21
France	24
Ireland	9
Italy	24
Luxembourg	6
Netherlands	12
Austria	12
Portugal	12
Finland	9
Sweden	12
United Kingdom	24

The members of the Committee shall be appointed by the Council, acting unanimously, for four years. Their appointments shall be renewable.

The members of the Committee may not be bound by any mandatory instructions. They shall be completely independent in the performance of their duties, in the general interest of the Community.

The Council, acting by a qualified majority, shall determine the allowances of members of the Committee.

Article 259 (ex Article 195)   1. For the appointment of the members of the Committee, each Member State shall provide the Council with a list containing twice as many candidates as there are seats allotted to its nationals.

The composition of the Committee shall take account of the need to ensure adequate representation of the various categories of economic and social activity.

2. The Council shall consult the Commission. It may obtain the opinion of European bodies which are representative of the various economic and social sectors to which the activities of the Community are of concern.

Article 260 (ex Article 196)   The Committee shall elect its chairman and officers from among its members for a term of two years.

It shall adopt its Rules of Procedure.

The Committee shall be convened by its chairman at the request of the Council or of the Commission. It may also meet on its own initiative.

Article 261 (ex Article 197)   The Committee shall include specialised sections for the principal fields covered by this Treaty.

These specialised sections shall operate within the general terms of reference of the Committee. They may not be consulted independently of the Committee.

Subcommittees may also be established within the Committee to prepare on specific questions or in specific fields, draft opinions to be submitted to the Committee for its consideration.

The Rules of Procedure shall lay down the methods of composition and the terms of reference of the specialised sections and of the subcommittees.

Article 262 (ex Article 198)   The Committee must be consulted by the Council or by the Commission where this Treaty so provides. The Committee may be consulted by these institutions in all cases in which they consider it appropriate. It may issue an opinion on its own initiative in cases in which it considers such action appropriate.

The Council or the Commission shall, if it considers it necessary, set the Committee, for the submission of its opinion, a time-limit which may not be less than one month from the date on which the chairman receives notification to this effect. Upon expiry of the time-limit, the absence of an opinion shall not prevent further action.

The opinion of the Committee and that of the specialised section, together with a record of the proceedings, shall be forwarded to the Council and to the Commission.

The Committee may be consulted by the European Parliament.

Chapter 4: The Committee of the Regions

Article 263 (ex Article 198a)   A Committee consisting of representatives of regional and local bodies, hereinafter referred to as 'the Committee of the Regions', is hereby established with advisory status.

The number of members of the Committee of the Regions shall be as follows:

Belgium	12
Denmark	9
Germany	24
Greece	12
Spain	21
France	24
Ireland	9
Italy	24
Luxembourg	6
Netherlands	12
Austria	12
Portugal	12
Finland	9
Sweden	12
United Kingdom	24

The members of the Committee and an equal number of alternate members shall be appointed for four years by the Council acting unanimously on proposals from the respective Member States. Their term of office shall be renewable. No member of the Committee shall at the same time be a Member of the European Parliament.

The members of the Committee may not be bound by any mandatory instructions. They shall be completely independent in the performance of their duties, in the general interest of Community.

Article 264 (ex Article 198b)   The Committee of the Regions shall elect its chairman and officers from among its members for a term of two years.

It shall adopt its Rules of Procedure.

The Committee shall be convened by its chairman at the request of the Council or of the Commission. It may also meet on its own initiative.

Article 265 (ex Article 198c)   The Committee of the Regions shall be consulted by the Council or by the Commission where this Treaty so provides and in all other cases, in particular those which concern cross-border cooperation, in which one of these two institutions considers it appropriate.

The Council or the Commission shall, if it considers it necessary, set the Committee, for the submission of its opinion, a time-limit which may not be less than one month from the date on which the chairman receives notification to this effect. Upon expiry of the time-limit, the absence of an opinion shall not prevent further action.

Where the Economic and Social Committee is consulted pursuant to Article 262, the Committee of the Regions shall be informed by the Council or the Commission of the request for an opinion. Where it considers that specific regional interests are involved, the Committee of the Regions may issue an opinion on the matter.

The Committee of the Regions may be consulted by the European Parliament.

It may issue an opinion on its own initiative in cases in which it considers such action appropriate.

The opinion of the Committee, together with a record of the proceedings, shall be forwarded to the Council and to the Commission.

Chapter 5: The European Investment Bank

Article 266 (ex Article 198d)   The European Investment Bank shall have legal personality.

The members of the European Investment Bank shall be the Member States.

The Statute of the European Investment Bank is laid down in a Protocol annexed to this Treaty.

Article 267 (ex Article 198e)   The task of the European Investment Bank shall be to contribute, by having recourse to the capital market and utilising its own resources, to the balanced and steady development of the common market in the interest of the Community. For this purpose the Bank shall, operating on a non-profit-making basis, grant loans and give guarantees which facilitate the financing of the following projects in all sectors of the economy:

(a) projects for developing less-developed regions;
(b) projects for modernising or converting undertakings or for developing fresh activities called for by the progressive establishment of the common market, where these projects are of such a size or nature that they cannot be entirely financed by the various means available in the individual Member States;
(c) projects of common interest to several Member States which are of such a size or nature that they cannot be entirely financed by the various means available in the individual Member States.

In carrying out its task, the Bank shall facilitate the financing of investment programmes in conjunction with assistance from the Structural Funds and other Community financial instruments.

Title II. Financial Provisions

Article 268 (ex Article 199)   All items of revenue and expenditure of the Community, including those relating to the European Social Fund, shall be included in estimates to be drawn up for each financial year and shall be shown in the budget.

Administrative expenditure occasioned for the institutions by the provisions of the Treaty on European Union relating to common foreign and security policy and to cooperation in the fields of justice and home affairs shall be charged to the budget. The operational expenditure occasioned by the implementation of the said provisions may, under the conditions referred to therein, be charged to the budget.

The revenue and expenditure shown in the budget shall be in balance.

Article 269 (ex Article 201)   Without prejudice to other revenue, the budget shall be financed wholly from own resources.

The Council, acting unanimously on a proposal from the Commission and after consulting the European Parliament, shall lay down provisions relating to the system of own resources of the Community, which it shall recommend to the Member States for adoption in accordance with their respective constitutional requirements.

Article 270 (ex Article 201a)   With a view to maintaining budgetary discipline, the Commission shall not make any proposal for a Community act, or alter its proposals, or adopt any implementing measure which is likely to have appreciable implications for the budget without providing the assurance that that proposal or that measure is capable of being financed within the limit of the Community's own resources arising under provisions laid down by the Council pursuant to Article 269.

Article 271 (ex Article 202)   The expenditure shown in the budget shall be authorised for one financial year, unless the regulations made pursuant to Article 279 provide otherwise.

In accordance with conditions to be laid down pursuant to Article 279, any appropriations, other than those relating to staff expenditure, that are unexpended at the end of the financial year may be carried forward to the next financial year only.

Appropriations shall be classified under different chapters grouping items of expenditure according to their nature or purpose and subdivided, as far as may be necessary, in accordance with the regulations made pursuant to Article 279.

The expenditure of the European Parliament, the Council, the Commission and the Court of Justice shall be set out in separate parts of the budget, without prejudice to special arrangements for certain common items of expenditure.

Article 272 (ex Article 203)   1. The financial year shall run from 1 January to 31 December.

2. Each institution of the Community shall, before 1 July, draw up estimates of its expenditure. The Commission shall consolidate these estimates in a preliminary draft budget. It shall attach thereto an opinion which may contain different estimates.

The preliminary draft budget shall contain an estimate of revenue and an estimate of expenditure.

3. The Commission shall place the preliminary draft budget before the Council not later than 1 September of the year preceding that in which the budget is to be implemented.

The Council shall consult the Commission and, where appropriate, the other institutions concerned whenever it intends to depart from the preliminary draft budget.

The Council, acting by a qualified majority, shall establish the draft budget and forward it to the European Parliament.

4. The draft budget shall be placed before the European Parliament not later than 5 October of the year preceding that in which the budget is to be implemented.

The European Parliament shall have the right to amend the draft budget, acting by a majority of its Members, and to propose to the Council, acting by an absolute majority of the votes cast, modifications to the draft budget relating to expenditure necessarily resulting from this Treaty or from acts adopted in accordance therewith.

If, within 45 days of the draft budget being placed before it, the European Parliament has given its approval, the budget shall stand as finally adopted. If within this period the European Parliament has not amended the draft budget nor proposed any modifications thereto, the budget shall be deemed to be finally adopted.

If within this period the European Parliament has adopted amendments or proposed modifications, the draft budget together with the amendments or proposed modifications shall be forwarded to the Council.

5. After discussing the draft budget with the Commission and, where appropriate, with the other institutions concerned, the Council shall act under the following conditions:

(a) the Council may, acting by a qualified majority, modify any of the amendments adopted by the European Parliament;

(b) with regard to the proposed modifications:

— where a modification proposed by the European Parliament does not have the effect of increasing the total amount of the expenditure of an institution, owing in particular to the fact that the increase in expenditure which it would involve would be expressly compensated by one or more proposed modifications correspondingly reducing expenditure, the Council may, acting by a qualified majority, reject the proposed modification. In the absence of a decision to reject it, the proposed modification shall stand as accepted;

— where a modification proposed by the European Parliament has the effect of increasing the total amount of the expenditure of an institution, the Council may, acting by a qualified majority, accept this proposed modification. In the absence of a decision to accept it, the proposed modification shall stand as rejected;

— where, in pursuance of one of the two preceding subparagraphs, the Council has rejected a proposed modification, it may, acting by a qualified majority, either retain the amount shown in the draft budget or fix another amount.

The draft budget shall be modified on the basis of the proposed modifications accepted by the Council.

If, within 15 days of the draft being placed before it, the Council has not modified any of the amendments adopted by the European Parliament and if the modifications proposed by the latter have been accepted, the budget shall be deemed to be finally adopted. The Council shall inform the European Parliament that it has not modified any of the amendments and that the proposed modifications have been accepted.

If within this period the Council has modified one or more of the amendments adopted by the European Parliament or if the modifications proposed by the latter have been rejected or modified, the modified draft budget shall again be forwarded to the European Parliament. The Council shall inform the European Parliament of the results of its deliberations.

6. Within 15 days of the draft budget being placed before it, the European Parliament, which shall have been notified of the action taken on its proposed modifications, may, acting by a majority of its Members and three-fifths of the votes cast, amend or reject the modifications to its amendments made by the Council and shall adopt the budget accordingly. If within this period the European Parliament has not acted, the budget shall be deemed to be finally adopted.

7. When the procedure provided for in this Article has been completed, the President of the European Parliament shall declare that the budget has been finally adopted.

8. However, the European Parliament, acting by a majority of its Members and two-thirds of the votes cast, may, if there are important reasons, reject the draft budget and ask for a new draft to be submitted to it.

9. A maximum rate of increase in relation to the expenditure of the same type to be incurred during the current year shall be fixed annually for the total expenditure other than that necessarily resulting from this Treaty or from acts adopted in accordance therewith.

The Commission shall, after consulting the Economic Policy Committee, declare what this maximum rate is as it results from:

— the trend, in terms of volume, of the gross national product within the Community;
— the average variation in the budgets of the Member States;

and

— the trend of the cost of living during the preceding financial year.

The maximum rate shall be communicated, before 1 May, to all the institutions of the Community. The latter shall be required to conform to this during the budgetary procedure, subject to the provisions of the fourth and fifth subparagraphs of this paragraph.

If, in respect of expenditure other than that necessarily resulting from this Treaty or from acts adopted in accordance therewith, the actual rate of increase in the draft budget established by the Council is over half the maximum rate, the European Parliament may, exercising its right of amendment, further increase the total amount of that expenditure to a limit not exceeding half the maximum rate.

Where the European Parliament, the Council or the Commission consider that the activities of the Communities require that the rate determined according to the procedure laid down in this paragraph should be exceeded, another rate may be fixed by agreement between the Council, acting by a qualified majority, and the European Parliament, acting by a majority of its Members and three-fifths of the votes cast.

10. Each institution shall exercise the powers conferred upon it by this Article, with due regard for the provisions of the Treaty and for acts adopted in accordance therewith, in particular those relating to the Communities' own resources and to the balance between revenue and expenditure.

Article 273 (ex Article 204)   If, at the beginning of a financial year, the budget has not yet been voted, a sum equivalent to not more than one-twelfth of the budget appropriations for the preceding financial year may be spent each month in respect of any chapter or other subdivision of the budget in accordance with the provisions of the Regulations made pursuant to Article 279; this arrangement shall not, however, have the effect of placing at the disposal of the Commission appropriations in excess of one-twelfth of those provided for in the draft budget in course of preparation.

The Council may, acting by a qualified majority, provided that the other conditions laid down in the first subparagraph are observed, authorise expenditure in excess of one-twelfth.

If the decision relates to expenditure which does not necessarily result from this Treaty or from acts adopted in accordance therewith, the Council shall forward it immediately to the European Parliament; within 30 days the European Parliament, acting by a majority of its Members and three-fifths of the votes cast, may adopt a different decision on the expenditure in excess of the one-twelfth referred to in the first subparagraph. This part of the decision of the Council shall be suspended until the European Parliament has taken its decision. If within the said period the European Parliament has not taken a decision which differs from the decision of the Council, the latter shall be deemed to be finally adopted.

The decisions referred to in the second and third subparagraphs shall lay down the necessary measures relating to resources to ensure application of this Article.

Article 274 (ex Article 205)   The Commission shall implement the budget, in accordance with the provisions of the regulations made pursuant to Article 279, on its own responsibility and within the limits of the appropriations, having regard to the principles of sound financial management. Member States shall cooperate with the Commission to ensure that the appropriations are used in accordance with the principles of sound financial management.

The regulations shall lay down detailed rules for each institution concerning its part in effecting its own expenditure.

Within the budget, the Commission may, subject to the limits and conditions laid down in the regulations made pursuant to Article 279, transfer appropriations from one chapter to another or from one subdivision to another.

Article 275 (ex Article 205a)   The Commission shall submit annually to the Council and to the European Parliament the accounts of the preceding financial year relating to the implementation of the budget. The Commission shall also forward to them a financial statement of the assets and liabilities of the Community.

Article 276 (ex Article 206)   1. The European Parliament, acting on a recommendation from the Council which shall act by a qualified majority, shall give a discharge to the Commission in respect of the implementation of the budget. To this end, the Council and the European Parliament in turn shall examine the accounts and the financial statement referred to in Article 275, the annual report by the Court of

Auditors together with the replies of the institutions under audit to the observations of the Court of Auditors, the statement of assurance referred to in Article 248(1), second subparagraph and any relevant special reports by the Court of Auditors.

2. Before giving a discharge to the Commission, or for any other purpose in connection with the exercise of its powers over the implementation of the budget, the European Parliament may ask to hear the Commission give evidence with regard to the execution of expenditure or the operation of financial control systems. The Commission shall submit any necessary information to the European Parliament at the latter's request.

3. The Commission shall take all appropriate steps to act on the observations in the decisions giving discharge and on other observations by the European Parliament relating to the execution of expenditure, as well as on comments accompanying the recommendations on discharge adopted by the Council.

At the request of the European Parliament or the Council, the Commission shall report on the measures taken in the light of these observations and comments and in particular on the instructions given to the departments which are responsible for the implementation of the budget. These reports shall also be forwarded to the Court of Auditors.

Article 277 (ex Article 207)   The budget shall be drawn up in the unit of account determined in accordance with the provisions of the regulations made pursuant to Article 279.

Article 278 (ex Article 208)   The Commission may, provided it notifies the competent authorities of the Member States concerned, transfer into the currency of one of the Member States its holdings in the currency of another Member State, to the extent necessary to enable them to be used for purposes which come within the scope of this Treaty. The Commission shall as far as possible avoid making such transfers if it possesses cash or liquid assets in the currencies which it needs.

The Commission shall deal with each Member State through the authority designated by the State concerned. In carrying out financial operations the Commission shall employ the services of the bank of issue of the Member State concerned or of any other financial institution approved by that State.

Article 279 (ex Article 209)   The Council, acting unanimously on a proposal from the Commission and after consulting the European Parliament and obtaining the opinion of the Court of Auditors, shall:
(a) make Financial Regulations specifying in particular the procedure to be adopted for establishing and implementing the budget and for presenting and auditing accounts;
(b) determine the methods and procedure whereby the budget revenue provided under the arrangements relating to the Community's own resources shall be made available to the Commission, and determine the measures to be applied, if need be, to meet cash requirements;
(c) lay down rules concerning the responsibility of financial controllers, authorising officers and accounting officers, and concerning appropriate arrangements for inspection.

Article 280 (ex Article 209a)   1. The Community and the Member States shall counter fraud and any other illegal activities affecting the financial interests of the Community through measures to be taken in accordance with this Article, which shall act as a deterrent and be such as to afford effective protection in the Member States.

2. Member States shall take the same measures to counter fraud affecting the financial interests of the Community as they take to counter fraud affecting their own financial interests.

3. Without prejudice to other provisions of this Treaty, the Member States shall coordinate their action aimed at protecting the financial interests of the Community against fraud. To this end they shall organise, together with the Commission, close and regular cooperation between the competent authorities.

4. The Council, acting in accordance with the procedure referred to in Article 251, after consulting the Court of Auditors, shall adopt the necessary measures in the fields of the prevention of and fight against fraud affecting the financial interests of the Community with a view to affording effective and equivalent protection in the Member States. These measures shall not concern the application of national criminal law or the national administration of justice.

5. The Commission, in cooperation with Member States, shall each year submit to the European Parliament and to the Council a report on the measures taken for the implementation of this Article.

PART SIX: GENERAL AND FINAL PROVISIONS

Article 281 (ex Article 210)   The Community shall have legal personality.

Article 282 (ex Article 211)   In each of the Member States, the Community shall enjoy the most extensive legal capacity accorded to legal persons under their laws; it may, in particular, acquire or dispose of movable and immovable property and may be a party to legal proceedings. To this end, the Community shall be represented by the Commission.

Article 283 (ex Article 212)   The Council shall, acting by a qualified majority on a proposal from the Commission and after consulting the other institutions concerned, lay down the Staff Regulations of officials of the European Communities and the Conditions of Employment of other servants of those Communities.

Article 284 (ex Article 213)   The Commission may, within the limits and under conditions laid down by the Council in accordance with the provisions of this Treaty, collect any information and carry out any checks required for the performance of the tasks entrusted to it.

Article 285 (ex Article 213a)   1. Without prejudice to Article 5 of the Protocol on the Statute of the European System of Central Banks and of the European Central Bank, the Council, acting in accordance with the procedure referred to in Article 251, shall adopt measures for the production of statistics where necessary for the performance of the activities of the Community.

2. The production of Community statistics shall conform to impartiality, reliability, objectivity, scientific independence, cost-effectiveness and statistical confidentiality; it shall not entail excessive burdens on economic operators.

Article 286 (ex Article 213b) 1. From 1 January 1999, Community acts on the protection of individuals with regard to the processing of personal data and the free movement of such data shall apply to the institutions and bodies set up by, or on the basis of, this Treaty.

2. Before the date referred to in paragraph 1, the Council, acting in accordance with the procedure referred to in Article 251, shall establish an independent supervisory body responsible for monitoring the application of such Community acts to Community institutions and bodies and shall adopt any other relevant provisions as appropriate.

Article 287 (ex Article 214) The members of the institutions of the Community, the members of committees, and the officials and other servants of the Community shall be required, even after their duties have ceased, not to disclose information of the kind covered by the obligation of professional secrecy, in particular information about undertakings, their business relations or their cost components.

Article 288 (ex Article 215) The contractual liability of the Community shall be governed by the law applicable to the contract in question.

In the case of non-contractual liability, the Community shall, in accordance with the general principles common to the laws of the Member States, make good any damage caused by its institutions or by its servants in the performance of their duties.

The preceding paragraph shall apply under the same conditions to damage caused by the ECB or by its servants in the performance of their duties.

The personal liability of its servants towards the Community shall be governed by the provisions laid down in their Staff Regulations or in the Conditions of Employment applicable to them.

Article 289 (ex Article 216) The seat of the institutions of the Community shall be determined by common accord of the Governments of the Member States.

Article 290 (ex Article 217) The rules governing the languages of the institutions of the Community shall, without prejudice to the provisions contained in the Rules of Procedure of the Court of Justice, be determined by the Council, acting unanimously.

Article 291 (ex Article 218) The Community shall enjoy in the territories of the Member States such privileges and immunities as are necessary for the performance of its tasks, under the conditions laid down in the Protocol of 8 April 1965 on the privileges and immunities of the European Communities. The same shall apply to the European Central Bank, the European Monetary Institute, and the European Investment Bank.

Article 292 (ex Article 219) Member States undertake not to submit a dispute concerning the interpretation or application of this Treaty to any method of settlement other than those provided for therein.

Article 293 (ex Article 220) Member States shall, so far as is necessary, enter into negotiations with each other with a view to securing for the benefit of their nationals:

— the protection of persons and the enjoyment and protection of rights under the same conditions as those accorded by each State to its own nationals;

— the abolition of double taxation within the Community;
— the mutual recognition of companies or firms within the meaning of the second paragraph of Article 48, the retention of legal personality in the event of transfer of their seat from one country to another, and the possibility of mergers between companies or firms governed by the laws of different countries;
— the simplification of formalities governing the reciprocal recognition and enforcement of judgments of courts or tribunals and of arbitration awards.

Article 294 (ex Article 221)   Member States shall accord nationals of the other Member States the same treatment as their own nationals as regards participation in the capital of companies or firms within the meaning of Article 48, without prejudice to the application of the other provisions of this Treaty.

Article 295 (ex Article 222)   This Treaty shall in no way prejudice the rules in Member States governing the system of property ownership.

Article 296 (ex Article 223)   1. The provisions of this Treaty shall not preclude the application of the following rules:
(a) no Member State shall be obliged to supply information the disclosure of which it considers contrary to the essential interests of its security;
(b) any Member State may take such measures as it considers necessary for the protection of the essential interests of its security which are connected with the production of or trade in arms, munitions and war material; such measures shall not adversely affect the conditions of competition in the common market regarding products which are not intended for specifically military purposes.

2. The Council may, acting unanimously on a proposal from the Commission, make changes to the list, which it drew up on 15 April 1958, of the products to which the provisions of paragraph 1(b) apply.

Article 297 (ex Article 224)   Member States shall consult each other with a view to taking together the steps needed to prevent the functioning of the common market being affected by measures which a Member State may be called upon to take in the event of serious internal disturbances affecting the maintenance of law and order, in the event of war, serious international tension constituting a threat of war, or in order to carry out obligations it has accepted for the purpose of maintaining peace and international security.

Article 298 (ex Article 225)   If measures taken in the circumstances referred to in Articles 296 and 297 have the effect of distorting the conditions of competition in the common market, the Commission shall, together with the State concerned, examine how these measures can be adjusted to the rules laid down in the Treaty.
   By way of derogation from the procedure laid down in Articles 226 and 227, the Commission or any Member State may bring the matter directly before the Court of Justice if it considers that another Member State is making improper use of the powers provided for in Articles 296 and 297. The Court of Justice shall give its ruling in camera.

Article 299 (ex Article 227)   1. This Treaty shall apply to the Kingdom of Belgium, the Kingdom of Denmark, the Federal Republic of Germany, the Hellenic Republic, the Kingdom of Spain, the French Republic, Ireland, the Italian Republic, the Grand

Duchy of Luxembourg, the Kingdom of the Netherlands, the Republic of Austria, the Portuguese Republic, the Republic of Finland, the Kingdom of Sweden and the United Kingdom of Great Britain and Northern Ireland.

2. The provisions of this Treaty shall apply to the French overseas departments, the Azores, Madeira and the Canary Islands.

However, taking account of the structural social and economic situation of the French overseas departments, the Azores, Madeira and the Canary Islands, which is compounded by their remoteness, insularity, small size, difficult topography and climate, economic dependence on a few products, the permanence and combination of which severely restrain their development, the Council, acting by a qualified majority on a proposal from the Commission and after consulting the European Parliament, shall adopt specific measures aimed, in particular, at laying down the conditions of application of the present Treaty to those regions, including common policies.

The Council shall, when adopting the relevant measures referred to in the second subparagraph, take into account areas such as customs and trade policies, fiscal policy, free zones, agriculture and fisheries policies, conditions for supply of raw materials and essential consumer goods, State aids and conditions of access to structural funds and to horizontal Community programmes.

The Council shall adopt the measures referred to in the second subparagraph taking into account the special characteristics and constraints of the outermost regions without undermining the integrity and the coherence of the Community legal order, including the internal market and common policies.

3. The special arrangements for association set out in Part Four of this Treaty shall apply to the overseas countries and territories listed in Annex II to this Treaty.

This Treaty shall not apply to those overseas countries and territories having special relations with the United Kingdom of Great Britain and Northern Ireland which are not included in the aforementioned list.

4. The provisions of this Treaty shall apply to the European territories for whose external relations a Member State is responsible.

5. The provisions of this Treaty shall apply to the Åland Islands in accordance with the provisions set out in Protocol No 2 to the Act concerning the conditions of accession of the Republic of Austria, the Republic of Finland and the Kingdom of Sweden.

6. Notwithstanding the preceding paragraphs:
(a) this Treaty shall not apply to the Faeroe Islands;
(b) this Treaty shall not apply to the Sovereign Base Areas of the United Kingdom of Great Britain and Northern Ireland in Cyprus;
(c) this Treaty shall apply to the Channel Islands and the Isle of Man only to the extent necessary to ensure the implementation of the arrangements for those islands set out in the Treaty concerning the accession of new Member States to the European Economic Community and to the European Atomic Energy Community signed on 22 January 1972.

Article 300 (ex Article 228)　1. Where this Treaty provides for the conclusion of agreements between the Community and one or more States or international organisations, the Commission shall make recommendations to the Council, which shall authorise the Commission to open the necessary negotiations. The Commission shall conduct these negotiations in consultation with special committees appointed by the Council to assist it in this task and within the framework of such directives as the Council may issue to it.

In exercising the powers conferred upon it by this paragraph, the Council shall act by a qualified majority, except in the cases where the first subparagraph of paragraph 2 provides that the Council shall act unanimously.

2. Subject to the powers vested in the Commission in this field, the signing, which may be accompanied by a decision on provisional application before entry into force, and the conclusion of the agreements shall be decided on by the Council, acting by a qualified majority on a proposal from the Commission. The Council shall act unanimously when the agreement covers a field for which unanimity is required for the adoption of internal rules and for the agreements referred to in Article 310.

By way of derogation from the rules laid down in paragraph 3, the same procedures shall apply for a decision to suspend the application of an agreement, and for the purpose of establishing the positions to be adopted on behalf of the Community in a body set up by an agreement based on Article 310, when that body is called upon to adopt decisions having legal effects, with the exception of decisions supplementing or amending the institutional framework of the agreement.

The European Parliament shall be immediately and fully informed on any decision under this paragraph concerning the provisional application or the suspension of agreements, or the establishment of the Community position in a body set up by an agreement based on Article 310.

3. The Council shall conclude agreements after consulting the European Parliament, except for the agreements referred to in Article 133(3), including cases where the agreement covers a field for which the procedure referred to in Article 251 or that referred to in Article 252 is required for the adoption of internal rules. The European Parliament shall deliver its opinion within a time-limit which the Council may lay down according to the urgency of the matter. In the absence of an opinion within that time-limit, the Council may act.

By way of derogation from the previous subparagraph, agreements referred to in Article 310, other agreements establishing a specific institutional framework by organising cooperation procedures, agreements having important budgetary implications for the Community and agreements entailing amendment of an act adopted under the procedure referred to in Article 251 shall be concluded after the assent of the European Parliament has been obtained.

The Council and the European Parliament may, in an urgent situation, agree upon a time-limit for the assent.

4. When concluding an agreement, the Council may, by way of derogation from paragraph 2, authorise the Commission to approve modifications on behalf of the Community where the agreement provides for them to be adopted by a simplified procedure or by a body set up by the agreement; it may attach specific conditions to such authorisation.

5. When the Council envisages concluding an agreement which calls for amendments to this Treaty, the amendments must first be adopted in accordance with the procedure laid down in Article 48 of the Treaty on European Union.

6. The Council, the Commission or a Member State may obtain the opinion of the Court of Justice as to whether an agreement envisaged is compatible with the provisions of this Treaty. Where the opinion of the Court of Justice is adverse, the agreement may enter into force only in accordance with Article 48 of the Treaty on European Union.

7. Agreements concluded under the conditions set out in this Article shall be binding on the institutions of the Community and on Member States.

Article 301 (ex Article 228a)   Where it is provided, in a common position or in a joint action adopted according to the provisions of the Treaty on European Union relating to the common foreign and security policy, for an action by the Community to interrupt or to reduce, in part or completely, economic relations with one or more third countries, the Council shall take the necessary urgent measures. The Council shall act by a qualified majority on a proposal from the Commission.

Article 302 (ex Article 229)   It shall be for the Commission to ensure the maintenance of all appropriate relations with the organs of the United Nations and of its specialised agencies.

   The Commission shall also maintain such relations as are appropriate with all international organisations.

Article 303 (ex Article 230)   The Community shall establish all appropriate forms of cooperation with the Council of Europe.

Article 304 (ex Article 231)   The Community shall establish close cooperation with the Organisation for Economic Cooperation and Development, the details of which shall be determined by common accord.

Article 305 (ex Article 232)   1. The provisions of this Treaty shall not affect the provisions of the Treaty establishing the European Coal and Steel Community, in particular as regards the rights and obligations of Member States, the powers of the institutions of that Community and the rules laid down by that Treaty for the functioning of the common market in coal and steel.

2. The provisions of this Treaty shall not derogate from those of the Treaty establishing the European Atomic Energy Community.

Article 306 (ex Article 233)   The provisions of this Treaty shall not preclude the existence or completion of regional unions between Belgium and Luxembourg, or between Belgium, Luxembourg and the Netherlands, to the extent that the objectives of these regional unions are not attained by application of this Treaty.

Article 307 (ex Article 234)   The rights and obligations arising from agreements concluded before 1 January 1958 or, for acceding States, before the date of their accession, between one or more Member States on the one hand, and one or more third countries on the other, shall not be affected by the provisions of this Treaty.

   To the extent that such agreements are not compatible with this Treaty, the Member State or States concerned shall take all appropriate steps to eliminate the incompatibilities established. Member States shall, where necessary, assist each other to this end and shall, where appropriate, adopt a common attitude.

   In applying the agreements referred to in the first paragraph, Member States shall take into account the fact that the advantages accorded under this Treaty by each Member State form an integral part of the establishment of the Community and are thereby inseparably linked with the creation of common institutions, the conferring of powers upon them and the granting of the same advantages by all the other Member States.

Article 308 (ex Article 235)   If action by the Community should prove necessary to attain, in the course of the operation of the common market, one of the objectives of the Community and this Treaty has not provided the necessary powers, the Council shall, acting unanimously on a proposal from the Commission and after consulting the European Parliament, take the appropriate measures.

Article 309 (ex Article 236)   1. Where a decision has been taken to suspend the voting rights of the representative of the government of a Member State in accordance with Article 7(2) of the Treaty on European Union, these voting rights shall also be suspended with regard to this Treaty.

2. Moreover, where the existence of a serious and persistent breach by a Member State of principles mentioned in Article 6(1) of the Treaty on European Union has been determined in accordance with Article 7(1) of that Treaty, the Council, acting by a qualified majority, may decide to suspend certain of the rights deriving from the application of this Treaty to the Member State in question. In doing so, the Council shall take into account the possible consequences of such a suspension on the rights and obligations of natural and legal persons.

The obligations of the Member State in question under this Treaty shall in any case continue to be binding on that State.

3. The Council, acting by a qualified majority, may decide subsequently to vary or revoke measures taken in accordance with paragraph 2 in response to changes in the situation which led to their being imposed.

4. When taking decisions referred to in paragraphs 2 and 3, the Council shall act without taking into account the votes of the representative of the government of the Member State in question. By way of derogation from Article 205(2) a qualified majority shall be defined as the same proportion of the weighted votes of the members of the Council concerned as laid down in Article 205(2).

This paragraph shall also apply in the event of voting rights being suspended in accordance with paragraph 1. In such cases, a decision requiring unanimity shall be taken without the vote of the representative of the government of the Member State in question.

Article 310 (ex Article 238)   The Community may conclude with one or more States or international organisations agreements establishing an association involving reciprocal rights and obligations, common action and special procedure.

Article 311 (ex Article 239)   The protocols annexed to this Treaty by common accord of the Member States shall form an integral part thereof.

Article 312 (ex Article 240)   This Treaty is concluded for an unlimited period.

FINAL PROVISIONS

Article 313 (ex Article 247)   This Treaty shall be ratified by the High Contracting Parties in accordance with their respective constitutional requirements. The instruments of ratification shall be deposited with the Government of the Italian Republic.

This Treaty shall enter into force on the first day of the month following the deposit of the instrument of ratification by the last signatory State to take this step. If, however, such deposit is made less than 15 days before the beginning of the following month, this Treaty shall not enter into force until the first day of the second month after the date of such deposit.

Article 314 (ex Article 248) This Treaty, drawn up in a single original in the Dutch, French, German, and Italian languages, all four texts being equally authentic, shall be deposited in the archives of the Government of the Italian Republic, which shall transmit a certified copy to each of the Governments of the other signatory States.

Pursuant to the Accession Treaties, the Danish, English, Finnish, Greek, Irish, Portuguese, Spanish and Swedish versions of this Treaty shall also be authentic.

IN WITNESS WHEREOF, the undersigned Plenipotentiaries have signed this Treaty.

Done at Rome this twenty-fifth day of March in the year one thousand nine hundred and fifty-seven.

P. H. SPAAK
ADENAUER
PINEAU
Antonio SEGNI
BECH
J. LUNS
J. Ch. SNOY ET D'OPPUERS
HALLSTEIN
M. FAURE
Gaetano MARTINO
Lambert SCHAUS
J. LINTHORST HOMAN

[*Annex I omitted*]

ANNEX II. OVERSEAS COUNTRIES AND TERRITORIES
to which the provisions of Part Four of the Treaty apply

Greenland,
New Caledonia and Dependencies,
French Polynesia,
French Southern and Antarctic Territories,
Wallis and Futuna Islands,
Mayotte,
Saint Pierre and Miquelon,
Aruba,
Netherlands Antilles:

— Bonaire,
— Curaçao,
— Saba,

— Sint Eustatius,
— Sint Maarten.

Anguilla,
Cayman Islands,
Falkland Islands,
South Georgia and the South Sandwich Islands,
Montserrat,
Pitcairn,
Saint Helena and Dependencies,
British Antarctic Territory,
British Indian Ocean Territory,
Turks and Caicos Islands,
British Virgin Islands,
Bermuda.

Treaty on European Union
(Consolidated Version)

HIS MAJESTY THE KING OF THE BELGIANS, HER MAJESTY THE QUEEN OF DENMARK, THE PRESIDENT OF THE FEDERAL REPUBLIC OF GERMANY, THE PRESIDENT OF THE HELLENIC REPUBLIC, HIS MAJESTY THE KING OF SPAIN, THE PRESIDENT OF THE FRENCH REPUBLIC, THE PRESIDENT OF IRELAND, THE PRESIDENT OF THE ITALIAN REPUBLIC, HIS ROYAL HIGHNESS THE GRAND DUKE OF LUXEMBOURG, HER MAJESTY THE QUEEN OF NETHERLANDS, THE PRESIDENT OF THE PORTUGUESE REPUBLIC, HER MAJESTY THE QUEEN OF THE UNITED KINGDOM OF GREAT BRITAIN AND NORTHERN IRELAND,[1]

RESOLVED to mark a new stage in the process of European integration undertaken with the establishment of the European Communities,

RECALLING the historic importance of the ending of the division of the European continent and the need to create firm bases for the construction of the future Europe,

CONFIRMING their attachment to the principles of liberty, democracy and respect for human rights and fundamental freedoms and of the rule of law,

CONFIRMING their attachment to fundamental social rights as defined in the European Social Charter signed at Turin on 18 October 1961 and in the 1989 Community Charter of the Fundamental Social Rights of Workers,

DESIRING to deepen the solidarity between their peoples while respecting their history, their culture and their traditions,

DESIRING to enhance further the democratic and efficient functioning of the institutions so as to enable them better to carry out, within a single institutional framework, the tasks entrusted to them,

RESOLVED to achieve the strengthening and the convergence of their economies and to establish an economic and monetary union including, in accordance with the provisions of this Treaty, a single and stable currency,

DETERMINED to promote economic and social progress for their peoples, taking into account the principle of sustainable development and within the context of the accomplishment of the internal market and of reinforced cohesion and environmental protection, and to implement policies ensuring that advances in economic integration are accompanied by parallel progress in other fields,

RESOLVED to establish a citizenship common to nationals of their countries,

RESOLVED to implement a common foreign and security policy including the progressive framing of a common defence policy, which might lead to a common defence in accordance with the provisions of Article 17, thereby reinforcing the European identity and its independence in order to promote peace, security and progress in Europe and in the world,

---

[1] The Republics of Austria and Finland, and the Kingdom of Sweden have since acceded to this Treaty.

RESOLVED to facilitate the free movement of persons, while ensuring the safety and security of their peoples, by establishing an area of freedom, security and justice, in accordance with the provisions of this Treaty,

RESOLVED to continue the process of creating an ever closer union among the peoples of Europe, in which decisions are taken as closely as possible to the citizen in accordance with the principle of subsidiarity,

IN VIEW of further steps to be taken in order to advance European integration,

HAVE DECIDED to establish a European Union and to this end have designated as their Plenipotentiaries [*names omitted*]:

WHO, having exchanged their full powers, found in good and due form, have agreed as follows.

Title I. Common Provisions

Article 1 (ex Article A)   By this Treaty, the HIGH CONTRACTING PARTIES establish among themselves a EUROPEAN UNION, hereinafter called 'the Union'.

This Treaty marks a new stage in the process of creating an ever closer union among the peoples of Europe, in which decisions are taken as openly as possible and as closely as possible to the citizen.

The Union shall be founded on the European Communities, supplemented by the policies and forms of cooperation established by this Treaty. Its task shall be to organise, in a manner demonstrating consistency and solidarity, relations between the Member States and between their peoples.

Article 2 (ex Article B)   The Union shall set itself the following objectives:

— to promote economic and social progress and a high level of employment and to achieve balanced and sustainable development, in particular through the creation of an area without internal frontiers, through the strengthening of economic and social cohesion and through the establishment of economic and monetary union, ultimately including a single currency in accordance with the provisions of this Treaty;

— to assert its identity on the international scene, in particular through the implementation of a common foreign and security policy including the progressive framing of a common defence policy, which might lead to a common defence, in accordance with the provisions of Article 17;

— to strengthen the promotion of the rights and interests of the nationals of its Member States through the introduction of a citizenship of the Union;

— to maintain and develop the Union as an area of freedom, security and justice, in which the free movement of persons is assured in conjunction with appropriate measures with respect to external border controls, asylum, immigration and the prevention and combating of crime;

— to maintain in full the acquis communautaire and build on it with a view to considering to what extent the policies and forms of cooperation introduced by this Treaty may need to be revised with the aim of ensuring the effectiveness of the mechanisms and the institutions of the Community.

The objectives of the Union shall be achieved as provided in this Treaty and in accordance with the conditions and the timetable set out therein while respecting the principle of subsidiarity as defined in Article 5 of the Treaty establishing the European Community.

Article 3 (ex Article C)   The Union shall be served by a single institutional framework which shall ensure the consistency and the continuity of the activities carried out in order to attain its objectives while respecting and building upon the acquis communautaire.

The Union shall in particular ensure the consistency of its external activities as a whole in the context of its external relations, security, economic and development policies. The Council and the Commission shall be responsible for ensuring such consistency and shall cooperate to this end. They shall ensure the implementation of these policies, each in accordance with its respective powers.

Article 4 (ex Article D)   The European Council shall provide the Union with the necessary impetus for its development and shall define the general political guidelines thereof.

The European Council shall bring together the Heads of State or Government of the Member States and the President of the Commission. They shall be assisted by the Ministers for Foreign Affairs of the Member States and by a Member of the Commission. The European Council shall meet at least twice a year, under the chairmanship of the Head of State or Government of the Member State which holds the Presidency of the Council.

The European Council shall submit to the European Parliament a report after each of its meetings and a yearly written report on the progress achieved by the Union.

Article 5 (ex Article E)   The European Parliament, the Council, the Commission, the Court of Justice and the Court of Auditors shall exercise their powers under the conditions and for the purposes provided for, on the one hand, by the provisions of the Treaties establishing the European Communities and of the subsequent Treaties and Acts modifying and supplementing them and, on the other hand, by the other provisions of this Treaty.

Article 6 (ex Article F)   1. The Union is founded on the principles of liberty, democracy, respect for human rights and fundamental freedoms, and the rule of law, principles which are common to the Member States.

2. The Union shall respect fundamental rights, as guaranteed by the European Convention for the Protection of Human Rights and Fundamental Freedoms signed in Rome on 4 November 1950 and as they result from the constitutional traditions common to the Member States, as general principles of Community law.

3. The Union shall respect the national identities of its Member States.

4. The Union shall provide itself with the means necessary to attain its objectives and carry through its policies.

Article 7 (ex Article F.1)   1. The Council, meeting in the composition of the Heads of State or Government and acting by unanimity on a proposal by one third of the Member States or by the Commission and after obtaining the assent of the European Parliament, may determine the existence of a serious and persistent breach by a Member State of principles mentioned in Article 6(1) after inviting the government of the Member State in question to submit its observations.

2. Where such a determination has been made, the Council, acting by a qualified majority, may decide to suspend certain of the rights deriving from the application of this Treaty to the Member State in question, including the voting rights of the representative of the government of that Member State in the Council. In doing so, the Council shall take into account the possible consequences of such a suspension on the rights and obligations of natural and legal persons.

The obligations of the Member State in question under this Treaty shall in any case continue to be binding on that State.

3. The Council, acting by a qualified majority, may decide subsequently to vary or revoke measures taken under paragraph 2 in response to changes in the situation which led to their being imposed.

4. For the purposes of this Article, the Council shall act without taking into account the vote of the representative of the government of the Member State in question. Abstentions by members present in person or represented shall not prevent the adoption of decisions referred to in paragraph 1. A qualified majority shall be defined as the same proportion of the weighted votes of the members of the Council concerned as laid down in Article 205(2) of the Treaty establishing the European Community.

This paragraph shall also apply in the event of voting rights being suspended pursuant to paragraph 2.

5. For the purposes of this Article, the European Parliament shall act by a two-thirds majority of the votes cast, representing a majority of its members.

[*Titles II–IV, Articles 8–10 amending the EC, ECSC, and EURATOM Treaties (not reproduced)*]

TITLE V. PROVISIONS ON A COMMON FOREIGN AND SECURITY POLICY

Article 11 (ex Article J.1)   1. The Union shall define and implement a common foreign and security policy covering all areas of foreign and security policy, the objectives of which shall be:
—   to safeguard the common values, fundamental interests, independence and integrity of the Union in conformity with the principles of the United Nations Charter;
—   to strengthen the security of the Union in all ways;
—   to preserve peace and strengthen international security, in accordance with the principles of the United Nations Charter, as well as the principles of the Helsinki Final Act and the objectives of the Paris Charter, including those on external borders;
—   to promote international cooperation;
—   to develop and consolidate democracy and the rule of law, and respect for human rights and fundamental freedoms.

2. The Member States shall support the Union's external and security policy actively and unreservedly in a spirit of loyalty and mutual solidarity.

The Member States shall work together to enhance and develop their mutual political solidarity. They shall refrain from any action which is contrary to the interests of the Union or likely to impair its effectiveness as a cohesive force in international relations.

The Council shall ensure that these principles are complied with.

Article 12 (ex Article J.2)   The Union shall pursue the objectives set out in Article 11 by:

— defining the principles and general guidelines for the common foreign and security policy;
— deciding on common strategies;
— adopting joint actions;
— adopting common positions;
— strengthening systematic cooperation between Member States in the conduct of policy.

Article 13 (ex Article J.3)   1. The European Council shall define the principles of and general guidelines for the common foreign and security policy, including for matters with defence implications.

2. The European Council shall decide on common strategies to be implemented by the Union in areas where the Member States have important interests in common.

Common strategies shall set out their objectives, duration and the means to be made available by the Union and the Member States.

3. The Council shall take the decisions necessary for defining and implementing the common foreign and security policy on the basis of the general guidelines defined by the European Council.

The Council shall recommend common strategies to the European Council and shall implement them, in particular by adopting joint actions and common positions.

The Council shall ensure the unity, consistency and effectiveness of action by the Union.

Article 14 (ex Article J.4)   1. The Council shall adopt joint actions. Joint actions shall address specific situations where operational action by the Union is deemed to be required. They shall lay down their objectives, scope, the means to be made available to the Union, if necessary their duration, and the conditions for their implementation.

2. If there is a change in circumstances having a substantial effect on a question subject to joint action, the Council shall review the principles and objectives of that action and take the necessary decisions. As long as the Council has not acted, the joint action shall stand.

3. Joint actions shall commit the Member States in the positions they adopt and in the conduct of their activity.

4. The Council may request the Commission to submit to it any appropriate proposals relating to the common foreign and security policy to ensure the implementation of a joint action.

5. Whenever there is any plan to adopt a national position or take national action pursuant to a joint action, information shall be provided in time to allow, if necessary, for prior consultations within the Council. The obligation to provide prior information shall not apply to measures which are merely a national transposition of Council decisions.

6. In cases of imperative need arising from changes in the situation and failing a Council decision, Member States may take the necessary measures as a matter of

urgency having regard to the general objectives of the joint action. The Member State concerned shall inform the Council immediately of any such measures.

7. Should there be any major difficulties in implementing a joint action, a Member State shall refer them to the Council which shall discuss them and seek appropriate solutions. Such solutions shall not run counter to the objectives of the joint action or impair its effectiveness.

Article 15 (ex Article J.5)   The Council shall adopt common positions. Common positions shall define the approach of the Union to a particular matter of a geographical or thematic nature. Member States shall ensure that their national policies conform to the common positions.

Article 16 (ex Article J.6)   Member States shall inform and consult one another within the Council on any matter of foreign and security policy of general interest in order to ensure that the Union's influence is exerted as effectively as possible by means of concerted and convergent action.

Article 17 (ex Article J.7)   1. The common foreign and security policy shall include all questions relating to the security of the Union, including the progressive framing of a common defence policy, in accordance with the second subparagraph, which might lead to a common defence, should the European Council so decide. It shall in that case recommend to the Member States the adoption of such a decision in accordance with their respective constitutional requirements.

The Western European Union (WEU) is an integral part of the development of the Union providing the Union with access to an operational capability notably in the context of paragraph 2. It supports the Union in framing the defence aspects of the common foreign and security policy as set out in this Article. The Union shall accordingly foster closer institutional relations with the WEU with a view to the possibility of the integration of the WEU into the Union, should the European Council so decide. It shall in that case recommend to the Member States the adoption of such a decision in accordance with their respective constitutional requirements.

The policy of the Union in accordance with this Article shall not prejudice the specific character of the security and defence policy of certain Member States and shall respect the obligations of certain Member States, which see their common defence realised in the North Atlantic Treaty Organisation (NATO), under the North Atlantic Treaty and be compatible with the common security and defence policy established within that framework.

The progressive framing of a common defence policy will be supported, as Member States consider appropriate, by cooperation between them in the field of armaments.

2. Questions referred to in this Article shall include humanitarian and rescue tasks, peacekeeping tasks and tasks of combat forces in crisis management, including peacemaking.

3. The Union will avail itself of the WEU to elaborate and implement decisions and actions of the Union which have defence implications.

The competence of the European Council to establish guidelines in accordance with Article 13 shall also obtain in respect of the WEU for those matters for which the Union avails itself of the WEU.

When the Union avails itself of the WEU to elaborate and implement decisions of the Union on the tasks referred to in paragraph 2 all Member States of the Union shall be entitled to participate fully in the tasks in question. The Council, in agreement with the institutions of the WEU, shall adopt the necessary practical arrangements to allow all Member States contributing to the tasks in question to participate fully and on an equal footing in planning and decision-taking in the WEU.

Decisions having defence implications dealt with under this paragraph shall be taken without prejudice to the policies and obligations referred to in paragraph 1, third subparagraph.

4. The provisions of this Article shall not prevent the development of closer cooperation between two or more Member States on a bilateral level, in the framework of the WEU and the Atlantic Alliance, provided such cooperation does not run counter to or impede that provided for in this Title.

5. With a view to furthering the objectives of this Article, the provisions of this Article will be reviewed in accordance with Article 48.

Article 18 (ex Article J.8) 1. The Presidency shall represent the Union in matters coming within the common foreign and security policy.

2. The Presidency shall be responsible for the implementation of decisions taken under this Title; in that capacity it shall in principle express the position of the Union in international organisations and international conferences.

3. The Presidency shall be assisted by the Secretary-General of the Council who shall exercise the function of High Representative for the common foreign and security policy.

4. The Commission shall be fully associated in the tasks referred to in paragraphs 1 and 2. The Presidency shall be assisted in those tasks if need be by the next Member State to hold the Presidency.

5. The Council may, whenever it deems it necessary, appoint a special representative with a mandate in relation to particular policy issues.

Article 19 (ex Article J.9) 1. Member States shall coordinate their action in international organisations and at international conferences. They shall uphold the common positions in such fora.

In international organisations and at international conferences where not all the Member States participate, those which do take part shall uphold the common positions.

2. Without prejudice to paragraph 1 and Article 14(3), Member States represented in international organisations or international conferences where not all the Member States participate shall keep the latter informed of any matter of common interest.

Member States which are also members of the United Nations Security Council will concert and keep the other Member States fully formed. Member States which are permanent members of the Security Council will, in the execution of their functions, ensure the defence of the positions and the interests of the Union, without prejudice to their responsibilities under the provisions of the United Nations Charter.

Article 20 (ex Article J.10)   The diplomatic and consular missions of the Member States and the Commission Delegations in third countries and international conferences, and their representations to international organisations, shall cooperate in ensuring that the common positions and joint actions adopted by the Council are complied with and implemented.

They shall step up cooperation by exchanging information, carrying out joint assessments and contributing to the implementation of the provisions referred to in Article 20 of the Treaty establishing the European Community.

Article 21 (ex Article J.11)   The Presidency shall consult the European Parliament on the main aspects and the basic choices of the common foreign and security policy and shall ensure that the views of the European Parliament are duly taken into consideration. The European Parliament shall be kept regularly informed by the Presidency and the Commission of the development of the Union's foreign and security policy.

The European Parliament may ask questions of the Council or make recommendations to it. It shall hold an annual debate on progress in implementing the common foreign and security policy.

Article 22 (ex Article J.12)   1. Any Member State or the Commission may refer to the Council any question relating to the common foreign and security policy and may submit proposals to the Council.

2. In cases requiring a rapid decision, the Presidency, of its own motion, or at the request of the Commission or a Member State, shall convene an extraordinary Council meeting within forty-eight hours or, in an emergency, within a shorter period.

Article 23 (ex Article J.13)   1. Decisions under this Title shall be taken by the Council acting unanimously. Abstentions by members present in person or represented shall not prevent the adoption of such decisions.

When abstaining in a vote, any member of the Council may qualify its abstention by making a formal declaration under the present subparagraph. In that case, it shall not be obliged to apply the decision, but shall accept that the decision commits the Union. In a spirit of mutual solidarity, the Member State concerned shall refrain from any action likely to conflict with or impede Union action based on that decision and the other Member States shall respect its position. If the members of the Council qualifying their abstention in this way represent more than one third of the votes weighted in accordance with Article 205(2) of the Treaty establishing the European Community, the decision shall not be adopted.

2. By derogation from the provisions of paragraph 1, the Council shall act by qualified majority:

— when adopting joint actions, common positions or taking any other decision on the basis of a common strategy;
— when adopting any decision implementing a joint action or a common position.

If a member of the Council declares that, for important and stated reasons of national policy, it intends to oppose the adoption of a decision to be taken by qualified majority, a vote shall not be taken. The Council may, acting by a qualified majority, request that the matter be referred to the European Council for decision by unanimity.

The votes of the members of the Council shall be weighted in accordance with Article 205(2) of the Treaty establishing the European Community. For their adoption, decisions shall require at least 62 votes in favour, cast by at least 10 members. This paragraph shall not apply to decisions having military or defence implications.

3. For procedural questions, the Council shall act by a majority of its members.

Article 24 (ex Article J.14)   When it is necessary to conclude an agreement with one or more States or international organisations in implementation of this Title, the Council, acting unanimously, may authorise the Presidency, assisted by the Commission as appropriate, to open negotiations to that effect. Such agreements shall be concluded by the Council acting unanimously on a recommendation from the Presidency. No agreement shall be binding on a Member State whose representative in the Council states that it has to comply with the requirements of its own constitutional procedure; the other members of the Council may agree that the agreement shall apply provisionally to them.

The provisions of this Article shall also apply to matters falling under Title VI.

Article 25 (ex Article J.15)   Without prejudice to Article 207 of the Treaty establishing the European Community, a Political Committee shall monitor the international situation in the areas covered by the common foreign and security policy and contribute to the definition of policies by delivering opinions to the Council at the request of the Council or on its own initiative. It shall also monitor the implementation of agreed policies, without prejudice to the responsibility of the Presidency and the Commission.

Article 26 (ex Article J.16)   The Secretary-General of the Council, High Representative for the common foreign and security policy, shall assist the Council in matters coming within the scope of the common foreign and security policy, in particular through contributing to the formulation, preparation and implementation of policy decisions, and, when appropriate and acting on behalf of the Council at the request of the Presidency, through conducting political dialogue with third parties.

Article 27 (ex Article J.17)   The Commission shall be fully associated with the work carried out in the common foreign and security policy field.

Article 28 (ex Article J.18)   1. Articles 189, 190, 196 to 199, 203, 204, 206 to 209, 213 to 219, 255 and 290 of the Treaty establishing the European Community shall apply to the provisions relating to the areas referred to in this Title.

2. Administrative expenditure which the provisions relating to the areas referred to in this Title entail for the institutions shall be charged to the budget of the European Communities.

3. Operational expenditure to which the implementation of those provisions gives rise shall also be charged to the budget of the European Communities, except for such expenditure arising from operations having military or defence implications and cases where the Council acting unanimously decides otherwise.

In cases where expenditure is not charged to the budget of the European Communities it shall be charged to the Member States in accordance with the gross national product scale, unless the Council acting unanimously decides otherwise. As for expenditure arising from operations having military or defence implications, Member States whose representatives in the Council have made a formal declaration under Article 23(1), second subparagraph, shall not be obliged to contribute to the financing thereof.

4. The budgetary procedure laid down in the Treaty establishing the European Community shall apply to the expenditure charged to the budget of the European Communities.

TITLE VI. PROVISIONS ON POLICE AND JUDICIAL COOPERATION IN CRIMINAL MATTERS

Article 29 (ex Article K.1) Without prejudice to the powers of the European Community, the Union's objective shall be to provide citizens with a high level of safety within an area of freedom, security and justice by developing common action among the Member States in the fields of police and judicial cooperation in criminal matters and by preventing and combating racism and xenophobia.

That objective shall be achieved by preventing and combating crime, organised or otherwise, in particular terrorism, trafficking in persons and offences against children, illicit drug trafficking and illicit arms trafficking, corruption and fraud, through:

— closer cooperation between police forces, customs authorities and other competent authorities in the Member States, both directly and through the European Police Office (Europol), in accordance with the provisions of Articles 30 and 32;
— closer cooperation between judicial and other competent authorities of the Member States in accordance with the provisions of Articles 31(a) to (d) and 32;
— approximation, where necessary, of rules on criminal matters in the Member States, in accordance with the provisions of Article 31(e).

Article 30 (ex Article K.2) 1. Common action in the field of police cooperation shall include:
(a) operational cooperation between the competent authorities, including the police, customs and other specialised law enforcement services of the Member States in relation to the prevention, detection and investigation of criminal offences;
(b) the collection, storage, processing, analysis and exchange of relevant information, including information held by law enforcement services on reports on suspicious financial transactions, in particular through Europol, subject to appropriate provisions on the protection of personal data;
(c) cooperation and joint initiatives in training, the exchange of liaison officers, secondments, the use of equipment, and forensic research;
(d) the common evaluation of particular investigative techniques in relation to the detection of serious forms of organised crime.

2. The Council shall promote cooperation through Europol and shall in particular, within a period of five years after the date of entry into force of the Treaty of Amsterdam:

(a) enable Europol to facilitate and support the preparation, and to encourage the coordination and carrying out, of specific investigative actions by the competent authorities of the Member States, including operational actions of joint teams comprising representative of Europol in a support capacity;
(b) adopt measures allowing Europol to ask the competent authorities of the Member States to conduct and coordinate their investigations in specific cases and to develop specific expertise which may be put at the disposal of Member States to assist them in investigating cases of organised crime;
(c) promote liaison arrangements between prosecuting/investigating officials specialising in the fight against organised crime in close cooperation with Europol;
(d) establish a research, documentation and statistical network on cross-border crime.

Article 31 (ex Article K.3)   Common action on judicial cooperation in criminal matters shall include:
(a) facilitating and accelerating cooperation between competent ministries and judicial or equivalent authorities of the Member States in relation to proceedings and the enforcement of decisions;
(b) facilitating extradition between Member States;
(c) ensuring compatibility in rules applicable in the Member States, as may be necessary to improve such cooperation;
(d) preventing conflicts of jurisdiction between Member States;
(e) progressively adopting measures establishing minimum rules relating to the constituent elements of criminal acts and to penalties in the fields of organised crime, terrorism and illicit drug trafficking.

Article 32 (ex Article K.4)   The Council shall lay down the conditions and limitations under which the competent authorities referred to in Articles 30 and 31 may operate in the territory of another Member State in liaison and in agreement with the authorities of that State.

Article 33 (ex Article K.5)   This Title shall not affect the exercise of the responsibilities incumbent upon Member States with regard to the maintenance of law and order and the safeguarding of internal security.

Article 34 (ex Article K.6)   1. In the areas referred to in this Title, Member States shall inform and consult one another within the Council with a view to coordinating their action. To that end, they shall establish collaboration between the relevant departments of their administrations.

2. The Council shall take measures and promote cooperation, using the appropriate form and procedures as set out in this Title, contributing to the pursuit of the objectives of the Union. To that end, acting unanimously on the initiative of any Member State or of the Commission, the Council may:
(a) adopt common positions defining the approach of the Union to a particular matter;
(b) adopt framework decisions for the purpose of approximation of the laws and regulations of the Member States. Framework decisions shall be binding upon the Member States as to the result to be achieved but shall leave to the national authorities the choice of form and methods. They shall not entail direct effect;

(c) adopt decisions for any other purpose consistent with the objectives of this Title, excluding any approximation of the laws and regulations of the Member States. These decisions shall be binding and shall not entail direct effect; the Council, acting by a qualified majority, shall adopt measures necessary to implement those decisions at the level of the Union;

(d) establish conventions which it shall recommend to the Member States for adoption in accordance with their respective constitutional requirements. Member States shall begin the procedures applicable within a time limit to be set by the Council.

Unless they provide otherwise, conventions shall, once adopted by at least half of the Member States, enter into force for those Member States. Measures implementing conventions shall be adopted within the Council by a majority of two-thirds of the Contracting Parties.

3. Where the Council is required to act by a qualified majority, the votes of its members shall be weighted as laid down in Article 205(2) of the Treaty establishing the European Community, and for their adoption acts of the Council shall require at least 62 votes in favour, cast by at least 10 members.

4. For procedural questions, the Council shall act by a majority of its members.

Article 35 (ex Article K.7)   1. The Court of Justice of the European Communities shall have jurisdiction, subject to the conditions laid down in this Article, to give preliminary rulings on the validity and interpretation of framework decisions and decisions, on the interpretation of conventions established under this Title and on the validity and interpretation of the measures implementing them.

2. By a declaration made at the time of signature of the Treaty of Amsterdam or at any time thereafter, any Member State shall be able to accept the jurisdiction of the Court of Justice to give preliminary rulings as specified in paragraph 1.

3. A Member State making a declaration pursuant to paragraph 2 shall specify that either:

(a) any court or tribunal of that State against whose decisions there is no judicial remedy under national law may request the Court of Justice to give a preliminary ruling on a question raised in a case pending before it and concerning the validity or interpretation of an act referred to in paragraph 1 if that court or tribunal considers that a decision on the question is necessary to enable it to give judgment, or

(b) any court or tribunal of that State may request the Court of Justice to give a preliminary ruling on a question raised in a case pending before it and concerning the validity or interpretation of an act referred to in paragraph 1 if that court or tribunal considers that a decision on the question is necessary to enable it to give judgment.

4. Any Member State, whether or not it has made a declaration pursuant to paragraph 2, shall be entitled to submit statements of case or written observations to the Court in cases which arise under paragraph 1.

5. The Court of Justice shall have no jurisdiction to review the validity or proportionality of operations carried out by the police or other law enforcement services of a Member State or the exercise of the responsibilities incumbent upon Member

States with regard to the maintenance of law and order and the safeguarding of internal security.

6. The Court of Justice shall have jurisdiction to review the legality of framework decisions and decisions in actions brought by a Member State or the Commission on grounds of lack of competence, infringement of an essential procedural requirement, infringement of this Treaty or of any rule of law relating to its application, or misuse of powers. The proceedings provided for in this paragraph shall be instituted within two months of the publication of the measure.

7. The Court of Justice shall have jurisdiction to rule on any dispute between Member States regarding the interpretation or the application of acts adopted under Article 34(2) whenever such dispute cannot be settled by the Council within six months of its being referred to the Council by one of its members. The Court shall also have jurisdiction to rule on any dispute between Member States and the Commission regarding the interpretation or the application of conventions established under Article 34(2)(d).

Article 36 (ex Article K.8)   1. A Coordinating Committee shall be set up consisting of senior officials. In addition to its coordinating role, it shall be the task of the Committee to:
— give opinions for the attention of the Council, either at the Council's request or on its own initiative;
— contribute, without prejudice to Article 207 of the Treaty establishing the European Community, to the preparation of the Council's discussions in the areas referred to in Article 29.

2. The Commission shall be fully associated with the work in the areas referred to in this Title.

Article 37 (ex Article K.9)   Within international organisations and at international conferences in which they take part, Member States shall defend the common positions adopted under the provisions of this Title.
   Articles 18 and 19 shall apply as appropriate to matters falling under this Title.

Article 38 (ex Article K.10)   Agreements referred to in Article 24 may cover matters falling under this Title.

Article 39 (ex Article K.11)   1. The Council shall consult the European Parliament before adopting any measure referred to in Article 34(2)(b), (c) and (d). The European Parliament shall deliver its opinion within a time-limit which the Council may lay down, which shall not be less than three months. In the absence of an opinion within that time-limit, the Council may act.

2. The Presidency and the Commission shall regularly inform the European Parliament of discussions in the areas covered by this Title.

3. The European Parliament may ask questions of the Council or make recommendations to it. Each year, it shall hold a debate on the progress made in the areas referred to in this Title.

Article 40 (ex Article K.12)   1. Member States which intend to establish closer cooperation between themselves may be authorised, subject to Articles 43 and 44, to make use of the institutions, procedures and mechanisms laid down by the Treaties provided that the cooperation proposed:

(a) respects the powers of the European Community, and the objectives laid down by this Title;

(b) has the aim of enabling the Union to develop more rapidly into an area of freedom, security and justice.

2. The authorisation referred to in paragraph 1 shall be granted by the Council, acting by a qualified majority at the request of the Member States concerned and after inviting the Commission to present its opinion; the request shall also be forwarded to the European Parliament.

If a member of the Council declares that, for important and stated reasons of national policy, it intends to oppose the granting of an authorisation by qualified majority, a vote shall not be taken. The Council may, acting by a qualified majority, request that the matter be referred to the European Council for decision by unanimity.

The votes of the members of the Council shall be weighted in accordance with Article 205(2) of the Treaty establishing the European Community. For their adoption, decisions shall require at least 62 votes in favour, cast by at least 10 members.

3. Any Member State which wishes to become a party to cooperation set up in accordance with this Article shall notify its intention to the Council and to the Commission, which shall give an opinion to the Council within three months of receipt of that notification, possibly accompanied by a recommendation for such specific arrangements as it may deem necessary for that Member State to become a party to the cooperation in question. Within four months of the date of that notification, the Council shall decide on the request and on such specific arrangements as it may deem necessary. The decision shall be deemed to be taken unless the Council, acting by a qualified majority, decides to hold it in abeyance; in this case, the Council shall state the reasons for its decision and set a deadline for re-examining it. For the purposes of this paragraph, the Council shall act under the conditions set out in Article 44.

4. The provisions of Articles 29 to 41 shall apply to the closer cooperation provided for by this Article, save as otherwise provided for in this Article and in Articles 43 and 44.

The provisions of the Treaty establishing the European Community concerning the powers of the Court of Justice of the European Communities and the exercise of those powers shall apply to paragraphs 1, 2 and 3.

5. This Article is without prejudice to the provisions of the Protocol integrating the Schengen acquis into the framework of the European Union.

Article 41 (ex Article K.13)   1. Articles 189, 190, 195, 196 to 199, 203, 204, 205(3), 206 to 209, 213 to 219, 255 and 290 of the Treaty establishing the European Community shall apply to the provisions relating to the areas referred to in this Title.

2. Administrative expenditure which the provisions relating to the areas referred to in this Title entail for the institutions shall be charged to the budget of the European Communities.

3. Operational expenditure to which the implementation of those provisions gives rise shall also be charged to the budget of the European Communities, except

where the Council acting unanimously decides otherwise. In cases where expenditure is not charged to the budget of the European Communities it shall be charged to the Member States in accordance with the gross national product scale, unless the Council acting unanimously decides otherwise.

4. The budgetary procedure laid down in the Treaty establishing the European Community shall apply to the expenditure charged to the budget of the European Communities.

Article 42 (ex Article K.14)   The Council, acting unanimously on the initiative of the Commission or a Member State, and after consulting the European parliament, may decide that action in areas referred to in Article 29 shall fall under Title IV of the Treaty establishing the European Community, and at the same time determine the relevant voting conditions relating to it. It shall recommend the Member States to adopt that decision in accordance with their respective constitutional requirements.

TITLE VII. (EX TITLE VIA) PROVISIONS ON CLOSER COOPERATION

Article 43 (ex Article K.15)   1. Member States which intend to establish closer cooperation between themselves may make use of the institutions, procedures and mechanisms laid down by this Treaty and the Treaty establishing the European Community provided that the cooperation:
(a) is aimed at furthering the objectives of the Union and at protecting and serving its interests;
(b) respects the principles of the said Treaties and the single institutional framework of the Union;
(c) is only used as a last resort, where the objectives of the said Treaties could not be attained by applying the relevant procedures laid down therein;
(d) concerns at least a majority of Member States;
(e) does not affect the 'acquis communautaire' and the measures adopted under the other provisions of the said Treaties;
(f) does not affect the competences, rights, obligations and interests of those Member States which do not participate therein;
(g) is open to all Member States and allows them to become parties to the cooperation at any time, provided that they comply with the basic decision and with the decisions taken within that framework;
(h) complies with the specific additional criteria laid down in Article 11 of the Treaty establishing the European Community and Article 40 of this Treaty, depending on the area concerned, and is authorised by the Council in accordance with the procedures laid down therein.

2. Member States shall apply, as far as they are concerned, the acts and decisions adopted for the implementation of the cooperation in which they participate. Member States not participating in such cooperation shall not impede the implementation thereof by the participating Member States.

Article 44 (ex Article K.16)   1. For the purpose of the adoption of the acts and decisions necessary for the implementation of the cooperation referred to in Article 43, the relevant institutional provisions of this Treaty and of the Treaty establishing the European Community shall apply. However, while all members of the Council shall be able to take part in the deliberations, only those representing participating Member States shall take part in the adoption of decisions. The qualified majority shall be defined as the same proportion of the weighted votes of the members of the Council concerned as laid down in Article 205(2) of the Treaty establishing the European Community. Unanimity shall be constituted by only those Council members concerned.

2. Expenditure resulting from implementation of the cooperation, other than administrative costs entailed for the institutions, shall be borne by the participating Member States, unless the Council, acting unanimously, decides otherwise.

Article 45 (ex Article K.17)   The Council and the Commission shall regularly inform the European Parliament of the development of closer cooperation established on the basis of this Title.

TITLE VIII. (EX TITLE VII) FINAL PROVISIONS

Article 46 (ex Article L)   The provisions of the Treaty establishing the European Community, the Treaty establishing the European Coal and Steel Community and the Treaty establishing the European Atomic Energy Community concerning the powers of the Court of Justice of the European Communities and the exercise of those powers shall apply only to the following provisions of this Treaty:
(a) provisions amending the Treaty establishing the European Economic Community with a view to establishing the European Community, the Treaty establishing the European Coal and Steel Community and the Treaty establishing the European Atomic Energy Community;
(b) provisions of Title VI, under the conditions provided for by Article 35;
(c) provisions of Title VII, under the conditions provided for by Article 11 of the Treaty establishing the European Community and Article 40 of this Treaty;
(d) Article 6(2) with regard to action of the institutions, insofar as the Court has jurisdiction under the Treaties establishing the European Communities and under this Treaty;
(e) Articles 46 to 53.

Article 47 (ex Article M)   Subject to the provisions amending the Treaty establishing the European Economic Community with a view to establishing the European Community, the Treaty establishing the European Coal and Steel Community and the Treaty establishing the European Atomic Energy Community, and to these final provisions, nothing in this Treaty shall affect the Treaties establishing the European Communities or the subsequent Treaties and Acts modifying or supplementing them.

Article 48 (ex Article N)   The government of any Member State or the Commission may submit to the Council proposals for the amendment of the Treaties on which the Union is founded.

   If the Council, after consulting the European Parliament and, where appropriate, the Commission, delivers an opinion in favour of calling a conference of representatives of the governments of the Member States, the conference shall be convened by the President of the Council for the purpose of determining by common accord the amendments to be made to those Treaties. The European Central Bank shall also be consulted in the case of institutional changes in the monetary area.

The amendments shall enter into force after being ratified by all the Member States in accordance with their respective constitutional requirements.

Article 49 (ex Article O)   Any European State which respects the principles set out in Article 6(1) may apply to become a member of the Union. It shall address its application to the Council, which shall act unanimously after consulting the Commission and after receiving the assent of the European Parliament, which shall act by an absolute majority of its component members.

The conditions of admission and the adjustments to the Treaties on which the Union is founded which such admission entails shall be the subject of an agreement between the Member States and the applicant State. This agreement shall be submitted for ratification by all the contracting states in accordance with their respective constitutional requirements.

Article 50 (ex Article P)   1. Articles 2 to 7 and 10 to 19 of the Treaty establishing a Single Council and a Single Commission of the European Communities, signed in Brussels on 8 April 1965, are hereby repealed.

2. Article 2, Article 3(2) and Title III of the Single European Act signed in Luxembourg on 17 February 1986 and in The Hague on 28 February 1986 are hereby repealed.

Article 51 (ex Article Q)   This Treaty is concluded for an unlimited period.

Article 52 (ex Article R)   1. This Treaty shall be ratified by the High Contracting Parties in accordance with their respective constitutional requirements. The instruments of ratification shall be deposited with the Government of the Italian Republic.

2. This Treaty shall enter into force on 1 January 1993, provided that all the instruments of ratification have been deposited, or, failing that, on the first day of the month following the deposit of the instrument of ratification by the last signatory State to take this step.[2]

Article 53 (ex Article S)   This Treaty, drawn up in a single original in the Danish, Dutch, English, French, German, Greek, Irish, Italian, Portuguese and Spanish languages, the texts in each of these languages being equally authentic, shall be deposited in the archives of the government of the Italian Republic, which will transmit a certified copy to each of the governments of the other signatory States.

Pursuant to the Accession Treaty of 1994, the Finnish and Swedish versions of this Treaty shall also be authentic.

IN WITNESS WHEREOF the undersigned Plenipotentiaries have signed this Treaty.

Done at Maastricht on the seventh day of February in the year one thousand nine hundred and ninety-two.

[*signatures omitted*]

---

[2] The Treaty entered into force on 1 November 1993.

Protocols

Only selected Protocols are given here. Recitals have been shortened or omitted, and short titles added. References to Treaty articles are to the new numbers used in the preceding texts of the consolidated versions of the Treaties. The Protocol texts printed here have been numbered consecutively but, in brackets, are added the number and year ascribed to each by the texts of the consolidated treaty versions given in OJ 1997 C 340/176–78.

Protocols annexed by Treaty on European Union to EC Treaty

1   EMU AND UNITED KINGDOM (PROTOCOL NO.25, 1992)

THE HIGH CONTRACTING PARTIES,

RECOGNIZING that the United Kingdom shall not be obliged or committed to move to the third stage of economic and monetary union without a separate decision to do so by its government and Parliament;

NOTING the practice of the government of the United Kingdom to fund its borrowing requirement by the sale of debt to the private sector;

HAVE AGREED the following provisions, which shall be annexed to the Treaty establishing the European Community:

1. The United Kingdom shall notify the Council whether it intends to move to the third stage before the Council makes its assessment under Article 121(2) of this Treaty;

Unless the United Kingdom notifies the Council that it intends to move to the third stage, it shall be under no obligation to do so.

If no date is set for the beginning of the third stage under Article 121(3) of this Treaty, the United Kingdom may notify its intention to move to the third stage before 1 January 1998.

2. Paragraphs 3 to 9 shall have effect if the United Kingdom notifies the Council that it does not intend to move to the third stage.

3. The United Kingdom shall not be included among the majority of Member States which fulfil the necessary conditions referred to in the second indent of Article 121(2) and the first indent of Article 121(3) of this Treaty.

4. The United Kingdom shall retain its powers in the field of monetary policy according to national law.

5. Articles 4(2), 104(1), (9) and (11), 105(1) to (5), 106, 108, 109, 110, 111, 112(1) and (2)(b) and 123(4) and (5) of this Treaty shall not apply to the United Kingdom. In these provisions references to the Community or the Member States shall not include the United Kingdom and references to national central banks shall not include the Bank of England.

6. Articles 116(4) and 119 and 120 of this Treaty shall continue to apply to the United Kingdom. Articles 114(4) and 124 shall apply to the United Kingdom as if it had a derogation.

7. The voting rights of the United Kingdom shall be suspended in respect of acts of the Council referred to in Articles listed in paragraph 5. For this purpose the weighted votes of the United Kingdom shall be excluded from any calculation of a qualified majority under Article 122(5) of this Treaty.

The United Kingdom shall also have no right to participate in the appointment of the President, the Vice-President and the other members of the Executive Board of the ECB under Articles 112(2)(b) and 123(1) of this Treaty.

8. Articles 3, 4, 6, 7, 9.2, 10.1, 10.3, 11.2, 12.1, 14, 16, 18 to 20, 22, 23, 26, 27, 30 to 34, 50 and 52 of the Protocol on the Statute of the European System of Central Banks and of the European Central Bank ('the Statute') shall not apply to the United Kingdom.

In those Articles, references to the Community or the Member States shall not include the United Kingdom and references to national central banks or shareholders shall not include the Bank of England.

References in Articles 10.3 and 30.2. of the Statute to 'subscribed capital of the ECB' shall not include capital subscribed by the Bank of England.

9. Article 111(3) of this Treaty and Articles 44 to 48 of the Statute shall have effect, whether or not there is any Member State with a derogation, subject to the following amendments:

(a) References in Article 44 to the tasks of the ECB and the EMI shall include those tasks that still need to be performed in the third stage owing to any decision of the United Kingdom not to move to that Stage.

(b) In addition to the tasks referred to in Article 47 the ECB shall also give advice in relation to and contribute to the preparation of any decision of the Council with regard to the United Kingdom taken in accordance with paragraphs 10(a) and 10(c).

(c) The Bank of England shall pay up its subscription to the capital of the ECB as a contribution of its operational costs on the same basis as national central banks of Member States with a derogation.

10. If the United Kingdom does not move to the third stage, it may change its notification at any time after the beginning of that stage. In that event:

(a) The United Kingdom shall have the right to move to the third stage provided only that it satisfies the necessary conditions. The Council, acting at the request of the United Kingdom and under the conditions and in accordance with the procedure laid down in Article 122(2) of this Treaty, shall decide whether it fulfills the necessary conditions.

(b) The Bank of England shall pay up its subscribed capital, transfer to the ECB foreign reserve assets and contribute to its reserves on the same basis as the national central bank of a Member State whose derogation has been abrogated.

(c) The Council, acting under the conditions and in accordance with the procedure laid down in Article 107(5) of this Treaty, shall take all other necessary decisions to enable the United Kingdom to move to the third stage.

If the United Kingdom moves to the third stage pursuant to the provisions of this protocol, paragraphs 3 to 9 shall cease to have effect.

11. Notwithstanding Articles 101 and 116(3) of this Treaty and Article 21.1. of the Statute, the government of the United Kingdom may maintain its ways and means

facility with the Bank of England if and so long as the United Kingdom does not move to the third stage.

2 EMU AND DENMARK (PROTOCOL No. 26, 1992)

THE HIGH CONTRACTING PARTIES,

DESIRING to settle, in accordance with the general objectives of the Treaty establishing the European Community, certain particular problems existing at the present time,

TAKING INTO ACCOUNT that the Danish Constitution contains provisions which may imply a referendum in Denmark prior to Danish participation in the third stage of Economic and Monetary Union,

HAVE AGREED on the following provisions, which shall be annexed to the Treaty establishing the European Community:

1. The Danish Government shall notify the Council of its position concerning participation in the third stage before the Council makes its assessment under Article 121(2) of this Treaty.

2. In the event of a notification that Denmark will not participate in the third stage, Denmark shall have an exemption. The effect of the exemption shall be that all Articles and provisions of this Treaty and the Statute of the ESCB referring to a derogation shall be applicable to Denmark.

3. In such case, Denmark shall not be included among the majority of Member States which fulfil the necessary conditions referred to in the second indent of Article 121(2) and the first indent of Article 121(3) of this Treaty.

4. As for the abrogation of the exemption, the procedure referred to in Article 122(2) shall only be initiated at the request of Denmark.

5. In the event of abrogation of the exemption status, the provisions of this Protocol shall cease to apply.

Protocols annexed by Treaty of Amsterdam to EC Treaty and Treaty on European Union

3 SCHENGEN ACQUIS (PROTOCOL No. 2, 1997)

Article 1 The Kingdom of Belgium, the Kingdom of Denmark, the Federal Republic of Germany, the Hellenic Republic, the Kingdom of Spain, the French Republic, the Italian Republic, the Grand Duchy of Luxembourg, the Kingdom of the Netherlands, the Republic of Austria, the Portuguese Republic, the Republic of Finland and the Kingdom of Sweden, signatories to the Schengen agreements, are authorised to establish closer cooperation among themselves within the scope of those agreements and related provisions, as they are listed in the Annex to this Protocol, hereinafter referred to as the 'Schengen acquis'. This cooperation shall be conducted within the institutional and legal framework of the European Union and with respect for the relevant provisions of the Treaty on European Union and of the Treaty establishing the European Community.

Article 2 1. From the date of entry into force of the Treaty of Amsterdam, the Schengen acquis, including the decisions of the Executive Committee established by the Schengen agreements which have been adopted before this date, shall immediately apply to the thirteen Member States referred to in Article 1, without prejudice to the provisions of paragraph 2 of this Article. From the same date, the Council will substitute itself for the said Executive Committee.

The Council, acting by the unanimity of its Members referred to in Article 1, shall take any measure necessary for the implementation of this paragraph. The Council, acting unanimously, shall determine, in conformity with the relevant provisions of the Treaties, the legal basis for each of the provisions or decisions which constitute the Schengen acquis.

With regard to such provisions and decisions and in accordance with that determination, the Court of Justice of the European Communities shall exercise the powers conferred upon it by the relevant applicable provisions of the Treaties. In any event, the Court of Justice shall have no jurisdiction on measures or decisions relating to the maintenance of law and order and the safeguarding of internal security.

As long as the measures referred to above have not been taken and without prejudice to Article 5(2), the provisions or decisions which constitute the Schengen acquis shall be regarded as acts based on Title VI of the Treaty on European Union.

2. The provisions of paragraph 1 shall apply to the Member States which have signed accession protocols to the Schengen agreements, from the dates decided by the Council, acting with the unanimity of its Members mentioned in Article 1, unless the conditions for the accession of any of those States to the Schengen acquis are met before the date of the entry into force of the Treaty of Amsterdam.

Article 3 Following the determination referred to in Article 2(1), second subparagraph, Denmark shall maintain the same rights and obligations in relation to the other signatories to the Schengen agreements, as before the said determination with regard to those parts of the Schengen acquis that are determined to have a legal basis in Title IV of the Treaty establishing the European Community.

With regard to those parts of the Schengen acquis that are determined to have legal base in Title VI of the Treaty on European Union, Denmark shall continue to have the same rights and obligations as the other signatories to the Schengen agreements.

Article 4 Ireland and the United Kingdom of Great Britain and Northern Ireland, which are not bound by the Schengen acquis, may at any time request to take part in some or all of the provisions of this acquis.

The Council shall decide on the request with the unanimity of its members referred to in Article 1 and of the representative of the Government of the State concerned.

Article 5 1. Proposals and initiatives to build upon the Schengen acquis shall be subject to the relevant provisions of the Treaties.

In this context, where either Ireland or the United Kingdom or both have not notified the President of the Council in writing within a reasonable period that they wish to take part, the authorisation referred to in Article 11 of the Treaty establishing the European Community or Article 40 of the Treaty on European Union shall be deemed to have been granted to the Members States referred to in Article 1 and to Ireland or the United Kingdom where either of them wishes to take part in the areas of cooperation in question.

2. The relevant provisions of the Treaties referred to in the first subparagraph of paragraph 1 shall apply even if the Council has not adopted the measures referred to in Article 2(1), second subparagraph.

Article 6   The Republic of Iceland and the Kingdom of Norway shall be associated with the implementation of the Schengen acquis and its further development on the basis of the Agreement signed in Luxembourg on 19 December 1996. Appropriate procedures shall be agreed to that effect in an Agreement to be concluded with those States by the Council, acting by the unanimity of its Members mentioned in Article 1. Such Agreement shall include provisions on the contribution of Iceland and Norway to any financial consequences resulting from the implementation of this Protocol.

  A separate Agreement shall be concluded with Iceland and Norway by the Council, acting unanimously, for the establishment of rights and obligations between Ireland and the United Kingdom of Great Britain and Northern Ireland on the one hand, and Iceland and Norway on the other, in domains of the Schengen acquis which apply to these States.

Article 7   The Council shall, acting by a qualified majority, adopt the detailed arrangements for the integration of the Schengen Secretariat into the General Secretariat of the Council.

Article 8   For the purposes of the negotiations for the admission of new Member States into the European Union, the Schengen acquis and further measures taken by the institutions within its scope shall be regarded as an acquis which must be accepted in full by all States candidates for admission.

ANNEX: SCHENGEN ACQUIS

1. The Agreement, signed in Schengen on 14 June 1985, between the Governments of the States of the Benelux Economic Union, the Federal Republic of Germany and the French Republic on the gradual abolition of checks at their common borders.

2. The Convention, signed in Schengen on 19 June 1990, between the Kingdom of Belgium, the Federal Republic of Germany, the French Republic, the Grand Duchy of Luxembourg and the Kingdom of the Netherlands, implementing the Agreement on the gradual abolition of checks at their common borders, signed in Schengen on 14 June 1985, with related Final Act and common declarations.

3. The Accession Protocols and Agreements to the 1985 Agreement and the 1990 Implementation Convention with Italy (signed in Paris on 27 November 1990), Spain and Portugal (signed in Bonn on 25 June 1991), Greece (signed in Madrid on 6 November 1992), Austria (signed in Brussels on 28 April 1995) and Denmark, Finland and Sweden (signed in Luxembourg on 19 December 1996), with related Final Acts and declarations.

4. Decisions and declarations adopted by the Executive Committee established by the 1990 Implementation Convention, as well as acts adopted for the implementation of the Convention by the organs upon which the Executive Committee has conferred decision making powers.

4   UNITED KINGDOM AND IRELAND: BORDER CONTROLS (PROTOCOL NO. 3, 1997)

Article 1   The United Kingdom shall be entitled, notwithstanding Article 14 of the Treaty establishing the European Community, any other provision of that Treaty or of the Treaty on European Union, any measure adopted under those Treaties, or any international agreement concluded by the Community or by the Community and its Member States with one or more third States, to exercise at its frontiers with other Member States such controls on persons seeking to enter the United Kingdom as it may consider necessary for the purpose:
(a) of verifying the right to enter the United Kingdom of citizens of States which are Contracting Parties to the Agreement on the European Economic Area and of their dependants exercising rights conferred by Community law, as well as citizens of other States on whom such rights have been conferred by an agreement by which the United Kingdom is bound; and
(b) of determining whether or not to grant other persons permission to enter the United Kingdom.

Nothing in Article 14 of the Treaty establishing the European Community or in any other provision of that Treaty or of the Treaty on European Union or in any measure adopted under them shall prejudice the right of the United Kingdom to adopt or exercise any such controls. References to the United Kingdom in this Article shall include territories for whose external relations the United Kingdom is responsible.

Article 2   The United Kingdom and Ireland may continue to make arrangements between themselves relating to the movement of persons between their territories ('the Common Travel Area'), while fully respecting the rights of persons referred to in Article 1, first paragraph, point (a) of this Protocol. Accordingly, as long as they maintain such arrangements, the provisions of Article 1 of this Protocol shall apply to Ireland under the same terms and conditions as for the United Kingdom. Nothing in Article 14 of the Treaty establishing the European Community, in any other provision of that Treaty or of the Treaty on European Union or in any measure adopted under them, shall affect any such arrangements.

Article 3   The other Member States shall be entitled to exercise at their frontiers or at any point of entry into their territory such controls on persons seeking to enter their territory from the United Kingdom or any territories whose external relations are under its responsibility for the same purposes stated in Article 1 of this Protocol, or from Ireland as long as the provisions of Article 1 of this Protocol apply to Ireland.

Nothing in Article 14 of the Treaty establishing the European Community or in any other provision of that Treaty or of the Treaty on European Union or in any measure adopted under them shall prejudice the right of the other Member States to adopt or exercise any such controls.

5   UNITED KINGDOM AND IRELAND: VISAS, ASYLUM ETC. (PROTOCOL NO. 4, 1997)

Article 1   Subject to Article 3, the United Kingdom and Ireland shall not take part in the adoption by the Council of proposed measures pursuant to Title IV of the Treaty establishing the European Community. By way of derogation from Article 205(2) of the Treaty establishing the European Community, a qualified majority shall be defined as the same proportion of the weighted votes of the members of the Council concerned as laid down in the said Article 205(2). The unanimity of the members of the Council, with the exception of the representatives of the governments of the United Kingdom and Ireland, shall be necessary for decisions of the Council which must be adopted unanimously.

Article 2   In consequence of Article 1 and subject to Articles 3, 4 and 6, none of the provisions of Title IV of the Treaty establishing the European Community, no measure adopted pursuant to that Title, no provision of any international agreement concluded by the Community pursuant to that Title, and no decision of the Court of Justice interpreting any such provision or measure shall be binding upon or applicable in the United Kingdom or Ireland; and no such provision, measure or decision shall in any way affect the competences, rights and obligations of those States; and no such provision, measure or decision shall in any way affect the acquis communautaire nor form part of Community law as they apply to the United Kingdom or Ireland.

Article 3   1. The United Kingdom or Ireland may notify the President of the Council in writing, within three months after a proposal or initiative has been presented to the Council pursuant to Title IV of the Treaty establishing the European Community, that it wishes to take part in the adoption and application of any such proposed measure, whereupon that State shall be entitled to do so. By way of derogation from Article 205(2) of the Treaty establishing the European Community, a qualified majority shall be defined as the same proportion of the weighted votes of the members of the Council concerned as laid down in the said Article 205(2).

    The unanimity of the members of the Council, with the exception of a member which has not made such a notification, shall be necessary for decisions of the Council which must be adopted unanimously. A measure adopted under this paragraph shall be binding upon all Member States which took part in its adoption.

2. If after a reasonable period of time a measure referred to in paragraph 1 cannot be adopted with the United Kingdom or Ireland taking part, the Council may adopt such measure in accordance with Article 1 without the participation of the United Kingdom or Ireland. In that case Article 2 applies.

Article 4   The United Kingdom or Ireland may at any time after the adoption of a measure by the Council pursuant to Title IV of the Treaty establishing the European Community notify its intention to the Council and to the Commission that it wishes to accept that measure. In that case, the procedure provided for in Article 11(3) of the Treaty establishing the European Community shall apply mutatis mutandis.

Article 5   A Member State which is not bound by a measure adopted pursuant to Title IV of the Treaty establishing the European Community shall bear no financial consequences of that measure other than administrative costs entailed for the institutions.

Article 6   Where, in cases referred to in this Protocol, the United Kingdom or Ireland is bound by a measure adopted by the Council pursuant to Title IV of the

Treaty establishing the European Community, the relevant provisions of that Treaty, including Article 68, shall apply to that State in relation to that measure.

Article 7 Articles 3 and 4 shall be without prejudice to the Protocol integrating the Schengen acquis into the framework of the European Union.

Article 8 Ireland may notify the President of the Council in writing that it no longer wishes to be covered by the terms of this Protocol. In that case, the normal treaty provisions will apply to Ireland.

6 Denmark: Border Controls and Defence (Protocol No. 5, 1997)

Part I

Article 1 Denmark shall not take part in the adoption by the Council of proposed measures pursuant to Title IV of the Treaty establishing the European Community. By way of derogation from Article 205(2) of the Treaty establishing the European Community, a qualified majority shall be defined as the same proportion of the weighted votes of the members of the Council concerned as laid down in the said Article 205(2). The unanimity of the members of the Council, with the exception of the representative of the government of Denmark, shall be necessary for the decisions of the Council which must be adopted unanimously.

Article 2 None of the provisions of Title IV of the Treaty establishing the European Community, no measure adopted pursuant to that Title, no provision of any international agreement concluded by the Community pursuant to that Title, and no decision of the Court of Justice interpreting any such provision or measure shall be binding upon or applicable in Denmark; and no such provision, measure or decision shall in any way affect the competences, rights and obligations of Denmark; and no such provision, measure or decision shall in any way affect the acquis communautaire nor form part of Community law as they apply to Denmark.

Article 3 Denmark shall bear no financial consequences of measures referred to in Article 1, other than administrative costs entailed for the institutions.

Article 4 Articles 1, 2 and 3 shall not apply to measures determining the third countries whose nationals must be in possession of a visa when crossing the external borders of the Member States, or measures relating to a uniform format for visas.

Article 5 1. Denmark shall decide within a period of 6 months after the Council has decided on a proposal or initiative to build upon the Schengen acquis under the provisions of Title IV of the Treaty establishing the European Community, whether it will implement this decision in its national law. If it decides to do so, this decision will create an obligation under international law between Denmark and the other Member States referred to in Article 1 of the Protocol integrating the Schengen acquis into the framework of the European Union as well as Ireland or the United Kingdom if those Member States take part in the areas of cooperation in question.

2. If Denmark decides not to implement a decision of the Council as referred to in paragraph 1, the Member States referred to in Article 1 of the Protocol integrating the Schengen acquis into the framework of the European Union will consider appropriate measures to be taken.

Part II

Article 6 With regard to measures adopted by the Council in the field of Articles 11 and 17 of the Treaty on European Union, Denmark does not participate in the elaboration and the implementation of decisions and actions of the Union which have defence implications, but will not prevent the development of closer cooperation between Member States in this area. Therefore Denmark shall not participate in their adoption. Denmark shall not be obliged to contribute to the financing of operational expenditure arising from such measures.

Part III

Article 7 At any time Denmark may, in accordance with its constitutional requirements, inform the other Member States that it no longer wishes to avail itself of all or part of this Protocol. In that event, Denmark will apply in full all relevant measures then in force taken within the framework of the European Union.

Protocols Annexed by Treaty of Amsterdam to EC Treaty

7 Asylum (Protocol No. 29, 1997)

SOLE Article Given the level of protection of fundamental rights and freedoms by the Member States of the European Union, Member States shall be regarded as constituting safe countries of origin in respect of each other for all legal and practical purposes in relation to asylum matters. Accordingly, any application for asylum made by a national of a Member State may be taken into consideration or declared admissible for processing by another Member State only in the following cases:
(a) if the Member State of which the applicant is a national proceeds after the entry into force of the Treaty of Amsterdam, availing itself of the provisions of Article 15 of the Convention for the Protection of Human Rights and Fundamental Freedoms, to take measures derogating in its territory from its obligations under that Convention;
(b) if the procedure referred to in Article 7(1) of the Treaty on European Union has been initiated and until the Council takes a decision in respect thereof;
(c) if the Council, acting on the basis of Article 7(1) of the Treaty on European Union, has determined, in respect of the Member State which the applicant is a national, the existence of a serious and persistent breach by that Member State of principles mentioned in Article 6(1);
(d) if a Member State should so decide unilaterally in respect of the application of a national of another Member State; in that case the Council shall be immediately informed; the application shall be dealt with on the basis of the presumption that it is manifestly unfounded without affecting in any way, whatever the cases may be, the decision-making power of the Member State.

8 Subsidiarity and Proportionality (Protocol No. 30, 1997)

(1) In exercising the powers conferred on it, each institution shall ensure that the principle of subsidiarity is complied with. It shall also ensure compliance with the principle of proportionality, according to which any action by the

Community shall not go beyond what is necessary to achieve the objectives of the Treaty.

(2) The application of the principles of subsidiarity and proportionality shall respect the general provisions and the objectives of the Treaty, particularly as regards the maintaining in full of the acquis communautaire and the institutional balance; it shall not affect the principles developed by the Court of Justice regarding the relationship between national and Community law, and it should take into account Article 6(4) of the Treaty on European Union, according to which 'the Union shall provide itself with the means necessary to attain its objectives and carry through its policies'.

(3) The principle of subsidiarity does not call into question the powers conferred on the European Community by the Treaty, as interpreted by the Court of Justice. The criteria referred to in the second paragraph of Article 5 of the Treaty shall relate to areas for which the Community does not have exclusive competence. The principle of subsidiarity provides a guide as to how those powers are to be exercised at the Community level. Subsidiarity is a dynamic concept and should be applied in the light of the objectives set out in the Treaty. It allows Community action within the limits of its powers to be expanded where circumstances so require, and conversely, to be restricted or discontinued where it is no longer justified.

(4) For any proposed Community legislation, the reasons on which it is based shall be stated with a view to justifying its compliance with the principles of subsidiarity and proportionality; the reasons for concluding that a Community objective can be better achieved by the Community must be substantiated by qualitative or, wherever possible, quantitative indicators.

(5) For Community action to be justified, both aspects of the subsidiarity principle shall be met: the objectives of the proposed action cannot be sufficiently achieved by Member States' action in the framework of their national constitutional system and can therefore be better achieved by action on the part of the Community.

The following guidelines should be used in examining whether the above-mentioned condition is fulfilled:

— the issue under consideration has transnational aspects which cannot be satisfactorily regulated by action by Member States;
— actions by Member States alone or lack of Community action would conflict with the requirements of the Treaty (such as the need to correct distortion of competition or avoid disguised restrictions on trade or strengthen economic and social cohesion) or would otherwise significantly damage Member States' interests;
— action at Community level would produce clear benefits by reason of its scale or effects compared with action at the level of the Member States.

(6) The form of Community action shall be as simple as possible, consistent with satisfactory achievement of the objective of the measure and the need for effective enforcement. The Community shall legislate only to the extent necessary. Other things being equal, directives should be preferred to regulations and framework directives to detailed measures. Directives as provided for in Article 249 of the Treaty, while binding upon each Member State to which they

are addressed as to the result to be achieved, shall leave to the national authorities the choice of form and methods.

(7) Regarding the nature and the extent of Community action, Community measures should leave as much scope for national decision as possible, consistent with securing the aim of the measure and observing the requirements of the Treaty. While respecting Community law, care should be taken to respect well established national arrangements and the organisation and working of Member States' legal systems. Where appropriate and subject to the need for proper enforcement, Community measures should provide Member States with alternative ways to achieve the objectives of the measures.

(8) Where the application of the principle of subsidiarity leads to no action being taken by the Community, Member States are required in their action to comply with the general rules laid down in Article 10 of the Treaty, by taking all appropriate measures to ensure fulfilment of their obligations under the Treaty and by abstaining from any measure which could jeopardise the attainment of the objectives of the Treaty.

(9) Without prejudice to its right of initiative, the Commission should:

— except in cases of particular urgency or confidentiality, consult widely before proposing legislation and, wherever appropriate, publish consultation documents;

— justify the relevance of its proposals with regard to the principle of subsidiarity; whenever necessary, the explanatory memorandum accompanying a proposal will give details in this respect. The financing of Community action in whole or in part from the Community budget shall require an explanation;

— take duly into account the need for any burden, whether financial or administrative, falling upon the Community, national governments, local authorities, economic operators and citizens, to be minimised and proportionate to the objective to be achieved;

— submit an annual report to the European Council, the European Parliament and the Council on the application of Article 3b of the Treaty. This annual report shall also be sent to the Committee of the Regions and to the Economic and Social Committee.

(10) The European Council shall take account of the Commission report referred to in the fourth indent of point 9 within the report on the progress achieved by the Union which it is required to submit to the European Parliament in accordance with Article 4 of the Treaty on European Union.

(11) While fully observing the procedures applicable, the European Parliament and the Council shall, as an integral part of the overall examination of Commission proposals, consider their consistency with Article 5 of the Treaty. This concerns the original Commission proposal as well as amendments which the European Parliament and the Council envisage making to the proposal.

(12) In the course of the procedures referred to in Articles 251 and 252 of the Treaty, the European Parliament shall be informed of the Council's position on the application of Article 5 of the Treaty, by way of a statement of the reasons which led the Council to adopt its common position. The Council shall inform the European Parliament of the reasons on the basis of which all or part of a

Commission proposal is deemed to be inconsistent with Article 5 of the Treaty.
(13) Compliance with the principle of subsidiarity shall be reviewed in accordance with the rules laid down by the Treaty.

9   EXTERNAL BORDERS (PROTOCOL NO. 31, 1997)

The provisions on the measures on the crossing of external borders included in Article 62(2)(a) of Title IV of the Treaty shall be without prejudice to the competence of Member States to negotiate or conclude agreements with third countries as long as they respect Community law and other relevant international agreements.

10   PUBLIC BROADCASTING (PROTOCOL NO. 32, 1997)

The provisions of the Treaty establishing the European Community shall be without prejudice to the competence of Member States to provide for the funding of public service broadcasting insofar as such funding is granted to broadcasting organisations for the fulfilment of the public service remit as conferred, defined and organised by each Member State, and insofar as such funding does not affect trading conditions and competition in the Community to an extent which would be contrary to the common interest, while the realisation of the remit of that public service shall be taken into account.

11   ANIMAL WELFARE (PROTOCOL NO. 33, 1997)

In formulating and implementing the Community's agriculture, transport, internal market and research policies, the Community and the Member States shall pay full regard to the welfare requirements of animals, while respecting the legislative or administrative provisions and customs of the Member States relating in particular to religious rites, cultural traditions and regional heritage.

Protocols annexed by Treaty of Amsterdam to Treaty on European Union and EC, ECSC, and Euratom Treaties

12   ENLARGEMENT (PROTOCOL NO. 7, 1997)

Article 1   At the date of entry into force of the first enlargement of the Union, notwithstanding Article 213(1) of the Treaty establishing the European Community, Article 9(1) of the Treaty establishing the European Coal and Steel Community and Article 126(1) of the Treaty establishing the European Atomic Energy Community, the Commission shall comprise one national of each of the Member States, provided that, by that date, the weighting of the votes in the Council has been modified, whether by reweighting of the votes or by dual majority, in a manner acceptable to all Member States, taking into account all relevant elements, notably compensating those Member States which give up the possibility of nominating a second member of the Commission.

Article 2   At least one year before the membership of the European Union exceeds twenty, a conference of representatives of the governments of the Member States shall be convened in order to carry out a comprehensive review of the provisions of the Treaties on the composition and functioning of the institutions.

13   Seats of the Institutions (Protocol No. 8, 1997)

SOLE Article

(a) The European Parliament shall have its seat in Strasbourg where the 12 periods of monthly plenary sessions, including the budget session, shall be held. The periods of additional plenary sessions shall be held in Brussels. The committees of the European Parliament shall meet in Brussels. The General Secretariat of the European Parliament and its departments shall remain in Luxembourg.

(b) The Council shall have its seat in Brussels. During the months of April, June and October, the Council shall hold its meetings in Luxembourg.

(c) The Commission shall have its seat in Brussels. The departments listed in Article s 7, 8 and 9 of the Decision of 8 April 1965 shall be established in Luxembourg.

(d) The Court of Justice and the Court of First Instance shall have their seats in Luxembourg.

(e) The Court of Auditors shall have its seat in Luxembourg.

(f) The Economic and Social Committee shall have its seat in Brussels.

(g) The Committee of the Regions shall have its seat in Brussels.

(h) The European Investment Bank shall have its seat in Luxembourg.

(i) The European Monetary Institute and the European Central Bank shall have their seat in Frankfurt.

(j) The European Police Office (Europol) shall have its seat in The Hague.

Ombudsman

Decision of the European Parliament of 9 March 1994
(Extracts)

THE EUROPEAN PARLIAMENT

HAVING REGARD to the Treaties establishing the European Communities and in particular Article 138e.4 [now 195.4] of the Treaty establishing the European Community

[recitals omitted]

HAVING REGARD to the opinion of the Commission;

HAVING REGARD to the Council's approval;

[recitals omitted]

HAS DECIDED:

Article 1   1. The regulations and general conditions of the Ombudsman's duties shall be as laid down by this decision [*text omitted*].

2. The Ombudsman shall perform his duties in accordance with the powers conferred on the Community institutions and bodies by the treaties.

3. The Ombudsman may not intervene in cases before courts or question the soundness of a court's ruling.

Article 2   1. Within the framework of the aforementioned Treaties and the conditions laid down therein, the Ombudsman shall help to uncover maladministration in the activities of the Community institutions and bodies, with the exception of the Court of Justice and the Court of First Instance acting in their judicial role, and make recommendations with a view to putting an end to it. No action by any other person or body may be the subject of a complaint to the Ombudsman.

2. Any citizen of the Union or any natural or legal person residing or having its office in a Member State of the Union may, directly or through a Member of the European Parliament, refer a complaint to the Ombudsman in respect of an instance of maladministration in the activities of Community institutions or bodies, with the exception of the Court of Justice and the Court of First Instance acting in their judicial role. The Ombudsman shall inform the institution or body concerned as soon as a complaint is referred to him,

3. The complaint must allow the person lodging the complaint and the object of the complaint to be identified; the person lodging the complaint may request that his complaint remain confidential.

4. A complaint shall be made within two years of the date on which the facts on which it is based came to the attention of the person lodging the complaint and must be preceded by the appropriate administrative approaches to the institutions and bodies concerned.

5. The Ombudsman may advise the person lodging the complaint to address it to another authority.

6. Complaints submitted to the Ombudsman shall not affect time limits for appeals in administrative or judicial proceedings.

7. When the Ombudsman, because of legal proceedings in progress or concluded concerning the facts which have been put forward, has to declare a complaint inadmissible or terminate consideration of it, the outcome of any enquiries he has carried out up to that points shall be filed without further action.

8. No complaint may be made to the Ombudsman that concerns work relationships between the Community institutions and bodies and their officials and other servants unless all the possibilities for the submission of internal administrative requests and complaints, in particular the procedures referred to in Article 90(1) and (2) of the Staff Regulations, have been exhausted by the person concerned, and the time limits for replies by the authority thus petitioned have expired.

9. The Ombudsman shall as soon as possible inform the person lodging the complaint of the action he has taken on it.

Article 3   1. The Ombudsman shall, on his own initiative or following a complaint, conduct all enquiries which he considers justified to clarify any suspected maladministration in the activities of Community institutions and bodies. He shall inform the institution or body concerned of the action he has taken on it.

2. The Community institutions and bodies shall be obliged to supply the Ombudsman with the information he has requested of them and give him access to the files concerned. They may refuse only on duly substantial grounds of secrecy.

They shall give access to documents originating in a Member State and classed as secret by law or regulation only where that Member State has given its prior agreement.

They shall give access to other documents originating in a Member State having informed the Member State concerned. In both cases, in accordance with Article 4, the Ombudsman may not divulge the content of such documents.

Officials and other servants of Community institutions and bodies must testify at the request of the Ombudsman; they shall speak on behalf of and in accordance with instructions from their administration and shall continue to be bound by their duty of professional secrecy.

3. The Member State authorities shall be obliged to provide the Ombudsman, whenever he may so request, via the Permanent Representations of the Member State to the European Communities, with any information that may help to clarify instances of maladministration by Community institutions or bodies unless such information is covered by laws or regulations on secrecy or by provisions preventing its being communicated. Nonetheless, in the latter case, the Member State concerned may allow the Ombudsman to have this information provided that he undertakes not to divulge it.

4. If the assistance which he requests is not forthcoming, the Ombudsman shall inform the European Parliament, which shall make appropriate representations.

5. As far as possible, the Ombudsman shall seek a solution with the institution or body concerned to eliminate the instance of maladministration and satisfy the complaint.

6. If the Ombudsman finds that there has been maladministration, he shall inform the institution or body concerned, where appropriate making draft recommenda-

tions. The institution or body so informed shall send the Ombudsman a detailed opinion within three months.

7. The Ombudsman shall then send a report to the European Parliament and to the institution or body concerned. he may make recommendations in his report. The person lodging the complaint shall be informed by the Ombudsman of the outcome of the enquiries, of the opinion expressed by the institution or body concerned and of any recommendations made by the Ombudsman.

8. At the end of each annual session, the Ombudsman shall submit to the European Parliament a report on the outcome of his enquiries.

Article 4   1. The Ombudsman and his staff [*text omitted*] shall be required not to divulge information or documents which they obtain in the course of their inquiries. They shall also be required to treat in confidence any information which could harm The person lodging the complaint or any other person involved, without prejudice to paragraph 2.

2. If, in the course of inquiries, he learns of facts which he considers might relate to criminal law, the Ombudsman shall immediately notify the competent national authorities. . . . The Ombudsman may also inform the Community institution or body concerned of the facts calling into question the conduct of a member of their staff from a disciplinary point of view.

Article 5   Insofar as it may help to make his enquiries more efficient and better safeguard the rights and interests of persons who make complaints to him, the Ombudsman may co-operate with authorities of the same type in certain Member State provided he complies with the national law applicable. The Ombudsman may not by this means demand to see documents to which he would not have access under Article 3.

Article 6   1. The Ombudsman shall be appointed by the European Parliament after each election to the European Parliament for the duration of the parliamentary term. He shall be eligible for reappointment.

2. The Ombudsman shall be chosen from among person who are Union citizens, have full civil and political rights, offer every guarantee of independence, and meet the conditions required for the exercise of the highest judicial office in their country or have the acknowledged competence and experience to undertake the duties of Ombudsman.

Article 7   1. The Ombudsman shall cease to exercise his duties either at the end of his term of office or on his resignation or dismissal.

2. Save in the event of his dismissal, the Ombudsman shall remain in office until his successor has been appointed.

3. In the event of early cessation of duties, a successor shall be appointed within three months of the office's falling vacant for the remainder of the parliamentary term.

Article 8   An Ombudsman who no longer fulfils the conditions required for the performance of his duties or is guilty of serious misconduct may be dismissed by the Court of Justice of the European Communities at the request of European Parliament.

Article 9   1. The Ombudsman shall perform his duties with complete independence, in the general interest of the Communities and of the citizens of the Union. In the performance of his duties he shall neither seek nor accept instructions from any government or other body. He shall refrain from any act incompatible with the nature of his duties.

2. When taking up his duties the Ombudsman shall give a solemn undertaking before the Court of Justice of the European Communities [*text omitted*].

Article 10   1. During his term of office, the Ombudsman may not engage in any other political or administrative duties, or any other occupation, whether gainful or not.
2. The Ombudsman shall have the same rank in terms of remuneration, allowances and pension as a judge at the CJ.
3. Articles 12 and 15 and Article 18 of the Protocol on the Privileges and Immunities of the European Communities shall apply to the Ombudsman and to the officials and servants of his secretariat.

Article 11   The Ombudsman shall be assisted by a secretariat, the principal officer of which he shall appoint.

[*Article 12 omitted*]

Article 13   The seat of the Ombudsman shall be that of the European Parliament.

Article 14   The Ombudsman shall adopt the implementing provisions for the Decision.

[*text omitted*]

Done at Strasbourg, 9 March 1994
[*Signature omitted*]

PART II

SECONDARY LEGISLATION AND OTHER DOCUMENTS

Free Movement of Goods

Commission Directive of 22 December 1969 based on the provisions of Article 33(7), on the abolition of measures which have an effect equivalent to quantitative restrictions on imports and are not covered by other provisions adopted in pursuance of the EEC Treaty
(70/50/EEC)[1]

The Commission of the European Communities,

HAVING REGARD to the provisions of the Treaty establishing the European Economic Community, and in particular Art. 33(7) thereof;

Whereas for the purpose of Art. 30 *et seq.* 'measures' means laws, regulations, administrative provisions, administrative practices, and all instruments issuing from a public authority, including recommendations;

Whereas for the purposes of this Directive 'administrative practices' means any standard and regularly followed procedure of a public authority; whereas 'recommendations' means any instruments issuing from a public authority which, while not legally binding on the addressees thereof, cause them to pursue a certain conduct;

Whereas the formalities to which imports are subject do not as a general rule have an effect equivalent to that of quantitative restrictions and, consequently, are not covered by this Directive;

Whereas certain measures adopted by Member States, other than those applicable equally to domestic and imported products, which were operative at the date of entry into force of the Treaty and are not covered by other provisions adopted in pursuance of the Treaty, either preclude importation or make it more difficult or costly than the disposal of domestic production;

Whereas such measures must be considered to include those which make access of imported products to the domestic market, at any marketing stage, subject to a condition which is not laid down for domestic products or to a condition differing from that laid down for domestic products, and more difficult to satisfy, so that a burden is thus placed on imported products only;

Whereas such measures must also be considered to include those which, at any marketing stage, grant to domestic products a preference, other than an aid, to which conditions may or may not be attached, and where such measures totally or partially preclude the disposal of imported products;

Whereas such measures hinder imports which could otherwise take place, and thus have an effect equivalent to quantitative restrictions on imports;

Whereas effects on the free movement of goods of measures which relate to the marketing of products and which apply equally to domestic and imported products are not as a general rule equivalent to those of quantitative restrictions, since

---
[1] OJ Sp. Ed., 1970 (I), 17.

such effects are normally inherent in the disparities between rules applied by Member States in this respect;

Whereas, however, such measures may have a restrictive effect on the free movement of goods over and above that which is intrinsic to such rules;

Whereas such is the case where imports are either precluded or made more difficult or costly than the disposal of domestic production and where such effect is not necessary for the attainment of an objective within the scope of the powers for the regulation of trade left to member states by the Treaty; whereas such is in particular the case where the said objective can be attained just as effectively by other means which are less of a hindrance to trade; whereas such is also the case where the restrictive effect of these provisions on the free movement of goods is out of proportion to their purpose;

Whereas these measures accordingly have an effect equivalent to that of quantitative restrictions on imports;

Whereas the customs union cannot be achieved without the abolition of such measures having an equivalent effect to quantitative restrictions on imports;

Whereas Member States must abolish all measures having equivalent effect by the end of the transitional period at the latest, even if no Commission Directive expressly requires them to do so;

Whereas the provisions concerning the abolition of quantitative restrictions and measures having equivalent effect between Member States apply both to products originating in and exported by Member States and to products originating in third countries and put into free circulation in the other Member States;

Whereas Art. 33(7) does not apply to measures of the kind referred to which fall under other provisions of the Treaty, and in particular those which fall under Arts. 37(1) and 44 of the Treaty or form an integral part of a national organisation of an agricultural market;

Whereas Art. 33(7) does not apply to the charges and taxation referred to in Art. 12 *et seq.* and Art. 95 *et seq.* or to the aids mentioned in Art. 92;

Whereas the provisions of Art. 33(7) do not prevent the application, in particular, of Arts. 36 and 233;

HAS ADOPTED this directive:

Article 1   The purpose of this Directive is to abolish the measures referred to in Arts. 2 and 3, which were operative at the date of entry into force of the EEC Treaty.

Article 2   1. This Directive covers measures, other than those applicable equally to domestic or imported products, which hinder imports which could otherwise take place including measures which make importation more difficult or costly than the disposal of domestic production.

2. In particular, it covers measures which make imports or the disposal, at any marketing stage, of imported products subject to a condition–other than a formality–which is required in respect of imported products only, or a condition differing from that required for domestic products and more difficult to satisfy. Equally, it covers, in particular, measures which favour domestic products or grant them a preference, other than an aid, to which conditions may or may not be attached.

3. The measures refered to must be taken to include those measures which:

(a) lay down, for imported products only, minimum or maximum prices below or above which imports are prohibited, reduced or made subject to conditions liable to hinder importation;

(b) lay down less favourable prices for imported products than for domestic products;

(c) fix profit margins or any other price components for imported products only or fix these differently for domestic products and for imported products, to the detriment of the latter;

(d) preclude any increase in the price of the imported product corresponding to the supplementary costs and charges inherent in importation;

(e) fix the prices of products solely on the basis of the cost price or the quality of domestic products at such a level as to create a hindrance to importation;

(f) lower the value of an imported product, in particular by causing a reduction in its intrinsic value, or increase its costs;

(g) make access of imported products to the domestic market conditional upon having an agent or representative in the territory of the importing Member State;

(h) lay down conditions of payment in respect of imported products only, or subject imported products to conditions which are different from those laid down for domestic products and more difficult to satisfy;

(i) require, for imports only, the giving of guarantees or making of payments on account;

(j) subject imported products only to conditions, in respect, in particular of shape, size, weight, composition, presentation, identification or putting up, or subject imported products to conditions which are different from those for domestic products and more difficult to satisfy;

(k) hinder the purchase by private individuals of imported products only, or encourage, require or give preference to the purchase of domestic products only;

(l) totally or partially preclude the use of national facilities or equipment in respect of imported products only, or totally or partially confine the use of such facilities or equipment to domestic products only;

(m) prohibit or limit publicity in respect of imported products only, or totally or partially confine publicity to domestic products only;

(n) prohibit, limit or require stocking in respect of imported products only; totally or partially confine the use of stocking facilities to domestic products only, or make the stocking of imported products subject to conditions which are different from those required for domestic products and more difficult to satisfy;

(o) make importation subject to the granting of reciprocity by one or more Member States;

(p) prescribe that imported products are to conform, totally or partially, to rules other than those of the importing country;

(q) specify time limits for imported products which are insufficient or excessive in relation to the normal course of the various transactions to which these time limits apply;

(r) subject imported products to controls, other than those inherent in the customs clearance procedure, to which domestic products are not subject or which are stricter in respect of imported products than they are in respect of domestic products, without this being necessary in order to ensure equivalent protection;

(s) confine names which are not indicative of origin or source to domestic products only.

Article 3   This Directive also covers measures governing the marketing of products which deal, in particular, with shape, size, weight, composition, presentation, identification or putting up and which are equally applicable to domestic and imported products, where the restrictive effect of such measures on the free movement of goods exceeds the effects intrinsic to trade rules.

This is the case, in particular, where:

— the restrictive effects on the free movement of goods are out of proportion to their purpose;
— the same objective can be attained by other means which are less of a hindrance to trade.

Article 4   1. Member States shall take all necessary steps in respect of products which must be allowed to enjoy free movement pursuant to Arts. 9 and 10 of the Treaty to abolish measures having an effect equivalent to quantitative restrictions on imports and covered by this Directive.

2. Member States shall inform the Commission of measures taken pursuant to this Directive.

Article 5   1. This Directive does not apply to measures:

(a) which fall under Art. 37(1) of the EEC Treaty;
(b) which are referred to in Art. 44 of the EEC Treaty or form an integral part of a national organisation of an agricultural market not yet replaced by a common organisation.

2. This Directive shall apply without prejudice to the application, in particular, of Arts. 36 and 223 of the EEC Treaty.

[final provisions omitted]

Communication from the Commission of 3 October 1980 concerning the consequences of the judgment given by the Court of Justice on 20 February 1979 in Case 120/78 ('Cassis de Dijon')[2]

The following is the text of a letter which has been sent to the Member States; the European Parliament and the Council have also been notified of it.

In the Commission's Communication of 6 November 1978 on 'Safeguarding free trade within the Community', it was emphasized that the free movement of goods is being affected by a growing number of restrictive measures.

The judgment delivered by the Court of Justice on 20 February 1979 in Case 120/78 (the 'Cassis de Dijon' case), and recently reaffirmed in the judgment of 26 June 1980 in Case 788/79, has given the Commission some interpretative guidance

[2] OJ 1980 C 256/2.

enabling it to monitor more strictly the application of the Treaty rules on the free movement of goods, particularly Articles 30 to 36 of the EEC Treaty.

The Court gives a very general definition of the barriers to free trade which are prohibited by the provisions of Article 30 et seq. of the EEC Treaty. These are taken to include 'any national measure capable of hindering, directly or indirectly, actually or potentially, intra-Community trade'.

In its judgment of 20 February 1979 the Court indicates the scope of this definition as it applies to technical and commercial rules.

Any product lawfully produced and marketed in one Member State must, in principle, be admitted to the market of any other Member State.

Technical and commercial rules, even those equally applicable to national and imported products, may create barriers to trade only where those rules are necessary to satisfy mandatory requirements and to serve a purpose which is in the general interest and for which they are an essential guarantee. This purpose must be such as to take precedence over the requirements of the free movement of goods, which constitutes one of the fundamental rules of the Community.

The conclusions in terms of policy which the Commission draws from this new guidance are set out below. - Whereas Member States may, with respect to domestic products and in the absence of relevant Community provisions, regulate the terms on which such products are marketed, the case is different for products imported from other Member States.

Any product imported from another Member State must in principle be admitted to the territory of the importing Member State if it has been lawfully produced, that is, conforms to rules and processes of manufacture that are customarily and traditionally accepted in the exporting country, and is marketed in the territory of the latter.

This principle implies that Member States, when drawing up commercial or technical rules liable to affect the free movement of goods, may not take an exclusively national viewpoint and take account only of requirements confined to domestic products. The proper functioning of the common market demands that each Member State also give consideration to the legitimate requirements of the other Member States.

— Only under very strict conditions does the Court accept exceptions to this principle; barriers to trade resulting from differences between commercial and technical rules are only admissible: - if the rules are necessary, that is appropriate and not excessive, in order to satisfy mandatory requirements (public health, protection of consumers or the environment, the fairness of commercial transactions, etc.);
— if the rules serve a purpose in the general interest which is compelling enough to justify an exception to a fundamental rule of the Treaty such as the free movement of goods;
— if the rules are essential for such a purpose to be attained, i.e. are the means which are the most appropriate and at the same time least hinder trade.

The Court's interpretation has induced the Commission to set out a number of guidelines.

—The principles deduced by the Court imply that a Member State may not in principle prohibit the sale in its territory of a product lawfully produced and marketed in another Member State even if the product is produced according to technical or quality requirements which differ from those imposed on its domestic products. Where a product 'suitably and satisfactorily' fulfils the legitimate objective of a Member State's own rules (public safety, protection of the consumer or the environment, etc.), the importing country cannot justify prohibiting its sale in its territory by claiming that the way it fulfils the objective is different from that imposed on domestic products.

In such a case, an absolute prohibition of sale could not be considered 'necessary' to satisfy a 'mandatory requirement' because it would not be an 'essential guarantee' in the sense defined in the Court's judgment.

The Commission will therefore have to tackle a whole body of commercial rules which lay down that products manufactured and marketed in one Member State must fulfil technical or qualitative conditions in order to be admitted to the market of another and specifically in all cases where the trade barriers occasioned by such rules are inadmissible according to the very strict criteria set out by the Court.

The Commission is referring in particular to rules covering the composition, designation, presentation and packaging of products as well as rules requiring compliance with certain technical standards.

The Commission's work of harmonization will henceforth have to be directed mainly at national laws having an impact on the functioning of the common market where barriers to trade to be removed arise from national provisions which are admissible under the criteria set by the Court.

The Commission will be concentrating on sectors deserving priority because of their economic relevance to the creation of a single internal market. To forestall later difficulties, the Commission will be informing Member States of potential objections, under the terms of Community law, to provisions they may be considering introducing which come to the attention of the Commission.

It will be producing suggestions soon on the procedures to be followed in such cases.

The Commission is confident that this approach will secure greater freedom of trade for the Community's manufacturers, so strengthening the industrial base of the Community, while meeting the expectations of consumers.

Freedom of Movement for Workers

Council Regulation of 15 October 1968 on freedom of movement for workers within the Community
(1612/68/EEC)[1]

The Council of the European Communities,

HAVING REGARD to the Treaty establishing the European Economic Community, and in particular Art. 49 thereof;

HAVING REGARD to the proposal from the Commission;

HAVING REGARD to the Opinion of the European Parliament;

HAVING REGARD to the Opinion of the Economic and Social Committee;

Whereas freedom of movement for workers should be secured within the Community by the end of the transitional period at the latest; whereas the attainment of this objective entails the abolition of any discrimination based on nationality between workers of the Member States as regards employment, remuneration and other conditions of work and employment, as well as the right of such workers to move freely within the Community in order to pursue activities as employed persons subject to any limitations justified on grounds of public policy, public security or public health;

Whereas by reason in particular of the early establishment of the customs union and in order to ensure the simultaneous completion of the principal foundations of the Community, provisions should be adopted to enable the objectives laid down in Arts. 48 and 49 of the Treaty in the field of freedom of movement to be achieved and to perfect measures adopted successively under Regulation No 15 on the first steps for attainment of freedom of movement and under Council Regulation No. 38/54/EEC of 25 March 1964 on freedom of movement for workers within the Community;

Whereas freedom of movement constitutes a fundamental right of workers and their families; whereas mobility of labour within the Community must be one of the means by which the worker is guaranteed the possibility of improving his living and working conditions and promoting his social advancement, while helping to satisfy the requirements of the economies of the Member States; whereas the right of all workers in the Member States to pursue the activity of their choice within the Community should be affirmed;

Whereas such right must be enjoyed without discrimination by permanent, seasonal and frontier workers and by those who pursue their activities for the purpose of providing services;

Whereas the right of freedom of movement, in order that it may be exercised, by objective standards, in freedom and dignity, requires that equality of treatment shall be ensured in fact and in law in respect of all matters relating to the actual pursuit of activities as employed persons and to eligibility for housing, and also

---

[1] OJ Sp. Ed., 1968 (II), 475. As last amended by Regulation 312/76, OJ 1976 L 39/2. Text not reproduced amended by Regulation 2434/92, OJ 1992 L 245/1.

that obstacles to the mobility of workers shall be eliminated, in particular as regards the worker's right to be joined by his family and the conditions for the integration of that family into the host country;

Whereas the principle of non-discrimination between Community workers entails that all nationals of Member States have the same priority as regards employment as is enjoyed by national workers;

[recitals omitted]

HAS ADOPTED this Regulation:

Part One: Employment and Workers' Families

Title I. Eligibility for Employment

Article 1   1. Any national of a Member State, shall, irrespective of his place of residence, have the right to take up a activity as an employed person, and to pursue such activity, within the territory of another Member State in accordance with the provisions laid down by law, regulation or administrative action governing the employment of nationals of that State.

2. He shall, in particular, have the right to take up available employment in the territory of another Member State with the same priority as nationals of that State.

Article 2   Any national of a Member State and any employer pursuing an activity in the territory of a Member State may exchange their applications for and offers of employment, and may conclude and perform contracts of employment in accordance with the provisions in force laid down by law, regulation or administrative action, without any discrimination resulting therefrom.

Article 3   1. Under this Regulation, provisions laid down by law, regulation or administrative action or administrative practices of a Member State shall not apply:

—   where they limit application for and offers of employment, or the right of foreign nationals to take up and pursue employment or subject these to conditions not applicable in respect of their own nationals; or
—   where, though applicable irrespective of nationality, their exclusive or principal aim or effect is to keep nationals of other Member States away from the employment offered.

This provision shall not apply to conditions relating to linguistic knowledge required by reason of the nature of the post to be filled.

2. There shall be included in particular among the provisions or practices of a Member State referred to in the first subparagraph of paragraph 1 those which:
(a) prescribe a special recruitment procedure for foreign nationals;
(b) limit or restrict the advertising of vacancies in the press or through any other medium or subject it to conditions other than those applicable in respect of employers pursuing their activities in the territory of that Member State;
(c) subject eligibility for employment to conditions of registration with employment offices or impede recruitment of individual workers, where persons who do not reside in the territory of that State are concerned.

Article 4 1. Provisions laid down by law, regulation or administrative action of the Member States which restrict by number or percentage the employment of foreign nationals in any undertaking, branch of activity or region, or at a national level, shall not apply to nationals of the other Member States.

2. When in a Member State the granting of any benefit to undertakings is subject to a minimum percentage of national workers being employed, nationals of the other Member States shall be counted as national workers, subject to the provisions of the Council Directive of 15 October 1963.[2]

Article 5 A national of a Member State who seeks employment in the territory of another Member State shall receive the same assistance there as that afforded by the employment offices in that State to their own nationals seeking employment.

Article 6 1. The engagement and recruitment of a national of one Member State for a post in another Member State shall not depend on medical, vocational or other criteria which are discriminatory on grounds of nationality by comparison with those applied to nationals of the other Member State who wish to pursue the same activity.

2. Nevertheless, a national who holds an offer in his name from an employer in a Member State other than that of which he is a national may have to undergo a vocational test, if the employer expressly requests this when making his offer of employment.

Title II. Employment and Equality of Treatment

Article 7 1. A worker who is a national of a Member State may not, in the territory of another Member State, be treated differently from national workers by reason of his nationality in respect of any conditions of employment and work, in particular as regards remuneration, dismissal, and should he become unemployed, reinstatement or re-employment.

2. He shall enjoy the same social and tax advantages as national workers.

3. He shall also, by virtue of the same right and under the same conditions as national workers, have access to training in vocational schools and retraining centres.

4. Any clause of a collective or individual agreement or of any other collective regulation concerning eligibility for employment, employment, remuneration and other conditions of work or dismissal shall be null and void in so far as it lays down or authorises discriminatory conditions in respect of workers who are nationals of the other Member States.

Article 8 1. A worker who is a national of a Member State and who is employed in the territory of another Member State shall enjoy equality of treatment as regards membership of trade unions and the exercise of rights attaching thereto, including the right to vote and to be eligible for the administration and management of bodies governed by public law and from holding an office governed by public law. Furthermore, he shall have the right of eligibility for workers' representative bodies in the undertaking. The provisions of this Article shall not affect laws or

---

[2] Directive 63/607, OJ Sp. Ed., 1963–64, 52.

regulations in certain Member States which grant more extensive rights to workers coming from the other Member States.

Article 9   1. A worker who is a national of a Member State and who is employed in the territory of another Member State shall enjoy all the rights and benefits accorded to national workers in matters of housing, including ownership of the housing he needs.

2. Such worker may, with the same right as nationals, put his name down on the housing lists in the region in which he is employed, where such lists exist; he shall enjoy the resultant benefits and priorities.

If his family has remained in the country whence he came, they shall be considered for this purpose as residing in the said region, where national workers benefit from a similar presumption.

TITLE III. WORKERS' FAMILIES

Article 10   1. The following shall, irrespective of their nationality, have the right to install themselves with a worker who is a national of one Member State and who is employed in the territory of another Member State:
(a) his spouse and their descendants who are under the age of 21 years or are dependants;
(b) dependent relatives in the ascending line of the worker and his spouse.

2. Member States shall facilitate the admission of any member of the family not coming within the provisions of paragraph 1 if dependent on the worker referred to above or living under his roof in the country whence he comes.

3. For the purposes of paragraphs 1 and 2, the worker must have available for his family housing considered as normal for national workers in the region where he is employed; this provision, however must not give rise to discrimination between national workers and workers from the other Member States.

Article 11   Where a national of a Member State is pursuing an activity as an employed or self-employed person in the territory of another Member State, his spouse and those of the children who are under the age of 21 years or dependent on him shall have the right to take up any activity as an employed person throughout the territory of that same State, even if they are not nationals of any Member State.

Article 12   The children of a national of a Member State who is or has been employed in the territory of another Member State shall be admitted to that State's general educational, apprenticeship and vocational training courses under the same conditions as the nationals of that State, if such children are residing in its territory.

Member States shall encourage all efforts to enable such children to attend these courses under the best possible conditions.

[*Remainder of the regulation omitted*]

Council Directive of 15 October 1968 on the abolition of restrictions on movement and residence within the Community for workers of Member States and their families (68/360/EEC)[3]

The Council of the European Communities,

HAVING REGARD to the Treaty establishing the European Economic Community, and in particular Art. 49 thereof;

HAVING REGARD to the proposal from the Commission;

HAVING REGARD to the Opinion of the European Parliament;

HAVING REGARD to the Opinion of the Economic and Social Committee;

Whereas Council Regulation (EEC) No. 1612/68 fixed the provisions governing freedom of movement for workers within the Community; whereas, consequently, measures should be adopted for the abolition of restrictions which still exist concerning movement and residence within the Community, which conform to the rights and privileges accorded by the said Regulation to nationals of any Member State who move in order to pursue activities as employed persons and to members of their families;

Whereas the rules applicable to residence should, as far as possible, bring the position of workers from other Member States and members of their families into line with that of nationals;

Whereas the co-ordination of special measures relating to the movement and residence of foreign nationals, justified on grounds of public policy, public security of public health, is the subject of the Council Directive of 25 February 1964, adopted in application of Art. 56 (2) of the Treaty;

HAS ADOPTED this Directive:

Article 1   Member States shall, acting as provided in this Directive, abolish restrictions on the movement and residence of nationals of the said States and of members of their families to whom Regulation (EEC) No 1612/68 applies.

Article 2   1. Member States shall grant the nationals referred to in Art 1 the right to leave their territory in order to take up activities as employed persons and to pursue such activities in the territory of another Member State. Such right shall be exercised simply on production of a valid identity card or passport. Members of the family shall enjoy the same right as the national on whom they are dependent.

2. Member States shall, acting in accordance with their laws, issue to such nationals, or renew, an identity card or passport, which shall state in particular the holder's nationality.

3. The passport must be valid at least for all Member States and for countries through which the holder must pass when travelling between Member States. Where a passport is the only document on which the holder may lawfully leave the country, its period of validity shall be not less than five years.

---

[3] OJ Sp. Ed., 1968 (II), 485. As last amended by Decision 95/1/EC, OJ 1995 L 1/1, Annex I, IV, B.

4. Member States may not demand from the nationals referred to in Art. 1 any exit visa or any equivalent document.

Article 3   1. Member States shall allow the persons referred to in Art. 1 to enter their territory simply on production of a valid identity card or passport.

2. No entry visa or equivalent document may be demanded save from members of the family who are not nationals of a Member State. Member States shall accord to such persons every facility for obtaining any necessary visas.

Article 4   1. Member States shall grant the right of residence in their territory to the persons referred to in Art. 1 who are able to produce the documents listed in paragraph 3.

2. As proof of the right of residence, a document entitled 'Residence Permit for a National of a Member State of the EEC' shall be issued. This document must include a statement that it has been issued pursuant to Regulation (EEC) No. 1612/68 and to the measures taken by the Member States for the implementation of the present Directive. The text of such statement is given in the Annex to this Directive.

3. For the issue of a Residence Permit for a National of a Member State of the EEC, Member States may require only the production of the following documents;
— by the worker:
  (a) the document with which he entered their territory;
  (b) a confirmation of engagement from the employer or a certificate of employment;
— by the members of the worker's family:
  (c) the document with which they entered the territory;
  (d) a document issued by the competent authority of the State of origin or the State whence they came, proving their relationship;
  (e) in the cases referred to in Art. 10(1) and (2) of Regulation (EEC) No. 1612/68, a document issued by the competent authority of the State of origin or the State whence they came, testifying that they are dependent on the worker or that they live under his roof in such country.

4. A member of the family who is not a national of a Member State shall be issued with a residence document which shall have the same validity as that issued to the worker on whom he is dependent.

Article 5   Completion of the formalities for obtaining a residence permit shall not hinder the immediate beginning of employment under a contract concluded by the applicants.

Article 6   1. The residence permit:
(a) must be valid throughout the territory of the Member State which issued it;
(b) must be valid for at least five years from the date of issue and be automatically renewable.

2. Breaks in residence not exceeding six consecutive months and absence on military service shall not affect the validity of a residence permit.

3. Where a worker is employed for a period exceeding three months but not exceeding a year in the service of an employer in the host State or in the employ of

a person providing services, the host Member State shall issue him a temporary residence permit, the validity of which may be limited to the expected period of the employment.

Subject to the provisions of Art. 8(1)(c), a temporary residence permit shall be issued also to a seasonal worker employed for a period of more than three months. The period of employment must be shown in the documents referred to in paragraph 4(3)(b).

Article 7   1. A valid residence permit may not be withdrawn from a worker solely on the ground that he is no longer in employment, either because he is temporarily incapable of work as a result of illness or accident, or because he is involuntarily unemployed, this being duly confirmed by the competent employment office.

2. When the residence permit is renewed for the first time, the period of residence may be restricted, but not to less than twelve months, where the worker has been involuntarily unemployed in the Member State for more than twelve consecutive months.

Article 8   1. Member States shall, without issuing a residence permit, recognise the right of residence in their territory of:
(a) a worker pursuing an activity as an employed person, where the activity is not expected to last for more than three months. The document with which the person concerned entered the territory and a statement by the employer on the expected duration of the employment shall be sufficient to cover his stay; a statement by the employer shall not, however, be required in the case of workers coming within the provisions of the Council Directive of 25 February 1964[4] on the attainment of freedom of establishment and freedom to provide services in respect of the activities of intermediaries in commerce, industry and small craft industries;
(b) a worker who, while having his residence in the territory of a Member State to which he returns as a rule, each day or at least once a week, is employed in the territory of another Member State. The competent authority of the State where he is employed may issue such worker with a special permit valid for five years and automatically renewable;
(c) a seasonal worker who holds a contract of employment stamped by the competent authority of the Member State on whose territory he has come to pursue his activity.

2. In all cases referred to in paragraph 1, the competent authorities of the host Member State may require the worker to report his presence in the territory.

Article 9   1. The residence documents granted to nationals of a Member State of the EEC referred to in this Directive shall be issued and renewed free of charge or on payment of an amount not exceeding the dues and taxes charged for the issue of identity cards to nationals.

2. The visa referred to in Art. 3(2) and the stamp referred to in Art. 8(1)(c) shall be free of charge.

3. Member States shall take the necessary steps to simplify as much as possible the formalities and procedure for obtaining the documents mentioned in paragraph 1.

---

[4] Directive 64/224, OJ Sp. Ed., 1963–64, 126.

Article 10   Member States shall not derogate from the provisions of this Directive save on grounds of public policy, public security or public health.

Article 11   1. This Directive shall not affect the provisions of the Treaty establishing the European Coal and Steel Community which relate to workers with recognised skills in coal mining and steel making, or the provisions of the Treaty establishing the European Atomic Energy Community which deal with the right to take up skilled employment in the field of nuclear energy, or any measures taken in implementation of those Treaties.

2. Nevertheless, this Directive shall apply to the categories of workers referred to in paragraph 1, and to members of their families, in so far as their legal position is not governed by the abovementioned Treaties or measures.

Article 12   1. Member States shall, within nine months of notification of this Directive, bring into force the measures necessary to comply with its provisions and shall forthwith inform the Commission thereof.

2. They shall notify the Commission of amendments made to provisions imposed by law, regulation or administrative action for the simplification of the formalities and procedure for issuing such documents as are still necessary for the entry, exit and residence of workers and members of their families.

Article 13   1. The Council Directive of 25 March 1964[5] on the abolition of restrictions on movement and on residence within the Community of workers and their families shall continue to have effect until this Directive is implemented by the Member States.

2. Residence permits issued pursuant to the Directive referred to in Paragraph 1 shall remain valid until the date on which they next expire.

[*final provisions omitted*]

ANNEX

Text of the statement referred to in Art. 4 (2):
'This permit is issued pursuant to Regulation (EEC) No. 1612/68 of the Council of the European Communities of 15 October 1968 and to the measures taken in implementation of the Council Directive of 15 October 1968.
In accordance with the provisions of the above-mentioned Regulation, the holder of this permit has the right to take up and pursue an activity as an employed person in . . . .* territory under the same conditions as . . . .* workers.'

* Austrian, Belgian, British, Danish, Finnish, German, Greek, Irish, French, Italian, Luxembourg, Netherlands, Portuguese, Spanish, Swedish, according to the country issuing the permit.

[5] OJ No. 62, 17 April 1964, 981/64.

Commission Regulation of 29 June 1970 on the right of workers to remain in the territory of a Member State after having been employed in that State (1251/70/EEC)[6]

The Commission of the European Communities,

HAVING REGARD to the Treaty establishing the European Economic Community, and in particular Art. 48 (3) (d) thereof, and Art. 2 of the Protocol on the Grand Duchy of Luxembourg;

HAVING REGARD to the Opinion of the European Parliament;

Whereas Council Regulation (EEC) No. 1612/68 of 15 October 1968 and Council Directive No. 68/360/EEC of 15 October 1968 enabled freedom of movement for workers to be secured at the end of a series of measures to be achieved progressively; whereas the right of residence acquired by workers in active employment has as a corollary the right, granted by the Treaty to such workers, to remain in the territory of a Member State after having been employed in that State; whereas it is important to lay down the conditions for the exercise of such right;

Whereas the said Council Regulation and Council Directive contain the appropriate provisions concerning the right of workers to reside in the territory of a Member State for the purposes of employment; whereas the right to remain, referred to in Art. 48(3)(d) of the Treaty, is interpreted therefore as the right of the worker to maintain his residence in the territory of a Member State when he ceases to be employed there;

Whereas the mobility of labour in the Community requires that workers may be employed successively in several Member States without thereby being placed at a disadvantage;

Whereas it is important, in the first place, to guarantee to the worker residing in the territory of a Member State the right to remain in that territory when he ceases to be employed in that State because he has reached retirement age or by reason of permanent incapacity to work; whereas, however, it is equally important to ensure that right for the worker who, after a period of employment and residence in the territory of a Member State, works as an employed person in the territory of another Member State, while still retaining his residence in the territory of the first State;

Whereas, to determine the conditions under which the right to remain arises, account should be taken of the reasons which have led to the termination of employment in the territory of the Member State concerned and, in particular, of the difference between retirement, the normal and foreseeable end of working life, and incapacity to work which leads to a premature and unforeseeable termination of activity; whereas special conditions must be laid down where termination of activity is the result of an accident at work or occupational disease, or where the worker's spouse is or was a national of the Member State concerned;

---

[6] OJ Sp. Ed., 1970 (II), 402.

Whereas the worker who has reached the end of his working life should have sufficient time in which to decide where he wishes to establish his final residence;

Whereas the exercise by the worker of the right to remain entails that such right shall be extended to members of his family; whereas in the case of the death of the worker during his working life, maintenance of the right of residence of the members of his family must also be recognised and be the subject of special conditions;

Whereas persons to whom the right to remain applies must enjoy equality of treatment with national workers who have ceased their working lives;

HAS ADOPTED this Regulation:

Article 1 The provisions of this Regulation shall apply to nationals of a Member State who have worked as employed persons in the territory of another Member State and to members of their families, as defined in Art. 10 of Council Regulation (EEC) No. 1612/68 on freedom of movement for workers within the Community.

Article 2   1. The following shall have the right to remain permanently in the territory of a Member State:

(a) a worker who, at the time of termination of his activity, has reached the age laid down by the law of that Member State for entitlement to an old-age pension and who has been employed in that State for at least the last twelve months and has resided there continuously for more than three years;

(b) a worker who, having resided continuously in the territory of that State for more than two years, ceases to work there as an employed person as a result of permanent incapacity to work. If such incapacity is the result of an accident at work or an occupational disease entitling him to a pension for which an institution of that State is entirely or partially responsible, no condition shall be imposed as to length of residence;

(c) a worker who, after three years' continuous employment and residence in the territory of that State, works as an employed person in the territory of another Member State, while retaining his residence in the territory of the first State, to which he returns, as a rule, each day or at least once a week.

Periods of employment completed in this way in the territory of the other Member State shall, for the purposes of entitlement to the rights referred to in subparagraphs (a) and (b), be considered as having been completed in the territory of the State of residence.

2. The conditions as to length of residence and employment laid down in paragraph 1(a) and the condition as to length of residence laid down in paragraph 1(b) shall not apply if the worker's spouse is a national of the Member State concerned or has lost the nationality of that State by marriage to that worker.

Article 3   1. The members of a worker's family referred to in Art. 1 of this Regulation who are residing with him in the territory of a Member State shall be entitled to remain there permanently if the worker has acquired the right to remain in the territory of that State in accordance with Art. 2, and to do so even after his death.

2. If, however, the worker dies during his working life and before having acquired the right to remain in the territory of the State concerned, members of his family shall be entitled to remain there permanently on condition that:

— the worker, on the date of his decease, had resided continuously in the territory of that Member State for at least 2 years; or
— his death resulted from an accident at work or an occupational disease; or
— the surviving spouse is a national of the State of residence or lost the nationality of that State by marriage to that worker.

Article 4   1. Continuity of residence as provided for in Arts. 2(1) and 3(2) may be attested by any means of proof in use in the country of residence. It shall not be affected by temporary absences not exceeding a total of three months per year, nor by longer absences due to compliance with the obligations of military service.

2. Periods of involuntary unemployment, duly recorded by the competent employment office, and absences due to illness or accident shall be considered as periods of employment within the meaning of Art. 2(1).

Article 5   1. The person entitled to the right to remain shall be allowed to exercise it within two years from the time of becoming entitled to such right pursuant to Art. 2(1)(a) and (b) and Art. 3. During such period he may leave the territory of the Member State without adversely affecting such right.

2. No formality shall be required on the part of the person concerned in respect of the exercise of the right to remain.

Article 6   1. Persons coming under the provisions of this Regulation shall be entitled to a residence permit which:
(a) shall be issued and renewed free of charge or on payment of a sum not exceeding the dues and taxes payable by nationals for the issue or renewal of identity documents;
(b) must be valid throughout the territory of the Member State issuing it; must be valid for at least five years and be renewable automatically.

2. Periods of non-residence not exceeding six consecutive months shall not affect the validity of the residence permit.

Article 7   The right to equality of treatment, established by Council Regulation (EEC) No. 1612/68, shall apply also to persons coming under the provisions of this Regulation.

Article 8   1. This Regulation shall not affect any provisions laid down by law, regulation or administrative action of one Member State which would be more favourable to nationals of other Member States.

2. Member States shall facilitate re-admission to their territories of workers who have left those territories after having resided there permanently for a long period and having been employed there and who wish to return there when they have reached retirement age or are permanently incapacitated for work.

Article 9   1. The Commission may, taking account of developments in the demographic situation of the Grand Duchy of Luxembourg, lay down, at the request of that State, different conditions from those provided for in this Regulation, in respect of the exercise of the right to remain in Luxembourg territory.

2. Within two months after the request supplying all appropriate details has been put before it, the Commission shall take a decision, stating the reasons on which it is based.

It shall notify the Grand Duchy of Luxembourg of such decision and inform the other Member States thereof;

[*final provisions omitted*]

Council Directive of 25 February 1964 on the coordination of special measures concerning the movement and residence of foreign nationals which are justified on grounds of public policy, public security or public health (64/221/EEC)[7]

The Council of the European Economic Community,

HAVING REGARD to the Treaty establishing the European Economic Community, and in particular Art. 56(2) thereof;

HAVING REGARD to Council Regulation No. 15 of 16 August 1961 on initial measures to bring about free movement of workers within the Community, and in particular Art. 47 thereof;

HAVING REGARD to Council Directive of 16 August 1961 on administrative procedures and practices governing the entry into and employment and residence in a Member State of workers and their families from other Member States of the Community;

HAVING REGARD to the General Programmes for the abolition of restrictions on freedom of establishment and on freedom to provide services, and in particular Title II of each such programme;

HAVING REGARD to the Council Directive of 25 February 1964 on the abolition of restrictions on movement and residence within the Community for nationals of Member States with regard to establishment and the provision of services;

HAVING REGARD to the proposal from the Commission;

HAVING REGARD to the Opinion of the European Parliament;

HAVING REGARD to the Opinion of the Economic and Social Committee;

Whereas co-ordination of provisions laid down by law, regulation or administrative action which provide for special treatment for foreign nationals on grounds of public policy, public security or public health should in the first place deal with the conditions for entry and residence of nationals of Member States moving within the Community either in order to pursue activities as employed or self-employed persons, or as recipients of services;

Whereas such co-ordination presupposes in particular an approximation of the procedures followed in each Member State when invoking grounds of public policy, public security or public health in matters connected with the movement or residence of foreign nationals;

[7] OJ Sp. Ed., 1963–64, 117.

Whereas, in each Member State, nationals of other Member States should have adequate legal remedies available to them in respect of the decisions of the administration in such matters;

Whereas it would be of little practical use to compile a list of diseases and disabilities which might endanger public health, public policy or public security and it would be difficult to make such a list exhaustive; whereas it is sufficient to classify such diseases and disabilities in groups;

HAS ADOPTED this Directive:

Article 1   1. The provisions of this Directive shall apply to any national of a Member State who resides in or travels to another Member State of the Community, either in order to pursue an activity as an employed or self-employed person, or as a recipient of services.[8]

2. These provisions shall apply also to the spouse and to members of the family who come within the provisions of the regulations and directives adopted in this field in pursuance of the Treaty.

Article 2   1. This Directive relates to all measures concerning entry into their territory, issue or renewal of residence permits, or expulsion from their territory, taken by Member States on grounds of public policy, public security or public health.

2. Such grounds shall not be invoked to service economic ends.

Article 3   1. Measures taken on grounds of public policy or of public security shall be based exclusively on the personal conduct of the individual concerned.

2. Previous criminal convictions shall not in themselves constitute grounds for the taking of such measures.

3. Expiry of the identity card or passport used by the person concerned to enter the host country and to obtain a residence permit shall not justify expulsion from the territory.

4. The State which issued the identity card or passport shall allow the holder of such documents to re-enter its territory without any formality even if the document is no longer valid or the nationality of the holder is in dispute.

Article 4   1. The only diseases or disabilities justifying refusal of entry into a territory or refusal to issue a first residence permit shall be those listed in the Annex to this Directive.

2. Diseases or disabilities occurring after a first residence permit has been issued shall not justify refusal to renew the residence permit or expulsion from the territory.

3. Member States shall not introduce new provisions or practices which are more restrictive than those in force at the date of notification of this Directive.

Article 5   1. A decision to grant or to refuse a first residence permit shall be taken as soon as possible and in any event not later than six months from the date of application for the permit.

---

[8] Pursuant to Directive 72/194, OJ 1972 L 121/32, Directive 64/221 also applies to nationals of Member States and members of their families who, pursuant to Regulation 1251/70, exercise the right to remain in the territory of a Member State. Directive 64/221 also applies to beneficiaries of Directive 90/364, OJ 1990 L 180/26; Directive 90/365, OJ 1990 L 180/28; and Directive 93/96, OJ 1993 L 317/59.

The person concerned shall be allowed to remain temporarily in the territory pending a decision either to grant or to refuse a residence permit.

2. The host country may, in cases where this is considered essential, request the Member State of origin of the applicant, and if need be other Member States, to provide information concerning any previous police record. Such enquiries shall not be made as a matter of routine. The Member State consulted shall give its reply within two months.

Article 6   The person concerned shall be informed of the grounds of public policy, public security, or public health upon which the decision taken in his case is based, unless this is contrary to the interests of the security of the State involved.

Article 7   The person concerned shall be officially notified of any decision to refuse the issue or renewal of a residence permit or to expel him from the territory. The period allowed for leaving the territory shall be stated in this notification. Save in cases of urgency, this period shall not be less than fifteen days if the person concerned has not yet been granted a residence permit and not less than one month in all other cases.

Article 8   The person concerned shall have the same legal remedies in respect of any decision concerning entry, or refusing the issue or renewal of a residence permit, or ordering expulsion from the territory, as are available to nationals of the State concerned in respect of acts of the administration.

Article 9   1. Where there is no right of appeal to a court of law, or where such appeal may be only in respect of the legal validity of the decision, or where the appeal cannot have suspensory effect, a decision refusing renewal of a residence permit or ordering the expulsion of the holder of a residence permit from the territory shall not be taken by the administrative authority, save in cases of urgency, until an opinion has been obtained from a competent authority of the host country before which the person concerned enjoys such rights of defence and of assistance or representation as the domestic law of that country provides for.

This authority shall not be the same as that empowered to take the decision refusing renewal of the residence permit or ordering expulsion.

2. Any decision refusing the issue of a first residence permit or ordering expulsion of the person concerned before the issue of the permit shall, where that person so requests, be referred for consideration to the authority whose prior opinion is required under paragraph 1. The person concerned shall then be entitled to submit his defence in person, except where this would be contrary to the interests of national security.

Article 10   1. Member States shall within six months of notification of this Directive put into force the measures necessary to comply with its provisions and shall forthwith inform the Commission thereof.

2. Member States shall ensure that the texts of the main provisions of national law which they adopt in the field governed by this Directive are communicated to the Commission.

[*final provisions omitted*]

ANNEX

A. Diseases which might endanger public health:

1. Diseases subject to quarantine listed in International Health Regulation No 2 of the World Health Organisation of 25 May 1951; Tuberculosis of the respiratory system in an active state or showing a tendency to develop;

2. Syphilis;

3. Other infectious diseases or contagious parasitic diseases if they are the subject of provisions for the protection of nationals of the host country.

B. Diseases and disabilities which might threaten public policy or public security:

1. Drug addiction;

2. Profound mental disturbance; manifest conditions of psychotic disturbance with agitation, delirium, hallucinations or confusion.

Freedom of movement of workers and access to employment in the public service of the Member States—Commission action in respect of the application of Article 48(4) of the EEC Treaty[9]

COMMISSION ACTION

The Commission, which is responsible under the Treaty for implementing Community rules and ensuring observance of the Court's judgments, seeks to ensure that the Member States apply the rules on freedom of movement and equal treatment of Community workers as regards access to employment on the basis of the principles of the Treaty, while avoiding the need to propose new Community legislation.

EXCLUSION OF SPECIFIC ACTIVITIES IN THE NATIONAL PUBLIC SERVICE

On the basis of current Court of Justice rulings, and bearing in mind the present conditions for establishing the single market, the Commission considers that the derogation in Article 48(4) covers specific functions of the State and similar bodies such as the armed forces, the police and other forces for the maintenance of order, the judiciary, the tax authorities and the diplomatic corps.

This derogation is also seen as covering posts in State Ministries, regional government authorities, local authorities and other similar bodies, central banks and other public bodies, where the duties of the post involve the exercise of State authority, such as the preparation of legal acts, the implementation of such acts, monitoring of their application and supervision of subordinate bodies. Accordingly, the action envisaged by the Commission does not concern such posts.

ACTIVITIES CONCERNED BY ACTION IN THE PUBLIC SERVICE SECTOR

The Commission considers that the functions involved in certain forms of public employment are for the most part sufficiently remote from the specific activities of

---

[9] OJ 1988 C 72/2.

the public service as defined by the Court of Justice that they would only in very rare cases be covered by the exception in Article 48(4) of the Treaty.

The Commission proposes therefore to implement its action in the following areas by order of priority:

— bodies responsible for administering commercial services (e.g., public transport, electricity and gas supply, airline and shipping companies, posts and telecommunications, radio and television companies),
— public health care services,
— teaching in state educational establishments,
— research for non-military purposes in public establishments.

Each of these activities also exists in the private sector, to which Article 48(4) does not apply, or may be exercise in the public sector without the imposition of nationality requirements.

The Commission proposes to inform the Member States of the conclusions of its review of the sectors chosen while requesting them to open access to employment in these sectors to workers who are nationals of other Member States. The Commission reserves the right of recourse, if necessary, to the procedure under Article 169 of the EEC Treaty providing for the opening of infringement proceedings against a Member State. Under this procedure Member States would have an opportunity to show that for a given post, and contrary to what might be expected, the post is indeed involved with the specific activities of the public service. In such cases, the Member States can continue to apply the nationality requirements for access to such posts, subject to any further decisions of the Court of Justice.

The sectoral actions will cover all posts in the sectors in question. The Commission would emphasize that in accordance with the case law of the Court of Justice discrimination on grounds of nationality with respect to access to subordinate posts in the public service, which do not involve activities specific to the public service, cannot be justified.

IMPORTANCE OF MEMBER STATES' COOPERATION

The Commission relies on active and effective cooperation by the Member States with a view to avoiding proceedings wherever possible.

In this connection, the Commission would request the Member States concerned—those whose national legislation restricts access to the posts in the sectors in question to their own nationals—to inform it concerning any objective difficulties they may have in securing compliance with the objectives of the Commissions' proposed action in this field so that, if necessary, the Commission can take them into account.

RECOURSE AVAILABLE TO COMMUNITY NATIONALS

In addition to the right to refer complaints[10] to the Commission, Community nationals are also entitled to seek redress in the national courts if they consider that

[10] In each Community Member State there is an Information Office—really a Commission 'branch office'—whose work is not just to inform citizens about their individual and collective rights, but also to receive complaints about infringements or omissions by the national authorities in the area of Community law. EEC nationals are also at liberty to make a complaint or indicate an apparent failure to comply with EEC legislation directly to the Commission's headquarters in Brussels.

the rejection of their application for employment in the public sector—or difference in the conditions of their employment in that sector—is not compatible with Community rules on freedom of movement as interpreted by the Court of Justice. These rules are in fact directly applicable in the legal systems of all the Member States and take precedence over al conflicting national provisions. A national court called on to interpret the rules on the freedom of movement of workers may, or in some cases must, refer the matter to the Court of Justice for a preliminary ruling under Article 177 of the EEC Treaty.

Right of Establishment and the Freedom to Provide Services

Council Directive of 21 May 1973 on the abolition of restrictions on movement and residence within the Community for nationals of Member States with regard to establishment and the provision of services (73/148/EEC)[1]

The Council of the European Communities,

HAVING REGARD to the Treaty establishing the European Economic Community, and in particular Art. 54(2) and Art. 63(2) thereof;

HAVING REGARD to the General Programmes for the abolition of restrictions on freedom of establishment and freedom to provide services, and in particular Title II thereof;

[recitals omitted]

HAS ADOPTED this Directive:

Article 1 1. The Member States shall, acting as provided in this Directive, abolish restrictions on the movement and residence of:
(a) nationals of a Member State who are established or who wish to establish themselves in another Member State in order to pursue activities as self-employed persons, or who wish to provide services in that State;
(b) nationals of Member States wishing to go to another Member State as recipients of services;
(c) the spouse and the children under twenty-one years of age of such nationals, irrespective of their nationality;
(d) the relatives in the ascending and descending lines of such nationals and of the spouse of such nationals, which relatives are dependent on them, irrespective of their nationality.

2. Member States shall favour the admission of any other member of the family of a national referred to in paragraph 1 (a) or (b) or of the spouse of that national, which member is dependent on that national or spouse of that national or who in the country of origin was living under the same roof.

Article 2 1. Member States shall grant the persons referred to in Art. 1 the right to leave their territory. Such right shall be exercised simply on production of a valid identity card or passport. Members of the family shall enjoy the same right as the national on whom they are dependent.

2. Member States shall, acting in accordance with their laws, issue to their nationals, or renew, an identity card or passport, which shall state in particular the holder's nationality.

---

[1] OJ 1973 L 172/14.

3. The passport must be valid at least for all Member States and for countries through which the holder must pass when travelling between Member States. Where a passport is the only document on which the holder may lawfully leave the country, its period of validity shall be not less than five years.

4. Member States may not demand from the persons referred to in Art. 1 any exit visa or any equivalent requirement.

Article 3 1. Member States shall grant to the persons referred to in Art. 1 the right to enter their territory merely on production of a valid identity card or passport.

2. No entry visa or equivalent requirement may be demanded save in respect of members of the family who do not have the nationality of a Member State. Member States shall afford to such persons every facility for obtaining any necessary visas.

Article 4 1. Each Member State shall grant the right of permanent residence to nationals of other Member States who establish themselves within its territory in order to pursue activities as self-employed persons, when the restrictions on these activities have been abolished pursuant to the Treaty.

As proof of the right of residence, a document entitled 'Residence Permit for a National of a Member State of the European Communiuties' shall be issued. This document shall be valid for not less than five years from the date of issue and shall be automatically renewable.

Breaks in residence not exceeding six consecutive months and absence on military service shall not affect the validity of a residence permit.

A valid residence permit may not be withdrawn from a national referred to in Art. 1 (1) (a) solely on the grounds that he is no longer in employment because he is temporarily incapable of work as a result of illness or accident.

Any national of a Member State who is not specified in the first subparagraph but who is authorised under the laws of another Member State to pursue an activity within its territory shall be granted a right of abode for a period not less than that of the authorisation granted for the pursuit of the activity in question.

However, any national referred to in subparagraph 1 and to whom the provisions of the preceding subparagraph apply as a result of a change of employment shall retain his residence permit until the date on which it expires.

2. The right of residence for persons providing and receiving services shall be of equal duration with the period during which the services are provided.

Where such period exceeds three months, the Member State in the territory of which the services are performed shall issue a right of abode as proof of the right of residence.

Where the period does not exceed three months, the identity card or passport with which the person concerned entered the territory shall be sufficient to cover his stay. The Member State may, however, require the person concerned to report his presence in the territory.

3. A member of the family who is not a national of a Member State shall be issued with a residence document which shall have the same validity as that issued to the national on whom he is dependent.

Article 5 The right of residence shall be effective throughout the territory of the Member State concerned.

Article 6   An applicant for a residence permit or right of abode shall not be required by a Member State to produce anything other than the following, namely:
(a) the identity card or passport with which he or she entered its territory;
(b) proof that he or she comes within one of the classes of person referred to in Arts. 1 and 4.

Article 7   1. The residence documents granted to nationals of a Member State shall be issued and renewed free of charge or on payment of an amount not exceeding the dues and taxes charged for the issue of identity cards to nationals. These provisions shall also apply to documents and certificates required for the issue and renewal of such residence documents.

2. The visas referred to in Art. 3(2) shall be free of charge.

3. Member States shall take the necessary steps to simplify as much as possible the formalities and the procedure for obtaining the documents mentioned in paragraph 1.

Article 8   Member States shall not derogate from the provisions of this Directive save on grounds of public policy, public security or public health.

[*remainder of the directive is omitted*]

Council Directive of 17 December 1974 concerning the right of nationals of a Member State to remain in the territory of another Member State after having pursued therein an activity in a self-employed capacity (75/34/EEC)[2]

The Council of the European Communities,

HAVING REGARD to the Treaty establishing the European Economic Community, and in particular Art. 235 thereof;

HAVING REGARD to the General Programme for the abolition of restrictions on freedom of establishment, and in particular Title II thereof;

[*recitals omitted*]

Whereas pursuant to Council Directive No. 73/148/EEC of 21 May 1973 on the abolition of restrictions on movement and residence within the Community for nationals of Member States with regard to establishment and the provision of services, each Member State grants the right of permanent residence to nationals of other Member States who establish themselves within its territory in order to pursue activities as self-employed persons, when the restrictions on these activities have been abolished pursuant to the Treaty;

Whereas it is normal for a person to prolong a period of permanent residence in the territory of a Member State by remaining there after having pursued an activity there; whereas the absence of a right so to remain in such circumstances is an obstacle to the attainment of freedom of establishment; whereas, as regards

---

[2] OJ 1975 L 14/10.

employed persons, the conditions under which such a right may be exercised have already been laid down by Regulation (EEC) No. 1251/70;

Whereas Art. 48(3)(d) of the Treaty recognises the right of workers to remain in the territory of a Member State after having been employed in that State; whereas Art. 54(2) does not expressly provide a similar right for self-employed persons; whereas, nevertheless, the nature of establishment, together with attachments formed to the countries in which they have pursued their activities, means that such persons have a definite interest in enjoying the same right to remain as that granted to workers; whereas in justification of this measure reference should be made to the Treaty provision enabling it to be taken;

[*recitals omitted*]

HAS ADOPTED this Directive:

Article 1 Member States shall, under the conditions laid down in this Directive, abolish restrictions on the right to remain in their territory in favour of nationals of another Member State who have pursued activities as self-employed persons in their territory, and members of their families, as defined in Art. 1 of Directive No. 3/148/EEC.

Article 2 1. Each Member State shall recognise the right to remain permanently in its territory of:

(a) any person who, at the time of termination of his activity, has reached the age laid down by the law of that State for entitlement to an old-age pension and who has pursued his activity in that State for at least the previous twelve months and has resided there continuously for more than three years.

   Where the law of that Member State does not grant the right to an old-age pension to certain categories of self-employed workers, the age requirement shall be considered as satisfied when the beneficiary reaches 65 years of age;

(b) any person who, having resided continuously in the territory of that State for more than two years, ceases to pursue his activity there as a result of permanent incapacity to work.

   If such incapacity is the result of an accident at work or an occupational illness entitling him to a pension which is payable in whole or in part by an institution of that State no condition shall be imposed as to length of residence;

(c) any person who, after three years' continuous activity and residence in the territory of that State, pursues his activity in the territory of another Member State, while retaining his residence in the territory of the first State, to which he returns, as a rule, each day or at least once a week.

Periods of activity so completed in the territory of the other Member State shall, for the purposes of entitlement to the rights referred to in (a) and (b), be considered as having been completed in the territory of the State of residence.

2. The conditions as to length of residence and activity laid down in paragraph 1(a) and the condition as to length of residence laid down in paragraph 1(b) shall not apply if the spouse of the self-employed person is a national of the Member State concerned or has lost the nationality of that State by marriage to that person.

Article 3 1. Each Member State shall recognise the right of the members of the self-employed person's family referred to in Art. 1 who are residing with him in the territory of that State to remain there permanently, if the person concerned has acquired the right to remain in the territory of that State in accordance with Art. 2. This provision shall continue to apply even after the death of the person concerned.

2. If, however, the self-employed person dies during his working life and before having acquired the right to remain in the territory of the State concerned, that State shall recognise the right of the members of his family to remain there permanently on condition that:

— the person concerned, on the date of his decease, had resided continuously in its territory for at least two years; or
— his death resulted from an accident at work or an occupational illness; or
— the surviving spouse is a national of that State or lost such nationality by marriage to the person concerned.

Article 4   1. Continuity of residence as provided for in Arts. 2(1) and 3(2) may be attested by any means of proof in use in the country of residence. It may not be affected by temporary absences not exceeding a total of three months per year, nor by longer absences due to compliance with the obligations of military service.

2. Periods of inactivity due to circumstances outside the control of the person concerned or of inactivity owing to illness or accident must be considered as periods of activity within the meaning of Art. 2(1).

Article 5   1. Member States shall allow the person entitled to the right to remain to exercise such right within two years from the time of becoming entitled thereto pursuant to Art. 2(1)(a) and (b) and Art. 3. During this period the beneficiary must be able to leave the territory of the Member State without adversely affecting such right.

2. Member States shall not require the person concerned to comply with any particular formality in order to exercise the right to remain.

Article 6   1. Member States shall recognise the right of persons having the right to remain in their territory to a residence permit, which must:
(a) be issued and renewed free of charge or on payment of a sum not exceeding the dues and taxes payable by nationals for the issue or renewal of identity cards;
(b) be valid throughout the territory of the Member State issuing it; be valid for five years and renewable automatically.

2. Periods of non-residence not exceeding six consecutive months and longer absences due to compliance with the obligations of military service may not affect the validity of a residence permit.

Article 7   Member States shall apply to persons having the right to remain in their territory the right of equality of treatment recognised by the Council Directives on the abolition of restrictions on freedom of establishment pursuant to Title III of the General Programme which provides for such abolition.

Article 8   1. This Directive shall not affect any provisions laid down by law, regulation or administrative action of any Member State which would be more favourable to nationals of other Member States.

2. Member States shall facilitate re-admission to their territories of self-employed persons who left those territories after having resided there permanently for a long

period while pursuing an activity there and who wish to return when they have reached retirement age as defined in Art. 2(1)(a) or are permanently incapacitated for work.

Article 9   Member States may not derogate from the provisions of this Directive save on grounds of public policy, public security or public health.

[*final provisions omitted*]

Council Directive of 17 December 1974 extending the scope of Directive 64/221/EEC[3] on the coordination of special measures concerning the movement and residence of foreign nationals which are justified on grounds of public policy, public security or public health to include nationals of a Member State who exercise the right to remain in the territory of another Member State after having pursued therein an activity in a self-employed capacity
(75/35/EEC)[4]

The Council of the European Communities,

HAVING REGARD to the Treaty establishing the European Economic Community, and in particular Art. 56 (2) and Art. 235 thereof;

HAVING REGARD to the proposal from the Commission;

HAVING REGARD to the Opinion of the European Parliament;

HAVING REGARD to the Opinion of the Economic and Social Committee;

Whereas Directive No. 64/221/EEC co-ordinated special measures concerning the movement and residence of foreign nationals which are justified on grounds of public policy, public security or public health and whereas Directive No. 75/34/EEC laid down conditions for the exercise of the right of nationals of a Member State to remain in the territory of another Member State after having pursued therein an activity in a self-employed capacity;

Whereas Directive No. 64/221/EEC should therefore apply to persons to whom Directive No. 75/34/EEC applies,

HAS ADOPTED this Directive:

Article 1   Directive No. 64/221/EEC shall apply to nationals of Member States and members of their families who have the right to remain in the territory of a Member State pursuant to Directive No. 75/34/EEC.

[*final provisions omitted*]

---

   [3] Article 1 of Directive 64/221 provides that that Directive applies to any national of a Member State who resides in or travels to another Member State, either in order to pursue an activity as a self-employed person, or as a recipient of services, see above at p. 150.
   [4] OJ 1975 L 14/14.

European Parliament and Council Directive of 16 December 1996 concerning the posting of workers in the framework of the provision of services (96/71/EC)[5]

The European Parliament and the Council of the European Union,

HAVING REGARD to the Treaty establishing the European Community, and in particular Articles 57(2) and 66 thereof,

[recitals omitted]

(1) Whereas, pursuant to Article 3(c) of the Treaty, the abolition, as between Member States, of obstacles to the free movement of persons and services constitutes one of the objectives of the Community;

(2) Whereas, for the provision of services, any restrictions based on nationality or residence requirements are prohibited under the Treaty with effect from the end of the transitional period;

(3) Whereas the completion of the internal market offers a dynamic environment for the transnational provision of services, prompting a growing number of undertakings to post employees abroad temporarily to perform work in the territory of a Member State other than the State in which they are habitually employed;

(4) Whereas the provision of services may take the form either of performance of work by an undertaking on its account and under its direction, under a contract concluded between that undertaking and the party for whom the services are intended, or of the hiring-out of workers for use by an undertaking in the framework of a public or a private contract;

(5) Whereas any such promotion of the transnational provision of services requires a climate of fair competition and measures guaranteeing respect for the rights of workers;

(6) Whereas the transnationalization of the employment relationship raises problems with regard to the legislation applicable to the employment relationship; whereas it is in the interests of the parties to lay down the terms and conditions governing the employment relationship envisaged;

(7) Whereas the Rome Convention of 19 June 1980 on the law applicable to contractual obligations, signed by 12 Member States, entered into force on 1 April 1991 in the majority of Member States;

(8) Whereas Article 3 of that Convention provides, as a general rule, for the free choice of law made by the parties; whereas, in the absence of choice, the contract is to be governed, according to Article 6(2), by the law of the country, in which the employee habitually carries out his work in performance of the contract, even if he is temporarily employed in another country, or, if the employee does not habitually carry out his work in any one country, by the law of the country in which the place of business through which he was engaged is situated, unless it appears from the circumstances as a whole that the contract is more closely connected with

5   OJ 1996 L 18/1.

another country, in which case the contract is to be governed by the law of that country;

(9) Whereas, according to Article 6(1) of the said Convention, the choice of law made by the parties is not to have the result of depriving the employee of the protection afforded to him by the mandatory rules of the law which would be applicable under paragraph 2 of that Article in the absence of choice;

(10) Whereas Article 7 of the said Convention lays down, subject to certain conditions, that effect may be given, concurrently with the law declared applicable, to the mandatory rules of the law of another country, in particular the law of the Member State within whose territory the worker is temporarily posted;

(11) Whereas, according to the principle of precedence of Community law laid down in its Article 20, the said Convention does not affect the application of provisions which, in relation to a particular matter, lay down choice-of-law rules relating to contractual obligations and which are or will be contained in acts of the institutions of the European Communities or in national laws harmonized in implementation of such acts;

(12) Whereas Community law does not preclude Member States from applying their legislation, or collective agreements entered into by employers and labour, to any person who is employed, even temporarily, within their territory, although his employer is established in another Member State; whereas Community law does not forbid Member States to guarantee the observance of those rules by the appropriate means;

(13) Whereas the laws of the Member States must be coordinated in order to lay down a nucleus of mandatory rules for minimum protection to be observed in the host country by employers who post workers to perform temporary work in the territory of a Member State where the services are provided; whereas such coordination can be achieved only by means of Community law;

(14) Whereas a 'hard core' of clearly defined protective rules should be observed by the provider of the services notwithstanding the duration of the worker's posting;

(15) Whereas it should be laid down that, in certain clearly defined cases of assembly and/or installation of goods, the provisions on minimum rates of pay and minimum paid annual holidays do not apply;

(16) Whereas there should also be some flexibility in application of the provisions concerning minimum rates of pay and the minimum length of paid annual holidays; whereas, when the length of the posting is not more than one month, Member States may, under certain conditions, derogate from the provisions concerning minimum rates of pay or provide for the possibility of derogation by means of collective agreements; whereas, where the amount of work to be done is not significant, Member States may derogate from the provisions concerning minimum rates of pay and the minimum length of paid annual holidays;

(17) Whereas the mandatory rules for minimum protection in force in the host country must not prevent the application of terms and conditions of employment which are more favourable to workers;

(18) Whereas the principle that undertakings established outside the Community must not receive more favourable treatment than undertakings established in the territory of a Member State should be upheld;

(19) Whereas, without prejudice to other provisions of Community law, this Directive does not entail the obligation to give legal recognition to the existence of temporary employment undertakings, nor does it prejudice the application by Member States of their laws concerning the hiring-out of workers and temporary employment undertakings to undertakings not established in their territory but operating therein in the framework of the provision of services;

(20) Whereas this Directive does not affect either the agreements concluded by the Community with third countries or the laws of Member States concerning the access to their territory of third-country providers of services; whereas this Directive is also without prejudice to national laws relating to the entry, residence and access to employment of third-country workers;

[footnotes and last recitals omitted]

HAVE ADOPTED this directive:

Article 1   Scope   1. This Directive shall apply to undertakings established in a Member State which, in the framework of the transnational provision of services, post workers, in accordance with paragraph 3, to the territory of a Member State.

2. This Directive shall not apply to merchant navy undertakings as regards seagoing personnel.

3. This Directive shall apply to the extent that the undertakings referred to in paragraph 1 take one of the following transnational measures:

(a) post workers to the territory of a Member State on their account and under their direction, under a contract concluded between the undertaking making the posting and the party for whom the services are intended, operating in that Member State, provided there is an employment relationship between the undertaking making the posting and the worker during the period of posting; or

(b) post workers to an establishment or to an undertaking owned by the group in the territory of a Member State, provided there is an employment relationship between the undertaking making the posting and the worker during the period of posting; or

(c) being a temporary employment undertaking or placement agency, hire out a worker to a user undertaking established or operating in the territory of a Member State, provided there is an employment relationship between the temporary employment undertaking or placement agency and the worker during the period of posting.

4. Undertakings established in a non-member State must not be given more favourable treatment than undertakings established in a Member State.
Definition

Article 2   Definition   1. For the purposes of this Directive, 'posted worker' means a worker who, for a limited period, carries out his work in the territory of a Member State other than the State in which he normally works.

2. For the purposes of this Directive, the definition of a worker is that which applies in the law of the Member State to whose territory the worker is posted.

Article 3   Terms and conditions of employment   1. Member States shall ensure that, whatever the law applicable to the employment relationship, the undertakings referred to in Article 1(1) guarantee workers posted to their territory the terms and conditions of employment covering the following matters which, in the Member State where the work is carried out, are laid down:
— by law, regulation or administrative provision, and/or
— by collective agreements or arbitration awards which have been declared universally applicable within the meaning of paragraph 8, insofar as they concern the activities referred to in the Annex:
   (a) maximum work periods and minimum rest periods;
   (b) minimum paid annual holidays;
   (c) the minimum rates of pay, including overtime rates; this point does not apply to supplementary occupational retirement pension schemes;
   (d) the conditions of hiring-out of workers, in particular the supply of workers by temporary employment undertakings;
   (e) health, safety and hygiene at work;
   (f) protective measures with regard to the terms and conditions of employment of pregnant women or women who have recently given birth, of children and of young people;
   (g) equality of treatment between men and women and other provisions on non-discrimination.

For the purposes of this Directive, the concept of minimum rates of pay referred to in paragraph 1(c) is defined by the national law and/or practice of the Member State to whose territory the worker is posted.

2. In the case of initial assembly and/or first installation of goods where this is an integral part of a contract for the supply of goods and necessary for taking the goods supplied into use and carried out by the skilled and/or specialist workers of the supplying undertaking, the first subparagraph of paragraph 1(b) and (c) shall not apply, if the period of posting does not exceed eight days.

This provision shall not apply to activities in the field of building work listed in the Annex.

3. Member States may, after consulting employers and labour, in accordance with the traditions and practices of each Member State, decide not to apply the first subparagraph of paragraph 1(c) in the cases referred to in Article 1(3)(a) and (b) when the length of the posting does not exceed one month.

4. Member States may, in accordance with national laws and/or practices, provide that exemptions may be made from the first subparagraph of paragraph 1(c) in the cases referred to in Article 1(3)(a) and (b) and from a decision by a Member State within the meaning of paragraph 3 of this Article, by means of collective agreements within the meaning of paragraph 8 of this Article, concerning one or more sectors of activity, where the length of the posting does not exceed one month.

5. Member States may provide for exemptions to be granted from the first subparagraph of paragraph 1(b) and (c) in the cases referred to in Article 1(3) (a) and (b) on the grounds that the amount of work to be done is not significant.

Member States availing themselves of the option referred to in the first subparagraph shall lay down the criteria which the work to be performed must meet in order to be considered as 'non-significant'.

6. The length of the posting shall be calculated on the basis of a reference period of one year from the beginning of the posting.

For the purpose of such calculations, account shall be taken of any previous periods for which the post has been filled by a posted worker.

7. Paragraphs 1 to 6 shall not prevent application of terms and conditions of employment which are more favourable to workers.

Allowances specific to the posting shall be considered to be part of the minimum wage, unless they are paid in reimbursement of expenditure actually incurred on account of the posting, such as expenditure on travel, board and lodging.

8. 'Collective agreements or arbitration awards which have been declared universally applicable' means collective agreements or arbitration awards which must be observed by all undertakings in the geographical area and in the profession or industry concerned.

In the absence of a system for declaring collective agreements or arbitration awards to be of universal application within the meaning of the first subparagraph, Member States may, if they so decide, base themselves on:

— collective agreements or arbitration awards which are generally applicable to all similar undertakings in the geographical area and in the profession or industry concerned, and/or
— collective agreements which have been concluded by the most representative employers' and labour organizations at national level and which are applied throughout national territory,

provided that their application to the undertakings referred to in Article 1(1) ensures equality of treatment on matters listed in the first subparagraph of paragraph 1 of this Article between those undertakings and the other undertakings referred to in this subparagraph which are in a similar position.

Equality of treatment, within the meaning of this Article, shall be deemed to exist where national undertakings in a similar position:

— are subject, in the place in question or in the sector concerned, to the same obligations as posting undertakings as regards the matters listed in the first subparagraph of paragraph 1, and
— are required to fulfil such obligations with the same effects.

9. Member States may provide that the undertakings referred to in Article 1(1) must guarantee workers referred to in Article 1(3)(c) the terms and conditions which apply to temporary workers in the Member State where the work is carried out.

10. This Directive shall not preclude the application by Member States, in compliance with the Treaty, to national undertakings and to the undertakings of other States, on a basis of equality of treatment, of:

— terms and conditions of employment on matters other than those referred to in the first subparagraph of paragraph 1 in the case of public policy provisions,

— terms and conditions of employment laid down in the collective agreements or arbitration awards within the meaning of paragraph 8 and concerning activities other than those referred to in the Annex.

Article 4   Cooperation on information   1. For the purposes of implementing this Directive, Member States shall, in accordance with national legislation and/or practice, designate one or more liaison offices or one or more competent national bodies.

2. Member States shall make provision for cooperation between the public authorities which, in accordance with national legislation, are responsible for monitoring the terms and conditions of employment referred to in Article 3. Such cooperation shall in particular consist in replying to reasoned requests from those authorities for information on the transnational hiring-out of workers, including manifest abuses or possible cases of unlawful transnational activities.
The Commission and the public authorities referred to in the first subparagraph shall cooperate closely in order to examine any difficulties which might arise in the application of Article 3(10).
    Mutual administrative assistance shall be provided free of charge.

3. Each Member State shall take the appropriate measures to make the information on the terms and conditions of employment referred to in Article 3 generally available.

4. Each Member State shall notify the other Member States and the Commission of the liaison offices and/or competent bodies referred to in paragraph 1.

Article 5   Measures   Member States shall take appropriate measures in the event of failure to comply with this Directive.
They shall in particular ensure that adequate procedures are available to workers and/or their representatives for the enforcement of obligations under this Directive.
Jurisdiction

Article 6   Jurisdiction   In order to enforce the right to the terms and conditions of employment guaranteed in Article 3, judicial proceedings may be instituted in the Member State in whose territory the worker is or was posted, without prejudice, where applicable, to the right, under existing international conventions on jurisdiction, to institute proceedings in another State.

Article 7   Implementation   Member States shall adopt the laws, regulations and administrative provisions necessary to comply with this Directive by 16 December 1999 at the latest. They shall forthwith inform the Commission thereof.
    When Member States adopt these provisions, they shall contain a reference to this Directive or shall be accompanied by such reference on the occasion of their official publication. The methods of making such reference shall be laid down by Member States.

Article 8   Commission review   By 16 December 2001 at the latest, the Commission shall review the operation of this Directive with a view to proposing the necessary amendments to the Council where appropriate.

[final provisions omitted]

ANNEX

The activities mentioned in Article 3 (1), second indent, include all building work relating to the construction, repair, upkeep, alteration or demolition of buildings, and in particular the following work:

1.　excavation
2.　earthmoving
3.　actual building work
4.　assembly and dismantling of prefabricated elements
5.　fitting out or installation
6.　alterations
7.　renovation
8.　repairs
9.　dismantling
10.　demolition
11.　maintenance
12.　upkeep, painting and cleaning work
13.　improvements.

Council Directive of 21 December 1988 on a general system for the recognition of higher-education diplomas awarded on completion of professional education and training of at least three years' duration (89/48/EEC)[6]

The Council of the European Communities,
HAVING REGARD to the Treaty establishing the European Economic Community, and in particular Arts. 49, 57 (1) and 66 thereof,

[recitals omitted]

Whereas, pursuant to Art. 3 (c) of the Treaty the abolition, as between Member States, of obstacles to freedom of movement for persons and services constitutes one of the objectives of the Community; whereas, for nationals of the Member States, this means in particular the possibility of pursuing a profession, whether in a self-employed or employed capacity, in a Member State other than that in which they acquired their professional qualifications;

Whereas the provisions so far adopted by the Council, and pursuant to which Member States recognise mutually and for professional purposes higher-education diplomas issued within their territory, concern only a few professions; whereas the level and duration of the education and training governing access to those professions have been regulated in a similar fashion in all the Member States or have been the subject of the minimal harmonisation needed to establish sectoral systems for the mutual recognition of diplomas;

---

[6]　OJ 1989 L 19/16.

Whereas, in order to provide a rapid response to the expectations of nationals of Community countries who hold higher-education diplomas awarded on completion of professional education and training issued in a Member State other than that in which they wish to pursue their profession, another method of recognition of such diplomas should also be put in place such as to enable those concerned to pursue all those professional activities which in a host Member State are dependent on the completion of post-secondary education and training provided they hold such a diploma preparing them for those activities awarded on completion of a course of studies lasting at least three years and issued in another Member State;

Whereas this objective can be achieved by the introduction of a general system for the recognition of higher-education diplomas awarded on completion of professional education and training of at least three years' duration;

Whereas, for those professions for the pursuit of which the Community has not laid down the necessary minimum level of qualification, Member States reserve the option of fixing such a level with a view to guaranteeing the quality of services provided in their territory; whereas, however, they may not, without infringing their obligations laid down in Art. 5 of the Treaty, require a national of a Member State to obtain those qualifications which in general they determine only by reference to diplomas issued under their own national education systems, where the person concerned has already acquired all or part of those qualifications in another Member State; whereas, as a result, any host Member State in which a profession is regulated is required to take account of qualifications acquired in another Member State and to determine whether those qualifications correspond to the qualifications which the Member State concerned requires;

Whereas collaboration between the Member States is appropriate in order to facilitate their compliance with those obligations; whereas, therefore, the means of organising such collaboration should be established;

Whereas the term 'regulated professional activity' should be defined so as to take account of differing national sociological situations; whereas the term should cover not only professional activities access to which is subject, in a Member State, to the possession of a diploma, but also professional activities, access to which is unrestricted when they are practised under a professional title reserved for the holders of certain qualifications; whereas the professional associations and organisations which confer such titles on their members and are recognised by the public authorities cannot invoke their private status to avoid application of the system provided for by this Directive;

Whereas it is also necessary to determine the characteristics of the professional experience or adaptation period which the host Member State may require of the person concerned in addition to the higher-education diploma, where the person's qualifications do not correspond to those laid down by national provisions;

Whereas an aptitude test may also be introduced in place of the adaptation period; whereas the effect of both will be to improve the existing situation with regard to the mutual recognition of diplomas between Member States and therefore to facilitate the free movement of persons within the Community; whereas their function is to assess the ability of the migrant, who is a person who has already received his professional training in another Member State, to adapt to this new professional environment; whereas, from the migrant's point of view, an aptitude test will have the advantage of reducing the length of the practice period; whereas, in principle, the choice between the adaptation period and the aptitude test should be made by the migrant; whereas, however, the nature of certain professions is such that Member States must be allowed to prescribe, under certain conditions, either the adaptation period or the test; whereas, in particular, the differences between the legal systems of the Member States, whilst they may vary in extent from one Member State to another, warrant special provisions since, as a rule, the education or training attested by the diploma, certificate or other evidence of formal qualifications in a field of law in the Member State of origin does not cover the legal knowledge required in the host Member State with respect to the corresponding legal field;

Whereas, moreover, the general system for the recognition of higher-education diplomas is intended neither to amend the rules, including those relating to professional ethics, applicable to any person pursuing a profession in the territory of a Member State nor to exclude migrants from the application of those rules; whereas that system is confined to laying down appropriate arrangements to ensure that migrants comply with the professional rules of the host Member State;

Whereas Arts. 49, 57 (1) and 66 of the Treaty empower the Community to adopt provisions necessary for the introduction and operation of such a system;

Whereas the general system for the recognition of higher-education diplomas is entirely without prejudice to the application of Art. 48 (4) and Art. 55 of the Treaty;

Whereas such a system, by strengthening the right of a Community national to use his professional skills in any Member State, supplements and reinforces his right to acquire such skills wherever he wishes;

Whereas this system should be evaluated, after being in force for a certain time, to determine how efficiently it operates and in particular how it can be improved or its field of application extended.

HAS ADOPTED this Directive:

Article 1   For the purposes of this Directive the following definitions shall apply:
(a) diploma: any diploma, certificate or other evidence of formal qualifications or any set of such diplomas, certificates or other evidence:
— which has been awarded by a competent authority in a Member State, designated in accordance with its own laws, regulations or administrative provisions;
— which shows that the holder has successfully completed a post-secondary course of at least three years' duration, or of an equivalent duration part-time, at a university or establishment of higher education or another establishment of similar level and, where appropriate, that he has successfully completed the professional training required in addition to the post-secondary course; and
— which shows that the holder has the professional qualifications required for the taking up or pursuit of a regulated profession in that Member State,

provided that the education and training attested by the diploma, certificate or other evidence of formal qualifications were received mainly in the Community, or the holder thereof has three years' professional experience certified by the Member State which recognised a third-country diploma, certificate or other evidence of formal qualifications.

The following shall be treated in the same way as a diploma, within the meaning of the first subparagraph: any diploma, certificate or other evidence of formal qualifications or any set of such diplomas, certificates or other evidence awarded by a competent authority in a Member State if it is awarded on the successful completion of education and training received in the Community and recognised by a competent authority in that Member State as being of an equivalent level and if it confers the same rights in respect of the taking up and pursuit of a regulated profession in that Member State;

(b) host Member State: any Member State in which a national of a Member State applies to pursue a profession subject to regulation in that Member State, other than the State in which he obtained his diploma or first pursued the profession in question;

(c) regulated profession: the regulated professional activity or range of activities which constitute this profession in a Member State;

(d) regulated professional activity: a professional activity, in so far as the taking up or pursuit of such activity or one of its modes of pursuit in a Member State is subject, directly or indirectly by virtue of laws, regulations or administrative provisions, to the possession of a diploma. The following in particular shall constitute a mode of pursuit of a regulated professional activity:

— pursuit of an activity under a professional title, in so far as the use of such a title is reserved to the holders of a diploma governed by laws, regulations or administrative provisions,

— pursuit of a professional activity relating to health, in so far as remuneration and/or reimbursement for such an activity is subject by virtue of national social security arrangements to the possession of a diploma.

Where the first subparagraph does not apply, a professional activity shall be deemed to be a regulated professional activity if it is pursued by the members of an association or organisation the purpose of which is, in particular, to promote and maintain a high standard in the professional field concerned and which, to achieve that purpose, is recognised in a special form by a Member State and:

— awards a diploma to its members,

— ensures that its members respect the rules of professional conduct which it prescribes, and

— confers on them the right to use a title or designatory letters, or to benefit from a status corresponding to that diploma.

A non-exhaustive list of associations or organisations which, when this Directive is adopted, satisfy the conditions of the second subparagraph is contained in the Annex. Whenever a Member State grants the recognition referred to in the second subparagraph to an association or organisation, it shall inform the Commission thereof, which shall publish this information in the *Official Journal of the European Communities*.

(e) professional experience: the actual and lawful pursuit of the profession concerned in a Member State;

(f) adaptation period: the pursuit of a regulated profession in the host Member State under the responsibility of a qualified member of that profession, such period of supervised practice possibly being accompanied by further training. This period of supervised practice shall be the subject of an assessment. The detailed rules governing the adaptation period and its assessment as well as the status of a migrant person under supervision shall be laid down by the competent authority in the host Member States;

(g) aptitude test: a test limited to the professional knowledge of the applicant, made by the competent authorities of the host Member State with the aim of assessing the ability of the applicant to pursue a regulated profession in that Member State.

In order to permit this test to be carried out, the competent authorities shall draw up a list of subjects which, on the basis of a comparison of the education and training required in the Member State and that received by the applicant, are not covered by the diploma or other evidence of formal qualifications possessed by the applicant.

The aptitude test must take account of the fact that the applicant is a qualified professional in the Member State of origin or the Member State from which he comes. It shall cover subjects to be selected from those on the list, knowledge of which is essential in order to be able to exercise the profession in the host Member State. The test may also include knowledge of the professional rules applicable to the activities in question in the host Member State. The detailed application of the aptitude test shall be determined by the competent authorities of that State with due regard to the rules of Community law.

The status, in the host Member State, of the applicant who wishes to prepare himself for the aptitude test in that State shall be determined by the competent authorities in that State.

Article 2   This Directive shall apply to any national of a Member State wishing to pursue a regulated profession in a host Member State in a self-employed capacity or as an employed person.

This Directive shall not apply to professions which are the subject of a separate Directive establishing arrangements for the mutual recognition of diplomas by Member States.

Article 3   Where, in a host Member State, the taking up or pursuit of a regulated profession is subject to possession of a diploma, the competent authority may not, on the grounds of inadequate qualifications, refuse to authorise a national of a Member State to take up or pursue that profession on the same conditions as apply to its own nationals:

(a) if the applicant holds the diploma required in another Member State for the taking up or pursuit of the profession in question in its territory, such diploma having been awarded in a Member State; or

(b) if the applicant has pursued the profession in question full-time for two years during the previous ten years in another Member State which does not regulate that profession, within the meaning of Art. 1(c) and the first subparagraph of Art. 1(d), and possesses evidence of one or more formal qualifications:

- which have been awarded by a competent authority in a Member State, designated in accordance with the laws, regulations or administrative provisions of such State,
- which show that the holder has successfully completed a post-secondary course of at least three years' duration, or of an equivalent duration part-time, at a university or establishment of higher education or another establishment of similar level of a Member State and, where appropriate, that he has successfully completed the professional training required in addition to the post-secondary course, and
- which have prepared the holder for the pursuit of his profession.

The following shall be treated in the same way as the evidence of formal qualifications referred to in the first subparagraph: any formal qualifications or any set of such formal qualifications awarded by a competent authority in a Member State if it is awarded on the successful completion of training received in the Community and is recognised by that Member State as being of an equivalent level, provided that the other Member States and the Commission have been noticed of this recognition.

Article 4   1. Notwithstanding Art. 3, the host Member State may also require the applicant:

(a) to provide evidence of professional experience, where the duration of the education and training adduced in support of his application, as laid down in Art. 3 (a) and (b), is at least one year less than that required in the host Member State. In this event, the period of professional experience required:

- may not exceed twice the shortfall in duration of education and training where the shortfall relates to post-secondary studies and/or to a period of probationary practice carried out under the control of a supervising professional person and ending with an examination,
- may not exceed the shortfall where the shortfall relates to professional practice acquired with the assistance of a qualified member of the profession.

In the case of diplomas within the meaning of the last subparagraph of Art. 1(a), the duration of education and training recognised as being of an equivalent level shall be determined as for the education and training defined in the first subparagraph of Art. 1(a).

When applying these provisions, account must be taken of the professional experience referred to in Art. 3(b).

At all events, the professional experience required may not exceed four years;

(b) to complete an adaptation period not exceeding three years or take an aptitude test:

- where the matters covered by the education and training he has received as laid down in Art. 3(a) and (b), differ substantially from those covered by the diploma required in the host Member State, or
- where, in the case referred to in Art. 3(a), the profession regulated in the host Member State comprises one or more regulated professional activities which are not in the profession regulated in the Member State from which the applicant originates or comes and that difference corresponds to

specific education and training required in the host Member State and covers matters which differ substantially from those covered by the diploma adduced by the applicant, or

— where, in the case referred to in Art. 3(b), the profession regulated in the host Member State comprises one or more regulated professional activities which are not in the profession pursued by the applicant in the Member State from which he originates or comes, and that difference corresponds to specific education and training required in the host Member State and covers matters which differ substantially from those covered by the evidence of formal qualifications adduced by the applicant.

Should the host Member State make use of this possibility, it must give the applicant the right to choose between an adaptation period and an aptitude test. By way of derogation from this principle, for professions whose practice requires precise knowledge of national law and in respect of which the provision of advice and/or assistance concerning national law is an essential and constant aspect of the professional activity, the host Member State may stipulate either an adaptation period or an aptitude test. Where the host Member State intends to introduce derogations for other professions as regards an applicant's right to choose, the procedure laid down in Art. 10 shall apply.

2. However, the host Member State may not apply the provisions of paragraph 1(a) and (b) cumulatively.

Article 5 Without prejudice to Arts. 3 and 4, a host Member State may allow the applicant, with a view to improving his possibilities of adapting to the professional environment in that State, to undergo there, on the basis of equivalence, that part of his professional education and training represented by professional practice, acquired with the assistance of a qualified member of the profession, which he has not undergone in his Member State of origin or the Member State from which he has come.

Article 6 1. Where the competent authority of a host Member State requires of persons wishing to take up a regulated profession proof that they are of good character or repute or that they have not been declared bankrupt, or suspends or prohibits the pursuit of that profession in the event of serious professional misconduct or a criminal offence, that State shall accept as sufficient evidence, in respect of nationals of Member States wishing to pursue that profession in its territory, the production of documents issued by competent authorities in the Member State of origin or the Member State from which the foreign national comes showing that those requirements are met.

Where the competent authorities of the Member State of origin or of the Member State from which the foreign national comes do not issue the documents referred to in the first subparagraph, such documents shall be replaced by a declaration on oath—or, in States where there is no provision for declaration on oath, by a solemn declaration—made by the person concerned before a competent judicial or administrative authority or, where appropriate, a notary or qualified professional body of the Member State of origin or the Member State from which the person comes; such authority or notary shall issue a certificate attesting the authenticity of the declaration on oath or solemn declaration.

2. Where the competent authority of a host Member State requires of nationals of that Member State wishing to take up or pursue a regulated profession a certificate of physical or mental health, that authority shall accept as sufficient evidence in this respect the production of the document required in the Member State of origin or the Member State from which the foreign national comes.

Where the Member State of origin or the Member State from which the foreign national comes does not impose any requirements of this nature on those wishing to take up or pursue the profession in question, the host Member State shall accept from such nationals a certificate issued by a competent authority in that State corresponding to the certificates issued in the host Member State.

3. The competent authorities of host Member States may require that the documents and certificates referred to in paragraphs 1 and 2 are presented no more than three months after their date of issue.

4. Where the competent authority of a host Member State requires nationals of that Member State wishing to take up or pursue a regulated profession to take an oath or make a solemn declaration and where the form of such oath or declaration cannot be used by nationals of other Member States, that authority shall ensure that an appropriate and equivalent form of oath or declaration is offered to the person concerned.

Article 7   1. The competent authorities of host Member States shall recognise the right of nationals of Member States who fulfil the conditions for the taking up and pursuit of a regulated profession in their territory to use the professional title of the host Member State corresponding to that profession.

2. The competent authorities of host Member States shall recognise the right of nationals of Member States who fulfil the conditions for the taking up and pursuit of a regulated profession in their territory to use their lawful academic title and, where appropriate, the abbreviation thereof deriving from their Member State of origin or the Member State from which they come, in the language of that State. Host Member State may require this title to be followed by the name and location of the establishment or examining board which awarded it.

3. Where a profession is regulated in the host Member State by an association or organisation referred to in Art. 1(d), nationals of Member States shall only be entitled to use the professional title or designatory letters conferred by that organisation or association on proof of membership.

Where the association or organisation makes membership subject to certain qualification requirements, it may apply these to nationals of other Member States who are in possession of a diploma within the meaning of Art. 1(a) or a formal qualification within the meaning of Art. 3(b) only in accordance with this Directive, in particular Arts. 3 and 4.

Article 8   1. The host Member State shall accept as proof that the conditions laid down in Arts. 3 and 4 are satisfied the certificates and documents issued by the competent authorities in the Member States, which the person concerned shall submit in support of his application to pursue the profession concerned.

2. The procedure for examining an application to pursue a regulated profession shall be completed as soon as possible and the outcome communicated in a

reasoned decision of the competent authority in the host Member State not later than four months after presentation of all the documents relating to the person concerned. A remedy shall be available against this decision, or the absence thereof, before a court or tribunal in accordance with the provisions of national law.

Article 9   1. Member States shall designate, within the period provided for in Art. 12, the competent authorities empowered to receive the applications and take the decisions referred to in this Directive.

They shall communicate this information to the other Member States and to the Commission.

2. Each Member State shall designate a person responsible for coordinating the activities of the authorities referred to in paragraph 1 and shall inform the other Member States and the Commission to that effect. His role shall be to promote uniform application of this Directive to all the professions concerned. A coordinating group shall be set up under the aegis of the Commission, composed of the coordinators appointed by each Member State or their deputies and chaired by a representative of the Commission.

The task of this group shall be:

— to facilitate the implementation of this Directive,
— to collect all useful information for its application in the Member States.

The group may be consulted by the Commission on any changes to the existing system that may be contemplated.

3. Member States shall take measures to provide the necessary information on the recognition of diplomas within the framework of this Directive. They may be assisted in this task by the information centre on the academic recognition of diplomas and periods of study established by the Member States within the framework of the Resolution of the Council and the Ministers of Education meeting within the Council of 9 February 1976,[7] and, where appropriate, the relevant professional associations or organisations. The Commission shall take the necessary initiatives to ensure the development and co-ordination of the communication of the necessary information.

Article 10   1. If, pursuant to the third sentence of the second subparagraph of Art. 4(1)(b), a Member State proposes not to grant applicants the right to choose between an adaptation period and an aptitude test in respect of a profession within the meaning of this Directive, it shall immediately communicate to the Commission the corresponding draft provision. It shall at the same time notify the Commission of the grounds which make the enactment of such a provision necessary.

The Commission shall immediately notify the other Member States of any draft it has received; it may also consult the coordinating group referred to in Art. 9(2) of the draft.

2. Without prejudice to the possibility for the Commission and the other Member States of making comments on the draft, the Member State may adopt the provi-

---

[7] OJ 1976 C 38/1.

sion only if the Commission has not taken a decision to the contrary within three months.

3. At the request of a Member State or the Commission, Member States shall communicate to them, without delay, the definitive text of a provision arising from the application of this Article.

Article 11   Following the expiry of the period provided for in Art. 12, Member States shall communicate to the Commission, every two years, a report on the application of the system introduced.

In addition to general remarks, this report shall contain a statistical summary of the decisions taken and a description of the main problems arising from application of the Directive.

Article 12   Member States shall take the measures necessary to comply with this Directive within two years of its notification.[8] They shall forthwith inform the Commission thereof.

Member States shall communicate to the Commission the texts of the main provisions of national law which they adopt in the field governed by this Directive.

Article 13   Five years at the latest following the date specified in Art. 12, the Commission shall report to the European Parliament and the Council on the state of application of the general system for the recognition of higher-education diplomas awarded on completion of professional education and training of at least three years' duration.

After conducting all necessary consultations, the Commission shall, on this occasion, present its conclusions as to any changes that need to be made to the system as it stands. At the same time the Commission shall, where appropriate, submit proposals for improvements in the present system in the interest of further facilitating the freedom of movement, right of establishment and freedom to provide services of the persons covered by this Directive.

[final provisions omitted]

Annex: List of Professional Associations or Organizations which Satisfy the Conditions of the Second Subparagraph of Article 1(D)

IRELAND[9]

1.   The Institute of Chartered Accountants in Ireland[10]

[8] This Directive was notified to Member States on 4 January 1989.
[9] Irish nationals are also members of the following United Kingdom chartered bodies:

Institute of Chartered Accountants in England and Wales
Institute of Chartered Accountants in Scotland
Institute of Actuaries
Faculty of Actuaries
Chartered Institute of Management Accountants
Institute of Chartered Secretaries and Administrators
Royal Town Planning Institute
Royal Institution of Chartered Surveyors
Chartered Institute of Building.

[10] For the purposes of the activity of auditing only.

2. The Institute of Certified Public Accountants in Ireland[10]
3. The Association of Certified Accountants[10]
4. Institution of Engineers of Ireland
5. Irish Planning Institute

UNITED KINGDOM
1. Institute of Chartered Accountants in England and Wales
2. Institute of Chartered Accountants of Scotland
3. Institute of Chartered Accountants in Ireland
4. Chartered Association of Certified Accountants
5. Chartered Institute of Loss Adjusters
6. Chartered Institute of Management Accountants
7. Institute of Chartered Secretaries and Administrators
8. Chartered Insurance Institute
9. Institute of Actuaries
10. Faculty of Actuaries
11. Chartered Institute of Bankers
12. Institute of Bankers in Scotland
13. Royal Institution of Chartered Surveyors
14. Royal Town Planning Institute
15. Chartered Society of Physiotherapy
16. Royal Society of Chemistry
17. British Psychological Society
18. Library Association
19. Institute of Chartered Foresters
20. Chartered Institute of Building
21. Engineering Council
22. Institute of Energy
23. Institution of Structural Engineers
24. Institution of Civil Engineers
25. Institution of Mining Engineers
26. Institution of Mining and Metallurgy
27. Institution of Electrical Engineers
28. Institution of Gas Engineers
29. Institution of Mechanical Engineers
30. Institution of Chemical Engineers
31. Institution of Production Engineers
32. Institution of Marine Engineers
33. Royal Institution of Naval Architects
34. Royal Aeronautical Society
35. Institute of Metals
36. Chartered Institution of Building Services Engineers
37. Institute of Measurement and Control
38. British Computer Society

Statement by the Council and the Commission

Re Article 9(1)

'The Council and the Commission agree that professional bodies and higher-education establishments should be consulted or be involved in an appropriate way in the decision-making process.'

Council Recommendation of 21 December 1988 concerning nationals of Member States who hold a diploma conferred in a third State (89/49/EEC)[11]

The Council of The European Communities,

APPROVING Council Directive 89/48/EEC of 21 December 1988 on a general system for the recognition of higher-education diplomas awarded on completion of professional education and training of at least three years' duration;

NOTING that this Directive refers only to diplomas, certificates and other evidence of formal qualifications awarded in Member States to nationals of Member States;

ANXIOUS, however, to take account of the special position of nationals of Member States who hold diplomas, certificates or other evidence of formal qualifications awarded in third States and who are thus in a positio comparable to one of those described in Art. 3 of the Directive,

HEREBY RECOMMENDS:

that the Governments of the Member States should allow the persons referred to above to take up and pursue regulated professions within the Community by recognising these diplomas, certificates and other evidence of formal qualifications in their territories.

[*final provisions omitted*]

Council Directive 18 June 1992 on a second general system for the recognition of professional education and training to supplement Directive 89/48/EEC (92/51/EEC)[12]

The Council of the European Communities,
HAVING REGARD to the Treaty establishing the European Economic Community, particular Articles 49, 57 (1) and 66 thereof,

[*recitals omitted*]

(1) Whereas, pursuant to Article 8a of the Treaty, the internal market shall comprise an area without internal frontiers and whereas, pursuant to Article 3(c) of the Treaty, the abolition, as between Member States, of obstacles to freedom of

---

[11] OJ 1989 L 19/24.   [12] OJ 1992 L 209/25.

movement for persons and services constitutes one of the objectives of the Community; whereas, for nationals of the Member States, this means in particular the possibility of pursuing a profession, whether in a self-employed or employed capacity, in a Member State other than that in which they acquired their professional qualifications;

(2) Whereas, for those professions for the pursuit of which the Community has not laid down the necessary minimum level of qualification, Member States reserve the option of fixing such a level with a view to guaranteeing the quality of services provided in their territory; whereas, however, they may not, without disregarding their obligations laid down in Articles 5, 48, 52 and 59 of the Treaty, require a national of a Member State to obtain those qualifications which in general they determine only by reference to those issued under their own national education and training systems, where the person concerned has already acquired all or part of those qualifications in another Member State; whereas, as a result, any host Member State in which a profession is regulated is required to take account of qualifications acquired in another Member State and to determine whether those qualifications correspond to the qualifications which the Member State concerned requires;

(3) Whereas Council Directive 89/48/EEC of 21 December 1988 on a general system for the recognition of higher education diplomas awarded on completion of professional education and training of at least three years' duration (4) facilitates compliance with such obligations; whereas, however, it is limited to higher education;

(4) Whereas, in order to facilitate the pursuit of all those professional activities which in a host Member State are dependent on the completion of a certain level of education and training, a second general system should be introduced to complement the first;

(5) Whereas the complementary general system must be based on the same principles and contain mutatis mutandis the same rules as the initial general system;

(6) Whereas this Directive is not applicable to those regulated professions which are covered by specific Directives principally concerned with introducing mutual recognition of training courses completed before entry into professional life;

(7) Whereas neither is it applicable, furthermore, to those activities covered by specific Directives principally intended to introduce recognition of technical skills based on experience acquired in another Member State; whereas certain of those Directives apply solely to the pursuit of activities in a self-employed capacity; whereas, in order to ensure that the pursuit of such activities as an employed person does not fall within the scope of this Directive, whereby the pursuit of the same activity would be subject to different legal recognition arrangements depending on whether it was pursued in a self-employed capacity or as an employed person, those Directives should be made applicable to persons pursuing the activities in question as employed persons;

(8) Whereas the complementary general system is entirely without prejudice to the application of Article 48(4) and Article 55 of the Treaty;

(9) Whereas this complementary system must cover the levels of education and training not covered by the initial general system, namely that corresponding to other post-secondary education and training courses and other equivalent educa-

tion and training, and that corresponding to long or short secondary courses, possibly complemented by professional training or experience;

(10) Whereas, where in most Member States pursuit of a given regulated profession is subject to either very short training or the possession of certain personal attributes or merely general knowledge, the normal mechanisms for recognition under this Directive may be excessively cumbersome; whereas in such cases there should be provision for simplified mechanisms;

(11) Whereas account should also be taken of the professional training system in the United Kingdom whereby standards for levels of performance for all professional activities are established via the 'National Framework of Vocational Qualifications';

(12) Whereas in some Member States there are only relatively few regulated professions; whereas, however, training for professions which are not regulated may be specifically geared to the pursuit of the profession, with the structure and level of training being monitored or approved by the competent authorities of the Member State concerned; whereas this provides guarantees equivalent to those provided in connection with a regulated profession;

(13) Whereas the competent authorities of the host Member State should be allowed to determine, in accordance with the relevant provisions of Community law, the detailed rules necessary for implementation of the adaptation period and the aptitude test;

(14) Whereas, since it covers two levels of education and training and since the initial general system covers a third level, the complementary general system must lay down whether and under what conditions a person possessing a certain level of education and training may pursue, in another Member State, a profession the qualifications for which are regulated at a different level;

(15) Whereas, for the pursuit of certain professions, certain Member States require the possession of a diploma within the meaning of Directive 89/48/EEC, while for the same profession other Member States require the completion of professional education or training with a different structure; whereas certain kinds of education and training, while not of a post-secondary nature of minimum duration within the meaning of this Directive, nevertheless result in a comparable professional level and prepare the person for similar responsibilities and activities; whereas such education and training should therefore be classed in the same category as that attested by a diploma; whereas such education and training is very varied and this classification can be achieved only by listing the courses in question; whereas such classification would, where appropriate, establish the recognition of equivalence between such education and training and that covered by Directive 89/48/EEC; whereas some regulated education and training should also be classed at diploma level in a second list;

(16) Whereas, in view of the constantly changing organization of professional training, there should be a procedure for amending those lists;

(17) Whereas, since it covers occupations the pursuit of which is dependent on the possession of professional or vocational education and training qualifications of secondary level and generally requires manual skills, the complementary general system must also provide for the recognition of such qualifications even where they

have been acquired solely through professional experience in a Member State which does not regulate such professions;

(18) Whereas the aim of this general system, like the first general system, is to eliminate obstacles to the taking up and pursuit of regulated professions; whereas work carried out pursuant to Council Decision 85/368/EEC of 16 July 1985 on the comparability of vocational training qualifications between the Member States of the European Community (5), while pursuing a different objective from the elimination of legal obstacles to freedom of movement, namely that of improving the transparency of the labour market, must be used, where appropriate, in the application of this Directive, particularly where it could provide information on the subject, content and duration of professional training;

(19) Whereas professional bodies and professional educational and training establishments should, where appropriate, be consulted or be involved in an appropriate way in the decision-making process;

(20) Whereas, like the initial system, such a system, by strengthening the right of a Community national to use his occupational skills in any Member State, supplements and reinforces his right to acquire such skills wherever he wishes;

(21) Whereas the two systems should be evaluated, after a certain period of application, in order to determine how efficiently they operate and, in particular, how they can both be improved,

HAS ADOPTED this Directive:

CHAPTER I. DEFINITIONS

Article 1 For the purposes of this Directive, the following definitions shall apply:
(a) diploma: any evidence of education and training or any set of such evidence:
— which has been awarded by a competent authority in a Member State, designated in accordance with the laws, regulations or administrative provisions of that State,
— which shows that the holder has successfully completed:
  (i) either a post-secondary course other than that referred to in the second indent of Article 1(a) of Directive 89/48/EEC, of at least one year's duration or of equivalent duration on a part-time basis, one of the conditions of entry of which is, as a general rule, the successful completion of the secondary course required to obtain entry to university or higher education, as well as the professional training which may be required in addition to that post-secondary course;
  (ii) or one of the education and training courses in Annex C, and
— which shows that the holder has the professional qualifications required for the taking up or pursuit of a regulated profession in that Member State,

provided that the education and training attested by this evidence was received mainly in the Community, or outside the Community at teaching establishments which provide education and training in accordance with the laws, regulations or administrative provisions of a Member State, or that the holder thereof has three years' professional experience certified by the Member State which recognized third-country evidence of education and training.

The following shall be treated in the same way as a diploma within the meaning of the first subparagraph: any evidence of education and training or any set of such evidence awarded by a competent authority in a Member State if it is awarded on the successful completion of education and training received in the Community and recognized by a competent authority in that member State as being of an equivalent level and if it confers the same rights in respect of the taking up and pursuit of a regulated profession in that Member State;

(b) certificate: any evidence of education and training or any set of such evidence:

— which has been awarded by a competent authority in a Member State, designated in accordance with the laws, regulations or administrative provisions of that State,

— which shows that the holder, after having followed a secondary course, has completed:
either a course of education or training other than courses referred to in point (a), provided at an educational or training establishment or on the job, or in combination at an educational or training establishment and on the job, and complemented, where appropriate, by the probationary or professional practice required in addition to this course,
or the probationary or professional practice required in addition to this secondary course, or

— which shows that the holder, after having followed a secondary course of a technical or vocational nature has completed, where necessary, either a course of education or training as referred to in the previous indent, or the probationary or professional practice required in addition to this secondary course of a technical or vocational nature and

— which shows that the holder has the professional qualifications required for the taking up or pursuit of a regulated profession in that Member State,

provided that the education and training attested by this evidence was received mainly in the Community, or outside the Community at teaching establishments which provide education and training in accordance with the laws, regulations or administrative provisions of a Member State, or that the holder thereof has two years' professional experience certified by the Member State which recognized third-country evidence of education and training.

The following shall be treated in the same was as a certificate, within the meaning of the first subparagraph: any evidence of education and training or any set of such evidence awarded by a competent authority in a Member State if it is awarded on the successful completion of education and training received in the Community and recognized by a competent authority in a Member State as being of an equivalent level and if it confers the same rights in respect of the taking up and pursuit of a regulated profession in that Member State;

(c) attestation of competence: any evidence of qualifications:

— attesting to education and training not forming part of a set constituting a diploma within the meaning of Directive 89/48/EEC or a diploma or certificate within the meaning of this Directive, or

— awarded following an assessment of the personal qualities, aptitudes or knowledge which it is considered essential that the applicant have for the pursuit of a profession by an authority designated in accordance with the laws, regulations or administrative provisions of a Member State, without proof of prior education and training being required;

(d) host Member State: any Member State in which a national of a Member State applies to pursue a profession subject to regulation in that Member State, other than the State in which he obtained his evidence of education and training or attestation of competence or first pursued the profession in question;

(e) regulated profession: the regulated professional activity or range of activities which constitute this profession in a Member State;

(f) regulated professional activity: a professional activity the taking up or pursuit of which, or one of its modes of pursuit in a Member State, is subject, directly or indirectly, by virtue of laws, regulations or administrative provisions, to the possession of evidence of education and training or an attestation of competence. The following in particular shall constitute a mode of pursuit of a regulated professional activity:

— pursuit of an activity under a professional title, in so far as the use of such a title is reserved to the holders of evidence of education and training or an attestation of competence governed by laws, regulations or administrative provisions,

— pursuit of a professional activity relating to health, in so far as remuneration and/or reimbursement for such an activity is subject by virtue of national social security arrangements to the possession of evidence of education and training or an attestation of competence.

Where the first subparagraph does not apply, a professional activity shall be deemed to be a regulated professional activity if it is pursued by the members of an association or organization the purpose of which is, in particular, to promote and maintain a high standard in the professional field concerned and which, to achieve that purpose, is recognized in a special form by a Member State and:

— awards evidence of education and training to its members,

— ensures that its members respect the rules of professional conduct which it prescribes, and

— confers on them the right to use a professional title or designatory letters, or to benefit from a status corresponding to that education and training.

Whenever a Member State grants the recognition referred to in the second subparagraph to an association or organization which satisfies the conditions of that subparagraph, it shall inform the Commission thereof;

(g) regulated education and training: any education and training which:

— is specifically geared to the pursuit of a given profession, and

— comprises a course or courses complemented, where appropriate, by professional training or probationary or professional practice, the structure and level of which are determined by the laws, regulations or administrative provisions of that Member State or which are monitored or approved by the authority designated for that purpose;

(h) professional experience: the actual and lawful pursuit of the profession concerned in a Member State;

(i) adaptation period: the pursuit of a regulated profession in the host Member State under the responsibility of a qualified member of that profession, such period of supervised practice possibly being accompanied by further education and training. This period of supervised practice shall be the subject of an assessment. The detailed rules governing the adaptation period and its assessment shall be laid down by the competent authorities in the host Member State.

The status enjoyed in the host Member State by the person undergoing the period of supervised practice, in particular in the matter of right of residence as well as of obligations, social rights and benefits, allowances and remuneration, shall be established by the competent authorities in that Member State in accordance with applicable Community law;

(j) aptitude test: a test limited to the professional knowledge of the applicant, made by the competent authorities of the host Member State with the aim of assessing the ability of the applicant to pursue a regulated profession in that Member State.

In order to permit this test to be carried out, the competent authorities shall draw up a list of subjects which, on the basis of a comparison of the education and training required in the Member State and that received by the applicant, are not covered by the evidence of education and training possessed by the applicant. These subjects may cover both theoretical knowledge and practical skills required for the pursuit of the profession.

This aptitude test must take account of the fact that the applicant is a qualified professional in the Member State of origin or the Member State from which he comes. It shall cover subjects to be selected from those on the list referred to in the second subparagraph, knowledge of which is essential to the pursuit of the profession in the host Member State. The test may also include knowledge of the professional rules applicable to the activities in question in the host Member State. The detailed application of the aptitude test shall be determined by the competent authorities of that State.

The status in the host Member State of the applicant who wishes to prepare himself for the aptitude test in that State shall be determined by the competent authorities in that State, in accordance with applicable Community law.

CHAPTER II. SCOPE

Article 2 This Directive shall apply to any national of a Member State wishing to pursue a regulated profession in a host Member State in a self-employed capacity or as an employed person.

This Directive shall apply to neither professions which are the subject of a specific Directive establishing arrangements for the mutual recognition of diplomas by Member States, nor activities covered by a Directive listed in Annex A.

The Directives listed in Annex B shall be made applicable to the pursuit as an employed person of the activities covered by those Directives.

CHAPTER III. SYSTEM FOR RECOGNITION WHERE A HOST MEMBER STATE REQUIRES POSSESSION OF A DIPLOMA WITHIN THE MEANING OF THIS DIRECTIVE OR DIRECTIVE 89/48/EEC

Article 3 Without prejudice to Directive 89/48/EEC, where, in a host Member State, the taking up or pursuit of a regulated profession is subject to possession of a diploma, as defined in this Directive or in Directive 89/48/EEC, the competent authority may not, on the grounds of inadequate qualifications, refuse to authorize a national of a Member State to take up or pursue that profession on the same conditions as those which apply to its own nationals:

(a) if the applicant holds the diploma, as defined in this Directive or in Directive 89/48/EEC, required in another Member State for the taking up or pursuit of the profession in question in its territory, such diploma having been awarded in a Member State; or

(b) if the applicant has pursued the profession in question full-time for two years, or for an equivalent period on a part-time basis, during the previous 10 years in another Member State which does not regulate that profession within the meaning of either Article 1(e) and the first subparagraph of Article 1(f) of this Directive or Article 1(c) and the first subparagraph of Article 1(d) of Directive 89/48/EEC, and possesses evidence of education and training which:

— has been awarded by a competent authority in a Member State, designated in accordance with the laws, regulations or administrative provisions of that State, and

— either shows that the holder has successfully completed a post-secondary course, other than that referred to in the second indent of Article 1 (a) of Directive 89/48/EEC, of at least one year's duration, or of equivalent duration on a part-time basis, one of the conditions of entry of which is, as a general rule, the successful completion of the secondary course required to obtain entry to university or higher education, as well as any professional training which is an integral part of that post-secondary course,

— or attests to regulated education and training referred to in Annex D, and

— has prepared the holder for the pursuit of his profession.

However, the two years' professional experience referred to above may not be required where the evidence of education and training held by the applicant and referred to in this point is awarded on completion of regulated education and training.

The following shall be treated in the same way as the evidence of education and training referred to in the first subparagraph of this point: any evidence of education and training or any set of such evidence awarded by a competent authority in a Member State if it is awarded on the completion of education and training received in the Community and is recognized by that Member State as being of an equivalent level, provided that the other Member States and the Commission have been notified of this recognition.

By way of derogation from the first subparagraph of this Article, the host Member State is not required to apply this Article where the taking up or pursuit of a regulated profession is subject in its country to possession of a diploma as defined in Directive 89/48/EEC, one of the conditions for the issue of which shall be the completion of a post-secondary course of more than four years duration.

Article 4 1. Notwithstanding Article 3, the host Member State may also require the applicant:

(a) to provide evidence of professional experience, where the duration of the education and training adduced in support of his application, as laid down in points (a) and (b) of the first subparagraph of Article 3, is at least one year less than that required in the host Member State. In this event, the period of professional experience required may not exceed:

— twice the shortfall in duration of education and training where the shortfall relates to a post-secondary course and/or to a period of probationary practice carried out under the control of a supervising professional person and ending with an examination,

— the shortfall where the shortfall relates to professional practice acquired with the assistance of a qualified member of the profession concerned.

In the case of diplomas within the meaning of the second subparagraph of Article 1(a), the duration of education and training recognized as being of an equivalent level shall be determined as for the education and training defined in the first subparagraph of Article 1(a).

When these provisions are applied, account must be taken of the professional experience referred to in point (b) of the first subparagraph of Article 3.

In any event, the professional experience required may not exceed four years. Professional experience may not, however, be required of an applicant holding a diploma attesting to a post-secondary course as referred to in the second indent of Article 1(a) or a diploma as defined in Article 1(a) of Directive 89/48/EEC who wishes to pursue his profession in a host Member State which requires the possession of a diploma attesting to one of the courses of education and training as referred to in Annex C.

(b) to complete an adaptation period not exceeding three years or take an aptitude test where:

— the theoretical and/or practical matters covered by the education and training which he has received as laid down in points (a) or (b) of the first subparagraph of Article 3 differ substantially from those covered by the diploma, as defined in this Directive or in Directive 89/48/EEC, required in the host Member State, or

— in the case referred to in point (a) of the first subparagraph of Article 3, the profession regulated in the host Member State comprises one or more regulated professional activities which do not form part of the profession regulated in the Member State from which the applicant originates or comes and that difference corresponds to specific education and training required in the host Member State and covers theoretical and/or practical matters which differ substantially from those covered by the diploma, as defined in this Directive or in Directive 89/48/EEC, adduced by the applicant, or

— in the case referred to in point (b) of the first subparagraph of Article 3, the profession regulated in the host Member State comprises one or more regulated professional activities which do not form part of the profession pursued by the applicant in the Member State from which he originates or comes, and that difference corresponds to specific education and training required in the host Member State and covers theoretical and/or practical matters which differ substantially from those covered by the evidence of education and training adduced by the applicant.

Should the host Member State make use of this possibility, it must give the applicant the right to choose between an adaptation period and an aptitude test. Where the host Member State, which requires a diploma as defined in

Directive 89/48/EEC or in this Directive, intends to introduce derogations from an applicant's right to choose, the procedure laid down in Article 14 shall apply.

By way of derogation from the second subparagraph of this point, the host Member State may reserve the right to choose between the adaptation period and the aptitude test if

— a profession is involved the pursuit of which requires a precise knowledge of national law and in respect of which the provision of advice and/or assistance concerning national law is an essential and constant feature of the professional activity, or

— where the host Member State makes access to the profession or its pursuit subject to the possession of a diploma as defined in Directive 89/48/EEC, one of the conditions for the award of which is the completion of a post-secondary course of more than three years' duration or an equivalent period on a part-time basis and the applicant holds either a diploma as defined in this Directive or evidence of education and training within the meaning of point (b) of the first subparagraph of Article 3 and not covered by Article 3(b) of Directive 89/48/EEC.

2. However, the host Member State may not apply the provisions of paragraph 1(a) and (b) cumulatively.

CHAPTER IV. SYSTEM FOR RECOGNITION WHERE A HOST MEMBER STATE REQUIRES POSSESSION OF A DIPLOMA AND THE APPLICANT IS THE HOLDER OF A CERTIFICATE OR HAS RECEIVED CORRESPONDING EDUCATION AND TRAINING

Article 5　Where, in a host Member State, the taking up or pursuit of a regulated profession is subject to possession of a diploma, the competent authority may not, on the grounds of inadequate qualifications, refuse to authorize a national of a Member State to take up or pursue that profession on the same conditions as those which apply to its own nationals:

(a) if the applicant holds the certificate required in another Member State for the taking up or pursuit of the same profession in its territory, such certificate having been awarded in a Member State; or

(b) if the applicant has pursued the same profession full-time for two years during the previous 10 years in another Member State which does not regulate that profession, within the meaning of Article 1(e) and the first subparagraph of Article 1(f), and possesses evidence of education and training:

— which was been awarded by a competent authority in a Member State, designated in accordance with the laws, regulations or administrative provisions of that State, and

— which shows that the holder, after having followed a secondary course, has completed:

either a course of professional education or training other than courses referred to in point (a), provided at an educational or training establishment or on the job, or in combination at an educational or training establishment and on the job and complemented, where appropriate, by the probationary or professional practice which is an integral part of that training course, or the probationary or professional practice which is an integral part of that secondary course, or

— which shows that the holder, after having followed a secondary course of a technical or vocational nature has completed, where necessary,
either a course of professional education or training as referred to in the previous indent,
or the period of probationary or professional practice which is an integral part of that secondary course of a technical or vocational nature and

— which has prepared the holder for the pursuit of this profession.

However, the two years' professional experience referred to above may not be required where the evidence of education and training held by the applicant and referred to in this point is awarded on completion of regulated education and training.

Nevertheless, the host Member State may require the applicant to undergo an adaptation period not exceeding three years or take an aptitude test. The host Member State must give the applicant the right to choose between an adaptation period and an aptitude test.

Where the host Member State intends to introduce derogations from an applicant's right to choose, the procedure laid down in Article 14 shall apply.

CHAPTER V. SYSTEM FOR RECOGNITION WHERE A HOST MEMBER STATE
REQUIRES POSSESSION OF A CERTIFICATE

Article 6   Where, in the host Member State, the taking up or pursuit of a regulated profession is subject to possession of a certificate, the competent authority may not, on the grounds of inadequate qualifications, refuse to authorize a national of a Member State to take up or pursue that profession on the same conditions as those which apply to its own nationals:

(a) if the applicant holds the diploma, as defined in this Directive or in Directive 89/48/EEC, or the certificate required in another Member State for the taking up or pursuit of the profession in question in its territory, such diploma having been awarded in a Member State; or

(b) if the applicant has pursued the profession in question full-time for two years or for an equivalent period on a part-time basis during the previous 10 years in another Member State which does not regulate that profession, within the meaning of Article 1(e) and the first subparagraph of Article 1(f), and possesses evidence of education and training:

— which has been awarded by a competent authority in a Member State, designated in accordance with the laws, regulations or administrative provisions of that State, and

— which shows that the holder has successfully completed a post-secondary course other than that referred to in the second indent of Article 1(a) of Directive 89/48/EEC, of at least one year's duration or of equivalent duration on a part-time basis, one of the conditions of entry of which is, as a general rule, the completion of the secondary course required to obtain entry to university or higher education, as well as any professional training which is an integral part of that post-secondary course, or

— which shows that the holder, after having followed a secondary course, has completed:
either a course of education or training for a profession other than courses referred to in point (a), provided at an educational establishment or on the job, or in combination at an educational establishment and on the job and complemented, where appropriate, by the probationary or professional practice which is an integral part of that training course,
or the probationary or professional practice which is an integral part of that secondary course, or

— which shows that the holder, after having followed a secondary course of a technical or vocational nature has completed, where necessary,
either a course of education or training for a profession as referred to in the previous indent,
or the period of probationary or professional practice which is an integral part of that secondary course of a technical or vocational nature and

— which has prepared the holder for the pursuit of this profession.

However, the two years' professional experience referred to above may not be required where the evidence of education and training held by the applicant and referred to in this point is awarded on completion or regulated education and training;

(c) if the applicant who does not hold any diploma, certificate or other evidence of education and training within the meaning of Article 3 (b) or of point (b) of this Article has pursued the profession in question full-time for three consecutive years, or for an equivalent period on a part-time basis, during the previous 10 years in another Member State which does not regulate that profession within the meaning of Article 1(e) and the first subparagraph of Article 1(f).

The following shall be treated in the same way as the evidence of education and training referred to under (b) in the first subparagraph: any evidence of education and training or any set of such evidence awarded by a competent authority in a Member State if it is awarded on the completion of education and training received in the Community and is recognized by that Member State as being of an equivalent level, provided that the other Member States and the Commission have been notified of this recognition.

Article 7   Without prejudice to Article 6, a host Member State may also require the applicant to:

(a) complete an adaptation period not exceeding two years or to take an aptitude test when the education and training which he received in accordance with points (a) or (b) of the first subparagraph of Article 6 relates to theoretical or practical matters differing substantially from those covered by the certificate required in the host Member State, or where there are differences in the fields of activity characterized in the host Member State by specific education and training relating to theoretical or practical matters differing substantially from those covered by the applicant's evidence of formal qualifications.

Should the host Member State make use of this possibility, it must give the applicant the right to choose between an adaptation period and an aptitude test. Where the host Member State which requires a certificate intends to introduce derogations as regards an applicant's right to choose, the procedure laid down in Article 14 shall apply;

(b) undergo an adaptation period not exceeding two years or take an aptitude test where, in the instance referred to in point (c) of the first subparagraph of Article 6, he does not hold a diploma, certificate or other evidence of education and training. The host Member State may reserve the right to choose between an adaptation period and an aptitude test.

Chapter VI. Special Systems for Recognition of Other Qualifications

Article 8 Where, in the host Member State, the taking up or pursuit of a regulated profession is subject to possession of

an attestation of competence, the competent authority may not, on the grounds of inadequate qualifications, refuse to authorize a national of a Member State to take up or pursue that profession on the same conditions as those which apply to its own nationals:

(a) if the applicant holds the attestation of competence required in another Member State for the taking up or pursuit of the same profession in its territory, such attestation having been awarded in a Member State; or

(b) if the applicant provides proof of qualifications obtained in other Member States, and giving guarantees, in particular in the matter of health, safety, environmental protection and consumer protection, equivalent to those required by the laws, regulations or administrative provisions of the host Member State.

If the applicant does not provide proof of such an attestation or of such qualifications the laws, regulations or administrative provisions of the host Member State shall apply.

Article 9 Where, in the host Member State, the taking up or pursuit of a regulated profession is subject only to possession of evidence of education attesting to general education at primary or secondary school level, the competent authority may not, on the grounds of inadequate qualifications, refuse to authorize a national of a Member State to take up or pursue that profession on the same conditions as those which apply to its own nationals if the applicant possesses formal qualifications of the corresponding level, awarded in another Member State.

This evidence of formal qualifications must have been awarded by a competent authority in that Member State, designated in accordance with its own laws, regulations or administrative provisions.

Chapter VII. Other Measures to Facilitate the Effective Exercise of the Right of Establishment, Freedom to Provide Services and Freedom of Movement of Employed persons

Article 10 1. Where the competent authority of the host Member State requires of persons wishing to take up a regulated profession proof that they are of good character or repute or that they have not been declared bankrupt, or suspends or prohibits the pursuit of that profession in the event of serious professional misconduct or a criminal offence, that State shall accept as sufficient evidence, in respect of nationals of Member States wishing to pursue that profession in its territory, the production of documents issued by competent authorities in the Member State of origin or the Member State from which the foreign national comes showing that those requirements are met.

Where the competent authorities of the Member State of origin or of the Member State from which the foreign national comes do not issue the documents referred to in the first subparagraph, such documents shall be replaced by a declaration on oath—or, in Member States where there is no provision for declaration on oath, by a solemn declaration—made by the person concerned before a competent judicial or administrative authority or, where appropriate, a notary or qualified professional body of the Member State of origin or the Member State from which the person comes; such authority or notary shall issue written confirmation attesting the authenticity of the declaration on oath or solemn declaration.

2. Where the competent authority of the host Member State requires of nationals of that Member State wishing to take up or pursue a regulated profession a statement of physical of mental health, that authority shall accept as sufficient evidence in this respect the production of the document required in the Member State of origin or the Member State from which the foreign national comes.

Where the Member State of origin or the Member State from which the foreign national comes does not impose any requirements of this nature on those wishing to take up or pursue the profession in question, the host Member State shall accept from such nationals a statement issued by a competent authority in that State corresponding to the statement issued in the host Member State.

3. The competent authority of the host Member State may require that the documents and statements referred to in paragraphs 1 and 2 are presented no more than three months after their date of issue.

4. Where the competent authority of the host Member State requires nationals of that Member State wishing to take up or pursue a regulated profession to take an oath or make solemn declaration and where the form of such oath or declaration cannot be used by nationals of other Member States, that authority shall ensure that an appropriate and equivalent form of oath or declaration is offered to the person concerned.

Article 11   1. The competent authorities of host Member States shall recognize the right of nationals of Member States who fulfil the conditions for the taking up and pursuit of a regulated profession in their territory to use the professional title of the host Member State corresponding to that profession.

2. The competent authority of the host Member State shall recognize the right of nationals of Member States who fulfil the conditions for the taking up and pursuit of a regulated profession in the territory to use their lawful academic title and, where appropriate, the abbreviation thereof deriving from their Member State of origin or the Member State from which they come, in the language of that State. The host Member State may require this title to be followed by the name and location of the establishment or examining board which awarded it.

3. Where a profession is regulated in the host Member State by an association or organization referred to in Article 1 (f), nationals of Member States shall be entitled to use the professional title or designatory letters conferred by that organization or association only on proof of membership.

Where the association or organization makes membership subject to certain qualification requirements, it may apply these to nationals of other Member States who are in possession of a diploma within the meaning of Article 1(a), a certificate within the meaning of Article 1(b) or evidence of education and training or qualification within the meaning of point (b) of the first subparagraph of Article 3, point (b) of the first subparagraph of Article 5 or Article 9 in accordance only with this Directive, in particular Articles 3, 4 and 5.

Article 12   1. The host Member State shall accept as means of proof that the conditions laid down in Articles 3 to 9 are satisfied the documents issued by the competent authorities in the Member States, which the person concerned shall submit in support of his application to pursue the profession concerned.

2. The procedure for examining an application to pursue a regulated profession shall be completed as soon as possible and the outcome communicated in a reasoned decision of the competent authority in the host Member State not later than four months after presentation of all the documents relating to the person concerned. A remedy shall be available against this decision or the absence thereof, before a court or tribunal in accordance with the provisions of national law.

CHAPTER VIII. PROCEDURE FOR COORDINATION

Article 13   1. Member States shall designate, within the period provided for in Article 17, the competent authorities empowered to receive the applications and take the decisions referred to in this Directive. They shall communicate this information to the other Member States and to the Commission.

2. Each Member State shall designate a person responsible for coordinating the activities of the authorities referred to in paragraph 1 and shall inform the other Member States and the Commission to that effect. His role shall be to promote uniform application of this Directive to all the professions concerned. This coordinator shall be a member of the coordinating group set up under the aegis of the Commission by Article 9(2) of Directive 89/48/EEC.

The coordinating group set up under the aforementioned provision of Directive 89/48/EEC shall also be required to:

— facilitate the implementation of this Directive,
— collect all useful information for its application in the Member States, particularly information relating to the establishment of an indicative list of regulated professions and to the disparities between the qualifications awarded in the Member States with a view to assisting the competent authorities of the Member States in their task of assessing whether substantial differences exist.

The group may be consulted by the Commission on any changes to the existing system which may be contemplated.

3. The Member States shall take measures to provide the necessary information on the recognition of diplomas and certificates and on other conditions governing the taking up of the regulated professions within the framework of this Directive. To carry out this task they may call upon the existing information networks and, where appropriate, the relevant professional associations or organizations. The Commission shall take the necessary initiatives to ensure the development and coordination of the communication of the necessary information.

Chapter IX. Procedure for Derogating from the Right to Choose Between Adaptation Period and Aptitude Test

Article 14   1. If, pursuant to the second sentence of the second subparagraph of Article 4(1)(b), the third subparagraph of Article 5, or the second sentence of the second subparagraph of Article 7(a), a Member State proposes not to grant applicants the right to choose between an adaptation period and an aptitude test, it shall immediately communicate to the Commission the corresponding draft provision. It shall at the same time notify the Commission of the grounds which make the enactment of such a provision necessary.

The Commission shall immediately notify the other Member States of any draft which it has received; it may also consult the coordinating group referred to in Article 13(2) on the draft.

2. Without prejudice to the possibility for the Commission and the other Member States to make comments on the draft, the Member State may adopt the provision only if the Commission has not taken a decision to the contrary within three months.

3. At the request of a Member State or the Commission, Member States shall communicate to them, without delay, the definitive text of any provision arising from the application of this Article.

[final provisions and annexes omitted]

Council Directive of 22 March 1977 to facilitate the effective exercise by lawyers of freedom to provide services (77/249/EEC)[13]

The Council of the European Communities,

HAVING REGARD to the Treaty establishing the European Economic Community, and in particular Arts. 57 and 66 thereof,

HAVING REGARD to the proposal from the Commission,

HAVING REGARD to the opinion of the European Parliament,

HAVING REGARD to the opinion of the Economic and Social Committee,

Whereas, pursuant to the Treaty, any restriction on the provision of services which is based on nationality or on conditions of residence has been prohibited since the end of the transitional period;

Whereas this Directive deals only with measures to facilitate the effective pursuit of the activities of lawyers by way of provision of services; whereas more detailed measures will be necessary to facilitate the effective exercise of the right of establishment;

Whereas if lawyers are to exercise effectively the freedom to provide services host Member States must recognise as lawyers those persons practising the profession in the various Member States;

---

[13] OJ 1977 L 78/17.

Whereas, since this Directive solely concerns provision of services and does not contain provisions on the mutual recognition of diplomas, a person to whom the Directive applies must adopt the professional title used in the Member State in which he is established, hereinafter referred to as 'the Member State from which he comes',

HAS ADOPTED this Directive:

Article 1   1. This Directive shall apply, within the limits and under the conditions laid down herein, to the activities of lawyers pursued by way of provision of services.

Notwithstanding anything contained in this Directive, Member States may reserve to prescribed categories of lawyers the preparation of formal documents for obtaining title to administer estates of deceased persons, and the drafting of formal documents creating or transferring interests in land.

2. 'Lawyer' means any person entitled to pursue his professional activities under one of the following designations:

Belgium:	Avocat—Advocaat
Denmark:	Advokat
Germany:	Rechtsanwalt
Greece:	[dikigoros]
France:	Avocat
Ireland:	Barrister
	Solicitor
Italy:	Avvocato
Luxembourg:	Avocat-avoué
Netherlands:	Advocaat
Portugal:	Advogado
Spain:	Abogado
United Kingdom:	Advocate
	Barrister
	Solicitor.
Austria:	Rechtsanwalt
Finland:	Asianajaja/Advokat
Sweden:	Advokat

Article 2   Each Member State shall recognise as a lawyer for the purpose of pursuing the activities specified in Art. 1(1) any person listed in paragraph 2 of that Article.

Article 3   A person referred to in Art. 1 shall adopt the professional title used in the Member State from which he comes, expressed in the language or one of the languages, of that State, with an indication of the professional organisation by which he is authorised to practise or the court of law before which he is entitled to practise pursuant to the laws of that State.

Article 4   1. Activities relating to the representation of a client in legal proceedings or before public authorities shall be pursued in each host Member State under the conditions laid down for lawyers established in that State, with the exception of any conditions requiring residence, or registration with a professional organisation, in that State.

2. A lawyer pursuing these activities shall observe the rules of professional conduct of the host Member State, without prejudice to his obligations in the Member State from which he comes.

3. When these activities are pursued in the United Kingdom, 'rules of professional conduct of the host Member State' means the rules of professional conduct applicable to solicitors, where such activities are not reserved for barristers and advocates. Otherwise the rules of professional conduct applicable to the latter shall apply. However, barristers from Ireland shall always be subject to the rules of professional conduct applicable in the United Kingdom to barristers and advocates.

When these activities are pursued in Ireland 'rules of professional conduct of the host Member State' means, in so far as they govern the oral presentation of a case in court, the rules of professional conduct applicable to barristers. In all other cases the rules of professional conduct applicable to solicitors shall apply. However, barristers and advocates from the United Kingdom shall always be subject to the rules of professional conduct applicable in Irelands to barristers.

4. A lawyer pursuing activities other than those referred to in paragraph 1 shall remain subject to the conditions and rules of professional conduct of the Member State from which he comes without prejudice to respect for the rules, whatever their source, which govern the profession in the host Member State, especially those concerning the incompatibility of the exercise of the activities of a lawyer with the exercise of other activities in that State, professional secrecy, relations with other lawyers, the prohibition on the same lawyer acting for parties with mutually conflicting interests, and publicity. The latter rules are applicable only if they are capable of being observed by a lawyer who is not established in the host Member State and to the extent to which their observance is objectively justified to ensure, in that State, the proper exercise of a lawyer's activities, the standing of the profession and respect for the rules concerning incompatibility.

Article 5 For the pursuit of activities relating to the representation of a client in legal proceedings, a Member State may require lawyers to whom Art. 1 applies:

— to be introduced, in accordance with local rules or customs, to the presiding judge and, where appropriate, to the President of the relevant Bar in the host Member State;
— to work in conjunction with a lawyer who practises before the judicial authority in question and who would, where necessary, be answerable to that authority, or with an 'avoué' or 'procuratore' practising before it.

Article 6 Any Member State may exclude lawyers who are in the salaried employment of a public or private undertaking from pursuing activities relating to the representation of that undertaking in legal proceedings in so far as lawyers established in that State are not permitted to pursue those activities.

Article 7 1. The competent authority of the host Member State may request the person providing the services to establish his qualifications as a lawyer.

2. In the event of non-compliance with the obligations referred to in Art. 4 and in force in the host Member State, the competent authority of the latter shall determine in accordance with its own rules and procedures the consequences of such non-compliance, and to this end may obtain any appropriate professional informa-

tion concerning the person providing services. It shall notify the competent authority of the Member State from which the person comes of any decision taken. Such exchanges shall not affect the confidential nature of the information supplied.

[*final provisions omitted*]

European Parliament and Council Directive of 16 February 1998 to Facilitate Practice of the Profession of Lawyer on a Permanent Basis in a Member State Other than that in which the Qualification was Obtained (98/5/EC)[14]

The European Parliament and the Council of the European Union,

HAVING REGARD to the Treaty establishing the European Community, and in particular Article 49, Article 57(1) and the first and third sentences of Article 57(2) thereof,

[*recitals omitted*]

(1) Whereas, pursuant to Article 7a of the Treaty, the internal market is to comprise an area without internal frontiers; whereas, pursuant to Article 3(c) of the Treaty, the abolition, as between Member States, of obstacles to freedom of movement for persons and services constitutes one of the objectives of the Community; whereas, for nationals of the Member States, this means among other things the possibility of practising a profession, whether in a self-employed or a salaried capacity, in a Member State other than that in which they obtained their professional qualifications;

(2) Whereas, pursuant to Council Directive 89/48/EEC of 21 December 1988 on a general system for the recognition of higher-education diplomas awarded on completion of professional education and training of at least three years' duration, a lawyer who is fully qualified in one Member State may already ask to have his diploma recognised with a view to establishing himself in another Member State in order to practise the profession of lawyer there under the professional title used in that State; whereas the objective of Directive 89/48/EEC is to ensure that a lawyer is integrated into the profession in the host Member State, and the Directive seeks neither to modify the rules regulating the profession in that State nor to remove such a lawyer from the ambit of those rules;

(3) Whereas while some lawyers may become quickly integrated into the profession in the host Member State, inter alia by passing an aptitude test as provided for in Directive 89/48/EEC, other fully qualified lawyers should be able to achieve such integration after a certain period of professional practice in the host Member State under their home-country professional titles or else continue to practise under their home-country professional titles;

(4) Whereas at the end of that period the lawyer should be able to integrate into the profession in the host Member States after verification that the possesses professional experience in that Member State;

14 OJ 1998 L 77/36.

(5) Whereas action along these lines is justified at Community level not only because, compared with the general system for the recognition of diplomas, it provides lawyers with an easier means whereby they can integrate into the profession in a host Member State, but also because, by enabling lawyers to practise under their home-country professional titles on a permanent basis in a host Member State, it meets the needs of consumers of legal services who, owing to the increasing trade flows resulting, in particular, from the internal market, seek advice when carrying out cross-border transactions in which international law, Community law and domestic laws often overlap;

(6) Whereas action is also justified at Community level because only a few Member States already permit in their territory the pursuit of activities of lawyers, otherwise than by way of provision of services, by lawyers from other Member States practising under their home-country professional titles; whereas, however, in the Member States where this possibility exists, the practical details concerning, for example, the area of activity and the obligation to register with the competent authorities differ considerably; whereas such a diversity of situations leads to inequalities and distortions in competition between lawyers from the Member States and practice of the profession, otherwise than by way of provision of services, by lawyers practising under their home-country professional titles is capable of resolving these difficulties and of affording the same opportunities to lawyers and consumers of legal services in all Member States;

(7) Whereas, in keeping with its objective, this Directive does not lay down any rules concerning purely domestic situations, and where it does affect national rules regulating the legal profession it does so no more than is necessary to achieve its purpose effectively; whereas it is without prejudice in particular to national legislation governing access to and practice of the profession of lawyer under the professional title used in the host Member State;

(8) Whereas lawyers covered by the Directive should be required to register with the competent authority in the host Member State in order that that authority may ensure that they comply with the rules of professional conduct in force in that State; whereas the effect of such registration as regards the jurisdictions in which, and the levels and types of court before which, lawyers may practise is determined by the law applicable to lawyers in the host Member State;

(9) Whereas lawyers who are not integrated into the profession in the host Member State should practise in that State under their home-country professional titles so as to ensure that consumers are properly informed and to distinguish between such lawyers and lawyers from the host Member State practising under the professional title used there;

(10) Whereas lawyers covered by this Directive should be permitted to give legal advice in particular on the law of their home Member States, on Community law, on international law and on the law of the host Member State; whereas this is already allowed as regards the provision of services under Council Directive 77/249/EEC of 22 March 1977 to facilitate the effective excercise by lawyers of freedom to provide services ; whereas, however, provision should be made, as in Directive 77/249/EEC, for the option of excluding from the activities of lawyers practising under their home-country professional titles in the United Kingdom and

Ireland the preparation of certain formal documents in the conveyancing and probate spheres; whereas this Directive in no way affects the provisions under which, in every Member State, certain activities are reserved for professions other than the legal profession; whereas the provision in Directive 77/249/EEC concerning the possibility of the host Member State to require a lawyer practising under his home-country professional title to work in conjunction with a local lawyer when representing or defending a client in legal proceedings should also be incorporated in this Directive; whereas that requirement must be interpreted in the light of the case law of the Court of Justice of the European Communities, in particular its judgment of 25 February 1988 in Case 427/85, *Commission v. Germany*;

(11) Whereas to ensure the smooth operation of the justice system Member States should be allowed, by means of specific rules, to reserve access to their highest courts to specialist lawyers, without hindering the integration of Member States' lawyers fulfilling the necessary requirements;

(12) Whereas a lawyer registered under his home-country professional title in the host Member State must remain registered with the competent authority in his home Member State if he is to retain his status of lawyer and be covered by this Directive; whereas for that reason close collaboration between the competent authorities is indispensable, in particular in connection with any disciplinary proceedings;

(13) Whereas lawyers covered by this Directive, whether salaried or self-employed in their home Member States, may practise as salaried lawyers in the host Member State, where that Member State offers that possibility to its own lawyers;

(14) Whereas the purpose pursued by this Directive in enabling lawyers to practise in another Member State under their home-country professional titles is also to make it easier for them to obtain the professional title of that host Member State; whereas under Articles 48 and 52 of the Treaty as interpreted by the Court of Justice the host Member State must take into consideration any professional experience gained in its territory; whereas after effectively and regularly pursuing in the host Member State an activity in the law of that State including Community law for a period of three years, a lawyer may reasonably be assumed to have gained the aptitude necessary to become fully integrated into the legal profession there; whereas at the end of that period the lawyer who can, subject to verification, furnish evidence of his professional competence in the host Member State should be able to obtain the professional title of that Member State; whereas if the period of effective and regular professional activity of at least three years includes a shorter period of practice in the law of the host Member State, the authority shall also take into consideration any other knowledge of that State's law, which it may verify during an interview; whereas if evidence of fulfilment of these conditions is not provided, the decision taken by the competent authority of the host State not to grant the State's professional title under the facilitation arrangements linked to those conditions must be substantiated and subject to appeal under national law;

(15) Whereas, for economic and professional reasons, the growing tendency for lawyers in the Community to practise jointly, including in the form of associations, has become a reality; whereas the fact that lawyers belong to a grouping in their home Member State should not be used as a pretext to prevent or deter them from establishing themselves in the host Member State; whereas Member States should

be allowed, however, to take appropriate measures with the legitimate aim of safe-guarding the profession's independence; whereas certain guarantees should be provided in those Member States which permit joint practice,

[*footnotes omitted*]

HAVE ADOPTED this Directive:

Article 1   Object, scope and definitions   1. The purpose of this Directive is to facilitate practice of the profession of lawyer on a permanent basis in a self-employed or salaried capacity in a Member State other than that in which the professional qualification was obtained.

2. For the purposes of this Directive:

(a) 'lawyer' means any person who is a national of a Member State and who is authorised to pursue his professional activities under one of the following professional titles:

Belgium	Avocat/Advocaat/Rechtsanwalt
Denmark	Advokat
Germany	Rechtsanwalt
Greece	Δικηγόρος [dikigoros]
Spain	Abogado/Advocat/Avogado/Abokatu
France	Avocat
Ireland	Barrister/Solicitor
Italy	Avvocato
Luxembourg	Avocat
Netherlands	Advocaat
Austria	Rechtsanwalt
Portugal	Advogado
Finland	Asianajaja/Advokat
Sweden	Advokat
United Kingdom	Advocate/Barrister/Solicitor

(b) 'home Member State' means the Member State in which a lawyer acquired the right to use one of the professional titles referred to in (a) before practising the profession of lawyer in another Member State;

(c) 'host Member State' means the Member State in which a lawyer practises pursuant to this Directive;

(d) 'home-country professional title' means the professional title used in the Member State in which a lawyer acquired the right to use that title before practising the profession of lawyer in the host Member State;

(e) 'grouping' means any entity, with or without legal personality, formed under the law of a Member State, within which lawyers pursue their professional activities jointly under a joint name;

(f) 'relevant professional title' or 'relevant profession' means the professional title or profession governed by the competent authority with whom a lawyer has registered under Article 3, and 'competent authority' means that authority.

3. This Directive shall apply both to lawyers practising in a self-employed capacity and to lawyers practising in a salarial capacity in the home Member State and, subject to Article 8, in the host Member State.

4. Practice of the profession of lawyer within the meaning of this Directive shall not include the provision of services, which is covered by Directive 77/249/EEC.

Article 2   Right to practise under the home-country professional title   Any lawyer shall be entitled to pursue on a permanent basis, in any other Member State under his home-country professional title, the activities specified in Article 5.

Integration into the profession of lawyer in the host Member State shall be subject to Article 10.

Article 3   Registration with the competent authority   1. A lawyer who wishes to practise in a Member State other than that in which he obtained his professional qualification shall register with the competent authority in that State.

2. The competent authority in the host Member State shall register the lawyer upon presentation of a certificate attesting to his registration with the competent authority in the home Member State. It may require that, when presented by the competent authority of the home Member State, the certificate be not more than three months old. It shall inform the competent authority in the home Member State of the registration.

3. For the purpose of applying paragraph 1:

—   in the United Kingdom and Ireland, lawyers practising under a professional title other than those used in the United Kingdom or Ireland shall register either with the authority responsible for the profession of barrister or advocate or with the authority responsible for the profession of solicitor,
—   in the United Kingdom, the authority responsible for a barrister from Ireland shall be that responsible for the profession of barrister or advocate, and the authority responsible for a solicitor from Ireland shall be that responsible for the profession of solicitor,
—   in Ireland, the authority responsible for a barrister or an advocate from the United Kingdom shall be that responsible for the profession of barrister, and the authority responsible for a solicitor from the United Kingdom shall be that responsible for the profession of solicitor.

4. Where the relevant competent authority in a host Member State publishes the names of lawyers registered with it, it shall also publish the names of lawyers registered pursuant to this Directive.

Article 4   Practice under the home-country professional title   1. A lawyer practising in a host Member State under his home-country professional title shall do so under that title, which must be expressed in the official language or one of the official languages of his home Member State, in an intelligible manner and in such a way as to avoid confusion with the professional title of the host Member State.

2. For the purpose of applying paragraph 1, a host Member State may require a lawyer practising under his home-country professional title to indicate the professional body of which he is a member in his home Member State or the judicial authority before which he is entitled to practise pursuant to the laws of his home Member State. A host Member State may also require a lawyer practising under his home-country professional title to include a reference to his registration with the competent authority in that State.

Article 5 Area of activity 1. Subject to paragraphs 2 and 3, a lawyer practising under his home-country professional title carries on the same professional activities as a lawyer practising under the relevant professional title used in the host Member State and may, inter alia, give advice on the law of his home Member State, on Community law, on international law and on the law of the host Member State. He shall in any event comply with the rules of procedure applicable in the national courts.

2. Member States which authorise in their territory a prescribed category of lawyers to prepare deeds for obtaining title to administer estates of deceased persons and for creating or transferring interests in land which, in other Member States, are reserved for professions other than that of lawyer may exclude from such activities lawyers practising under a home-country professional title conferred in one of the latter Member States.

3. For the pursuit of activities relating to the representation or defence of a client in legal proceedings and insofar as the law of the host Member State reserves such activities to lawyers practising under the professional title of that State, the latter may require lawyers practising under their home-country professional titles to work in conjunction with a lawyer who practises before the judicial authority in question and who would, where necessary, be answerable to that authority or with an 'avoué' practising before it.

 Nevertheless, in order to ensure the smooth operation of the justice system, Member States may lay down specific rules for access to supreme courts, such as the use of specialist lawyers.

Article 6 Rules of professional conduct applicable 1. Irrespective of the rules of professional conduct to which he is subject in his home Member State, a lawyer practising under his home-country professional title shall be subject to the same rules of professional conduct as lawyers practising under the relevant professional title of the host Member State in respect of all the activities he pursues in its territory.

2. Lawyers practising under their home-country professional titles shall be granted appropriate representation in the professional associations of the host Member State. Such representation shall involve at least the right to vote in elections to those associations' governing bodies.

3. The host Member State may require a lawyer practising under his home-country professional title either to take out professional indemnity insurance or to become a member of a professional guarantee fund in accordance with the rules which that State lays down for professional activities pursued in its territory. Nevertheless, a lawyer practising under his home-country professional title shall be exempted from that requirement if he can prove that he is covered by insurance taken out or a guarantee provided in accordance with the rules of his home Member State, insofar as such insurance or guarantee is equivalent in terms of the conditions and extent of cover. Where the equivalence is only partial, the competent authority in the host Member State may require that additional insurance or an additional guarantee be contracted to cover the elements which are not already covered by the insurance or guarantee contracted in accordance with the rules of the home Member State.

Article 7 Disciplinary proceedings 1. In the event of failure by a lawyer practising under his home-country professional title to fulfil the obligations in force in the host Member State, the rules of procedure, penalties and remedies provided for in the host Member State shall apply.

2. Before initiating disciplinary proceedings against a lawyer practising under his home-country professional title, the competent authority in the host Member State shall inform the competent authority in the home Member State as soon as possible, furnishing it with all the relevant details.

The first subparagraph shall apply *mutatis mutandis* where disciplinary proceedings are initiated by the competent authority of the home Member State, which shall inform the competent authority of the host Member State(s) accordingly.

3. Without prejudice to the decision-making power of the competent authority in the host Member State, that authority shall cooperate throughout the disciplinary proceedings with the competent authority in the home Member State. In particular, the host Member State shall take the measures necessary to ensure that the competent authority in the home Member State can make submissions to the bodies responsible for hearing any appeal.

4. The competent authority in the home Member State shall decide what action to take, under its own procedural and substantive rules, in the light of a decision of the competent authority in the host Member State concerning a lawyer practising under his home-country professional title.

5. Although it is not a prerequisite for the decision of the competent authority in the host Member State, the temporary or permanent withdrawal by the competent authority in the home Member State of the authorisation to practise the profession shall automatically lead to the lawyer concerned being temporarily or permanently prohibited from practising under his home-country professional title in the host Member State.

Article 8   Salaried practice   A lawyer registered in a host Member State under his home-country professional title may practise as a salaried lawyer in the employ of another lawyer, an association or firm of lawyers, or a public or private enterprise to the extent that the host Member State so permits for lawyers registered under the professional title used in that State.

Article 9   Statement of reasons and remedies   Decisions not to effect the registration referred to in Article 3 or to cancel such registration and decisions imposing disciplinary measures shall state the reasons on which they are based.

A remedy shall be available against such decisions before a court or tribunal in accordance with the provisions of domestic law.

Article 10   Like treatment as a lawyer of the host Member State   1. A lawyer practising under his home-country professional title who has effectively and regularly pursued for a period of at least three years an activity in the host Member State in the law of that State including Community law shall, with a view to gaining admission to the profession of lawyer in the host Member State, be exempted from the conditions set out in Article 4(1)(b) of Directive 89/48/EEC. 'Effective and regular pursuit' means actual exercise of the activity without any interruption other than that resulting from the events of everyday life.

It shall be for the lawyer concerned to furnish the competent authority in the host Member State with proof of such effective regular pursuit for a period of at least three years of an activity in the law of the host Member State. To that end:

(a) the lawyer shall provide the competent authority in the host Member State with any relevant information and documentation, notably on the number of matters he has dealt with and their nature;

(b) the competent authority of the host Member State may verify the effective and regular nature of the activity pursued and may, if need be, request the lawyer to provide, orally or in writing, clarification of or further details on the information and documentation mentioned in point (a).

Reasons shall be given for a decision by the competent authority in the host Member State not to grant an exemption where proof is not provided that the requirements laid down in the first subparagraph have been fulfilled, and the decision shall be subject to appeal under domestic law.

2. A lawyer practising under his home-country professional title in a host Member State may, at any time, apply to have his diploma recognised in accordance with Directive 89/48/EEC with a view to gaining admission to the profession of lawyer in the host Member State and practising it under the professional title corresponding to the profession in that Member State.

3. A lawyer practising under his home-country professional title who has effectively and regularly pursued a professional activity in the host Member State for a period of at least three years but for a lesser period in the law of that Member State may obtain from the competent authority of that State admission to the profession of lawyer in the host Member State and the right to practise it under the professional title corresponding to the profession in that Member State, without having to meet the conditions referred to in Article 4(1)(b) of Directive 89/48/EEC, under the conditions and in accordance with the procedures set out below:

(a) The competent authority of the host Member State shall take into account the effective and regular professional activity pursued during the abovementioned period and any knowledge and professional experience of the law of the host Member State, and any attendance at lectures or seminars on the law of the host Member State, including the rules regulating professional practice and conduct.

(b) The lawyer shall provide the competent authority of the host Member State with any relevant information and documentation, in particular on the matters he has dealt with. Assessment of the lawyer's effective and regular activity in the host Member State and assessment of his capacity to continue the activity he has pursued there shall be carried out by means of an interview with the competent authority of the host Member State in order to verify the regular and effective nature of the activity pursued.

Reasons shall be given for a decision by the competent authority in the host Member State not to grant authorisation where proof is not provided that the requirements laid down in the first subparagraph have been fulfilled, and the decision shall be subject to appeal under domestic law.

4. The competent authority of the host Member State may, by reasoned decision subject to appeal under domestic law, refuse to allow the lawyer the benefit of the provisions of this Article if it considers that this would be against public policy, in a particular because of disciplinary proceedings, complaints or incidents of any kind.

5. The representatives of the competent authority entrusted with consideration of the application shall preserve the confidentiality of any information received.

6. A lawyer who gains admission to the profession of lawyer in the host Member State in accordance with paragraphs 1, 2 and 3 shall be entitled to use his home-country professional title, expressed in the official language or one of the official languages of his home Member State, alongside the professional title corresponding to the profession of lawyer in the host Member State.

Article 11   Joint practice   Where joint practise is authorised in respect of lawyers carrying on their activities under the relevant professional title in the host Member State, the following provisions shall apply in respect of lawyers wishing to carry on activities under that title or registering with the competent authority:

(1) One or more lawyers who belong to the same grouping in their home Member State and who practise under their home-country professional title in a host Member State may pursue their professional activities in a branch or agency of their grouping in the host Member State. However, where the fundamental rules governing that grouping in the home Member State are incompatible with the fundamental rules laid down by law, regulation or administrative action in the host Member State, the latter rules shall prevail insofar as compliance therewith is justified by the public interest in protecting clients and third parties.

(2) Each Member State shall afford two or more lawyers from the same grouping or the same home Member State who practise in its territory under their home-country professional titles access to a form of joint practice. If the host Member State gives its lawyers a choice between several forms of joint practice, those same forms shall also be made available to the aforementioned lawyers. The manner in which such lawyers practise jointly in the host Member State shall be governed by the laws, regulations and administrative provisions of that State.

(3) The host Member State shall take the measures necessary to permit joint practice also between:
  (a) several lawyers from different Member States practising under their home-country professional titles;
  (b) one or more lawyers covered by point (a) and one or more lawyers from the host Member State.

  The manner in which such lawyers practice jointly in the host Member State shall be governed by the laws, regulations and administrative provisions of that State.

(4) A lawyer who wishes to practise under his home-country professional title shall inform the competent authority in the host Member State of the fact that he is a member of a grouping in his home Member State and furnish any relevant information on that grouping.

(5) Notwithstanding points 1 to 4, a host Member State, insofar as it prohibits lawyers practising under its own relevant professional title from practising the profession of lawyer within a grouping in which some persons are not members of the profession, may refuse to allow a lawyer registered under his home-country professional title to practice in its territory in his capacity as a member of his grouping. The grouping is deemed to include persons who are not members of the profession if

— the capital of the grouping is held entirely or partly, or
— the name under which it practises is used, or
— the decision-making power in that grouping is exercised, de facto or de jure,

by persons who do not have the status of lawyer within the meaning of Article 1(2).

Where the fundamental rules governing a grouping of lawyers in the home Member State are incompatible with the rules in force in the host Member State or with the provisions of the first subparagraph, the host Member State may oppose the opening of a branch or agency within its territory without the restrictions laid down in point (1).

Article 12   Name of the grouping   Whatever the manner in which lawyers practise under their home-country professional titles in the host Member State, they may employ the name of any grouping to which they belong in their home Member State.

The host Member State may require that, in addition to the name referred to in the first subparagraph, mention be made of the legal form of the grouping in the home Member State and/or of the names of any members of the grouping practising in the host Member State.

Article 13   Cooperation between the competent authorities in the home and host Member States and confidentiality   In order to facilitate the application of this Directive and to prevent its provisions from being misapplied for the sole purpose of circumventing the rules applicable in the host Member State, the competent authority in the host Member State and the competent authority in the home Member State shall collaborate closely and afford each other mutual assistance.

They shall preserve the confidentiality of the information they exchange.

Article 14   Designation of the competent authorities   Member States shall designate the competent authorities empowered to receive the applications and to take the decisions referred to in this Directive by 14 March 2000. They shall communicate this information to the other Member States and to the Commission.

Article 15   Report by the Commission   Ten years at the latest from the entry into force of this Directive, the Commission shall report to the European Parliament and to the Council on progress in the implementation of the Directive.

After having held all the necessary consultations, it shall on that occasion present its conclusions and any amendments which could be made to the existing system.

Article 16   Implementation   1. Member States shall bring into force the laws, regulations and administrative provisions necessary to comply with this Directive by 14 March 2000. They shall forthwith inform the Commission thereof.

When Member States adopt these measures, they shall contain a reference to this Directive or shall be accompanied by such reference on the occasion of their official publication. The methods of making such reference shall be adopted by Member States.

2. Member States shall communicate to the Commission the texts of the main provisions of domestic law which they adopt in the field covered by this Directive.

[*final provisions omitted*]

Other Rights of Residence

Council Directive of 28 June 1990 on the right of residence for employees and self-employed persons who have ceased their occupational activity
(90/365/EEC)[1]

The Council of the European Communities,

HAVING REGARD to the Treaty establishing the European Economic Community, and in particular Art. 235 thereof,

[recitals omitted]

Whereas Art. 3(c) of the Treaty provides that the activities of the Community shall include, as provided in the Treaty, the abolition, as between Member States, of obstacles to freedom of movement for persons;

Whereas Art. 8a of the Treaty provides that the internal market must be established by 31 December 1992; whereas the internal market comprises an area without internal frontiers in which the free movement of goods, persons, services and capital is ensured, in accordance with the provisions of the Treaty;

Whereas Arts. 48 and 52 of the Treaty provide for freedom of movement for workers and self-employed persons, which entails the right of residence in the Member States in which they pursue their occupational activity; whereas it is desirable that this right of residence also be granted to persons who have ceased their occupational activity even if they have not exercise their right to freedom of movement during their working life;

Whereas beneficiaries of the right of residence must not become an unreasonable burden on the public finances of the host Member State;

Whereas under Art. 10 of Regulation (EEC) No. 1408/71,[2] as amended by Regulation (EEC) No. 1390/81,[3] recipients of invalidity or old age cash benefits or pensions for accidents at work or occupational diseases are entitled to continue to receive these benefits and pensions even if they reside in the territory of a Member State other than that in which the institution responsible for payment is situated;

Whereas this right can only be genuinely exercised if it is also granted to members of the family;

Whereas the beneficiaries of this Directive should be covered by administrative arrangements similar to those laid down in particular by Directive 68/360/EEC[4] and Directive 64/221/EEC;[5]

Whereas the Treaty does not provide, for the action concerned, powers other than those of Art. 235,

---

[1] OJ 1990 L 180/28.
[2] OJ Sp. Ed. 1971 (II), 416. As amended and up-dated (and consolidated) by Regulation 2001/83, OJ 1983 L 230/6, and subsequently amended.
[3] OJ 1981 L 143/1.   [4] OJ Sp. Ed. 1968 (II), above at p. 143.
[5] OJ Sp. Ed. 1963–64, 117, above at p. 150.

HAS ADOPTED this Directive:

Article 1   1. Member States shall grant the right of residence to nationals of Member States who have pursued an activity as an employee or self-employed person and to members of their families as defined in paragraph 2, provided that they are recipients of an invalidity or early retirement pension, or old age benefits, or of a pension in respect of an industrial accident or disease of an amount sufficient to avoid becoming a burden on the social security system of the host Member State during their period of residence and provided they are covered by sickness insurance in respect of all risks in the host Member State.

The resources of the applicant shall be deemed sufficient where they are higher than the level of resources below which the host Member State may grant social assistance to its nationals, taking into account the personal circumstances of persons admitted pursuant to paragraph 2.

Where the second subparagraph cannot be applied in a Member State, the resources of the applicant shall be deemed sufficient if they are higher than the level of the minimum social security pension paid by the host Member State.

2. The following shall, irrespective of their nationality, have the right to install themselves in another Member State with the holder of the right of residence:
(a) his or her spouse and their descendants who are dependants;
(b) dependent relatives in the ascending line of the holder of the right of residence and his or her spouse.

Article 2   1. Exercise of the right of residence shall be evidenced by means of the issue of a document known as a 'Residence permit for a national of a Member State of the EEC', whose validity may be limited to five years on a renewable basis. However, the Member States may, when they deem it to be necessary, require revalidation of the permit at the end of the first two years of residence. Where a member of the family does not hold the nationality of a Member State, he or she shall be issued with a residence document of the same validity as that issued to the national on whom he or she depends.

For the purposes of issuing the residence permit or document, the Member State may require only that the applicant present a valid identity card or passport and provide proof that he or she meets the conditions laid down in Art. 1.

2. Arts. 2, 3, 6(1)(a) and 2 and Art. 9 of Directive 68/360/EEC shall apply *mutatis mutandis* to the beneficiaries of this Directive.

The spouse and the dependent children of a national of a Member State entitled to the right of residence within the territory of a Member State shall be entitled to take up any employed or self-employed activity anywhere within the territory of that Member State, even if they are not nationals of a Member State.

Member States shall not derogate from the provisions of this Directive save on grounds of public policy, public security or public health. In that event, Directive 64/221/EEC shall apply.

3. This Directive shall not affect existing law on the acquisition of second homes.

Article 3   The right of residence shall remain for as long as beneficiaries of that right fulfil the conditions laid down in Art. 1.

Article 4   The Commission shall, not more than three years after the date of implementation of this Directive, and at three-yearly intervals thereafter, draw up a report on the application of this Directive and submit it to the European Parliament and the Council.

[*final provisions omitted*]

Council Directive of 29 October 1993 on the right of residence for students (93/96/EEC)[6]

The Council of the European Communities,

HAVING REGARD to the Treaty establishing the European Economic Community, and in particular Art. 7 thereof,

[*recitals omitted*]

Whereas Art. 3(c) of the Treaty provides that the activities of the Community shall include, as provided in the Treaty, the abolition, as between Member States, of obstacles to freedom of movement for persons;

Whereas Art. 8a of the Treaty provides that the internal market must be established by 31 December 1992; whereas the internal market comprises an area without internal frontiers in which the free movement of goods, persons, services and capital is ensured in accordance with the provisions of the Treaty;

Whereas, as the Court of Justice has ruled, Arts. 128 and 7 of the Treaty prohibit any discrimination between nationals of the Member States as regards access to vocational training in the Community; whereas access by a national of one Member State to vocational training in another Member State implies, for that national, a right of residence in that other Member State;

Whereas, accordingly, in order to guarantee access to vocational training, the conditions likely to facilitate the effective exercise of that right of residence should be laid down;

Whereas the right of residence for students forms part of a set of related measures designed to promote vocational training;

Whereas beneficiaries of the right of residence must not become an unreasonable burden on the public finances of the host Member State;

Whereas, in the present state of Community law, as established by the case law of the Court of Justice, assistance granted to students, does not fall within the scope of the Treaty within the meaning of Art. 7 thereof;

Whereas the right of residence can only be genuinely exercised if it is also granted to the spouse and their dependent children;

Whereas the beneficiaries of this Directive should be covered by administrative arrangements similar to those laid down in particular in Directive 68/360/EEC of 15 October 1968 on the abolition of restrictions on movement and residence within the Community for workers of Member States and their families and

---

[6] OJ 1993 L 317/59, as amended by Decision 95/1/EC, OJ 1995 L 1/1.

Council Directive 64/221/EEC of 25 February 1964 on the coordination of special measures concerning the movement and residence of foreign nationals which are justified on grounds of public policy, public security or public health;

Whereas this Directive does not apply to students who enjoy the right of residence by virtue of the fact that they are or have been effectively engaged in economic activities or are members of the family of a migrant worker;

Whereas, by its judgment of 7 July 1992 in Case C-295/90, the Court of Justice annulled Council Directive 90/366/EEC of 28 June 1990 on the right of residence for students, while maintaining the effects of the annulled Directive until the entry into force of a directive adopted on the appropriate legal basis;

Whereas the effects of Directive 90/366/EEC should be maintained during the period up to 31 December 1993, the date by which Member States are to have adopted the laws, regulations and administrative provisions necessary to comply with this Directive.

HAS ADOPTED this Directive:

Article 1   In order to lay down conditions to facilitate the exercise of the right of residence and with a view to guaranteeing access to vocational training in a non-discriminatory manner for a national of a Member State who has been accepted to attend a vocational training course in another Member State, the Member States shall recognize the right of residence for any student who is a national of a Member State and who does not enjoy that right under other provisions of Community law, and for student's spouse and their dependent children, where the student assures the relevant national authority, by means of a declaration or by such alternative means as the student may choose that are at least equivalent, that he has sufficient resources to avoid becoming a burden on the social assistance system of the host Member State during their period of residence, provided that the student is enrolled in a recognized educational establishment for the principal purpose of following a vocational training course there and that he is covered by sickness insurance in respect of all risks in the host Member State.

Article 2   1. The right of residence shall be restricted to the duration of the course of studies in question.

The right of residence shall be evidenced by means of the issue of a document known as a 'residence permit for a national of a Member State of the Community', the validity of which may be limited to the duration of the course of studies or to one year where the course lasts longer; in the latter event it shall be renewable annually. Where a member of the family does not hold the nationality of a Member State, he or she shall be issued with a residence document of the same validity as that issued to the national on whom he or she depends.

For the purpose of issuing the residence permit or document, the Member State may require only that the applicant present a valid identity card or passport and provide proof that he or she meets the conditions laid down in Art. 1.

2. Arts. 2, 3 and 9 of Directive 68/360/EEC shall apply *mutatis mutandis* to the beneficiaries of this Directive.

The spouse and the dependent children of a national of a Member State entitled to the right of residence within the territory of a Member State shall be entitled to take up any employed or self-employed activity anywhere within the territory of that Member State, even if they are not nationals of a Member State.

Member States shall not derogate from the provisions of this Directive save on grounds of public policy, public security or public health; in that event, Arts. 2 and 9 of Directive 64/221/EEC shall apply.

Article 3   This Directive shall not establish any entitlement to the payment of maintenance grants by the host Member State on the part of students benefiting from the right of residence.

Article 4   The right of residence shall remain for as long as beneficiaries of that right fulfil the conditions laid down in Art. 1.

Article 5   The Commission shall, not more than three years after the date of implementation of this Directive, and at three-yearly intervals thereafter, draw up a report on the application of this Directive and submit it to the European Parliament and the Council.

The Commission shall pay particular attention to any difficulties to which the implementation of Art. 1 might give rise in the Member State; it shall, if appropriate, submit proposals to the Council with the aim of remedying such difficulties.

[*final provisions omitted*]

Council Directive of 28 June 1990 on the right of residence (90/364/EEC)[7]

The Council of the European Communities,

HAVING REGARD to the Treaty establishing the European Economic Community, and in particular Art. 235 thereof,

[*recitals omitted*]

Whereas Art. 3(c) of the Treaty provides that the activities of the Community shall include, as provided in the Treaty, the abolition, as between Member States, of obstacles to freedom of movement for persons;

Whereas Art. 8a of the Treaty provides that the internal market must be established by 31 December 1992; whereas the internal market comprises an area without internal frontiers in which the free movement of goods, persons, services and capital is ensured in accordance with the provisions of the Treaty;

Whereas national provisions on the right of nationals of the Member States to reside in a Member State other than their own must be harmonised to ensure such freedom of movement;

Whereas beneficiaries of the right of residence must not become an unreasonable burden on the public finances of the host Member State;

Whereas this right can only be genuinely exercised if it is also granted to members of the family;

---

[7] OJ 1990 L 180/26.

Whereas the beneficiaries of this Directive should be covered by administrative arrangements similar to those laid down in particular in Directive 68/360/EEC and Directive 64/221/EEC;

Whereas the Treaty does not provide, for the action concerned, powers other than those of Art. 235,

HAS ADOPTED this Directive:

Article 1   1. Member States shall grant the right of residence to nationals of Member States who do not enjoy this right under the provisions of Community law and to members of their families as defined in paragraph 2, provided that they themselves and the members of their families are covered by sickness insurance in respect of all risks in the host Member State and have sufficient resources to avoid becoming a burden on the social assistance system of the host Member State during their period of residence.

The resources referred to in the first subparagraph shall be deemed sufficient where they are higher than the level of resources below which the host Member State may grant social assistance to its nationals, taking into account the personal circumstances of the applicant and, where appropriate, the personal circumstances of persons admitted pursuant to paragraph 2.

Where the second subparagraph cannot be applied in a Member State, the resources of the applicant shall be deemed sufficient if they are higher than the level of the minimum social security pension paid by the host Member State.

2. The following shall, irrespective of their nationality, have the right to install themselves in another Member State with the holder of the right of residence:
(a) his or her spouse and their descendants who are dependants;
(b) dependent relatives in the ascending line of the holder of the right of residence
     and his or her spouse.

Article 2   1. Exercise of the right of residence shall be evidenced by means of the issue of a document known as a 'Residence permit for a national of a Member State of the EEC, the validity of which may be limited to five years on a renewable basis. However, the Member States may, when they deem it to be necessary, require revalidation of the permit at the end of the first two years of residence. Where a member of the family does not hold the nationality of a Member State, he or she shall be issued with a residence document of the same validity as that issued to the national on whom he or she depends.

For the purpose of issuing the residence permit or document, the Member State may require only that the applicant present a valid identity card or passport and provide proof that he or she meets the conditions laid down in Art. 1.

2. Arts. 2, 3, 6 (1) (a) and (2) and Art. 9 of Directive 68/360/EEC shall apply *mutatis mutandis* to the beneficiaries of this Directive.

The spouse and the dependent children of a national of a Member State entitled to the right of residence within the territory of a Member State shall be entitled to take up any employed or self-employed activity anywhere within the territory of that Member State, even if they are not nationals of a Member State.

Member States shall not derogate from the provisions of this Directive save on grounds of public policy, public security or public health. In that event, Directive 64/221/EEC shall apply.

3. This Directive shall not affect existing law on the acquisition of second homes.

Article 3 The right of residence shall remain for as long as beneficiaries of that right fulfil the conditions laid down in Art. 1.

Article 4 The Commission shall, not more than three years after the date of implementation of this Directive, and at three-yearly intervals thereafter, draw up a report on the application of this Directive and submit it to the European Parliament and the Council.

[final provisions omitted]

Competition

First Council Regulation implementing Articles 85 and 86 of the EC Treaty (Regulation 17)[1]

The Council of the European Economic Community,

HAVING REGARD to the Treaty establishing the European Economic Community, and in particular Art. 87 thereof;

[recitals omitted]

Whereas this Regulation may enter into force without prejudice to any other provisions that may hereafter be adopted pursuant to Art. 87;

HAS ADOPTED this Regulation:

Article 1   Basic provision   Without prejudice to Arts. 6, 7 and 23 of this Regulation, agreements, decisions and concerted practices of the kind described in Art. 85(1) of the Treaty and the abuse of a dominant position in the market, within the meaning of Art. 86 of the Treaty, shall be prohibited, no prior decision to that effect being required.

Article 2   Negative clearance   Upon application by the undertakings or associations of undertakings concerned, the Commission may certify that, on the basis of the facts in its possession, there are no grounds under Art. 85(1) or Art. 86 of the Treaty for action on its part in respect of an agreement, decision or practice.

Article 3   Termination of infringements   1. Where the Commission, upon application or upon its own initiative, finds that there is infringement of Art. 85 or Art. 86 of the Treaty, it may by decision require the undertakings or associations of undertakings concerned to bring such infringement to an end.

2. Those entitled to make application are:
(a) Member States;
(b) natural or legal persons who claim a legitimate interest.

3. Without prejudice to the other provisions of this Regulation, the Commission may, before taking a decision under paragraph 1, address to the undertakings or associations of undertakings concerned recommendations for termination of the infringement.

Article 4   Notification of new agreements, decisions and practices   1. Agreements, decisions and concerted practices of the kind described in Art. 85(1) of the Treaty which come into existence after the entry into force of this Regulation and in respect of which the parties seek application of Art. 85(3) must be notified to the Commission. Until they have been notified, no decision in application of Art. 85(3) may be taken.

2. Paragraph 1 shall not apply to agreements, decisions or concerted practices where:

---

[1] OJ Sp. Ed. 1959-62, 87. As last amended by Decision 95/1/EC, OJ 1995 L 1/1.

(1) the only parties thereto are undertakings from one Member State and the agreements, decisions or practices do not relate either to imports or to exports between Member States;

(2) not more than two undertakings are party thereto, and the agreements only:
  (a) restrict the freedom of one party to the contract in determining the prices or conditions of business upon which the goods which he has obtained from the other party to the contract may be resold; or
  (b) impose restrictions on the exercise of the rights of the assignee or user of industrial property rights–in particular patents, utility models, designs or trade marks–or of the person entitled under a contract to the assignment, or grant, of the right to use a method of manufacture or knowledge relating to the use and to the application of industrial processes;

(3) they have as their sole object:
  (a) the development or uniform application of standards or types; or
  (b) joint research and development;
  (c) specialisation in the manufacture of products, including agreements necessary for achieving this,
    — where the products which are the subject of specialisation do not, in a substantial part of the common market, represent more than 15% of the volume of business done in identical products or those considered by consumers to be similar by reason of their characteristics, price and use,
    and
    — where the total annual turnover of the participating undertakings does not exceed 200 million units of account.

These agreements, decisions and practices may be notified to the Commission.

Article 5   Notification of existing agreements, decisions and practices   1. Agreements, decisions and concerted practices of the kind described in Art. 85(1) of the Treaty which are in existence at the date of entry into force of this Regulation and in respect of which the parties seek application of Art. 85(3) shall be notified to the Commission before 1 November 1962. However, notwithstanding the foregoing provisions, any agreements, decisions and concerted practices to which not more than two undertakings are party shall be notified before 1 February 1963.

2. Paragraph 1 shall not apply to agreements, decisions or concerted practices falling within Art. 4(2); these may be notified to the Commission.

Article 6   Decisions pursuant to Art. 85(3)   1. Whenever the Commission takes a decision pursuant to Art. 85(3) of the Treaty, it shall specify therein the date from which the decision shall take effect. Such date shall not be earlier than the date of notification.

2. The second sentence of paragraph 1 shall not apply to agreements, decisions or concerted practices falling within Art. 4(2) and Art. 5(2), nor to those falling within Art. 5(1) which have been notified within the time limit specified in Art. 5(1).

Article 7   Special provisions for existing agreements, decisions and practices   1. Where agreements, decisions and concerted practices in existence at the date of entry into force of this Regulation and notified within the time limits specified in Art. 5(1) do

not satisfy the requirements of Art. 85(3) of the Treaty and the undertakings or associations of undertakings concerned cease to give effect to them or modify them in
such manner that they no longer fall within the prohibition contained in Art. 85(1)
or that they satisfy the requirements of Art. 85(3), the prohibition contained in Art.
85(1) shall apply only for a period fixed by the Commission. A decision by the
Commission pursuant to the foregoing sentence shall not apply as against undertakings and associations of undertakings which did not expressly consent to the
notification.

2. Paragraph 1 shall apply to agreements, decisions and concerted practices falling
within Art. 4(2) which are in existence at the date of entry into force of this
Regulation if they are notified before 1 January 1967.

Article 8   Duration and revocation of decisions under Art. 85(3)   1. A decision in application of Art. 85(3) of the Treaty shall be issued for a specified period and conditions
and obligations may be attached thereto.

2. A decision may on application be renewed if the requirements of Art. 85(3) of the
Treaty continue to be satisfied.

3. The Commission may revoke or amend its decision or prohibit specified acts by
the parties:
(a) where there has been a change in any of the facts which were basic to the mak-
    ing of the decision;
(b) where the parties commit a breach of any obligation attached to the decision;
(c) where the decision is based on incorrect information or was induced by
    deceit;
(d) where the parties abuse the exemption from the provisions of Art. 85(1) of the
    Treaty granted to them by the decision.

   In cases to which subparagraphs (b), (c) or (d) apply, the decision may be revoked
with retroactive effect.

Article 9   Powers   1. Subject to review of its decision by the Court of Justice, the
Commission shall have sole power to declare Art. 85(1) inapplicable pursuant to Art.
85(3) of the Treaty.

2. The Commission shall have power to apply Art. 85(1) and Art. 86 of the Treaty;
this power may be exercised notwithstanding that the time limits specified in Art.
5(1) and in Art. 7(2) relating to notification have not expired.

3. As long as the Commission has not initiated any procedure under Arts. 2, 3 or 6,
the authorities of the Member States shall remain competent to apply Art. 85(1) and
Art. 86 in accordance with Art. 88 of the Treaty; they shall remain competent in this
respect notwithstanding that the time limits specified in Art. 5(1) and in Art. 7(2)
relating to notification have not expired.

Article 10   Liaison with the authorities of the Member States   1. The Commission shall
forthwith transmit to the competent authorities of the Member States a copy of the
application and notifications together with copies of the most important documents lodged with the Commission for the purpose of establishing the existence of
infringements of Arts. 85 or 86 of the Treaty or of obtaining negative clearance or a
decision in application of Art. 85(3).

2. The Commission shall carry out the procedure set out in paragraph 1 in close and constant liaison with the competent authorities of the Member States; such authorities shall have the right to express their views upon that procedure.

3. An Advisory Committee on Restrictive Practices and Monopolies shall be consulted prior to the taking of any decision following upon a procedure under paragraph 1, and of any decision concerning the renewal, amendment or revocation of a decision pursuant to Art. 85(3) of the Treaty.

4. The Advisory Committee shall be composed of officials competent in the matter of restrictive practices and monopolies. Each Member State shall appoint an official to represent it who, if prevented from attending, may be replaced by another official.

5. The consultation shall take place at a joint meeting convened by the Commission; such meeting shall be held not earlier than fourteen days after dispatch of the notice convening it. The notice shall, in respect of each case to be examined, be accompanied by a summary of the case together with an indication of the most important documents, and a preliminary draft decision.

6. The Advisory Committee may deliver an opinion notwithstanding that some of its members or their alternates are not present. A report of the outcome of the consultative proceedings shall be annexed to the draft decision. It shall not be made public.

Article 11   Request for information   1. In carrying out the duties assigned to it by Art. 89 and by provisions adopted under Art. 87 of the Treaty, the Commission may obtain all necessary information from the Governments and competent authorities of the Member States and from undertakings and associations of undertakings.

2. When sending a request for information to an undertaking or association of undertakings, the Commission shall at the same time forward a copy of the request to the competent authority of the Member State in whose territory the seat of the undertaking or association of undertakings is situated.

3. In its request the Commission shall state the legal basis and the purpose of the request and also the penalties provided for in Art. 15(1)(b) for supplying incorrect information.

4. The owners of the undertakings or their representatives and, in the case of legal persons, companies or firms, or of associations having no legal personality, the persons authorised to represent them by law or by their constitution shall supply the information requested.

5. Where an undertaking or association of undertakings does not supply the information requested within the time limit fixed by the Commission, or supplies incomplete information, the Commission shall by decision require the information to be supplied. The decision shall specify what information is required, fix an appropriate time limit within which it is to be supplied and indicate the penalties provided for in Art. 15(1)(b) and Art. 16(1)(c) and the right to have the decision reviewed by the Court of Justice.

6. The Commission shall at the same time forward a copy of its decision to the competent authority of the Member State in whose territory the seat of the undertaking or association of undertakings is situated.

Article 12   Inquiry into sectors of the economy   1. If in any sector of the economy the trend of trade between Member States, price movements, inflexibility of prices or other circumstances suggest that in the economic sector concerned competition is being restricted or distorted within the common market, the Commission may decide to conduct a general inquiry into that economic sector and in the course thereof may request undertakings in the sector concerned to supply the information necessary for giving effect to the principles formulated in Arts. 85 and 86 of the Treaty and for carrying out the duties entrusted to the Commission.

2. The Commission may in particular request every undertaking or association of undertakings in the economic sector concerned to communicate to it all agreements, decisions and concerted practices which are exempt from notification by virtue of Art. 4(2) and Art. 5(2).

3. When making inquiries pursuant to paragraph 2, the Commission shall also request undertakings or groups of undertakings whose size suggests that they occupy a dominant position within the common market or a substantial part thereof to supply to the Commission such particulars of the structure of the undertakings and of their behaviour as are requisite to an appraisal of their position in the light of Art. 86 of the Treaty.

4. Art. 10(3) to (6) and Arts. 11, 13, and 14 shall apply correspondingly.

Article 13   Investigations by the authorities of the Member States   1. At the request of the Commission, the competent authorities of the Member States shall undertake the investigations which the Commission considers to be necessary under Art. 14(1), or which it has ordered by decision pursuant to Art. 14(3). The officials of the competent authorities of the Member States responsible for conducting these investigations shall exercise their powers upon production of an authorisation in writing issued by the competent authority of the Member State in whose territory the investigation is to be made. Such authorisation shall specify the subject-matter and purpose of the investigation.

2. If so requested by the Commission or by the competent authority of the Member State in whose territory the investigation is to be made, the officials of the Commission may assist the officials of such authorities in carrying out their duties.

Article 14   Investigating powers of the Commission   1. In carrying out the duties assigned to it by Art. 89 and by provisions adopted under Art. 87 of the Treaty, the Commission may undertake all necessary investigations into undertakings and associations of undertakings. To this end the officials authorised by the Commission are empowered:
(a) to examine the books and other business records;
(b) to take copies of or extracts from the books and business records;
(c) to ask for oral explanations on the spot;
(d) to enter any premises, land and means of transport of undertakings.

2. The officials of the Commission authorised for the purpose of these investigations shall exercise their powers upon production of an authorisation in writing specifying the subject-matter and purpose of the investigation and the penalties provided for in Art. 15(1)(c) in cases where production of the required books or other business records is incomplete. In good time before the investigation, the

Commission shall inform the competent authority of the Member State in whose territory the same is to be made of the investigation and of the identity of the authorised officials.

3. Undertakings and associations of undertakings shall submit to investigations ordered by decision of the Commission. The decision shall specify the subject-matter and purpose of the investigation, appoint the date on which it is to begin and indicate the penalties provided for in Art. 15(1)(c) and Art. 16(1)(d) and the right to have the decision reviewed by the Court of Justice.

4. The Commission shall take decisions referred to in paragraph 3 after consultation with the competent authority of the Member State in whose territory the investigation is to be made.

5. Officials of the competent authority of the Member State in whose territory the investigation is to be made may, at the request of such authority or of the Commission, assist the officials of the Commission in carrying out their duties.

6. Where an undertaking opposes an investigation ordered pursuant to this Article, the Member State concerned shall afford the necessary assistance to the officials authorised by the Commission to enable them to make their investigation. Member States shall, after consultation with the Commission, take the necessary measures to this end before 1 October 1962.

Article 15   Fines   1. The Commission may by decision impose on undertakings or associations of undertakings fines of from 100 to 5000 units of account where, intentionally or negligently:
(a) they supply incorrect or misleading information in an application pursuant to Art. 2 or in a notification pursuant to Arts. 4 or 5; or
(b) they supply incorrect information in response to a request made pursuant to Art. 11(3) or (5) or to Art. 12, or do not supply information within the time limit fixed by a decision taken under Art. 11(5); or
(c) they produce the required books or other business records in incomplete form during investigations under Arts. 13 or 14, or refuse to submit to an investigation ordered by decision issued in implementation of Art. 14(3).

2. The Commission may by decision impose on undertakings or associations of undertakings fines from 1,000 to 1,000,000 units of account, or a sum in excess thereof but not exceeding 10% of the turnover in the preceding business year of each of the undertakings participating in the infringement where, either intentionally or negligently:
(a) they infringe Art. 85(1) or Art. 86 of the Treaty; or
(b) they commit a breach of any obligation imposed pursuant to Art. 8(1).

   In fixing the amount of the fine, regard shall be had both to the gravity and to the duration of the infringement.

3. Art. 10(3) to (6) shall apply.

4. Decisions taken pursuant to paragraphs 1 and 2 shall not be of a criminal law nature.

5. The fines provided for in paragraph 2(a) shall not be imposed in respect of acts taking place:

(a) after notification to the Commission and before its decision in application of Art. 85(3) of the Treaty, provided they fall within the limits of the activity described in the notification;

(b) before notification and in the course of agreements, decisions or concerted practices in existence at the date of entry into force of this Regulation, provided that notification was effected within the time limits specified in Art. 5(1) and Art. 7(2).

6. Paragraph 5 shall not have effect where the Commission has informed the undertakings concerned that after preliminary examination it is of opinion that Art. 85(1) of the Treaty applies and that application of Art. 85(3) is not justified.

Article 16   Periodic penalty payments   1. The Commission may by decision impose on undertakings or associations of undertakings periodic penalty payments of from 50 to 1000 units of account per day, calculated from the date appointed by the decision, in order to compel them:

(a) to put an end to an infringement of Arts. 85 or 86 of the Treaty, in accordance with a decision taken pursuant to Art. 3 of this Regulation;

(b) to refrain from any act prohibited under Art. 8(3);

(c) to supply complete and correct information which it has requested by decision taken pursuant to Art. 11(5);

(d) to submit to an investigation which it has ordered by decision taken pursuant to Art. 14(3).

2. Where the undertakings or associations of undertakings have satisfied the obligation which it was the purpose of the periodic penalty payment to enforce, the Commission may fix the total amount of the periodic penalty payment at a lower figure than that which would arise under the original decision.

3. Art. 10(3) to (6) shall apply.

Article 17   Review by the Court of Justice   The Court of Justice shall have unlimited jurisdiction within the meaning of Art. 172 of the Treaty to review decisions whereby the Commission has fixed a fine or periodic penalty payment; it may cancel, reduce or increase the fine or periodic penalty payment imposed.

Article 18   Unit of account   For the purposes of applying Arts. 15 to 17 the unit of account shall be that adopted in drawing up the budget of the Community in accordance with Arts. 207 and 209 of the Treaty.

Article 19   Hearing of the parties and of third persons   1. Before taking decisions as provided for in Arts. 2, 3, 6, 7, 8, 15 and 16, the Commission shall give the undertakings or associations of undertakings concerned the opportunity of being heard on the matters to which the Commission has taken objection.

2. If the Commission or the competent authorities of the Member States consider it necessary, they may also hear other natural or legal persons. Applications to be heard on the part of such persons shall, where they show a sufficient interest, be granted.

3. Where the Commission intends to give negative clearance pursuant to Art. 2 or take a decision in application of Art. 85(3) of the Treaty, it shall publish a summary of the relevant application or notification and invite all interested third parties to

submit their observations within a time limit which it shall fix being not less than one month. Publication shall have regard to the legitimate interest of undertakings in the protection of their business secrets.

Article 20   Professional secrecy   1. Information acquired as a result of the application of Arts. 11, 12, 13 and 14 shall be used only for the purpose of the relevant request or investigation.

2. Without prejudice to the provisions of Arts. 19 and 21, the Commission and the competent authorities of the Member States, their officials and other servants shall not disclose information acquired by them as a result of the application of this Regulation and of the kind covered by the obligation of professional secrecy.

3. The provisions of paragraphs 1 and 2 shall not prevent publication of general information or surveys which do not contain information relating to particular undertakings or associations of undertakings.

Article 21   Publication of decisions   1. The Commission shall publish the decisions which it takes pursuant to Arts. 2, 3, 6, 7, and 8.

2. The publication shall state the names of the parties and the main content of the decision; it shall have regard to the legitimate interest of undertakings in the protection of their business secrets.

Article 22 Special provisions   1. The Commission shall submit to the Council proposals for making certain categories of agreement, decision and concerted practice falling within Art. 4(2) or Art. 5(2) compulsorily notifiable under Art. 4 or 5.

2. Within one year from the date of entry into force of this Regulation, the Council shall examine, on a proposal from the Commission, what special provisions might be made for exempting from the provisions of this Regulation agreements, decisions and concerted practices falling within Art. 4(2) or Art. 5(2).

Article 23   Transitional provisions applicable to decisions of authorities of the Member States
1. Agreements, decisions and concerted practices of the kind described in Art. 85(1) of the Treaty to which, before the entry into force of this Regulation, the competent authority of a Member State has declared Art. 85(1) to be inapplicable pursuant to Art. 85(3) shall not be subject to compulsory notification under Art. 5. The decision of the competent authority of the Member State shall be deemed to be a decision within the meaning of Art. 6; it shall cease to be valid upon expiration of the period fixed by such authority but in any event not more than three years after the entry into force of this Regulation. Art. 8(3) shall apply.

2. Applications for renewal of decisions of the kind described in paragraph 1 shall be decided upon by the Commission in accordance with Art. 8(2).

Article 24   Implementing provisions   The Commission shall have power to adopt implementing provisions concerning the form, content and other details of applications pursuant to Arts. 2 and 3 and of notifications pursuant to Arts. 4 and 5, and concerning hearings pursuant to Art. 19(1) and (2).

Article 25   1. As regards agreements, decisions and concerted practices to which Art. 85 of the Treaty applies by virtue of accession, the date of accession shall be substituted for the date of entry into force of this Regulation in every place where reference is made in this Regulation to this latter date.

2. Agreements, decisions and concerted practices existing at the date of accession to which Art. 85 of the Treaty applies by virtue of accession shall be notified pursuant to Art. 5(1) or Art. 7(1) and (2) within six months from the date of accession.

3. Fines under Art. 15(2)(a) shall not be imposed in respect of any act prior to notification of the agreements, decisions and practices to which paragraph 2 applies and which have been notified within the period therein specified.

4. New Member States shall take the measures referred to in Art. 14(6) within six months from the date of accession after consulting the Commission.

5. The provisions of paragraphs 1 to 4 above shall apply in the same way in the case of the accession of the Hellenic Republic, the Kingdom of Spain and of the Portuguese Republic.

6. The provisions of paragraphs 1 to 4 still apply in the same way in the case of the accession of Austria, Finland and Sweden. However, they do not apply to agreements, decisions and concerted practices which at the date of accession already fall under Article 53 of the EEA Agreement.

[final provisions omitted]

Commission Notice (1968) Regarding Agreements, Decisions and Concerted Practices in the Field of Co-operation between Enterprises (Extracts)[2]

The Commission of the European Communities has frequently been asked as to the position it intends to adopt, within the framework of the application of the competition rules in the Treaties of Rome and Paris, on co-operation between enterprises. For this reason, this Notice attempts to furnish enterprises with certain guidance which, while not being exhaustive, should nonetheless provide them with useful tips on the interpretation to be given to the provisions of Art. 85(1) of the EEC Treaty and Art. 65(1) of the ECSC Treaty.

I

The Commission is favourably disposed to co-operation between small and medium-sized enterprises to the extent to which they are thereby enabled to work more rationally and to increase their productivity and competitiveness in a larger market. While recognising that its task is to facilitate such co-operation in particular, the Commission recognises that co-operation between large enterprises may also be economically justifiable without giving rise to objections from the point of view of competition policy.

[text reciting the effect of EEC Article 85(1) and ECSC Article 65(1) omitted]

The Commission feels it appropriate, and of particular interest to small and medium-sized enterprises, to explain the considerations which it will take into account in the interpretation of EEC 85(1) and ECSC 65(1) and in their application to certain co-operation arrangements between enterprises and to indicate which thereof do

---

[2] JO 1968 C 75/3 amended C 84/4 translated by the Editors. The notice is undated.

not, in its opinion, fall under them. This Notice applies to all enterprises, whatever their size.

Forms of co-operation other than those mentioned below may also not be prohibited by EEC 85(1) or ECSC 65(1). This applies in particular if the global market position of the co-operating enterprises is too weak to lead, because of the agreement, to appreciable restraint on competition within the common market or, in the context of EEC 85(1), to affect trade between Member States.

It should also be pointed out that other forms of inter-enterprise co-operation, or agreements containing additional clauses, to which the competition rules of the Treaties apply, may still be exempted under EEC 85(3) or authorised under ECSC 65(2).

The Commission intends, by individual decisions where appropriate, or by general notices, to establish rapidly the status of various types of co-operation in relation to the rules of the Treaties.

At this stage no general guidance can be given on the application of EEC 86 concerning the abuse of a dominant position in the common market or part thereof. The same is true of ECSC 66(7).

The present Notice should, as a general rule, allay the need to obtain negative clearance for the agreements listed in Regulation 17 Art. 2. Nor should it be necessary to seek clarification of the legal position by a Commission decision on an individual case; there is therefore no need to notify, for that purpose, such agreements. If, however, there is doubt in a particular case, as to whether a co-operation agreement restricts competition, or if other types of inter-enterprise co-operation which, in the opinion of the enterprises, do not restrict competition are not mentioned herein, the enterprises may request negative clearance of EEC 85(1) or, where ECSC 65(1) applies, file, as a precaution, an application under ECSC 65(2).

This Notice does not pre-judge interpretation by the Court of Justice of the European Communities.

II

The Commission considers that the following agreements do not restrict competition.

1. Agreements having as their sole object:
(a) the exchange of opinions or experience,
(b) joint market research,
(c) the joint carrying out of comparative studies of enterprises or industries,
(d) the joint preparation of statistics and calculation models.

Agreements whose sole purpose is the joint acquisition of information necessary to enable the various enterprises to determine their future market behaviour freely and independently or to have individual recourse to a joint advisory body do not have, as their object or effect, the restriction of competition. But such may occur if the enterprises' freedom of action is limited or their market behaviour co-ordinated expressly or through concerted practices. This is particularly the case where concrete recommendations are made or conclusions expressed in such a way as to induce identical market behaviour in at least some of the enterprises.

The exchange of information may take place among the enterprises themselves or through a third party acting as an intermediary body. However, the distinction between information which has no bearing on competition and behaviour in restraint thereof is particularly difficult to draw when such bodies are required to register orders, turnover figures, investments and prices so that, as a general rule, it is impossible, without more, to assume the inapplicability of EEC 85(1) or ECSC 65(1). A restriction of competition may occur, in particular, where there is an oligopolist market for homogeneous products.

In the absence of more extensive co-operation between participating enterprises, mere joint market research and comparative studies of enterprises and industries in order to collect information and ascertain facts and market conditions do not of themselves affect competition. Other steps of this type such as, for example, the joint establishment of conjunctural and structural analyses are so obviously untainted that there is no need to give them special mention.

Calculation models containing specific rates of calculation must be considered recommendations which may lead to a restraint of competition.

2. Agreements having as their sole object:
(a) co-operation in accounting matters,
(b) joint credit guarantees,
(c) joint debt-collection offices,
(d) the consultation of joint bodies as to business organisation or tax matters.

These cases involve co-operation in fields which concern neither the supply of goods and services nor economic decisions of enterprises involved so that they cannot lead to any restriction of competition.

Co-operation in accounting matters is neutral from the point of view of competition since it deals only with the technical handling of accounting. Similarly the creation of credit guarantee pools does not come under competition rules since it does not modify the relationship between supply and demand.

Debt-collecting offices which do not limit their activity to collecting payment at the instance and on the instructions of participants, or which fix prices or exercise any influence on price formation, may restrict competition. Application of conditions which are uniform for all participants may constitute a concerted practice, as may joint comparison of prices. In this connection there is no objection to the use of standard forms; their use, however, must not be tied to an agreement or tacit understanding on uniform prices, rebates or conditions of sale.

3. Agreements having as their sole object:
(a) joint research and development projects,
(b) joint allocation of research and development contracts,
(c) the sharing-out of research and development projects among the participants.

Similarly, in the field of research the mere exchange of experience and findings is for information only and does not restrict competition. It does not need special mention.

Agreements made for joint research or the joint development of research results to the stage of their industrial application do not affect the competitive position of the parties. This is equally the case when research fields and development work are shared out provided that the results remain accessible to all participants. But the Treaties' competition rules may be infringed if enterprises contract obligations restricting their own research and development activity or their exploitation of the results of joint work so that, outside the joint project, they are no longer free to carry out research and development for their own account. In the absence of joint research, any contractual obligation or undertaking to give up their own research in full or in part may have the effect of restricting competition.

Specialisation which may restrict competition occurs when research fields are shared out without an agreement providing for reciprocal access to the results.

Competition may also be restricted by the making of agreements, or corresponding concerted practices, as to the practical exploitation of joint research and development work particularly when the participants undertake or agree to manufacture only the products, or type of products, developed jointly or to split future production amongst themselves.

The idea of joint research is that its results be exploited by the participating enterprises in proportion to their participation. If the participation of certain enterprises is limited to a defined field of joint research or to the provision of a fixed financial contribution then–in so far as one can speak here of joint research–there are no restraints on competition merely because the participants have access to the research results only in proportion to their participation. On the other hand, competition may be restricted if certain participants are excluded from exploitation of the results either *in toto* or to an extent incommensurate with their participation.

If the granting of licences to third parties is expressly or tacitly excluded, competition may be restricted; however the pooling of research justifies the obligation not to grant licences to third parties save by common agreement or majority decision.

The legal form taken by joint research and development does not affect any assessment of the compatibility of the agreement with the rules on competition.

4. Agreements whose sole object is the joint use of plant and storage and transport facilities.

These types of co-operation do not restrict competition since they are limited to organisational matters and to the technical use of facilities. There may, however, be restriction of competition if the enterprises involved do not themselves bear the cost of utilising plant and equipment or if agreements are made, or concerted practices applied, regarding joint production or the sharing out of production or the establishment or running of a joint enterprise.

5. Agreements whose sole object is the setting-up of working partnerships for the joint filling of orders when the participating enterprises do not compete with each other as regards the work to be done or where each alone is unable to fill the orders.

Enterprises which do not compete with each other cannot, by setting up temporary associations, restrict competition *inter se*. This is true not only for enterprises belonging to different industries but also for those of the same sector to the extent to which they participate in the working partnership only by providing products or services which the other participants cannot. It matters little that the enterprises compete with each other in other sectors; what matters is to know if, given the concrete circumstances of the particular case, competition in the products or services at issue is possible in the foreseeable future. If the absence of competition between the enterprises and the persistence of this situation rest on agreements or concerted practices there may be a restraint on competition.

Furthermore, even in the case of working partnerships of enterprises which do compete with each other, competition is not restricted when the participants could not alone and by themselves fill a particular order. This is especially so when, because of lack of experience, specialised knowledge, capacity or adequate financial cover, the enterprise by itself is operating with no hope of success or without being able to finish the work on time or bear the financial risk.

Nor is there restriction of competition if the establishment of a working partnership is the only way in which the enterprises can make a tempting offer. Competition may, however, be restricted if the enterprises undertake to operate solely within the framework of a working partnership.

6. Agreements having as their sole object:

(a) joint selling,

(b) joint after-sales and repair services, provided the enterprises participating are not in competition *inter se* for the products or services covered by the agreement.

As already explained in full under section 5, co-operation between enterprises cannot restrict competition if they are not competing with each other.

Very often joint selling carried out by small or medium enterprises does not constitute an appreciable restriction on competition, even when they are in competition *inter se*; it is, however, impossible to lay down in this Notice general criteria or to fix precisely the extent of 'small' or 'medium-sized'.

There is no joint after-sales and repair service if several producers, without acting in concert, entrust the after-sales and repair service of their products to the same enterprise which is independent of them.

7. Agreements whose sole object is joint advertising.

Joint advertising aims to draw the buyers' attention to the products of an industry or to a common brand; as such it does not restrict competition between participating enterprises. Competition may, however, be restricted when through an agreement or concerted policy participants are prevented, entirely or in part, from doing their own advertising or when other restrictions are imposed on them.

8. Agreements whose sole object is the use of a common label to denominate products of a certain quality where the label is available to all competitors on the same conditions.

Such labelling associations do not restrict competition if other competitors, whose products meet objectively the required quality standards, may use the label on the same conditions as members. Similarly the obligation to submit to quality control the products bearing the label or to prescribe uniform instructions for use or to use the label for products meeting the quality standards do not constitute a restraint on competition. But there may be restraint on competition if the right to use the label is tied to obligations regarding production, marketing, price formation or other matters as when, for example, the participating enterprises are obliged to manufacture or sell only products of guaranteed quality.

Commission Notice of 9 December 1997 on agreements of minor importance which do not fall under Article 85(1) of the EC Treaty[3]

1. The Commission considers it important to facilitate cooperation between undertakings where such cooperation is economically desirable without presenting difficulties from the point of view of competition policy. To this end, it published the 'Notice concerning agreements, decisions and concerted practices in the field of cooperation between enterprises'[4] listing a number of agreements that by their nature cannot be regarded as being in restraint of competition. Furthermore, in the Notice concerning its assessment of certain subcontracting agreements[5] the Commission considered that that type of contract, which offers all undertakings opportunities for development, does not automatically fall within the scope of Article 85(1). The Notice concerning the assessment of cooperative joint ventures pursuant to Article 85 of the EEC Treaty[6] describes in detail the conditions under which the agreements in question do not fall under the prohibition of restrictive agreements. By issuing this Notice which replaces the Commission Notice of 3 September 1986,[7] the Commission is taking a further step towards defining the scope of Article 85(1), in order to facilitate cooperation between undertakings.

2. Article 85(1) prohibits agreements which may affect trade between Member States and which have as their object or effect the prevention, restriction or distortion of competition within the common market. The Court of Justice of the European Communities has clarified that this provision is not applicable where the impact of the agreement on intracommunity trade or on competition is not appreciable. Agreements which are not capable of significantly affecting trade between Member States are not caught by Article 85. They should therefore be examined on the basis, and within the framework, of national legislation alone. This is also the case for agreements whose actual or potential effect remains limited to the territory of only one Member State or of one or more third countries. Likewise, agreements which do not have as their object or their effect an appreciable restriction of competition are not caught by the prohibition contained in Article 85(1).

3. In this Notice the Commission, by setting quantitative criteria and by explaining their application, has given a sufficiently concrete meaning to the term 'appreciable' for undertakings to be able to judge for themselves whether their agreements do not fall within the p rohibition under Article 85(1) by virtue of their minor importance. The quantitative definition of appreciab ility, however, serves only as a guideline: in individual cases even agreements between undertakings which exceed the threshold set out below may still have only a negligible effect on trade between Member States or on competition within the common market and are therefore not caught by Article 85(1). This Notice does not contain an exhaustive description of restictions which fall outside Article 85(1). It is generally recognized that even agreements which are not of minor importance can escape the prohibition on agreements on account of their exclusively favourable impact on competition.

---

[3] OJ 1997 C 372/13.   [4] OJ 1968 C 75/3, as corrected in OJ 1968 C 84/14.
[5] OJ 1979 C1/2.   [6] OJ 1993 C 43/2.   [7] OJ 1986 C 231/2.

4. The benchmarks provided by the Commission in this Notice should eliminate the need to have the legal status of agreements covered by it established through individual Commission decisions; notification for this purpose will no longer be necessary for such agreements. However, if it is doubtful whether, in an individual case, an agreement is likely to affect trade between Member States or to restrict competition to any significant extent, undertakings are free to apply for negative clearance or to notify the agreement pursuant to Council Regulations No. 17,[8] (EEC) No. 1017/68,[9] (EEC) No. 4056/86[10] and (EEC) No. 3975/87.[11]

5. In cases covered by this Notice, and subject to points 11 and 20 , the Commission will not institute any proceedings either upon application or on its own initiative. Where undertakings have failed to notify an agreement falling within the scope of Article 85(1) because they assumed in good faith that the agreement was covered by this Notice, the Commission will not consider imposing fines.

6. This Notice is likewise applicable to decisions by associations of undertakings and to concerted practices.

7. This Notice is without prejudice to the competence of national courts to apply Article 85. However, it constitutes a factor which th os e courts may take into account when deciding a pending case. It is also without prejudice to any interpretation of Article 85 which may be given by the Court of Justice or the Court of First Instance of the European Communities.

8. This Notice is without prejudice to the application of national competition laws.

II

9. The Commission holds the view that agreements between undertakings engaged in the production or distribution of goods or in the provision of services do not fall under the prohibition in Article 85(1) if the aggregate market shares held by all of the participating undertakings do not exceed, on any of the relevant markets:
(a) the 5% threshold, where the agreement is made between undertakings operating at the same level of production or of marketing ('horizontal' agreement);
(b) the 10% threshold, where the agreement is made between undertakings operating at different economic levels ('vertical' agreement).

   In the case of a mixed horizontal/vertical agreement or where it is difficult to classify the agreement as either horizontal or vertical, the 5% threshold is applicable.

10. The Commission also holds the view that the said agreements do not fall under the prohibition of Article 85(1) if the market shares g iven at point 9 are exceeded by no more than one-tenth during two successive financial years.

11. With regard to:
(a) horizontal agreements which have as their object

   — to fix prices or to limit production or sales; or
   — to share markets or sources of supply,

(b) vertical agreements which have as their object

   — to fix resale prices or

---

[8] OJ No. 13, 21.2.1962, 204/62.   [9] OJ 1968 L 175/1.   [10] OJ 1986 L 378/4.
[11] OJ 1987 L 374/1.

— to confer territorial protection on the participating undertakings or third undertakings,

the applicability of Article 85(1) cannot be ruled out even where the aggregate market shares held by all of the participating undertakings remain below the thresholds mentioned in points 9 and 10.

The Commission considers, however, that in the first instance it is for the authorities and courts of the Member States to take action on any agreements envisaged above in (a) and (b). Accordingly, it will only intervene in such cases when it considers that the interest of the Community so demands, and in particular if the agreements impair the proper functioning of the internal market.

12. For the purposes of this Notice, 'participating undertakings' are:

(a) undertakings being parties to the agreement;

(b) undertakings in which a party to the agreement, directly or indirectly,

— owns more than half of the capital or business assets, or
— has the power to exercise more than half of the voting rights, or
— has the power to appoint more than half of the members of the supervisory board, board of management or bodies legally representing the undertakings, or
— has to the right to manage the undertaking's business;

(c) undertakings which directly or indirectly have over a party to the agreement the rights or powers listed in (b);

(d) undertakings over which an undertaking referred to in (c) has, directly or indirectly, the rights or powers listed in (b).

Undertakings over which several undertakings as referred to in (a) to (d) jointly have, directly or indirectly, the rights or powers set out in (b) shall also be considered to be participating undertakings.

13. In order to calculate the market share, it is necessary to determine the relevant market; for this, the relevant product market and the relevant geographic market must be de fined.

14. The relevant product market comprises any products or services which are regarded as interchangeable or substitutable by the consumer, by reason of their characteristics, prices and intended use.

15. The relevant geographic market comprises the area in which the participating undertakings are involved in the supply of relevant products or services, in which the conditions of competition are sufficiently homogeneous, and which can be distinguished from neighbouring geographic areas because, in particular, conditions of competition are appreciably different in those areas.

16. When applying points 14 and 15, reference should be had to the Notice [on the definition of the relevant market under Community competition law].[12]

17. In the case of doubt about the de limitation of the relevant geographic market, undertakings may take the view that the i r agreement has no appreciable effect on intracommunity trade or on competition when the market share thresholds indicated in points 9 and 10 are not exceeded in any Member State. This view,

[12] OJ 1997 C 372/5.

however, does not preclude the application of national competition law to the agreements in question.

18. Chapter II of this Notice shall not apply where in a relevant market competition is restricted by the cumulative effects of parallel networks of similar agreements established by several manufacturers or dealers.

III

19. Agreements between small and medium sized undertakings, as defined in the Annex to Commission Recommendation 96/280/EC[13] are rarely capable of significantly affecting trade between Member States and competition within the common market. Consequently, as a general rule, they are not caught by the prohibition in Article 85(1). In cases where such agreements exceptionally meet the conditions for the application of that provision, they will not be of sufficient Community interest to justify any intervention. This is why the Commission will not institute any proceedings, either upon request or on its own initiative, to apply the provisions of Article 85(1) to such agreements, even if the thresholds set out in points 9 and 10 above are exceeded.

20. The Commission nevertheless reserves the right to intervene in such agreements:
(a) where they significantly impede competition in a substantial part of the relevant market,
(b) where, in the relevant market, competition is restricted by the cumulative effect of parallel networks of similar agreements made between several producers or dealers.

Commission Notice (1997) on the definition of the relevant market for the purposes of Community Competition Law[14]

I. Introduction

The purpose of this notice is to provide guidance as to how the Commission applies the concept of relevant product and geographic market in its ongoing enforcement of Community competition law, in particular the application of Regulations 17/62 and 4064/89, their equivalents in other sectoral applications such as transport, coal and steel, and agriculture, and the relevant provisions of the EEA agreement.[15] Throughout this notice, references to Articles 85 and 86 of the Treaty and to merger control are to be understood as referring to the equivalent provisions in the EEA agreement and the ECSC Treaty.

Market definition is a tool to identify and define the boundaries of competition between firms. It allows to establish the framework within which competition policy is applied by the Commission. The main purpose of market definition is to identify in a systematic way the competitive constraints that the undertakings

---

[13] OJ 1996 L 107/4.   [14] OJ 1997 C 372/5.

[15] The focus of assessment in state aid cases is the aid recipient and the industry/sector concerned rather than identification of competitive constraints faced by the aid recipient. When consideration of market power and therefore of the relevant market are raised in any particular case, elements of the approach outlined here might serve as a basis for the assessment of state aid cases.

involved[16] face. The objective of defining a market in both its product and geographic dimension is to identify those actual competitors of the undertakings involved that are capable of constraining their behaviour and of preventing them from behaving independently of an effective competitive pressure. It is from this perspective, that the market definition makes it possible, inter alia, to calculate market shares that would convey meaningful information regarding market power for the purposes of assessing dominance or for the purposes of applying Article 85.

It follows from the above, that the concept of relevant market is different from other concepts of market often used in other contexts. For instance, companies often use the term market to refer to the area where it sells its products or to refer broadly to the industry or sector where it belongs

The definition of the relevant market in both its product and geographic dimensions often has a decisive influence on the assessment of a competition case. By rendering public the procedures the Commission follows when considering market definition and by indicating the criteria and evidence on which it relies to reach a decision, the Commission expects to increase the transparency of its policy and decision making in the area of competition policy.

Increased transparency will also result in companies and their advisors being able to better anticipate the possibility that the Commission would raise competition concerns in an individual case. Companies could, therefore, take such a possibility into account in their own internal decision making when contemplating for instance, acquisitions, the creation of joint ventures or the establishment of certain agreements. It is also intended that companies are in a better position to understand what sort of information the Commission considers relevant for the purposes of market definition.

The Commission's interpretation of the notion of relevant market is without prejudice to the interpretation which may be given by the Court of Justice or the Court of First Instance of the European Communities.

II. Definition of Relevant Market

Definition of Relevant Product and Relevant Geographic Market

The regulations based on Articles 85 and 86 of the Treaty, in particular in section 6 of Form A/B with respect to Regulation 17, as well as in section 6 of Form CO with respect to regulation 4064/89 on the control of concentrations of a Community dimension have laid down the following definitions. Relevant product markets are defined as follows:

'A relevant product market comprises all those products and/or services which are regarded as interchangeable or substitutable by the consumer, by reason of the products' characteristics, their prices and their intended use'.

Relevant geographic markets are defined as follows:

'The relevant geographic market comprises the area in which the undertakings concerned are involved in the supply and demand of products or services, in which the conditions of competition are sufficiently homogeneous and which

---

[16] For the purposes of this notice, the undertakings involved will be in the case of a concentration, the parties to the concentration; in investigations under Article 86 of the Treaty, the undertaking being investigated or the complainants; for investigations under Article 85, the parties to the agreement.

can be distinguished from neighbouring areas because the conditions of competition are appreciably different in those areas'.

The relevant market within which to assess a given competition issue is therefore established by the combination of the product and geographic markets. The Commission interprets the definitions at paragraphs 7 and 8 (which reflect the jurisprudence of the Court of Justice and the Court of First Instance as well as its own decisional practice) according to the orientations defined in this Notice.

Concept of Relevant Market and Objectives of Community Competition Policy

The concept of relevant market is closely related to the objectives pursued under Community competition policy. For example under the Community's merger control, the objective in controlling structural changes in the supply of a product/service is to prevent the creation or reinforcement of a dominant position as a result of which effective competition would be significantly impeded in a substantial part of the common market. Under the Community's competition policy, a dominant position is such that a firm or group of firms would be in a position to behave to an appreciable extent independently of its competitors, customers and ultimately of its consumers.[17] Such a position would usually arise when a firm or group of firms would account for a large share of the supply in any given market, provided that other factors analysed in the assessment (such as entry barriers, capacity of reaction of customers, etc.) point in the same direction.

The same approach is followed by the Commission in its application of Article 86 of the Treaty to firms that enjoy a single or collective dominant position. Under Regulation 17 the Commission has the power to investigate and bring to an end abuses of such a dominant position, which must also be defined by reference to the relevant market. Markets may also need to be defined in the application of Article 85 of the Treaty, in particular, in determining whether an appreciable restriction of competition exists or in establishing if the condition under Article 85 (3)(b) for an exemption from the application of article 85(1) is met.

The criteria to define the relevant market are applied generally for the analysis of certain behaviours in the market and for the analysis of structural changes in the supply of products. This methodology, though, might lead to different results depending on the nature of the competition issue being examined. For instance, the scope of the geographic market might be different when analysing a concentration, where the analysis is essentially prospective, than when analysing past behaviour. The different time horizon considered in each case might lead to the result that different geographic markets are defined for the same products depending on whether the Commission is examining a change in the structure of supply, such as a concentration or a cooperative joint venture, or issues relating to certain past behaviour.

Basic Principles for Market Definition

COMPETITIVE CONSTRAINTS

Firms are subject to three main sources of competitive constraints: demand substitutability, supply substitutability and potential competition. From an economic

---

[17] Definition given by the Court of Justice in Hoffmann La Roche (CJEC Sentence of 13 February 1979, Case 85/76), and confirmed in subsequent judgments.

point of view, for the definition of the relevant market, demand substitution constitutes the most immediate and effective disciplinary force on the suppliers of a given product, in particular in relation to their pricing decisions. A firm or a group of firms cannot have a significant impact on the prevailing conditions of sale, such as prices, if its customers are in a position to switch easily to available substitute products or to suppliers located elsewhere. Basically, the exercise of market definition consists in identifying the effective alternative sources of supply for the customers of the undertakings involved, both in terms of products/services and geographic location of suppliers.

The competitive constraints arising from supply side substitutability other then those described in para 20–23 and from potential competition are in general less immediate and in any case require an analysis of additional factors. As a result such constraints are taken into account at the assessment stage of competition analysis.

DEMAND SUBSTITUTION

The assessment of demand substitution entails a determination of the range of products which are viewed as substitutes by the consumer. One way of making this determination can be viewed, as a thought experiment, postulating a hypothetical small, non-transitory change in relative prices and evaluating the likely reactions of customers to that increase. The exercise of market definition focuses on prices for operational and practical purposes, and more precisely on demand substitution arising from small, permanent changes in relative prices. This concept can provide clear indications as to the evidence that is relevant to define markets.

Conceptually, this approach implies that starting from the type of products that the undertakings involved sell and the area in which they sell them, additional products and areas will be included into or excluded from the market definition depending on whether competition from these other products and areas affect or restrain sufficiently the pricing of the parties' products in the short term.

The question to be answered is whether the parties' customers would switch to readily available substitutes or to suppliers located elsewhere in response to an hypothetical small (in the range 5%–10%), permanent relative price increase in the products and areas being considered. If substitution would be enough to make the price increase unprofitable because of the resulting loss of sales, additional substitutes and areas are included in the relevant market. This would be done until the set of products and geographic areas is such that small, permanent increases in relative prices would be profitable. The equivalent analysis is applicable in cases concerning the concentration of buying power, where the starting point would then be the supplier and the price test allows to identify the alternative distribution channels or outlets for the supplier's products. In the application of these principles, careful account should be taken of certain particular situations as described under paragraphs 56 and 58.

A practical example of this test can be provided by its application to a merger of, for instance, soft drink bottlers. An issue to examine in such a case would be to decide whether different flavours of soft drinks belong to the same market. In practice, the question to address would be if consumers of flavour A would switch to other flavours when confronted with a permanent price increase of 5% to 10% for flavour A. If a sufficient number of consumers would switch to, say, flavour B, to such an extent that the price increase for flavour A would not be profitable due to the resulting loss of sales, then the market would comprise at least flavours A and B. The process would have to be extended in addition to other available flavours until a set of products is identified for which a price rise would not induce a sufficient substitution in demand.

Generally, and in particular for the analysis of merger cases, the price to take into account will be the prevailing market price. This might not be the case where the prevailing price has been determined in the absence of sufficient competition. In particular for investigation of abuses of dominant positions, the fact that the prevailing price might already have been substantially increased will be taken into account.

SUPPLY SUBSTITUTION

Supply-side substitutability may also be taken into account when defining markets in those situations in which its effects are equivalent to those of demand substitution in terms of effectiveness and immediacy. This requires that suppliers be able to switch production to the relevant products and market them in the short term[18] without incurring significant additional costs or risks in response to small and permanent changes in relative prices. When these conditions are met, the additional production that is put on the market will have a disciplinary effect on the competitive behaviour of the companies involved. Such an impact in terms of effectiveness and immediacy is equivalent to the demand substitution effect.

These situations typically arise when companies market a wide range of qualities or grades of one product; even if for a given final customer or group of consumers, the different qualities are not substitutable, the different qualities will be grouped into one product market provided that most of the suppliers are able to offer and sell the various qualities under the conditions of immediacy and absence of significant increase in costs described above. In such cases, the relevant product market will encompass all products that are substitutable in demand and supply, and the current sales of those products will be summed to calculate the total value or volume of the market. The same reasoning may lead to group different geographic areas.

A practical example of the approach to supply side substitutability when defining product markets is to be found in the case of paper. Paper is usually supplied in a range of different qualities, from standard writing paper to high quality papers to be used for instance to publish art books. From a demand point of view, different qualities of paper cannot be used for a specific use, i.e. an art book or a high quality publication cannot be based on lower quality papers. However, paper plants are prepared to manufacture the different qualities, and production can be adjusted with negligible costs and in a short time frame. In the absence of particular difficulties in distribution, paper manufacturers are able therefore to compete for orders of the various qualities, in particular if orders are passed with a sufficient lead time to allow to modify production plans. Under such circumstances, the Commission would not define a separate market for each quality of paper and respective usage.

---

[18] i.e. the period which does not imply a significant adjustment of existing tangible and intangible assets (see para. 23).

The various qualities of paper are included in the relevant market, and their sales added up to estimate total market value and volume.

When supply side substitutability would imply the need to adjust significantly existing tangible and intangible assets, additional investments, strategic decisions or time delays, it will not be considered at the stage of market definition. Examples where supply side substitution did not lead the Commission to enlarge the market are offered in the area of consumer products, in particular for branded beverages. Although bottling plants may in principle bottle different beverages, there are costs and lead times involved (in terms of advertising, product testing and distribution) before the products can actually be sold. In these cases, the effects of supply side substitutability and other forms of potential competition would then be examined at a later stage.

POTENTIAL COMPETITION

The third source of competitive constraint, potential competition, is not taken into account when defining markets, since the conditions under which potential competition will actually represent an effective competitive constraint depend on the analysis of specific factors and circumstances related to the conditions of entry. If required, this analysis is only carried out at a subsequent stage, in general once the position of the companies involved in the relevant market has already been ascertained, and such position is indicative of concerns from a competition point of view.

III. EVIDENCE RELIED UPON TO DEFINE RELEVANT MARKETS

The Process of Defining the Relevant Market in Practice

PRODUCT DIMENSION

There is a range of evidence permitting to assess the extent to which substitution would take place. In individual cases, certain types of evidence will be determinant, depending very much on the characteristics and specificity of the industry and products or services that are being examined. The same type of evidence may be of no importance in other cases. In most cases, a decision will have to be based on the consideration of a number of criteria and different items of evidence. The Commission follows an open approach to empirical evidence, aimed at making an effective use of all available information which may be relevant in individual cases. The Commission does not follow a rigid hierarchy of different sources of information or types of evidence.

The process of defining relevant markets may be summarised as follows: on the basis of the preliminary information available or information submitted by the undertakings involved, the Commission will usually be in a position to broadly establish the possible relevant markets within which, for instance a concentration or a restriction of competition has to be assessed. In general, and for all practical purposes when handling individual cases, the question will usually be to decide on a few alternative possible relevant markets. For instance, with respect to the product market, the issue will often be to establish whether product A and product B belong or do not belong to the same product market. It is often the case that the inclusion of product B would be enough to remove any competition concerns.

In such situations it is not necessary to consider whether the market also includes additional products and reach a definitive conclusion on the precise product market. If under the conceivable alternative market definitions the operation in question does not raise competition concerns, the question of market definition will be left open, reducing thereby the burden on companies to supply information.

GEOGRAPHIC DIMENSION

The Commission's approach to geographic market definition might be summarised as follows: it will take a preliminary view of the scope of the geographic market on the basis of broad indications regarding the distribution of market shares of the parties and their competitors as well as a preliminary analysis of pricing and price differences at national and EU or EEA level. This initial view is used basically as a working hypothesis to focus the Commission's enquiries for the purposes of arriving at a precise geographic market definition.

The reasons behind any particular configuration of prices and market shares need to be explored. Companies might enjoy high market shares in their domestic markets just because of the weight of the past, and conversely, a homogeneous presence of companies throughout the EEA might be consistent with national or regional geographic markets. The initial working hypothesis will therefore be checked against an analysis of demand characteristics (importance of national or local preferences, current patterns of purchases of customers, product differentiation/brands, other) in order to establish whether companies in different areas do really constitute an actual alternative source of supply for consumers. The theoretical experiment is again based on substitution arising from changes in relative prices, and the question to answer is again whether the customers of the parties would switch their orders to companies located elsewhere in the short term and at a negligible cost..

If necessary, a further check on supply factors will be carried out to ensure that those companies located in distinct areas do not face impediments to develop their sales on competitive terms throughout the whole geographic market. This analysis will include an examination of requirements for a local presence in order to sell in that area, the conditions of access to distribution channels, costs associated with setting up a distribution network, and the existence or absence of regulatory barriers arising from public procurement, price regulations, quotas and tariffs limiting trade or production, technical standards, monopolies, freedom of establishment, requirements for administrative authorisations, packaging regulations, etc.

In short, the Commission will identify possible obstacles and barriers isolating companies located in a given area from the competitive pressure of companies located outside that area, so as to determine the precise degree of market interpenetration at national, European or global level.

The actual pattern and evolution of trade flows offers useful supplementary indications as to the economic importance of each demand or supply factors mentioned above, and the extent to which they may or may not constitute actual barriers creating different geographic markets. The analysis of trade flows will generally address the question of transport costs and the extent to which these may hinder trade between different areas, having regard to plant location, costs of production and relative price levels.

MARKET INTEGRATION IN THE EUROPEAN UNION

Finally, the Commission also takes into account the continuing process of market integration in particular in the European Union when defining geographic markets, especially in the area of concentrations and structural joint ventures. The measures adopted and implemented in the internal market programme to remove barriers to trade and further integrate the community markets cannot be ignored when assessing the effects on competition of a concentration or a structural joint venture. A situation where national markets have been artificially isolated from each other because of the existence of legislative barriers that have now been removed, will generally lead to a cautious assessment of past evidence regarding prices, market shares or trade patterns. A process of market integration that would, in the short term, lead to wider geographic markets may therefore be taken into consideration when defining the geographic market for the purposes of assessing concentrations and joint ventures.

The Process of Gathering Evidence

When a precise market definition is deemed necessary, the Commission will often contact the main customers and the main companies in the industry to enquire into their views about the boundaries of product and geographic markets and to obtain the necessary factual evidence to reach a conclusion. The Commission might also contact the relevant professional associations, and where appropriate, companies active in upstream markets, so as to be able to define, insofar as necessary, separate product and geographic markets, for different levels of production or distribution of the products/services in question. It might also request additional information to the undertakings involved.

Where appropriate, the Commission services will address written requests for information to the market players mentioned above. These requests will usually include questions relating to the perceptions of companies about reactions to hypothetical price increases and their views of the boundaries of the relevant market. They will also include requests to provide the factual information the Commission deems necessary to reach a conclusion on the extent of the relevant market. The Commission services might also discuss with marketing directors or other officers of those companies to gain a better understanding on how negotiations between suppliers and customers take place and better understand issues relating to the definition of the relevant market. Where appropriate, they might also carry out visits or inspections to the premises of the parties, their customers and/or their competitors, in order to better understand how products are manufactured and sold.

The type of evidence relevant to reach a conclusion as to the product market can be categorised as follows.

EVIDENCE TO DEFINE MARKETS—PRODUCT DIMENSION

An analysis of the product characteristics and its intended use allows the Commission, in a first step, to limit the field of investigation of possible substitutes. However, product characteristics and intended use are insufficient to conclude whether two products are demand substitutes. Functional interchangeability or similarity in characteristics may not provide in themselves sufficient criteria because the responsiveness of customers to relative price changes may be determined by other considerations also. For example, there may be different competitive constraints in the original equipment market for car components and in spare parts, thereby leading to a distinction of two relevant markets. Conversely, differences in product characteristics are not in themselves sufficient to exclude demand substitutability, since this will depend to a large extent on how customers value different characteristics.

The type of evidence the Commission considers relevant to assess whether two products are demand substitutes can be categorised as follows:

Evidence of substitution in the recent past   In certain cases, it is possible to analyse evidence relating to recent past events or shocks in the market that offer actual examples of substitution between two products. When available, this sort of information will normally be fundamental for market definition. If there have been changes in relative prices in the past (all else being equal), the reactions in terms of quantities demanded will be determinant in establishing substitutability. Launches of new products in the past can also offer useful information, when it is possible to precisely analyse which products lost sales to the new product.

There are a number of quantitative tests that have specifically been designed for the purpose of delineating markets. These tests consist of various econometric and statistical approaches: estimates of elasticities and cross-price elasticities[19] for the demand of a product, tests based on similarity of price movements over time, the analysis of causality between price series and similarity of price levels and/or their convergence. The Commission takes into account the available quantitative evidence capable of withstanding rigorous scrutiny for the purposes of establishing patterns of substitution in the past.

Views of customers and competitors   The Commission often contacts the main customers and competitors of the companies involved in its enquiries, to gather their views on the boundaries of the product market as well as most of the factual information it requires to reach a conclusion on the scope of the market. Reasoned answers of customers and competitors as to what would happen if relative prices for the candidate products would increase in the candidate geographic area by a small amount (for instance of 5%–10%) are taken into account when they are sufficiently backed by factual evidence.

Consumer preferences   In cases of consumer goods, it might be difficult for the Commission to gather the direct views of end consumers about substitute products. Marketing studies that companies have commissioned in the past and that are used by companies in their own decision making as to pricing of their products and/or marketing actions may provide useful information for the Commission's delineation of the relevant market. Consumer surveys on usage patterns and attitudes, data from consumer's purchasing patterns, the views expressed by retailers and more generally, market research studies submitted by the parties and their competitors are taken into account to establish whether an economically significant proportion of consumers consider two products as substitutable, taking also into

---

[19] Own price elasticity of demand for product X is a measure of the responsiveness of demand for X to percentage change in its own price. Cross-price elasticity between products X and Y is the resposiveness of demand for product X to percentage change in the price of product Y.

account the importance of brands for the products in question. The methodology followed in consumer surveys carried out ad-hoc by the undertakings involved or their competitors for the purposes of a merger procedure or a procedure under Regulation 17 will usually be scrutinized with utmost care. Unlike pre-existing studies, they have not been prepared in the normal course of business for the adoption of business decisions.

Barriers and costs associated with switching demand to potential substitutes There are a number of barriers and costs that might prevent the Commission from considering two prima facie demand substitutes as belonging to one single product market. It is not possible to provide an exhaustive list of all the possible barriers to substitution and of switching costs. These barriers or obstacles might have a wide range of origins, and in its decisions, the Commission has been confronted with regulatory barriers or other forms of State intervention, constraints arising in downstream markets, need to incur specific capital investment or loss in current output in order to switch to alternative inputs, the location of customers, specific investment in production process, learning and human capital investment, retooling costs or other investments, uncertainty about quality and reputation of unknown suppliers, and others.

Different categories of customers and price discrimination The extent of the product market might be narrowed in the presence of distinct groups of customers. A distinct group of customers for the relevant product may constitute a narrower, distinct market when such group could be subject to price discrimination. This will usually be the case when two conditions are met: a) it is possible to identify clearly which group an individual customer belongs to at the moment of selling the relevant products to him, and b) trade among customers or arbitrage by third parties should not be feasible.

Evidence to define markets—Geographic dimension

The type of evidence the Commission considers relevant to reach a conclusion as to the geographic market can be categorised as follows:

Past evidence of diversion of orders to other areas In certain cases, evidence on changes in prices between different areas and consequent reactions by customers might be available. Generally, the same quantitative tests used for product market definition might as well be used in geographic market definition, bearing in mind that international comparisons of prices might be more complex due to a number of factors such as exchange rate movements, taxation and product differentiation.

Basic demand characteristics The nature of demand for the relevant product may in itself determine the scope of the geographical market. Factors such as national preferences or preferences for national brands, language, culture and life style, and the need for a local presence have a strong potential to limit the geographic scope of competition.

Views of customers and competitors Where appropriate, the Commission will contact the main customers and competitors of the parties in its enquiries, to gather their views on the boundaries of the geographic market as well as most of the factual information it requires to reach a conclusion on the scope of the market when they are sufficiently backed by factual evidence.

Current geographic pattern of purchases   ʌn examination of the customers' current geographic pattern of purchases provides useful evidence as to the possible scope of the geographic market. When customers purchase from companies located anywhere in the EU or the EEA on similar terms, or they procure their supplies through effective tendering procedures in which companies from anywhere in the EU or the EEA do submit bids, the geographic market will be usually considered to be Community-wide.

Trade flows/pattern of shipments   When the number of customers is so large that it is not possible to obtain through them a clear picture of geographic purchasing patterns, information on trade flows might be used alternatively, provided that the trade statistics are available with a sufficient degree of detail for the relevant products. Trade flows, and above all, the rational behind trade flows provide useful insights and information for the purpose of establishing the scope of the geographic market but are not in themselves conclusive.

Barriers and switching costs associated to divert orders to companies located in other areas The absence of transborder purchases or trade flows, for instance, does not necessarily mean that the market is at most national in scope. Still, barriers isolating the national market have to identified before concluding that the relevant geographic market in such a case is national. Perhaps the clearest obstacle for a customer to divert its orders to other areas is the impact of transport costs and transport restrictions arising from legislation or from the nature of the relevant products. The impact of transport costs will usually limit the scope of the geographic market for bulky, low value products, bearing in mind that a transport disadvantage might also be compensated by a comparative advantage in other costs (labour costs or raw materials). Access to distribution in a given area, regulatory barriers still existing in certain sectors, quotas and custom tariffs might also constitute barriers isolating a geographic area from the competitive pressure of companies located outside that area. Significant switching costs in procuring supplies from companies located in other countries constitute additional sources of such barriers.

On the basis of the evidence gathered, the Commission will then define a geographic market that could range from a local dimension to a global one, and there are examples of both local and global markets in past decisions of the Commission.

The paragraphs above describe the different factors which might be relevant to define markets. This does not imply that in each individual case it will be necessary to obtain evidence and assess each of these factors. Often in practice the evidence provided by a subset of these factors will be sufficient to reach a conclusion, as shown in the past decisional practice of the Commission.

IV. Calculation of Market Shares

The definition of the relevant market in both its product and geographic dimensions allows to identify the suppliers and the customers/consumers active on that market. On that basis, a total market size and market shares for each supplier can be calculated on the basis of their sales of the relevant products on the relevant area. In practice, the total market size and market shares are often available from market sources, i.e. companies' estimates, studies commissioned to industry consultants and/or trade associations. When this is not the case, or also when available estimates are not reliable, the Commission will usually ask each supplier in the relevant market to provide its own sales in order to calculate total market size and market shares.

If sales are usually the reference to calculate market shares, there are nevertheless other indications that, depending on the specific products or industry in question, can offer useful information such as, in particular, capacity, the number of players in bidding markets, units of fleet as in aerospace, or the reserves held in the case of sectors such as mining.

As a rule of thumb, both volume sales and value sales provide useful information. In cases of differentiated products, sales in value and their associated market share will usually be considered to better reflect the relative position and strength of each supplier.

V. ADDITIONAL CONSIDERATIONS

There are certain areas where the application of the principles above has to be undertaken with care. This is the case when considering primary and secondary markets, in particular, when the behaviour of undertakings at a point in time has to be analysed under Article 86. The method to define markets in these cases is the same, i.e. to assess the responses of customers based on their purchasing decisions to relative price changes, but taking into account as well constraints on substitution imposed by conditions in the connected markets. A narrow definition of market for secondary products, for instance, spare parts, may result when compatibility with the primary product is important. Problems of finding compatible secondary products together with the existence of high prices and a long life time of the primary products may render relative price increases of secondary products profitable. A different market definition may result if significant substitution between secondary products is possible or if the characteristics of the primary products make quick and direct consumer responses to relative price increases of the secondary products feasible.

In certain cases, the existence of chains of substitution might lead to the definition of a relevant market where products or areas at the extreme of the market are not directly substitutable. An example might be provided by the geographic dimension of a product with significant transport costs. In such cases, deliveries from a given plant are limited to a certain area around each plant by the impact of transport costs. In principle, such area could constitute the relevant geographic market. However, if the distribution of plants is such that there are considerable overlaps between the areas around different plants, it is possible that the pricing of those products will be constrained by a chain substitution effect, and lead to define a broader geographic market. The same reasoning may apply if product B is a demand substitute for products A and C. Even if products A and C are not direct demand substitutes they might be found to be in the same relevant product market since their respective pricing might be constrained by substitution to B.

From a practical perspective, the concept of chains of substitution has to be corroborated by actual evidence, for instance related to price interdependence at the extremes of the chains of substitution, in order to lead to an extension of the relevant market in an individual case. Price levels at the extremes of the chains would have to be as well of the same magnitude

Commission Regulation of 22 June 1983 on the application of Article 85(3) of the EC Treaty to categories of exclusive distribution agreements (1983/83/EEC)[20]

The Commission of the European Communities,

[recitals omitted]

(1) Whereas Regulation No. 19/65/EEC empowers the Commission to apply Art. 85(3) of the Treaty by regulation to certain categories of bilateral exclusive distribution agreements and analogous concerted practices falling within Art. 85(1);

(2) Whereas experience to date makes it possible to define a category of agreements and concerted practices which can be regarded as normally satisfying the conditions laid down in Art. 85(3);

(3) Whereas exclusive distribution agreements of the category defined in Art. 1 of this Regulation may fall within the prohibition contained in Art. 85(1) of the Treaty; whereas this will apply in exceptional cases to exclusive agreements of this kind to which only undertakings from one Member State are party and which concern the resale of goods within that Member State; whereas, however, to the extent that such agreements may affect trade between Member States and also satisfy all the requirements set out in this Regulation there is no reason to withhold from them the benefit of the exemption by category;

(4) Whereas it is not necessary expressly to exclude from the defined category those agreements which do not fulfil the conditions of Art. 85(1) of the Treaty;

(5) Whereas exclusive distribution agreements lead in general to an improvement in distribution because the undertaking is able to concentrate its sales activities, does not need to maintain numerous business relations with a larger number of dealers and is able, by dealing with only one dealer, to overcome more easily distribution difficulties in international trade resulting from linguistic, legal and other differences;

(6) Whereas exclusive distribution agreements facilitate the promotion of sales of a product and lead to intensive marketing and to continuity of supplies while at the same time rationalising distribution; whereas they stimulate competition between the products of different manufacturers; whereas the appointment of an exclusive distributor who will take over sales promotion, customer services and carrying of stocks is often the most effective way, and sometimes indeed the only way, for the manufacturer to enter a market and compete with other manufacturers already present; whereas this is particularly so in the case of small and medium-sized undertakings; whereas it must be left to the contracting parties to decide whether and to what extent they consider it desirable to incorporate in the agreements terms providing for the promotion of sales;

---

[20] OJ 1983 L 173/1, as last amended by Commission Regulation 1582/97/EC, OJ 1997 L 214/27.

(7) Whereas, as a rule, such exclusive distribution agreements also allow consumers a fair share of the resulting benefit as they gain directly from the improvement in distribution, and their economic and supply position is improved as they can obtain products manufactured in particular in other countries more quickly and more easily;

(8) Whereas this Regulation must define the obligations restricting competition which may be included in exclusive distribution agreements; whereas the other restrictions on competition allowed under this Regulation in addition to the exclusive supply obligation produce a clear division of functions between the parties and compel the exclusive distributor to concentrate his sales efforts on the contract goods and the contract territory; whereas they are, where they are agreed only for the duration of the agreement, generally necessary in order to attain the improvement in the distribution of goods sought through exclusive distribution; whereas it may be left to the contracting parties to decide which of these obligations they include in their agreements; whereas further restrictive obligations and in particular those which limit the exclusive distributor's choice of customers or his freedom to determine his prices and conditions of sale cannot be exempted under this Regulation;

(9) Whereas the exemption by category should be reserved for agreements for which it can be assumed with sufficient certainty that they satisfy the conditions of Art. 85(3) of the Treaty;

(10) Whereas it is not possible, in the absence of a case-by-case examination, to consider that adequate improvements in distribution occur where a manufacturer entrusts the distribution of his goods to another manufacturer with whom he is in competition; whereas such agreements should, therefore, be excluded from the exemption by category; whereas certain derogations from this rule in favour of small and medium-sized undertakings can be allowed;

(11) Whereas consumers will be assured of a fair share of the benefits resulting from exclusive distribution only if parallel imports remain possible; whereas agreements relating to goods which the user can obtain only from the exclusive distributor should therefore be excluded from the exemption by category; whereas the parties cannot be allowed to abuse industrial property rights or other rights in order to create absolute territorial protection; whereas this does not prejudice the relationship between competition law and industrial property rights, since the sole object here is to determine the conditions for exemption by category;

(12) Whereas, since competition at the distribution stage is ensured by the possibility of parallel imports, the exclusive distribution agreements covered by this Regulation will not normally afford any possibility of eliminating competition in respect of a substantial part of the products in question; whereas this is also true of agreements that allot to the exclusive distributor a contract territory covering the whole of the common market;

(13) Whereas, in particular cases in which agreements or concerted practices satisfying the requirements of this Regulation nevertheless have effects incompatible with Art. 85(3) of the Treaty, the Commission may withdraw the benefit of the exemption by category from the undertakings party to them;

(14) Whereas agreements and concerted practices which satisfy the conditions set out in this Regulation need not be notified; whereas an undertaking may

nonetheless in a particular case where real doubt exists, request the Commission to declare whether its agreements comply with this Regulation;

(15) Whereas this Regulation does not affect the applicability of Commission Regulation (EEC) No. 3604/82 of 23 December 1982 on the application of Art. 85(3) of the Treaty to categories of specialisation agreements, whereas it does not exclude the application of Art. 86 of the Treaty.

HAS ADOPTED this Regulation:

Article 1 Pursuant to Art. 85(3) of the Treaty and subject to the provisions of this Regulation, it is hereby declared that Art. 85(1) of the Treaty shall not apply to agreements to which only two undertakings are party and whereby one party agrees with the other to supply certain goods for resale within the whole or a defined area of the common market only to that other.

Article 2 1. Apart from the obligation referred to in Art. 1 no restriction on competition shall be imposed on the supplier other than the obligation not to supply the contract goods to users in the contract territory.

2. No restriction on competition shall be imposed on the exclusive distributor other than:
(a) the obligation not to manufacture or distribute goods which compete with the contract goods;
(b) the obligation to obtain the contract goods for resale only from the other party;
(c) the obligation to refrain, outside the contract territory and in relation to the contract goods, from seeking customers, from establishing any branch and from maintaining any distribution depot.

3. Art. 1 shall apply notwithstanding that the exclusive distributor undertakes all or any of the following obligations:
(a) to purchase complete ranges of goods or minimum quantities;
(b) to sell the contract goods under trademarks or packed and present as specified by the other party;
(c) to take measures for promotion of sales, in particular:

— to advertise,
— to maintain a sales network or stock of goods,
— to provide customer and guarantee services,
— to employ staff having specialised or technical training.

Article 3 Art. 1 shall not apply where:
(a) manufacturers of identical goods or of goods which are considered by users as equivalent in view of their characteristics, price and intended use enter into reciprocal exclusive distribution agreements between themselves in respect of such goods;
(b) manufacturers of identical goods or of goods which are considered by users as equivalent in view of their characteristics, price and intended use enter into a non-reciprocal exclusive distribution agreement between themselves in respect of such goods unless at least one of them has a total annual turnover of no more than 100 million ECU;

(c) users can obtain the contract goods in the contract territory only from the exclusive distributor and have no alternative source of supply outside the contract territory;

(d) one or both of the parties makes it difficult for intermediaries or users to obtain the contract goods from other dealers inside the common market or, in so far as no alternative source of supply is available there, from outside the common market, in particular where one or both of them:

    1. exercises industrial property rights so as to prevent dealers or users from obtaining outside, or from selling in, the contract territory properly marked or otherwise properly marketed contract goods;

    2. exercises other rights or takes other measures so as to prevent dealers or users from obtaining outside, or from selling in, the contract territory contract goods.

Article 4　1. Art. 3(a) and (b) shall also apply where the goods there referred to are manufactured by an undertaking connected with a party to the agreement.

2. Connected undertakings are:

(a) undertakings in which a party to the agreement, directly or indirectly:

owns more than half the capital or business assets, or

  — has the power to exercise more than half the voting rights, or
  — has the power to appoint more than half the members of the supervisory board, board of directors or bodies legally representing the undertaking, or
  — has the right to manage the affairs;

(b) undertakings which directly or indirectly have in or over a party to the agreement the rights or powers listed in (a);

(c) undertakings in which an undertaking referred to in (b) directly or indirectly has the rights or powers listed in (a).

3. Undertakings in which the parties to the agreement or undertakings connected with them jointly have the rights or powers set out in paragraph 2 (a) shall be considered to be connected with each of the parties to the agreement.

Article 5　1. For the purpose of Art. 3(b), the ECU is the unit of account used for drawing up the budget of the Community pursuant to Arts. 207 and 209 of the Treaty.

2. Article 1 shall remain applicable where during any period of two consecutive financial years the total turnover referred to in Art. 3(b) is exceeded by no more than 10%.

3. For the purpose of calculating total turnover within the meaning of Art. 3(b), the turnovers achieved during the last financial year by the party to the agreement and connected undertakings in respect of all goods and services, excluding all taxes and other duties, shall be added together. For this purpose no account shall be taken of dealings between the party to the agreement and its connected undertakings or between its connected undertakings.

Article 6　The Commission may withdraw the benefit of this Regulation, pursuant to Art. 7 of Regulation No. 19/65/EEC, when it finds in a particular case that an agreement which is exempted by this Regulation nevertheless has certain effects

which are incompatible with the conditions set out in Art. 85(3) of the Treaty, and in particular where;
(a) the contract goods are not subject, in the contract territory, to effective competition from identical goods or goods considered by users as equivalent in view of their characteristics, price and intended use;
(b) access by other suppliers to the different stages of distribution within the contract territory is made difficult to a significant extent;
(c) for reasons other than those referred to in Art. 3(c) and (d) it is not possible for intermediaries or users to obtain supplies of the contract goods from dealers outside the contract territory on the terms there customary;
(d) the exclusive distributor:

1. without any objectively justified reason refuses to supply in the contract territory categories of purchasers who cannot obtain contract goods elsewhere on suitable terms or applies to them differing prices or conditions of sale;
2. sells the contract goods at excessively high prices.

Article 7   In the period 1 July 1983 to 31 December 1986, the prohibition in Art. 85(1) of the Treaty shall not apply to agreements which were in force on 1 July 1983 or entered into force between 1 July and 31 December 1983 and which satisfy the exemption conditions of Regulation No. 67/67/EEC.

The provisions of the proceeding paragraph shall apply in the same way to agreements which were in force on the date of accession of the Kingdom of Spain and of the Portuguese Republic and which, as a result of accession fall within the scope of Art. 85(1) of the Treaty.

Article 7a   The prohibition in Article 85(1) of the Treaty shall not apply to agreements which were in existence at the date of accession of Austria, Finland and Sweden and which, by reason of this accession, fall within the scope of Article 85(1) if, within six months from the date of accession, they are so amended that they comply with the conditions laid down in this Regulation. However, this Article shall not apply to agreements which at the date of accession already fall under Article 53 of the EEA Agreement.

Article 8   This Regulation shall not apply to agreements entered into for the resale of drinks in premises used for the sale and consumption of beer or for the resale of petroleum products in service stations.

Article 9   This Regulation shall apply *mutatis mutandis* to concerted practices of the type defined in Art. 1.

Article 10   This Regulation shall enter into force on 1 July 1983. It shall expire on 31 December 1999.

[*final provisions omitted*]

Commission Regulation of 22 June 1983 on the application of Article 85(3) of the EC Treaty to categories of exclusive purchasing agreements (1984/83/EEC)[21]

The Commission of the European Communities,

[recitals omitted]

(1) Whereas Regulation No. 19/65/EEC empowers the Commission to apply Art. 85(3) of the Treaty by regulation to certain categories of bilateral exclusive purchasing agreements entered into for the purpose of the resale of goods and corresponding concerted practices falling within Art. 85;

(2) Whereas experience to date makes it possible to define three categories of agreements and concerted practices which can be regarded as normally satisfying the conditions laid down in Art. 85(3); whereas the first category comprises exclusive purchasing agreements of short and medium duration in all sectors of the economy; whereas the other two categories comprise long-term exclusive purchasing agreements entered into for the resale of beer in premises used for the sale and consumption of drinks (beer supply agreements) and of petroleum products in service stations (service-station agreements);

(3) Whereas exclusive purchasing agreements of the categories defined in this Regulation may fall within the prohibition contained in Art. 85(1) of the Treaty; whereas this will often be the case with agreements concluded between undertakings from different Member States; whereas an exclusive purchasing agreement to which undertakings from only one Member State are party and which concerns the resale of goods within that Member State may also be caught by the prohibition; whereas this is in particular the case where it is one of a number of similar agreements which together may affect trade between Member States;

(4) Whereas it is not necessary expressly to exclude from the defined categories those agreements which do not fulfil the conditions of Art. 85(1) of the Treaty;

(5) Whereas the exclusive purchasing agreements defined in this Regulation lead in general to an improvement in distribution; whereas they enable the supplier to plan the sales of his goods with greater precision and for a longer period and ensure that the reseller's requirements will be met on a regular basis for the duration of the agreement; whereas this allows the parties to limit the risk to them of variations in market conditions and to lower distribution costs;

(6) Whereas such agreements also facilitate the promotion of the sales of a product and lead to intensive marketing because the supplier, in consideration for the exclusive purchasing obligation, is as a rule under an obligation to contribute to the improvement of the structure of the distribution network, the quality of the promotional effort or the sales success; whereas, at the same time, they stimulate competition between the products of different manufacturers; whereas the appointment of several resellers, who are bound to purchase exclusively from the manufacturer and who take over sales promotion, customer services and carrying

---

[21] OJ 1983 L 173/5, as last amended by Commission Regulation 1582/97/EC, OJ 1997 L 214/27.

of stock, is often the most effective way, and sometimes the only way, for the manufacturer to penetrate a market and compete with other manufacturers already present; whereas this is particularly so in the case of small and medium-sized undertakings; whereas it must be left to the contracting parties to decide whether and to what extent they consider it desirable to incorporate in their agreements terms concerning the promotion of sales;

(7) Whereas, as a rule, exclusive purchasing agreements between suppliers and resellers also allow consumers a fair share of the resulting benefit as they gain the advantages of regular supply and are able to obtain the contract goods more quickly and more easily;

(8) Whereas this Regulation must define the obligations restricting competition which may be included in an exclusive purchasing agreement; whereas the other restrictions of competition allowed under this Regulation in addition to the exclusive purchasing obligation lead to a clear division of functions between the parties and compel the reseller to concentrate his sales efforts on the contract goods; whereas they are, where they are agreed only for the duration of the agreement, generally necessary in order to attain the improvement in the distribution of goods sought through exclusive purchasing; whereas further restrictive obligations and in particular those which limit the reseller's choice of customers or his freedom to determine his prices and conditions of sale cannot be exempted under this Regulation;

(9) Whereas the exemption by categories should be reserved for agreements for which it can be assumed with sufficient certainty that they satisfy the conditions of Art. 85(3) of the Treaty;

(10) Whereas it is not possible, in the absence of a case-by-case examination, to consider that adequate improvements in distribution occur where a manufacturer imposes an exclusive purchasing obligation with respect to his goods on a manufacturer with whom he is in competition; whereas such agreements should, therefore, be excluded from the exemption by categories; whereas certain derogations from this rule in favour of small and medium-sized undertakings can be allowed;

(11) Whereas certain conditions must be attached to the exemption by categories so that access by other undertakings to the different stages of distribution can be ensured; whereas, to this end, limits must be set to the scope and to the duration of the exclusive purchasing obligation; whereas it appears appropriate as a general rule to grant the benefit of a general exemption from the prohibition on restrictive agreements only to exclusive purchasing agreements which are concluded for a specified product or range of products and for not more than five years;

(12) Whereas, in the case of beer supply agreements and service-station agreements, different rules should be laid down which take account of the particularities of the markets in question;

(13) Whereas these agreements are generally distinguished by the fact that, on the one hand, the supplier confers on the reseller special commercial or financial advantages by contributing to his financing, granting him or obtaining for him a loan on favourable terms, equipping him with a site or premises for conducting his business, providing him with equipment or fittings, or undertaking other investments for his benefit and that, on the other hand, the reseller enters into a long-

term exclusive purchasing obligation which in most cases is accompanied by a ban on dealing in competing products;

(14) Whereas beer supply and service-station agreements, like the other exclusive purchasing agreements dealt with in this Regulation, normally produce an appreciable improvement in distribution in which consumers are allowed a fair share of the resulting benefit;

(15) Whereas the commercial and financial advantages conferred by the supplier on the reseller make it significantly easier to establish, modernize, maintain and operate premises used for the sale and consumption of drinks and service stations; whereas the exclusive purchasing obligation and the ban on dealing in competing products imposed on the reseller incite the reseller to devote all the resources at his disposal to the sale of the contract goods; whereas such agreements lead to durable cooperation between the parties allowing them to improve or maintain the quality of the contract goods and of the services to the customer and sales efforts of the reseller; whereas they allow long-term planning of sales and consequently a cost effective organisation of production and distribution; whereas the pressure of competition between products of different makes obliges the undertakings involved to determine the number and character of premises used for the sale and consumption of drinks and service stations, in accordance with the wishes of customers;

(16) Whereas consumers benefit from the improvements described, in particular because they are ensured supplies of goods of satisfactory quality at fair prices and conditions while being able to choose between the products of different manufacturers;

(17) Whereas the advantages produced by beer supply agreements and service-station agreements cannot otherwise be secured to the same extent and with the same degree of certainty; whereas the exclusive purchasing obligation on the reseller and the non-competition clause imposed on him are essential components of such agreements and thus usually indispensable for the attainment of these advantages; whereas, however, this is true only as long as the reseller's obligation to purchase from the supplier is confined in the case of premises used for the sale and consumption of drinks to beers and other drinks of the types offered by the supplier, and in the case of service stations to petroleum-based fuel for motor vehicles and other petroleum-based fuels; whereas the exclusive purchasing obligation for lubricants and related petroleum-based products can be accepted only on condition that the supplier provides for the reseller or finances the procurement of specific equipment for the carrying out of lubrication work; whereas this obligation should only relate to products intended for use within the service station;

(18) Whereas, in order to maintain the reseller's commercial freedom and to ensure access to the retail level of distribution on the part of other suppliers, not only the scope but also the duration of the exclusive purchasing obligation must be limited; whereas it appears appropriate to allow drinks suppliers a choice between a medium-term exclusive purchasing agreement covering a range of drinks and a long-term exclusive purchasing agreement for beer; whereas it is necessary to provide special rules for those premises used for the sale and consumption of drinks which the supplier lets to the reseller; whereas, in this case, the reseller must have the right to obtain from other undertakings, under the conditions specified in this

Regulation, other drinks, except beer, supplied under the agreement or of the same type but bearing a different trademark; whereas a uniform maximum duration should be provided for service-station agreements, with the exception of tenancy agreements between the supplier and the reseller, which takes account of the long-term character of the relationship between the parties;

(19) Whereas to the extent that Member States provide, by law or administrative measures, for the same upper limit of duration for the exclusive purchasing obligation upon the reseller in service-station agreements as laid down in this Regulation but provide for a permissible duration which varies in proportion to the consideration provided by the supplier or generally provide for a shorter duration than that permitted by this Regulation, such laws or measures are not contrary to the objectives of this Regulation which, in this respect, merely sets an upper limit to the duration of service-station agreements; whereas the application and enforcement of such national laws or measures must therefore be regarded as compatible with the provisions of this Regulation;

(20) Whereas the limitations and conditions provided for in this Regulation are such as to guarantee effective competition on the markets in question; whereas, therefore, the agreements to which the exemption by category applies do not normally enable the participating undertakings to eliminate competition for a substantial part of the products in question;

(21) Whereas, in particular cases in which agreements or concerted practices satisfying the conditions of this Regulation nevertheless have effects incompatible with Art. 85(3) of the Treaty, the Commission may withdraw the benefit of the exemption by category from the undertakings party thereto;

(22) Whereas agreements and concerted practices which satisfy the conditions set out in this Regulation need not be notified; whereas an undertaking may nonetheless, in a particular case where real doubt exists, request the Commission to declare whether its agreements comply with this Regulation;

(23) Whereas this Regulation does not affect the applicability of Commission Regulation (EEC) No. 3604/82 of 23 December 1982 on the application of Art. 85(3) of the Treaty to categories of specialisation agreements; whereas it does not exclude the application of Art. 86 of the Treaty;

HAS ADOPTED this Regulation:

TITLE I. GENERAL PROVISIONS

Article 1   Pursuant to Art. 85(3) of the Treaty, and subject to the conditions set out in Arts. 2 to 5 of this Regulation, it is hereby declared that Art. 85(1) of the Treaty shall not apply to agreements to which only two undertakings are party and whereby one party, the reseller, agrees with the other, the supplier, to purchase certain goods specified in the agreement for resale only from the supplier or from a connected undertaking or from another undertaking which the supplier has entrusted with the sale of his goods.

Article 2   1. No other restriction of competition shall be imposed on the supplier than the obligation not to distribute the contract goods or goods which compete with the contract goods in the reseller's principal sales area and at the reseller's level of distribution.

2. Apart from the obligation described in Art. 1, no other restriction of competition shall be imposed on the reseller than the obligation not to manufacture or distribute goods which compete with the contract goods.

3. Art. 1 shall apply notwithstanding that the reseller undertakes any or all of the following obligations:
(a) to purchase complete ranges of goods;
(b) to purchase minimum quantities of goods which are subject to the exclusive purchasing obligation;
(c) to sell the contract goods under trademarks, or packed and presented as specified by the supplier;
(d) to take measures for the promotion of sales, in particular:

— to advertise,
— to maintain a sales network or stock of goods,
— to provide customer and guarantee services,
— to employ staff having specialised or technical training.

Article 3   Art. 1 shall not apply where:
(a) manufacturers of identical goods or of goods which are considered by users as equivalent in view of their characteristics, price and intended use enter into reciprocal exclusive purchasing agreements between themselves in respect of such goods;
(b) manufacturers of identical goods or of goods which are considered by users as equivalent in view of their characteristics, price and intended use enter into a non-reciprocal exclusive purchasing agreement between themselves in respect of such goods, unless at least one of them has a total annual turnover of no more than 100 million ECU;
(c) the exclusive purchasing obligation is agreed for more than one type of goods where these are neither by their nature nor according to commercial usage connected to each other;
(d) the agreement is concluded for an indefinite duration or for a period of more than five years.

Article 4   1. Art. 3(a) and (b) shall also apply where the goods there referred to are manufactured by an undertaking connected with a party to the agreement.

2. Connected undertakings are:
(a) undertakings in which a party to the agreement, directly or indirectly:

— owns more than half the capital or business assets, or
— has the power to exercise more than half the voting rights, or
— has the power to appoint more than half the members of the supervisory board, board of directors or bodies legally representing the undertaking, or
— has the right to manage the affairs;

(b) undertakings which directly or indirectly have in or over a party to the agreement the rights or powers listed in (a);
(c) undertakings in which an undertaking referred to in (b) directly or indirectly has the rights or powers listed in (a).

3. Undertakings in which the parties to the agreement or undertakings connected with them jointly have the rights or powers set out in paragraph 2(a) shall be considered to be connected with each of the parties to the agreement.

Article 5   1. For the purpose of Art. 3(b), the ECU is the unit of account used for drawing up the budget of the Community pursuant to Arts. 207 and 209 of the Treaty.

2. Art. 1 shall remain applicable where during any period of two consecutive financial years the total turnover referred to in Art. 3(b) is exceeded by no more than 10%.

3. For the purpose of calculating total turnover within the meaning of Art. 3(b), the turnovers achieved during the last financial year by the party to the agreement and connected undertakings in respect of all goods and services, excluding all taxes and other duties, shall be added together. For this purpose no account shall be taken of dealings between the party to the agreement and its connected undertakings or between its connected undertakings.

TITLE II. SPECIAL PROVISIONS FOR BEER SUPPLY AGREEMENTS

Article 6   1. Pursuant to Art. 85(3) of the Treaty, and subject to Arts. 7 to 9 of this Regulation, it is hereby declared that Art. 85(1) of the Treaty shall not apply to agreements to which only two undertakings are party and whereby one party, the reseller, agrees with the other, the supplier, in consideration for the according of special commercial or financial advantages, to purchase only from the supplier, an undertaking connected with the supplier or another undertaking entrusted by the supplier with the distribution of his goods, certain beers, or certain beers and certain other drinks, specified in the agreement for resale in premises used for the sale and consumption of drinks and designated in the agreement.

2. The declaration in paragraph 1 shall also apply where exclusive purchasing obligations of the kind described in paragraph 1 are imposed on the reseller in favour of the supplier by another undertaking which is itself not a supplier.

Article 7   1. Apart from the obligation referred to in Art. 6, no restriction on competition shall be imposed on the reseller other than:
(a) the obligation not to sell beers and other drinks which are supplied by other undertakings and which are of the same type as the beers or other drinks supplied under the agreement in the premises designated in the agreement;
(b) the obligation, in the event that the reseller sells in the premises designated in the agreement beers which are supplied by other undertakings and which are of a different type from the beers supplied under the agreement, to sell such beers only in bottles, cans or other small packages, unless the sale of such beers in draught form is customary or is necessary to satisfy a sufficient demand from consumers;
(c) the obligation to advertise goods supplied by other undertakings within or outside the premises designated in the agreement only in proportion to the share of these goods in the total turnover realised in the premises.

2. Beers or other drinks are of different types where they are clearly distinguishable by their composition, appearance or taste.

Article 8   1. Art. 6 shall not apply where:

(a) the supplier or a connected undertaking imposes on the reseller exclusive purchasing obligations for goods other than drinks or for services;
(b) the supplier restricts the freedom of the reseller to obtain from an undertaking of his choice either services or goods for which neither an exclusive purchasing obligation nor a ban on dealing in competing products may be imposed;
(c) the agreement is concluded for an indefinite duration or for a period of more than five years and the exclusive purchasing obligation relates to specified beers and other drinks;
(d) the agreement is concluded for an indefinite duration or for a period of more than 10 years and the exclusive purchasing obligation relates only to specified beers;
(e) the supplier obliges the reseller to impose the exclusive purchasing obligation on his successor for a longer period than the reseller would himself remain tied to the supplier.

2. Where the agreement relates to premises which the supplier lets to the reseller or allows the reseller to occupy on some other basis in law or in fact, the following provisions shall also apply:

(a) notwithstanding paragraphs (1)(c) and (d), the exclusive purchasing obligations and bans on dealing in competing products specified in this Title may be imposed on the reseller for the whole period for which the reseller in fact operates the premises;
(b) the agreement must provide for the reseller to have the right to obtain:
  — drinks, except beer, supplied under the agreement from other undertakings where these undertakings offer them on more favourable conditions which the supplier does not meet,
  — drinks, except beer, which are of the same type as those supplied under the agreement but which bear different trade marks, from other undertakings where the supplier does not offer them.

Article 9   Arts. 2(1) and (3), 3(a) and (b), 4 and 5 shall apply *mutatis mutandis*.

TITLE III. SPECIAL PROVISIONS FOR SERVICE-STATION AGREEMENTS

Article 10   Pursuant to Art. 85(3) of the Treaty and subject to Arts. 11 to 13 of this Regulation, it is hereby declared that Art. 85(1) of the Treaty shall not apply to agreements to which only two undertakings are party and whereby one party, the reseller, agrees with the other, the supplier, in consideration for the according of special commercial or financial advantages, to purchase only from the supplier, an undertaking connected with the supplier or another undertaking entrusted by the supplier with the distribution of his goods, certain petroleum-based motor-vehicle fuels or certain petroleum-based motor-vehicle and other fuels specified in the agreement for resale in a service station designated in the agreement.

Article 11   Apart from the obligation referred to in Art. 10, no restriction on competition shall be imposed on the reseller other than:
(a) the obligation not to sell motor-vehicle fuel and other fuels which are supplied by other undertakings in the service station designated in the agreement;
(b) the obligation not to use lubricants or related petroleum-based products which are supplied by other undertakings within the service station designated in the

agreement where the supplier or a connected undertaking has made available to the reseller, or financed, a lubrication bay or other motor-vehicle lubrication equipment;

(c) the obligation to advertise goods supplied by other undertakings within or outside the service station designated in the agreement only in proportion to the share of these goods in the total turnover realised in the service station;

(d) the obligation to have equipment owned by the supplier or a connected undertaking or financed by the supplier or a connected undertaking serviced by the supplier or an undertaking designated by him.

Article 12   1. Art. 10 shall not apply where:

(a) the supplier or a connected undertaking imposes on the reseller exclusive purchasing obligations for goods other than motor-vehicle and other fuels or for services, except in the case of the obligations referred to in Art. 11(b) and (d);

(b) the supplier restricts the freedom of the reseller to obtain from an undertaking of his choice goods or services for which under the provisions of this Title neither an exclusive purchasing obligation nor a ban on dealing in competing products may be imposed;

(c) the agreement is concluded for an indefinite duration or for a period of more than 10 years;

(d) the supplier obliges the reseller to impose the exclusive purchasing obligation on his successor for a longer period than the reseller would himself remain tied to the supplier.

2. Where the agreement relates to a service station which the supplier lets to the reseller, or allows the reseller to occupy on some other basis, in law or in fact, exclusive purchasing obligations or bans on dealing in competing products specified in this Title may, notwithstanding paragraph 1(c), be imposed on the reseller for the whole period for which the reseller in fact operates the premises.

Article 13   Arts. 2(1) and (3), 3(a) and (b), 4 and 5 of this Regulation shall apply *mutatis mutandis.*

TITLE IV. MISCELLANEOUS PROVISIONS

Article 14   The Commission may withdraw the benefit of this Regulation, pursuant to Art. 7 of Regulation No. 19/65/EEC, when it finds in a particular case that an agreement which is exempted by this Regulation nevertheless has certain effects which are incompatible with the conditions set out in Art. 85(3) of the Treaty, and in particular where:

(a) the contract goods are not subject, in a substantial part of the common market, to effective competition from identical goods or goods considered by users as equivalent in view of their characteristics, price and intended use;

(b) access by other suppliers to the different stages of distribution in a substantial part of the common market is made difficult to a significant extent;

(c) the supplier without any objectively justified reason:

  1. refuses to supply categories of resellers who cannot obtain the contract goods elsewhere on suitable terms or applies to them differing prices or conditions of sale;

  2. applies less favourable prices or conditions of sale to resellers bound by an

exclusive purchasing obligation as compared with other resellers at the same level of distribution.

Article 15   1. In the period 1 July 1983 to 31 December 1986, the prohibition in Art. 85(1) of the Treaty shall not apply to agreements of the kind described in Art. 1 which either were in force on 1 July 1983 or entered into force between 1 July and 31 December 1983 and which satisfy the exemption conditions of Regulation No. 67/67/EEC.

2. In the period 1 July 1983 to 31 December 1988, the prohibition in Art. 85(1) of the Treaty shall not apply to agreements of the kinds described in Arts. 6 and 10 which either were in force on 1 July 1983 or entered into force between 1 July and 31 December 1983 and which satisfy the exemption conditions of Regulation No. 67/67/EEC.

3. In the case of agreements of the kinds described in Arts. 6 and 10, which were in force on 1 July 1983 and which expire after 31 December 1988, the prohibition in Art. 85(1) of the Treaty shall not apply in the period from 1 January 1989 to the expiry of the agreement but at the latest to the expiry of this Regulation to the extent that the supplier releases the reseller, before 1 January 1989, from all obligations which would prevent the application of the exemption under Titles II and III.

4. The provisions of the preceding paragraphs shall apply in the same way to the agreements referred to respectively in those paragraphs, which were in force on the date of accession of the Kingdom of Spain and of the Portuguese Republic and which, as a result of accession, fall within the scope of Art. 85(1) of the Treaty.

Article 15a   The prohibition in Article 85(1) of the Treaty shall not apply to agreements which were in existence at the date of accession of Austria, Finland and Sweden and which, by reason of this accession, fall within the scope of Article 85(1) if, within six months from the date of accession, they are so amended that they comply with the conditions laid down in the Regulation. However, this Article shall not apply to agreements which at the date of accession already fall under Article 53(1) of the EEA Agreement.

Article 16   This Regulation shall not apply to agreements by which the supplier undertakes with the reseller to supply only to the reseller certain goods for resale, in the whole or in a defined part of the Community, and the reseller undertakes with the supplier to purchase these goods only from the supplier.

Article 17   This Regulation shall not apply where the parties or connected undertakings, for the purpose of resale in one and the same premises used for the sale and consumption of drinks or service station, enter into agreements both of the kind referred to in Title I and of a kind referred to in Title II or III.

Article 18   This Regulation shall apply *mutatis mutandis* to the categories of concerted practices defined in Arts. 1, 6 and 10.

[*final provisions omitted*]

Commission Regulation of 19 December 1984 on the application of Article 85(3) of the EC Treaty to categories of specialisation agreements (417/85/EEC)[22]

The Commission of the European Communities,

[recitals omitted]

Whereas:

(1) Regulation (EEC) No. 2821/71 empowers the Commission to apply Art. 85(3) of the Treaty by Regulation to certain categories of agreements, decisions and concerted practices falling within the scope of Art. 85 (1) which relate to specialisation, including agreements necessary for achieving it.

(2) Agreements on specialisation in present or future production may fall within the scope of Art. 85(1).

(3) Agreements on specialisation in production generally contribute to improving the production or distribution of goods, because undertakings concerned can concentrate on the manufacture of certain products and thus operate more efficiently and supply the products more cheaply. It is likely that, given effective competition, consumers will receive a fair share of the resulting benefit.

(4) Such advantages can arise equally from agreements whereby each participant gives up the manufacture of certain products in favour of another participant and from agreements whereby the participants undertake to manufacture certain products or have them manufactured only jointly.

(5) The Regulation must specify what restrictions of competition may be included in specialisation agreements. The restrictions of competition that are permitted in the Regulation in addition to reciprocal obligations to give up manufacture are normally essential for the making and implementation of such agreements. These restrictions are therefore, in general, indispensable for the attainment of the desired advantages for the participating undertakings and consumers. It may be left to the parties to decide which of these provisions they include in their agreements.

(6) The exemption must be limited to agreements which do not give rise to the possibility of eliminating competition in respect of a substantial part of the products in question. The Regulation must therefore apply only as long as the market share and turnover of the participating undertakings do not exceed a certain limit.

(7) It is, however, appropriate to offer undertakings which exceed the turnover limit set in the Regulation a simplified means of obtaining the legal certainty provided by the block exemption. This must allow the Commission to exercise effective supervision as well as simplifying its administration of such agreements.

(8) In order to facilitate the conclusion of long-term specialisation agreements, which can have a bearing on the structure of the participating undertakings, it is appropriate to fix the period of validity of the Regulation at 13 years. If the circumstances on the basis of which the Regulation was adopted should change significantly within this period, the Commission will make the necessary amendments.

---

[22] OJ 1985 L 53/1, as last amended by Commission Regulation 2236/97/EC, OJ 1997 L 306/12.

(9) Agreements, decisions and concerted practices which are automatically exempted pursuant to this Regulation need not be notified. Undertakings may none the less in an individual case request a decision pursuant to Council Regulation No. 17, as last amended by the Act of Accession of Greece,

HAS ADOPTED this regulation:

Article 1   Pursuant to Art. 85(3) of the Treaty and subject to the provisions of this Regulation, it is hereby declared that Art. 85(1) of the Treaty shall not apply to agreements on specialisation whereby, for the duration of the agreement, undertakings accept reciprocal obligations:
(a) not to manufacture certain products or to have them manufactured, but to leave it to other parties to manufacture the products or have them manufactured; or
(b) to manufacture certain products or have them manufactured only jointly.

Article 2   1. Article 1 shall also apply to the following restrictions of competition:
(a) an obligation not to conclude with third parties specialisation agreements relating to identical products or to products considered by users to be equivalent in view of their characteristics, price and intended use;
(b) an obligation to procure products which are the subject of the specialisation exclusively from another party, a joint undertaking or an undertaking jointly charged with their manufacture, except where they are obtainable on more favourable terms elsewhere and the other party, the joint undertaking or the undertaking charged with manufacture is not prepared to offer the same terms;
(c) an obligation to grant other parties the exclusive right, within the whole or a defined areas of the common market, to distribute products which are the subject of the specialisation provided that intermediaries and users can also obtain the products from other suppliers and the parties do not render it difficult for intermediaries or users thus to obtain the products;
(d) an obligation to grant one of the parties the exclusive right to distribute products which are the subject of the specialisation provided that the party does not distribute products of a third undertaking which compete with the contract products;
(e) an obligation to grant the exclusive right to distribute products which are the subject of the specialisation to a joint undertaking or to a third undertaking, provided that the joint undertaking or third under taking does not manufacture or distribute products which compete with the contract products;
(f) an obligation to grant the exclusive right to distribute within the whole or a defined area of the common market the products which are the subject of the specialisation to joint undertakings or third undertakings which do not manufacture or distribute products which compete with the contract products, provided that users and intermediaries can also obtain the contract products from other suppliers and that neither the parties nor the joint undertakings or third undertakings entrusted with the exclusive distribution of the contract products render it difficult for users and intermediaries to thus obtain the contract products.

2a. Article 1 shall not apply if restrictions of competition other than those set out in paragraphs 1 and 2 are imposed upon the parties by agreement, decision or concerted practice;

2. Art. 1 shall also apply where the parties undertake obligations of the types referred to in paragraph 1 but with a more limited scope than is permitted by that paragraph.

3. Art. 1 shall apply notwithstanding that any of the following obligations, in particular, are imposed:

(a) an obligation to supply other parties with products which are the subject of the specialisation and in so doing to observe minimum standards of quality;

(b) an obligation to maintain minimum stocks of products which are the subject of the specialisation and of replacement parts for them;

(c) an obligation to provide customer and guarantee services for products which are the subject of the specialisation.

Article 3   1. Art. 1 shall apply only if:

(a) the products which are the subject of the specialisation together with the participating undertakings' other products which are considered by users to be equivalent in view of their characteristics, price and intended use do not represent more than 20% of the market for all such products in the common market or a substantial part thereof; and

(b) the aggregate turnover of all the participating undertakings does not exceed ECU 1000 million.

2. If pursuant to point (d), (e) or (f) of Article 2(1), one of the parties, a joint undertaking, a third undertaking or more than one joint undertaking or third undertaking are entrusted with the distribution of the products which are the subject of the specialisation, Article 1 shall apply only if:

(a) the products which are the subject of the specialisation together with the participating undertakings' other products which are considered by users to be equivalent in view of their characteristics, price and intended use do not represent more than 10% of the market for all such products in the common market or a substantial part thereof; and

(b) the aggregate annual turnover of all the participating undertakings does not exceed ECU 1000 million.

3. Article 1 shall continue to apply if the market shares and turnover referred to in paragraphs 1 and 2 are exceeded during any period of two consecutive financial years by not more than one-tenth.

4. Where the limits laid down in paragraphs 3 are also exceeded, Art. 1 shall continue to apply for a period of six months following the end of the financial year during which it was exceeded.

Article 4   1. The exemption provided for in Art. 1 shall also apply to agreements involving participating undertakings whose aggregate turn-over exceeds the limits laid down in Art. 3 (1)(b), 2(b) and (3), on condition that the agreements in question are notified to the Commission in accordance with the provisions of Commission Regulation No. 27, and that the Commission does not oppose such exemption within a period of six months.

2. The period of six months shall run from the date on which the notification is received by the Commission. Where, however, the notification is made by registered post, the period shall run from the date shown on the postmark of the place of posting.

3. Paragraph 1 shall apply only if:

(a) express reference is made to this Article in the notification or in a communication accompanying it; and

(b) the information furnished with the notification is complete and in accordance with the facts.

4. The benefit of paragraph 1 may be claimed for agreements notified before the entry into force of this Regulation by submitting a communication to the Commission referring expressly to this Art. and to the notification. Paragraphs 2 and 3(b) shall apply *mutatis mutandis*.

5. The Commission may oppose the exemption. It shall oppose exemption if it receives a request to do so from a Member State within three months of the forwarding to the Member State of the notification referred to in paragraph 1 or of the communication referred to in paragraph 4. This request must be justified on the basis of considerations relating to the competition rules of the Treaty.

6. The Commission may withdraw the opposition to the exemption at any time. However, where the opposition was raised at the request of a Member State and this request is maintained, it may be withdrawn only after consultation of the Advisory Committee on Restrictive Practices and Dominant Positions.

7. If the opposition is withdrawn because the undertakings concerned have shown that the conditions of Art. 85(3) are fulfilled, the exemption shall apply from the date of notification.

8. If the opposition is withdrawn because the undertakings concerned have amended the agreement so that the conditions of Art. 85(3) are fulfilled, the exemption shall apply from the date on which the amendments take effect.

9. If the Commission opposes exemption and the opposition is not withdrawn, the effects of the notification shall be governed by the provisions of Regulation No. 17.

Article 5   1. Information acquired pursuant to Art. 4 shall be used only for the purposes of this Regulation.

2. The Commission and the authorities of the Member States, their officials and other servants shall not disclose information acquired by them pursuant to this Regulation of a kind that is covered by the obligation of professional secrecy.

3. Paragraphs 1 and 2 shall not prevent publication of general information or surveys which do not contain information relating to particular undertakings or associations of undertakings.

Article 6   For the purpose of calculating total annual turnover within the meaning of Art. 3(1)(b) and (2)(b), the turnovers achieved during the last financial year by the participating undertakings in respect of all goods and services excluding tax shall be added together. For this purpose, no account shall be taken of dealings between the participating undertakings or between these undertakings and a third undertaking jointly charged with manufacture or sale.

Article 7   1. For the purposes of Art. 3(1) and (2) and Art. 6, participating undertakings are:

(a) undertakings party to the agreement;

(b) undertakings in which a party to the agreement, directly or indirectly:

— owns more than half the capital or business assets,
— has the power to exercise more than half the voting rights,
— has the power to appoint at least half the members of the supervisory board, board of management or bodies legally representing the undertakings, or
— has the right to manage the affairs;

(c) undertakings which directly or indirectly have in or over a party to the agreement the rights or powers listed in (b);

(d) undertakings in or over which an undertaking referred to in (c) directly or indirectly has the rights or powers listed in (b).

2. Undertakings in which the undertakings referred to in paragraph 1(a) to (d) directly or indirectly jointly have the rights or powers set out in paragraph 1(b) shall also be considered to be participating undertakings.

Article 8   The Commission may withdraw the benefit of this Regulation, pursuant to Art. 7 of Regulation (EEC) No. 2821/71, where it finds in a particular case that an agreement exempted by this Regulation nevertheless has effects which are incompatible with the conditions set out in Art. 85(3) of the Treaty, and in particular where:

(a) the agreement is not yielding significant results in terms of rationalisation or consumers are not receiving a fair share of the resulting benefit; or

(b) the products which are the subject of the specialisation are not subject in the common market or a substantial part thereof to effective competition from identical products or products considered by users to be equivalent in view of their characteristics, price and intended use.

Article 9   This Regulation shall apply *mutatis mutandis* to decisions of associations of undertakings and concerted practices.

Article 9a   The prohibition in Art. 85(1) of the Treaty shall not apply to the specialisation agreements which were in existence at the date of the accession of the Kingdom of Spain and of the Portuguese Republic and which, by reason of this accession, fall within the scope of Art. 85(1), if, before 1 July 1986, they are so amended that they comply with the conditions laid down in this Regulation.

As regards agreements to which Article 85 of the Treaty applies as a result of the accession of Austria, Finland and Sweden, the preceding paragraph shall apply *mutatis mutandis* on the understanding that the relevant dates shall be the date of accession of those countries and six months after the date of accession respectively. However, this paragraph shall not apply to agreements which at the date of accession already fall under Article 53(1) of the EEA Agreement.

Article 10   1. This Regulation shall enter into force on 1 March 1985. It shall apply until 31 December 2000.

2. Commission Regulation (EEC) No. 3604/82 is hereby repealed.

[final provisions omitted]

Commission Regulation of 19 December 1984 on the application of Article 85 (3) of the EC Treaty to categories of research and development agreements (418/85/EEC)[23]

The Commission of the European Communities,

[recitals omitted]

Whereas:

(1) Regulation (EEC) No. 2821/71 empowers the Commission to apply Art. 85(3) of the Treaty by Regulation to certain categories of agreements, decisions and concerted practices falling within the scope of Art. 85(1) which have as their object the research and development of products or processes up to the stage of industrial application, and exploitation of the results, including provisions regarding industrial property rights and confidential technical knowledge.

(2) As stated in the Commission's 1968 notice concerning agreements, decisions and concerted practices in the field of cooperation between enterprises, agreements on the joint execution of research work or the joint development of the results of the research, up to but not including the stage of industrial application, generally do not fall within the scope of Art. 85(1) of the Treaty. In certain circumstances, however, such as where the parties agree not to carry out other research and development in the same field, thereby forgoing the opportunity of gaining competitive advantages over the other parties, such agreements may fall within Art. 85(1) and should therefore not be excluded from this Regulation.

(3) Agreements providing for both joint research and development and joint exploitation of the results may fall within Art. 85(1) because the parties jointly determine how the products developed are manufactured or the processes developed are applied or how related intellectual property rights or know-how are exploited.

(4) Cooperation in research and development and in the exploitation of the results generally promotes technical and economic progress by increasing the dissemination of technical knowledge between the parties and avoiding duplication of research and development work, by stimulating new advances through the exchange of complementary technical knowledge, and by rationalising the manufacture of the products or application of the processes arising out of the research and development. These aims can be achieved only where the research and development programme and its objectives are clearly defined and each of the parties is given the opportunity of exploiting any of the results of the programme that interest it; where universities or research institutes participate and are not interested in the industrial exploitation of the results, however, it may be agreed that they may use the said results solely for the purpose of further research.

(5) Consumers can generally be expected to benefit from the increased volume and effectiveness of research and development through the introduction of new or improved products or services or the reduction of prices brought about by new or improved processes.

---

[23] OJ 1985 L 53/5, as last amended by Commission Regulation 2236/97/EC, OJ 1997 L 306/12.

(6) This Regulation must specify the restrictions of competition which may be included in the exempted agreements. The purpose of the permitted restrictions is to concentrate the research activities of the parties in order to improve their chances of success, and to facilitate the introduction of new products and services onto the market. These restrictions are generally necessary to secure the desired benefits for the parties and consumers.

(7) The joint exploitation of results can be considered as the natural consequence of joint research and development. It can take different forms ranging from manufacture to the exploitation of intellectual property rights or know-how that substantially contributes to technical or economic progress. In order to attain the benefits and objectives described above and to justify the restrictions of competition which are exempted, the joint exploitation must relate to products or processes for which the use of the results of the research and development is decisive. Joint exploitation is not therefore justified where it relates to improvements which were not made within the framework of a joint research and development programme but under an agreement having some other principal objective, such as the licensing of intellectual property rights, joint manufacture or specialisation, and merely containing ancillary provisions on joint research and development.

(8) The exemption granted under the Regulation must be limited to agreements which do not afford the undertakings the possibility of eliminating competition in respect of a substantial part of the products in question. In order to guarantee that several independent poles of research can exist in the common market in any economic sector, it is necessary to exclude from the block exemption agreements between competitors whose combined share of the market for products capable of being improved or replaced by the results of the research and development exceeds a certain level at the time the agreement is entered into.

(9) In order to guarantee the maintenance of effective competition during joint exploitation of the results, it is necessary to provide that the block exemption will cease to apply if the parties' combined shares of the market for the products arising out of the joint research and development become too great. However, it should be provided that the exemption will continue to apply, irrespective of the parties' market shares, for a certain period after the commencement of joint exploitation, so as to await stabilisation of their market shares, particularly after the introduction of an entirely new product, and to guarantee a minimum period of return on the generally substantial investments involved.

(10) Agreements between undertakings which do not fulfil the market share conditions laid down in the Regulation may, in appropriate cases, be granted an exemption by individual decision, which will in particular take account of world competition and the particular circumstances prevailing in the manufacture of high technology products.

(11) It is desirable to list in the Regulation a number of obligations that are commonly found in research and development agreements but that are normally not restrictive of competition and to provide that, in the event that, because of the particular economic or legal circumstances, they should fall within Art. 85(1), they also would be covered by the exemption. This list is not exhaustive.

(12) The Regulation must specify what provisions may not be included in agreements if these are to benefit from the block exemption by virtue of the fact that such provisions are restrictions falling within Art. 85(1) for which there can be no general presumption that they will lead to the positive effects required by Art. 85(3).

(13) Agreements which are not automatically covered by the exemption because they include provisions that are not expressly exempted by the Regulation and are not expressly excluded from exemption are none the less capable of benefiting from the general presumption of compatibility with Art. 85(3) on which the block exemption is based. It will be possible for the Commission rapidly to establish whether this is the case for a particular agreement. Such an agreement should therefore be deemed to be covered by the exemption provided for in this Regulation where it is notified to the Commission and the Commission does not oppose the application of the exemption within a specified period of time.

(14) Agreements covered by this Regulation may also take advantage of provisions contained in other block exemption Regulations of the Commission, and in particular Regulation (EEC) No. 417/85 on specialisation agreements, Regulation (EEC) No. 1983/83 on exclusive distribution agreements, Regulation (EEC) No. 1984/83, on exclusive purchasing agreements and Regulation (EEC) No. 2349/84 on patent licensing agreements, if they fulfil the conditions set out in these Regulations. The provisions of the aforementioned Regulations are, however, not applicable in so far as this Regulation contains specific rules.

(15) If individual agreements exempted by this Regulation nevertheless have effects which are incompatible with Art. 85(3), the Commission may withdraw the benefit of the block exemption.

(16) The Regulation should apply with retroactive effect to agreements in existence when the Regulation comes into force where such agreements already fulfil its conditions or are modified to do so. The benefit of these provisions may not be claimed in actions pending at the date of entry into force of this Regulation, nor may it be relied on as grounds for claims for damages against third parties.

(17) Since research and development cooperation agreements are often of a long-term nature, especially where the cooperation extends to the exploitation of the results, it is appropriate to fix the period of validity of the Regulation at 13 years. If the circumstances on the basis of which the Regulation was adopted should change significantly within this period, the Commission will make the necessary amendments.

(18) Agreements which are automatically exempted pursuant to this Regulation need not be notified. Undertakings may nevertheless in a particular case request a decision pursuant to Council Regulation No. 17, as last amended by the Act of Accession of Greece,

HAS ADOPTED this Regulation:

Article 1 1. Pursuant to Art. 85(3) of the Treaty and subject to the provisions of this Regulation, it is hereby declared that Art. 85(1) of the Treaty shall not apply to agreements entered into between undertakings for the purpose of:
(a) joint research and development of products or processes and joint exploitation of the results of that research and development;

(b) joint exploitation of the results of research and development of products or processes jointly carried out pursuant to a prior agreement between the same undertakings; or

(c) joint research and development of products or processes excluding joint exploitation of the results, in so far as such agreements fall within the scope of Art. 85(1).

2. For the purposes of this Regulation:

(a) *research and development of products or processes* means the acquisition of technical knowledge and the carrying out of theoretical analysis, systematic study or experimentation, including experimental production, technical testing of products or processes, the establishment of the necessary facilities and the obtaining of intellectual property rights for the results;

(b) *contract processes* means processes arising out of the research and development;

(c) *contract products* means products or services arising out of the research and development or manufactured or provided applying the contract processes;

(d) *exploitation of the results* means the manufacture of the contract products or the application of the contract processes or the assignment or licensing of intellectual property rights or the communication of know-how required for such manufacture or application;

(e) *technical knowledge* means technical knowledge which is either protected by an intellectual property right or is secret (know-how).

3. Research and development of the exploitation of the results are carried out *jointly* where:

(a) the work involved is:

    — carried out by a joint team, organisation or undertaking,
    — jointly entrusted to a third party, or
    — allocated between the parties by way of specialisation in research, development or production;

(b) the parties collaborate in any way in the assignment or the licensing of intellectual property rights or the communication of know-how, within the meaning of paragraph 2(d), to third parties.

Article 2   The exemption provided for in Art. 1 shall apply on condition that:

(a) the joint research and development work is carried out within the framework of a programme defining the objectives of the work and the field in which it is to be carried out;

(b) all the parties have access to the results of the work;

(c) where the agreement provides only for joint research and development, each party is free to exploit the results of the joint research and development and any pre-existing technical knowledge necessary therefor independently;

(d) the joint exploitation relates only to results which are protected by intellectual property rights or constitute know-how which substantially contributes to technical or economic progress and that the results are decisive for the manufacture of the contract products or the application of the contract processes;

(f) undertakings charged with manufacture by way of specialisation in production are required to fulfil orders for supplies from all the parties.

Article 3 1. Where the parties are not competing manufacturers of products capable of being improved or replaced by the contract products, the exemption provided for in Article 1 shall apply for the duration of the research and development programme and, where the results are jointly exploited, for five years from the time the contract products are first put on the market within the common market.

2. Where two or more of the parties are competing manufacturers within the meaning of paragraph 1, the exemption provided for in Art. 1 shall apply for the period specified in paragraph 1 only if, at the time the agreement is entered into, the parties' combined production of the products capable of being improved or replaced by the contract products does not exceed 20% of the market for such products in the common market or a substantial part thereof.

3. After the end of the period referred to in paragraph 1, the exemption provided for in Art. 1 shall continue to apply as long as the production of the contract products together with the parties' combined production of other products which are considered by users to be equivalent in view of their characteristics, price and intended use does not exceed 20% of the total market for such products in the common market or a substantial part thereof. Where contract products are components used by the parties of the manufacture of other products, reference shall be made to the markets for such of those latter products for which the components represent a significant part.

3a. Where one of the parties, a joint undertaking, a third undertaking or more than one joint undertaking or third undertaking are entrusted with the distribution of the products which are the subject of the agreement under Article 4(1)(fa), (fb) or (fc), the exemption provided for in Article 1 shall apply only if the parties production of the products referred to in paragraphs 2 and 3 does not exceed 10% of the market for all such products in the common market or a substantial part thereof.

4. The exemption provided for in Article 1 shall continue to apply where the market shares referred to in paragraph 3 and 4 is exceeded during any period of two consecutive financial years by not more than one-tenth.

5. Where the limits laid down in paragraph 5 are also exceeded, the exemption provided for in Article 1 shall continue to apply for a period of six months following the end of the financial year during which they were exceeded.

Article 4 1. The exemption provided for in Art. 1 shall also apply to the following restrictions of competition imposed on the parties:
(a) an obligation not to carry out independently research and development in the field to which the programme relates or in a closely connected field during the execution of the programme;
(b) an obligation not to enter into agreements with third parties on research and development in the field to which the programme relates or in a closely connected field during the execution of the programme;
(c) an obligation to procure the contract products exclusively from parties, joint organisations or undertakings or third parties, jointly charged with their manufacture;
(d) an obligation not to manufacture the contract products or apply the contract processes in territories reserved for other parties;

(e) an obligation to restrict the manufacture of the contract products or application of the contract processes to one or more technical fields of application, except where two or more of the parties are competitors within the meaning of Art. 3 at the time the agreement is entered into;

(f) an obligation not to pursue, for a period of five years from the time the contract products are first put on the market within the common market, an active policy of putting the products on the market in territories reserved for other parties, and in particular not to engage in advertising specifically aimed at such territories or to establish any branch or maintain any distribution depot there for the distribution of the products, provided that users and intermediaries can obtain the contract products from other suppliers and the parties do not render it difficult for intermediaries and users to thus obtain the products;

(fa) an obligation to grant one of the parties the exclusive right to distribute the contract products, provided that that party does not distribute products manufactured by a third producer which compete with the contract products;

(fb) an obligation to grant the exclusive right to distribute the contract products to a joint undertaking or a third undertaking, provided that the joint undertaking or third undertaking does not manufacture or distribute products which compete with the contract products;

(fc) an obligation to grant the exclusive right to distribute the contract products in the whole or defined area of the common market to joint undertakings or third undertakings which do not manufacture or distribute products which compete with the contract products, provided that users and intermediaries are also able to obtain the contract products from other suppliers and neither the parties nor the joint undertakings or third undertakings entrusted with the exclusive distribution of the contract products render it difficult for users and intermediaries to thus obtain the contract products.

(g) an obligation on the parties to communicate to each other any experience they may gain in exploiting the results and to grant each other non-exclusive licences for inventions relating to improvements or new applications.

2. The exemption provided for in Art. 1 shall also apply where in a particular agreement the parties undertake obligations of the types referred to in paragraph 1 but with a more limited scope than is permitted by that paragraph.

Article 5   1. Art. 1 shall apply notwithstanding that any of the following obligations, in particular, are imposed on the parties during the currency of the agreement:

(a) an obligation to communicate patented or non-patented technical knowledge necessary for the carrying out of the research and development programme for the exploitation of its results;

(b) an obligation not to use any know-how received from another party for purposes other than carrying out the research and development programme and the exploitation of its results;

(c) an obligation to obtain and maintain in force intellectual property rights for the contract products or processes;

(d) an obligation to preserve the confidentiality of any know-how received or jointly developed under the research and development programme; this obligation may be imposed even after the expiry of the agreement;

(e) an obligation:
  - (i) to inform other parties of infringements of their intellectual property rights,
  - (ii) to take legal action against infringers, and
  - (iii) to assist in any such legal action or share with the other parties in the cost thereof;

(f) an obligation to pay royalties or render services to other parties to compensate for unequal contributions to the joint research and development or unequal exploitation of its results;

(g) an obligation to share royalties received from third parties with other parties;

(h) an obligation to supply other parties with minimum quantities of contract products and to observe minimum standards of quality.

2. In the event that, because of particular circumstances, the obligations referred to in paragraph 1 fall within the scope of Art. 85(1), they also shall be covered by the exemption. The exemption provided for in this paragraph shall also apply where in a particular agreement the parties undertake obligations of the types referred to in paragraph 1 but with a more limited scope than is permitted by that paragraph.

Article 6   The exemption provided for in Art. 1 shall not apply where the parties, by agreement, decision or concerted practice:

(a) are restricted in their freedom to carry out research and development independently or in cooperation with third parties in a field unconnected with that to which the programme relates or, after its completion, in the field to which the programme relates or in a connected field;

(b) are prohibited after completion of the research and development programme from challenging the validity of intellectual property rights which the parties hold in the common market and which are relevant to the programme or, after the expiry of the agreement, from challenging the validity of intellectual property rights which the parties hold in the common market and which protect the results of the research and development;

(c) are restricted as to the quantity of the contract products they may manufacture or sell or as to the number of operations employing the contract process they may carry out;

(d) are restricted in their determination of prices, components of prices or discounts when selling the contract products to third parties;

(e) are restricted as to the customers they may serve, without prejudice to Art. 4(1)(e);

(f) are prohibited from putting the contract products on the market or pursuing an active sales policy for them in territories within the common market that are reserved for other parties after the end of the period referred to in Art. 4(1)(f);

(g) are required not to grant licences to third parties to manufacture the contract products or to apply the contract processes even though the exploitation by the parties themselves of the results of the joint research and development is not provided for or does not take place;

(h) are required:
  - — to refuse without any objectively justified reason to meet demand from users or dealers established in their respective territories who would

> market the contract products in other territories within the common market, or
> — to make it difficult for users or dealers to obtain the contract products from other dealers within the common market, and in particular to exercise intellectual property rights or take measures so as to prevent users or dealers from obtaining, or from putting on the market within the common market, products which have been lawfully put on the market within the common market by another party or with its consent.

Article 7   1. The exemption provided for in this Regulation shall also apply to agreements of the kinds described in Art. 1 which fulfil the conditions laid down in Arts. 2 and 3 and which contain obligations restrictive of competition which are not covered by Arts. 4 and 5 and do not fall within the scope of Art. 6, on condition that the agreements in question are notified to the Commission in accordance with the provisions of Commission Regulation No. 27, and that the Commission does not oppose such exemption within a period of six months.

2. The period of six months shall run from the date on which the notification is received by the Commission. Where, however, the notification is made by registered post, the period shall run from the date shown on the postmark of the place of posting.

3. Paragraph 1 shall apply only if:
(a) express reference is made to this Article in the notification or in a communication accompanying it, and
(b) the information furnished with the notification is complete and in accordance with the facts.

4. The benefit of paragraph 1 may be claimed for agreements notified before the entry into force of this Regulation by submitting a communication to the Commission referring expressly to this Article and to the notification. Paragraphs 2 and 3 (b) shall apply *mutatis mutandis*.

5. The Commission may oppose the exemption. It shall oppose exemption if it receives a request to do so from a Member State within three months of the forwarding to the Member State of the notification referred to in paragraph 1 or of the communication referred to in paragraph 4. This request must be justified on the basis of considerations relating to the competition rules of the Treaty.

6. The Commission may withdraw the opposition to the exemption at any time. However, where the opposition was raised at the request of a Member State and this request is maintained, it may be withdrawn only after consultation of the Advisory Committee on Restrictive Practices and Dominant Positions.

7. If the opposition is withdrawn because the undertakings concerned have shown that the conditions of Art. 85(3) are fulfilled, the exemption shall apply from the date of notification.

8. If the opposition is withdrawn because the undertakings concerned have amended the agreement so that the conditions of Art. 85(3) are fulfilled, the exemption shall apply from the date on which the amendments take effect.

9. If the Commission opposes exemption and the opposition is not withdrawn, the effects of the notification shall be governed by the provisions of Regulation No. 17.

Article 8   1. Information acquired pursuant to Art. 7 shall be used only for the purposes of this Regulation.

2. The Commission and the authorities of the Member States, their officials and other servants shall not disclose information acquired by them pursuant to this Regulation of a kind that is covered by the obligation of professional secrecy.

3. Paragraphs 1 and 2 shall not prevent publication of general information or surveys which do not contain information relating to particular undertakings or associations of undertakings.

Article 9   1. The provisions of this Regulation shall also apply to rights and obligations which the parties create for undertakings connected with them. The market shares held and the actions and measures taken by connected undertakings shall be treated as those of the parties themselves.

2. Connected undertakings for the purposes of this Regulation are:
(a) undertakings in which a party to the agreement, directly or indirectly:
   — owns more than half the capital or business assets,
   — has the power to exercise more than half the voting rights,
   — has the power to appoint more than half the members of the supervisory board, board of directors or bodies legally representing the undertakings, or
   — has the right to manage the affairs;
(b) undertakings which directly have in or over a party to the agreement the rights or powers listed in (a);
(c) undertakings in or over which an undertaking referred to in (b) directly or indirectly has the rights or powers listed in (a).

3. Undertakings in which the parties to the agreement or undertakings connected with them jointly have, directly or indirectly, the rights or powers set out in paragraph 2(a) shall be considered to be connected with each of the parties to the agreement.

Article 10   The Commission may withdraw the benefit of this Regulation, pursuant to Art. 7 of Regulation (EEC) No. 2821/71, where it finds in a particular case that an agreement exempted by this Regulation nevertheless has certain effects which are incompatible with the conditions laid down in Art. 85(3) of the Treaty, and in particular where:
(a) the existence of the agreement substantially restricts the scope for third parties to carry out research and development in the relevant field because of the limited research capacity available elsewhere;
(b) because of the particular structure of supply, the existence of the agreement substantially restricts the access of third parties to the market for the contract products;
(c) without any objectively valid reason, the parties do not exploit the results of the joint research and development;
(d) the contract products are not subject in the whole or a substantial part of the common market to effective competition from identical products or products considered by users as equivalent in view of their characteristics, price and intended use.

Article 11   1. In the case of agreements notified to the Commission before 1 March 1985, the exemption provided for in Art. 1 shall have retroactive effect from the time at which the conditions for application of this Regulation were fulfilled or, where the agreement does not fall within Art. 4(2)(3)(b) of Regulation No. 17, not earlier than the date of notification.

2. In the case of agreements existing on 13 March 1962 and notified to the Commission before 1 February 1963, the exemption shall have retroactive effect from the time at which the conditions for application of this Regulation were fulfilled.

3. Where agreements which were in existence on 13 March 1962 and which were notified to the Commission before 1 February 1963, or which are covered by Art. 4 (2)(3)(b) of Regulation No. 17 and were notified to the Commission before 1 January 1967, are amended before 1 September 1985 so as to fulfil the conditions for application of this Regulation, such amendment being communicated to the Commission before 1 October 1985, the prohibition laid down in Art. 85(1) of the Treaty shall not apply in respect of the period prior to the amendment. The communication of amendments shall take effect from the date of their receipt by the Commission. Where the communication is sent by registered post, it shall take effect from the date shown on the postmark of the place of posting.

4. In the case of agreements to which Art. 85 of the Treaty applies as a result of the accession of the United Kingdom, Ireland and Denmark, paragraphs 1 to 3 shall apply except that the relevant dates shall be 1 January 1973 instead of 13 March 1962 and 1 July 1973 instead of 1 February 1963 and 1 January 1967.

5. In the case of agreements to which Art. 85 of the Treaty applies as a result of the accession of Greece, paragraphs 1 to 3 shall apply except that the relevant dates shall be 1 January 1981 instead of 13 March 1962 and 1 July 1981 instead of 1 February 1963 and 1 January 1967.

6. As regards agreements to which Art. 85 of the Treaty applies as a result of the accession of the Kingdom of Spain and of the Portuguese Republic, paragraphs 1 to 3 shall apply except that the relevant dates should be 1 January 1986 instead of 13 March 1962 and 1 July 1986 instead of 1 February 1963, 1 January 1967, 1 March 1985 and 1 September 1985. The amendments made to the agreements in accordance with the provisions of paragraph 3 need not be notified to the Commission.

7. As regards agreements to which Article 85 of the Treaty applies as a result of the accession of Austria, Finland and Sweden, paragraphs 1 to 3 shall apply *mutatis mutandis* on the understanding that the relevant dates shall be the date of accession instead of 13 March 1962 and six months after the date of accession instead of 1 February 1963, 1 January 1967, 1 March 1985 and 1 September 1985. The amendment made to these agreements in accordance with the provisions of paragraph 3 need not be notified to the Commission. However, this paragraph shall not apply to agreements which at the date of accession already fall under Article 53(1) of the EEA Agreement.

Article 12   This Regulation shall apply *mutatis mutandis* to decisions of associations of undertakings.

Article 13 This Regulation shall enter into force on 1 March 1985. It shall apply until 31 December 2000.

[*final provisions omitted*]

Commission Regulation of 30 November 1988 on the application of Article 85(3) of the EC Treaty to categories of franchise agreements (4087/88/EEC)[24]

The Commission of the European Communities,

[*recitals omitted*]

Whereas:

(1) Regulation No. 19/65/EEC empowers the Commission to apply Art. 85(3) of the Treaty by Regulation to certain categories of bilateral exclusive agreements falling within the scope of Art. 85(1) which either have as their object the exclusive distribution or exclusive purchase of goods, or include restrictions imposed in relation to the assignment or use of industrial property rights.

(2) Franchise agreements consist essentially of licences of industrial or intellectual property rights relating to trade marks or signs and know-how, which can be combined with restrictions relating to supply or purchase of goods.

(3) Several types of franchise can be distinguished according to their object: industrial franchise concerns the manufacturing of goods, distribution franchise concerns the sale of goods, and service franchise concerns the supply of services.

(4) It is possible on the basis of the experience of the Commission to define categories of franchise agreements which fall under Art. 85(1) but can normally be regarded as satisfying the conditions laid down in Art. 85(3). This is the case for franchise agreements whereby one of the parties supplies goods or provides services to end users. On the other hand, industrial franchise agreements should not be covered by this Regulation. Such agreements, which usually govern relationships between producers, present different characteristics than the other types of franchise. They consist of manufacturing licences based on patents and/or technical know-how, combined with trade-mark licences. Some of them may benefit from other block exemptions if they fulfil the necessary conditions.

(5) This Regulation covers franchise agreements between two undertakings, the franchisor and the franchisee, for the retailing of goods or the provision of services to end users, or a combination of these activities, such as the processing or adaptation of goods to fit specific needs of their customers. It also covers cases where the relationship between franchisor and franchisees is made through a third undertaking, the master franchisee. It does not cover wholesale franchise agreements because of the lack of experience of the Commission in that field.

(6) Franchise agreements as defined in this Regulation can fall under Art. 85(1). They may in particular affect intra-Community trade where they are concluded between undertakings from different Member States or where they form the basis of a network which extends beyond the boundaries of a single Member State.

[24] OJ 1988 L 359/46, as last amended by Declaration 95/1/EC, OJ 1995 L 1/1.

(7) Franchise agreements as defined in this Regulation normally improve the distribution of goods and/or the provision of services as they give franchisors the possibility of establishing a uniform network with limited investments, which may assist the entry of new competitors on the market, particularly in the case of small and medium-sized undertakings, thus increasing interbrand competition. They also allow independent traders to set up outlets more rapidly and with higher chance of success than if they had to do so without the franchisor's experience and assistance. They have therefore the possibility of competing more efficiently with large distribution undertakings.

(8) As a rule, franchise agreements also allow consumers and other end users a fair share of the resulting benefit, as they combine the advantage of a uniform network with the existence of traders personally interested in the efficient operation of their business. The homogeneity of the network and the constant cooperation between the franchisor and the franchisees ensures a constant quality of the products and services. The favourable effect of franchising on interbrand competition and the fact that consumers are free to deal with any franchisee in the network guarantees that a reasonable part of the resulting benefits will be passed on to the consumers.

(9) This Regulation must define the obligations restrictive of competition which may be included in franchise agreements. This is the case in particular for the granting of an exclusive territory to the franchisees combined with the prohibition on actively seeking customers outside that territory, which allows them to concentrate their efforts on their allotted territory. The same applies to the granting of an exclusive territory to a master franchisee combined with the obligation not to conclude franchise agreements with third parties outside that territory. Where the franchisees sell or use in the process of providing services, goods manufactured by the franchisor or according to its instructions and/or bearing its trade mark, an obligation on the franchisees not to sell, or use in the process of the provision of services, competing goods, makes it possible to establish a coherent network which is identified with the franchised goods. However, this obligation should only be accepted with respect to the goods which form the essential subject-matter of the franchise. It should notably not relate to accessories or spare parts for these goods.

(10) The obligations referred to above thus do not impose restrictions which are not necessary for the attainment of the abovementioned objectives. In particular, the limited territorial protection granted to the franchisees is indispensable to protect their investment.

(11) It is desirable to list in the Regulation a number of obligations that are commonly found in franchise agreements and are normally not restrictive of competition and to provide that if, because of the particular economic or legal circumstances, they fall under Art. 85(1), they are also covered by the exemption. This list, which is not exhaustive, includes in particular clauses which are essential either to preserve the common identity and reputation of the network or to prevent the know-how made available and the assistance given by the franchisor from benefiting competitors.

(12) The Regulation must specify the conditions which must be satisfied for the exemption to apply. To guarantee that competition is not eliminated for a substantial part of the goods which are the subject of the franchise, it is necessary that par-

allel imports remain possible. Therefore, cross deliveries between franchisees should always be possible. Furthermore, where a franchise network is combined with another distribution system, franchisees should be free to obtain supplies from authorised distributors. To better inform consumers, thereby helping to ensure that they receive a fair share of the resulting benefits, it must be provided that the franchisee shall be obliged to indicate its status as an independent undertaking, by any appropriate means which does not jeopardize the common identity of the franchised network. Furthermore, where the franchisees have to honour guarantees for the franchisor's goods, this obligation should also apply to goods supplied by the franchisor, other franchisees or other agreed dealers.

(13) The Regulation must also specify restrictions which may not be included in franchise agreements if these are to benefit from the exemption granted by the Regulation, by virtue of the fact that such provisions are restrictions falling under Art. 85(1) for which there is no general presumption that they will lead to the positive effects required by Art. 85(3). This applies in particular to market sharing between competing manufacturers, to clauses unduly limiting the franchisee's choice of suppliers or customers, and to cases where the franchisee is restricted in determining its prices. However, the franchisor should be free to recommend prices to the franchisees, where it is not prohibited by national laws and to the extent that it does not lead to concerted practices for the effective application of these prices.

(14) Agreements which are not automatically covered by the exemption because they contain provisions that are not expressly exempted by the Regulation and not expressly excluded from exemption may nonetheless generally be presumed to be eligible for application of Art. 85(3). It will be possible for the Commission rapidly to establish whether this is the case for a particular agreement. Such agreements should therefore be deemed to be covered by the exemption provided for in this Regulation where they are notified to the Commission and the Commission does not oppose the application of the exemption within a specified period of time.

(15) If individual agreements exempted by this Regulation nevertheless have effects which are incompatible with Art. 85(3), in particular as interpreted by the administrative practice of the Commission and the case law of the Court of Justice, the Commission may withdraw the benefit of the block exemption. This applies in particular where competition is significantly restricted because of the structure of the relevant market.

(16) Agreements which are automatically exempted pursuant to this Regulation need not be notified. Undertakings may nevertheless in a particular case request a decision pursuant to Council Regulation No. 17[25] as last amended by the Act of Accession of Spain and Portugal.

(17) Agreements may benefit from the provisions either of this Regulation or of another Regulation, according to their particular nature and provided that they fulfil the necessary conditions of application. They may not benefit from a combination of the provisions of this Regulation with those of another block exemption Regulation,

---

[25] OJ Sp. Ed. 1959–62, 87.

HAS ADOPTED this Regulation:

Article 1 1. Pursuant to Art. 85(3) of the Treaty and subject to the provisions of this Regulation, it is hereby declared that Art. 85(1) of the Treaty shall not apply to franchise agreements to which two undertakings are party, which include one or more of the restrictions listed in Art. 2.

2. The exemption provided for in paragraph 1 shall also apply to master franchise agreements to which two undertakings are party. Where applicable, the provisions of this Regulation concerning the relationship between franchisor and franchisee shall apply *mutatis mutandis* to the relationship between franchisor and master franchisee and between master franchisee and franchisee.

3. For the purposes of this Regulation:
(a) 'franchise' means a package of industrial or intellectual property rights relating to trade marks, trade names, shop signs, utility models, designs, copyrights, know-how or patents, to be exploited for the resale of goods or the provision of services to end users;
(b) 'franchise agreement' means an agreement whereby one undertaking, the franchisor, grants the other, the franchisee, in exchange for direct or indirect financial consideration, the right to exploit a franchise for the purposes of marketing specified types of goods and/or services; it includes at least obligations relating to:
   — the use of a common name or shop sign and a uniform presentation of contract premises and/or means of transport,
   — the communication by the franchisor to the franchisee of know-how,
   — the continuing provision by the franchisor to the franchisee of commercial or technical assistance during the life of the agreement;
(c) 'master franchise agreement' means an agreement whereby one undertaking, the franchisor, grants the other, the master franchisee, in exchange for direct or indirect financial consideration, the right to exploit a franchise for the purposes of concluding franchise agreements with third parties, the franchisees;
(d) 'franchisor's goods' means goods produced by the franchisor or according to its instructions, and/or bearing the franchisor's name or trade mark;
(e) 'contract premises' means the premises used for the exploitation of the franchise or, when the franchise is exploited outside those premises, the base from which the franchisee operates the means of transport used for the exploitation of the franchise (contract means of transport);
(f) 'know-how' means a package of non-patented practical information, resulting from experience and testing by the franchisor, which is secret, substantial and identified;
(g) 'secret' means that the know-how, as a body or in the precise configuration and assembly of its components, is not generally known or easily accessible; it is not limited in the narrow sense that each individual component of the know-how should be totally unknown or unobtainable outside the franchisor's business;
(h) 'substantial' means that the know-how includes information which is of importance for the sale of goods or the provision of services to end users, and in particular for the presentation of goods for sale, the processing of goods in connection with the provision of services, methods of dealing with customers, and

administration and financial management; the know-how must be useful for the franchisee by being capable, at the date of conclusion of the agreement, of improving the competitive position of the franchisee, in particular by improving the franchisee's performance or helping it to enter a new market;

(i) 'identified' means that the know-how must be described in a sufficiently comprehensive manner so as to make it possible to verify that it fulfils the criteria of secrecy and substantiality; the description of the know-how can either be set out in the franchise agreement or in a separate document or recorded in any other appropriate form.

Article 2 The exemption provided for in Art. 1 shall apply to the following restrictions of competition:

(a) an obligation on the franchisor, in a defined area of the common market, the contract territory, not to:
  — grant the right to exploit all or part of the franchise to third parties,
  — itself exploit the franchise, or itself market the goods or services which are the subject-matter of the franchise under a similar formula,
  — itself supply the franchisor's goods to third parties;

(b) an obligation on the master franchisee not to conclude franchise agreements with third parties outside its contract territory;

(c) an obligation on the franchisee to exploit the franchise only from the contract premises;

(d) an obligation on the franchisee to refrain, outside the contract territory, from seeking customers for the goods or the services which are the subject-matter of the franchise;

(e) an obligation on the franchisee not to manufacture, sell or use in the course of the provision of services, goods competing with the franchisor's goods which are the subject-matter of the franchise; where the subject-matter of the franchise is the sale or use in the course of the provision of services both certain types of goods and spare parts or accessories therefor, that obligation may not be imposed in respect of these spare parts or accessories.

Article 3 1. Art. 1 shall apply notwithstanding the presence of any of the following obligations on the franchisee, in so far as they are necessary to protect the franchisor's industrial or intellectual property rights or to maintain the common identity and reputation of the franchised network:

(a) to sell, or use in the course of the provision of services, exclusively goods matching minimum objective quality specifications laid down by the franchisor;

(b) to sell, or use in the course of the provision of services, goods which are manufactured only by the franchisor or by third parties designed by it, where it is impracticable, owing to the nature of the goods which are the subject-matter of the franchise, to apply objective quality specifications;

(b) not to engage, directly or indirectly, in any similar business in a territory where it would compete with a member of the franchised network, including the franchisor; the franchisee may be held to this obligation after termination of the agreement, for a reasonable period which may not exceed one year, in the territory where it has exploited the franchise;

(d) not to acquire financial interests in the capital of a competing undertaking, which would give the franchisee the power to influence the economic conduct of such undertaking;

(e) to sell the goods which are the subject-matter of the franchise only to end users, to other franchisees and to resellers within other channels of distribution supplied by the manufacturer of these goods or with its consent;

(f) to use is best endeavours to sell the goods or provide the services that are the subject-matter of the franchise; to offer for sale a minimum range of goods, achieve a minimum turnover, plan its orders in advance, keep minimum stocks and provide customer and warranty services;

(g) to pay to the franchisor a specified proportion of its revenue for advertising and itself carry out advertising for the nature of which it shall obtain the franchisor's approval.

2. Art. 1 shall apply notwithstanding the presence of any of the following obligations on the franchisee:

(a) not to disclose to third parties the know-how provided by the franchisor; the franchisee may be held to this obligation after termination of the agreement;

(b) to communicate to the franchisor any experience gained in exploiting the franchise and to grant it, and other franchisees, a non-exclusive licence for the know-how resulting from that experience;

(c) to inform the franchisor of infringements of licensed industrial or intellectual property rights, to take legal action against infringers or to assist the franchisor in any legal action against infringers:

(d) not to use know-how licensed by the franchisor for purposes other than the exploitation of the franchise; the franchisee may be held to this obligation after termination of the agreement;

(e) to attend or have its staff attend training courses arranged by the franchisor;

(f) to apply the commercial methods devised by the franchisor, including any subsequent modification thereof, and use the licensed industrial or intellectual property rights;

(g) to comply with the franchisor's standards for the equipment and presentation of the contract premises and/or means of transport;

(h) to allow the franchisor to carry out checks of the contract premises and/or means of transport, including the goods sold and the services provided, and the inventory and accounts of the franchisee;

(i) not without the franchisor's consent to change the location of the contract premises;

(j) not without the franchisor's consent to assign the rights and obligations under the franchise agreement.

3. In the event that, because of particular circumstances, obligations referred to in paragraph 2 fall within the scope of Art. 85 (1), they shall also be exempted even if they are not accompanied by any of the obligations exempted by Art. 1.

Article 4   The exemption provided for in Art. 1 shall apply on condition that:
(a) the franchisee is free to obtain the goods that are the subject-matter of the franchise from other franchisees; where such goods are also distributed through

another network of authorised distributors, the franchisee must be free to obtain the goods from the latter;

(b) where the franchisor obliges the franchisee to honour guarantees for the franchisor's goods, that obligation shall apply in respect of such goods supplied by any member of the franchised network or other distributors which give a similar guarantee, in the common market;

(c) the franchisee is obliged to indicate its status as an independent undertaking; this indication shall however not interfere with the common identity of the franchised network resulting in particular from the common name or shop sign and uniform appearance of the contract premises and/or means of transport.

Article 5   The exemption granted by Art. 1 shall not apply where:

(a) undertakings producing goods or providing services which are identical or are considered by users as equivalent in view of their characteristics, price and intended use, enter into franchise agreements in respect of such goods or services;

(b) without prejudice to Art. 2(e) and Art. 3(1)(b), the franchisee is prevented from obtaining supplies of goods of a quality equivalent to those offered by the franchisor;

(c) without prejudice to Art. 2(e), the franchisee is obliged to sell, or use in the process of providing services, goods manufactured by the franchisor or third parties designated by the franchisor and the franchisor refuses, for reasons other than protecting the franchisor's industrial or intellectual property rights, or maintaining the common identity and reputation of the franchised network, to designate as authorised manufacturers third parties proposed by the franchisee;

(d) the franchisee is prevented from continuing to use the licensed know-how after termination of the agreement where the know-how has become generally known or easily accessible, other than by breach of an obligation by the franchisee;

(e) the franchisee is restricted by the franchisor, directly or indirectly, in the determination of sale prices for the goods or services which are the subject-matter of the franchise, without prejudice to the possibility for the franchisor of recommending sale prices;

(f) the franchisor prohibits the franchisee from challenging the validity of the industrial or intellectual property rights which form part of the franchise, without prejudice to the possibility for the franchisor of terminating the agreement in such a case;

(g) franchisees are obliged not to supply within the common market the goods or services which are the subject-matter of the franchise to end users because of their place of residence.

Article 6   1. The exemption provided for in Art. 1 shall also apply to franchise agreements which fulfil the conditions laid down in Art. 4 and include obligations restrictive of competition which are not covered by Arts. 2 and 3(3) and do not fall within the scope of Art. 5, on condition that the agreements in question are notified to the Commission in accordance with the provisions of Commission Regulation No. 27[26] and that the Commission does not oppose such exemption within a period of six months.

---

[26] OJ 1987 C 229/3.

2. The period of six months shall run from the date on which the notification is received by the Commission. Where, however, the notification is made by registered post, the period shall run from the date shown on the postmark of the place of posting.

3. Paragraph 1 shall apply only if:

(a) express reference is made to this Article in the notification or in a communication accompanying it; and

(b) the information furnished with the notification is complete and in accordance with the facts.

4. The benefit of paragraph 1 can be claimed for agreements notified before the entry into force of this Regulation by submitting a communication to the Commission referring expressly to this Article and to the notification. Paragraphs 2 and 3(b) shall apply *mutatis mutandis*.

5. The Commission may oppose exemption. It shall oppose exemption if it receives a request to do so from a Member State within three months of the forwarding to the Member State of the notification referred to in paragraph 1 or the communication referred to in paragraph 4. This request must be justified on the basis of considerations relating to the competition rules of the Treaty.

6. The Commission may withdraw its opposition to the exemption at any time. However, where that opposition was raised at the request of a Member State, it may be withdrawn only after consultation of the advisory Committee on Restrictive Practices and Dominant Positions.

7. If the opposition is withdrawn because the undertakings concerned have shown that the conditions of Art. 85(3) are fulfilled, the exemption shall apply from the date of the notification.

8. If the opposition is withdrawn because the undertakings concerned have amended the agreement so that the conditions of Art. 85(3) are fulfilled, the exemption shall apply from the date on which the amendments take effect.

9. If the Commission opposes exemption and its opposition is not withdrawn, the effects of the notification shall be governed by the provisions of Regulation No. 17.

Article 7 1. Information acquired pursuant to Art. 6 shall be used only for the purposes of this Regulation.

2. The Commission and the authorities of the Member States, their officials and other servants shall not disclose information acquired by them pursuant to this Regulation of a kind that is covered by the obligation of professional secrecy.

3. Paragraphs 1 and 2 shall not prevent publication of general information or surveys which do not contain information relating to particular undertakings or associations of undertakings.

Article 8 The Commission may withdraw the benefit of this Regulation, pursuant to Art. 7 of Regulation No. 19/65/EEC, where it finds in a particular case that an agreement exempted by this Regulation nevertheless has certain effects which are incompatible with the conditions laid down in Art. 85(3) of the EEC Treaty, and in particular where territorial protection is awarded to the franchisee and:

(a) access to the relevant market or competition therein is significantly restricted by the cumulative effect of parallel networks of similar agreements established by competing manufacturers or distributors;
(b) the goods or services which are the subject-matter of the franchise do not face, in a substantial part of the common market, effective competition from goods or services which are identical or considered by users as equivalent in view of their characteristics, price and intended use;
(c) the parties, or one of them, prevent end users, because of their place of residence, from obtaining, directly or through intermediaries, the goods or services which are the subject-matter of the franchise within the common market, or use differences in specifications concerning those goods or services in different Member States, to isolate markets;
(d) franchisees engage in concerted practices relating to the sale prices of the goods or services which are the subject-matter of the franchise;
(e) the franchisor uses its right to check the contract premises and means of transport, or refuses its agreement to requests by the franchisee to move the contract premises or assign its rights and obligations under the franchise agreement, for reasons other than protecting the franchisor's industrial or intellectual property rights, maintaining the common identity and reputation of the franchised network or verifying that the franchisee abides by its obligations under the agreement.

Article 8a   The prohibition in Article 85(1) of the Treaty shall not apply to the franchise agreements which were in existence at the date of accession of Austria, Finland and Sweden and which, by reason of this accession fall within the scope of Article 85(1) if, within six months from the date of accession, they are so amended that they comply with the conditions laid down in this Regulation. However, this Article shall not apply to agreements which at the date of accession already fall under Article 53(1) of the EEA Agreement.

Article 9   This Regulation shall enter into force on 1 February 1989.
   It shall remain in force until 31 December 1999.

[final provisions omitted]

Council Regulation of 21 December 1989 on the control of concentrations between undertakings (4064/89/EEC)[27]

The Council of the European Communities,

HAVING REGARD to the Treaty establishing the European Economic Community, and in particular Arts. 87 and 235 thereof,

---

[27] OJ 1990 L 257/14 (corrigendum to OJ 1989 L 395/1), as last amended by Regulation 1310/97/EC, OJ 1997 L 180/1. Pursuant to Article 2 of the latter Regulation, it shall not apply to any concentration which was the subject of an agreement or announcement or where control was acquired within the meaning of Article 4(1) of Regulation 4064/89/EEC, before 1 March 1998 and it shall not in any circumstances apply to any concentration in respect of which proceedings were initiated before 1 March 1998 by a Member State's authority with responsibility for competition.

(1) Whereas, for the achievement of the aims of the Treaty establishing the European Economic Community, Art. 3(f) gives the Community the objective of instituting 'a system ensuring that competition in the common market is not distorted';

(2) Whereas this system is essential for the achievement of the internal market by 1992 and its further development;

(3) Whereas the dismantling of internal frontiers is resulting and will continue to result in major corporate reorganisations in the Community, particularly in the form of concentrations;

(4) Whereas such a development must be welcomed as being in line with the requirements of dynamic competition and capable of increasing the competitiveness of European industry, improving the conditions of growth and raising the standard of living in the Community;

(5) Whereas, however, it must be ensured that the process of reorganisation does not result in lasting damage to competition; whereas Community law must therefore include provisions governing those concentrations which may significantly impede effective competition in the common market or in a substantial part of it;

(6) Whereas Arts. 85 and 86, while applicable, according to the case-law of the Court of Justice, to certain concentrations, are not, however, sufficient to control all operations which may prove to be incompatible with the system of undistorted competition envisaged in the Treaty;

(7) Whereas a new legal instrument should therefore be created in the form of a Regulation to permit effective control of all concentrations from the point of view of their effect on the structure of competition in the Community and to be the only instrument applicable to such concentrations;

(8) Whereas this Regulation should therefore be based not only on Art. 87 but, principally, on Art. 235 of the Treaty, under which the Community may give itself the additional powers of action necessary for the attainment of its objectives, including with regard to concentrations on the markets for agricultural products listed in Annex II to the Treaty;

(9) Whereas the provisions to be adopted in this Regulation should apply to significant structural changes the impact of which on the market goes beyond the national borders of any one Member State;

(10) Whereas the scope of application of this Regulation should therefore be defined according to the geographical area of activity of the undertakings concerned and be limited by quantitative thresholds in order to cover those concentrations which have a Community dimension; whereas, at the end of an initial phase of the application of this Regulation, these thresholds should be reviewed in the light of the experience gained;

(11) Whereas a concentration with a Community dimension exists where the combined aggregate turnover of the undertakings concerned exceeds given levels worldwide and within the Community and where at least two of the undertakings concerned have their sole or main fields of activities in different Member States or where, although the undertakings in question act mainly in one and the same Member State, at least one of them has substantial operations in at least one other

Member State; whereas that is also the case where the concentrations are effected by undertakings which do not have their principal fields of activities in the Community but which have substantial operations there;

(12) Whereas the arrangements to be introduced for the control of concentrations should, without prejudice to Art. 90(2) of the Treaty, respect the principle of non-discrimination between the public and the private sectors; whereas, in the public sector, calculation of the turnover of an undertaking concerned in a concentration needs, therefore, to take account of undertakings making up an economic unit with an independent power of decision, irrespective of the way in which their capital is held or of the rules of administrative supervision applicable to them;

(13) Whereas it is necessary to establish whether concentrations with a Community dimension are compatible or not with the common market from the point of view of the need to maintain and develop effective competition in the common market; whereas, in so doing, the Commission must place its appraisal within the general framework of the achievement of the fundamental objectives referred to in Art. 2 of the Treaty, including that of strengthening the Community's economic and social cohesion, referred to in Art. 130a;

(14) Whereas this Regulation should establish the principle that a concentration with a Community dimension which creates or strengthens a position as a result of which effective competition in the common market or in a substantial part of it is significantly impeded is to be declared incompatible with the common market;

(15) Whereas concentrations which, by reason of the limited market share of the undertakings concerned, are not liable to impede effective competition may be presumed to be compatible with the common market; whereas, without prejudice to Arts. 85 and 86 of the Treaty, an indication to this effect exists, in particular, where the market share of the undertakings concerned does not exceed 25% either in the common market or in a substantial part of it;

(16) Whereas the Commission should have the task of taking all the decisions necessary to establish whether or not concentrations with a Community dimension are compatible with the common market, as well as decisions designed to restore effective competition;

(17) Whereas to ensure effective control undertakings should be obliged to give prior notification of concentrations with a Community dimension and provision should be made for the suspension of concentrations for a limited period, and for the possibility of extending or waiving a suspension where necessary; whereas in the interests of legal certainty the validity of transactions must nevertheless be protected as much as necessary;

(18) Whereas a period within which the Commission must initiate proceedings in respect of a notified concentration and periods within which it must give a final decision on the compatibility or incompatibility with the common market of a notified concentration should be laid down;

(19) Whereas the undertakings concerned must be afforded the right to be heard by the Commission when proceedings have been initiated; whereas the members of the management and supervisory bodies and the recognised representatives of the employees of the undertakings concerned, and third parties showing a legitimate interest, must also be given the opportunity to be heard;

(20) Whereas the Commission should act in close and constant liaison with the competent authorities of the Member States from which it obtains comments and information;

(21) Whereas, for the purposes of this Regulation, and in accordance with the case-law of the Court of Justice, the Commission must be afforded the assistance of the Member States and must also be empowered to require information to be given and to carry out the necessary investigations in order to appraise concentrations;

(22) Whereas compliance with this Regulation must be enforceable by means of fines and periodic penalty payments; whereas the Court of Justice should be given unlimited jurisdiction in that regard pursuant to Art. 172 of the Treaty;

(23) Whereas it is appropriate to define the concept of concentration in such a manner as to cover only operations bringing about a lasting change in the structure of the undertakings concerned; whereas it is therefore necessary to exclude from the scope of this Regulation those operations which have as their object or effect the coordination of the competitive behaviour of undertakings which remain independent, since such operations fall to be examined under the appropriate provisions of the Regulations implementing Arts. 85 and 86 of the Treaty; whereas it is appropriate to make this distinction specifically in the case of the creation of joint ventures;

(24) Whereas there is no coordination of competitive behaviour within the meaning of this Regulation where two or more undertakings agree to acquire jointly control of one or more other undertakings with the object and effect of sharing amongst themselves such undertakings or their assets;

(25) Whereas this Regulation should still apply where the undertakings concerned accept restrictions directly related and necessary to the implementation of the concentration;

(26) Whereas the Commission should be given exclusive competence to apply this Regulation, subject to review by the Court of Justice;

(27) Whereas the Member States may not apply their national legislation on competition to concentrations with a Community dimension, unless this Regulation makes provision therefor; whereas the relevant powers of national authorities should be limited to cases where, failing intervention by the Commission, effective competition is likely to be significantly impeded within the territory of a Member State and where the competition interests of that Member State cannot be sufficiently protected otherwise by this Regulation; whereas the Member States concerned must act promptly in such cases; whereas this Regulation cannot, because of the diversity of national law, fix a single deadline for the adoption of remedies;

(28) Whereas, furthermore, the exclusive application of this Regulation to concentrations with a Community dimension is without prejudice to Art. 223 of the Treaty, and does not prevent the Member States from taking appropriate measures to protect legitimate interests other than those pursued by this Regulation, provided that such measures are compatible with the general principles and other provisions of Community law;

(29) Whereas concentrations not covered by this Regulation come, in principle, within the jurisdiction of the Member States; whereas, however, the Commission

should have the power to act, at the request of a Member State concerned, in cases where effective competition could be significantly impeded within that Member State's territory;

(30) Whereas the conditions in which concentrations involving Community undertakings are carried out in non-member countries should be observed, and provision should be made for the possibility of the Council giving the Commission an appropriate mandate for negotiation with a view to obtaining non-discriminatory treatment for Community undertakings;

(31) Whereas this Regulation in no way detracts from the collective rights of employees as recognised in the undertakings concerned,

HAS ADOPTED this Regulation:

Article 1 Scope   1. Without prejudice to Art. 22, this Regulation shall apply to all concentrations with a Community dimension as defined in paragraphs 2 and 3.

2. For the purposes of this Regulation, a concentration has a Community dimension where:
(a) the combined aggregate worldwide turnover of all the undertakings concerned is more than ECU 5000 million; and
(b) the aggregate Community-wide turnover of each of at least two of the undertakings concerned is more than ECU 250 million,

unless each of the undertakings concerned achieves more than two-thirds of its aggregate Community-wide turnover within one and the same Member State.

3. For the purposes of this Regulation, a concentration that does not meet the thresholds laid down in paragraph 2 has a Community dimension where:
(a) the combined aggregate worldwide turnover of all the undertakings concerned is more than ECU 2 500 million;
(b) in each of at least three Member States, the combined aggregate turnover of all the undertakings concerned is more than ECU 100 million;
(c) in each of at least three Member States included for the purpose of point (b), the aggregate turnover of each of at least two of the undertakings concerned is more than ECU 25 million; and
(d) the aggregate Community-wide turnover of each of at least two of the undertakings concerned is more than ECU 100 million;

unless each of the undertakings concerned achieves more than two-thirds of its aggregate Community-wide turnover within one and the same Member State.

4. Before 1 July 2000 the Commission shall report to the Council on the operation of the thresholds and criteria set out in paragraphs 2 and 3.

5. Following the report referred to in paragraph 4 and on a proposal from the Commission, the Council, acting by a qualified majority, may revise the thresholds and criteria mentioned in paragraph 3.

Article 2 Appraisal of concentrations   1. Concentrations within the scope of this Regulation shall be appraised in accordance with the following provisions with a view to establishing whether or not they are compatible with the common market. In making this appraisal, the Commission shall take into account:

(a) the need to maintain and develop effective competition within the common market in view of, among other things, the structure of all the markets concerned and the actual or potential competition from undertakings located either within or outwith the Community;

(b) the market position of the undertakings concerned and their economic and financial power, the alternatives available to suppliers and users, their access to supplies or markets, any legal or other barriers to entry, supply and demand trends for the relevant goods and services, the interests of the intermediate and ultimate consumers, and the development of technical and economic progress provided that it is to consumers' advantage and does not form an obstacle to competition.

2. A concentration which does not create or strengthen a dominant position as a result of which effective competition would be significantly impeded in the common market or in a substantial part of it shall be declared compatible with the common market.

3. A concentration which creates or strengthens a dominant position as a result of which effective competition would be significantly impeded in the common market or in a substantial part of it shall be declared incompatible with the common market.

4. To the extent that the creation of a joint venture constituting a concentration pursuant to Article 3 has as its object or effect the coordination of the competitive behaviour of undertakings that remain independent, such coordination shall be appraised in accordance with the criteria of Article 85(1) and (3) of the Treaty, with a view to establishing whether or not the operation is compatible with the common market.

In making the appraisal, the Commission shall take into account in particular:

— whether two or more parent companies retain to a significant extent activities in the same market as the joint venture or in a market which is downstream or upstream from that of the joint venture or in a neighbouring market closely related to this market,

— whether the coordination which is the direct consequence of the creation of the joint venture affords the undertakings concerned the possibility of eliminating competition in respect of a substantial part of the products or services in question.

Article 3   Definition of concentration   1. A concentration shall be deemed to arise where:

(a) two or more previously independent undertakings merge, or

(b) one or more persons already controlling at least one undertaking, or one or more undertakings

acquire, whether by purchase of securities or assets, by contract or by any other means, direct or indirect control of the whole or parts of one or more other undertakings.

2. The creation of a joint venture performing on a lasting basis all the functions of an autonomous economic entity shall constitute a concentration within the meaning of paragraph 1(b).

3. For the purposes of this Regulation, control shall be constituted by rights, contracts or any other means which, either separately or in combination and having regard to the considerations of fact or law involved, confer the possibility of exercising decisive influence on an undertaking, in particular by:

(a) ownership or the right to use all or part of the assets of an undertaking;

(b) rights or contracts which confer decisive influence on the composition, voting or decisions of the organs of an undertaking.

4. Control is acquired by persons or undertakings which:

(a) are holders of the rights or entitled to rights under the contracts concerned; or

(b) while not being holders of such rights or entitled to rights under such contracts, have the power to exercise the rights deriving therefrom.

5. A concentration shall not be deemed to arise where:

(a) credit institutions or other financial institutions or insurance companies, the normal activities of which include transactions and dealing in securities for their own account or for the account of others, hold on a temporary basis securities which they have acquired in an undertaking with a view to reselling them, provided that they do not exercise voting rights in respect of those securities with a view to determining the competitive behaviour of that undertaking or provided that they exercise such voting rights only with a view to preparing the disposal of all or part of that undertaking or of its assets or the disposal of those securities and that any such disposal takes place within one year of the date of acquisition; that period may be extended by the Commission on request where such institutions or companies can show that the disposal was not reasonably possible within the period set;

(b) control is acquired by an office-holder according to the law of a Member State relating to liquidation, winding up, insolvency, cessation of payments, compositions or analogous proceedings;

(c) the operations referred to in paragraph 1(b) are carried out by the financial holding companies referred to in Art. 5(3) of the Fourth Council Directive 78/660/EEC of 25 July 1978 on the annual accounts of certain types of companies,[28] as last amended by Directive 84/569/EEC,[29] provided however that the voting rights in respect of the holding are exercised, in particular in relation to the appointment of members of the management and supervisory bodies of the undertakings in which they have holdings, only to maintain the full value of those investments and not to determine directly or indirectly the competitive conduct of those undertakings.

Article 4   Prior notification of concentrations   1. Concentrations with a Community dimension defined in this Regulation shall be notified to the Commission not more than one week after the conclusion of the agreement, or the announcement of the public bid, or the acquisition of a controlling interest. That week shall begin when the first of those events occurs.

2. A concentration which consists of a merger within the meaning of Art. 3(1)(a) or in the acquisition of joint control within the meaning of Art. 3(1)(b) shall be notified jointly by the parties to the merger or by those acquiring joint control as the case

---

[28] OJ 1978 L 222/11.   [29] OJ 1985 L 314/28.

may be. In all other cases, the notification shall be effected by the person or undertaking acquiring control of the whole or parts of one or more undertakings.

3. Where the Commission finds that a notified concentration falls within the scope of this Regulation, it shall publish the fact of the notification, at the same time indicating the names of the parties, the nature of the concentration and the economic sectors involved. The Commission shall take account of the legitimate interest of undertakings in the protection of their business secrets.

Article 5 *Calculation of turnover* 1. Aggregate turnover within the meaning of Art. 1(2) shall comprise the amounts derived by the undertakings concerned in the preceding financial year from the sale of products and the provision of services falling within the undertakings' ordinary activities after deduction of sales rebates and of value added tax and other taxes directly related to turnover. The aggregate turnover of an undertaking concerned shall not include the sale of products or the provision of services between any of the undertakings referred to in paragraph 4.

Turnover, in the Community or in a Member State, shall comprise products sold and services provided to undertakings or consumers, in the Community or in that Member State as the case may be.

2. By way of derogation from paragraph 1, where the concentration consists in the acquisition of parts, whether or not constituted as legal entities, of one or more undertakings, only the turnover relating to the parts which are the subject of the transaction shall be taken into account with regard to the seller or sellers.

However, two or more transactions within the meaning of the first subparagraph which take place within a two-year period between the same persons or undertakings shall be treated as one and the same concentration arising on the date of the last transaction.

3. In place of turnover the following shall be used:
(a) for credit institutions and other financial institutions, as regards Article 1(2) and (3), the sum of the following income items as defined in Council Directive 86/635/EEC of 8 December 1986[30] on the annual accounts and consolidated accounts of banks and other financial institutions, after deduction of value added tax and other taxes directly related to those items, where appropriate:

   (i) interest income and similar income;
   (ii) income from securities:

   — income from shares and other variable yield securities,
   — income from participating interests,
   — income from shares in affiliated undertakings;

   (iii) commissions receivable;
   (iv) net profit on financial operations;
   (v) other operating income.

   The turnover of a credit or financial institution in the Community or in a Member State shall comprise the income items, as defined above, which are received by the branch or division of that institution established in the Community or in the Member State in question, as the case may be;

---

[30] OJ 1986 L 372/1.

(b) for insurance undertakings, the value of gross premiums written which shall comprise all amounts received and receivable in respect of insurance contracts issued by or on behalf of the insurance undertakings, including also outgoing reinsurance premiums, and after deduction of taxes and parafiscal contributions or levies charged by reference to the amounts of individual premiums or the total volume of premiums; as regards Article 1(2)(b) and (3)(b), (c) and (d) and the final part of Article 1(2) and (3), gross premiums received from Community residents and from residents of one Member State respectively shall be taken into account.

4. Without prejudice to paragraph 2, the aggregate turnover of an undertaking concerned within the meaning of Art. 1(2) and (3) shall be calculated by adding together the respective turnovers of the following:
(a) the undertaking concerned;
(b) those undertakings in which the undertaking concerned, directly or indirectly:

— owns more than half the capital or business assets, or
— has the power to exercise more than half the voting rights, or
— has the power to appoint more than half the members of the supervisory board, the administrative board or bodies legally representing the undertakings, or
— has the right to manage the undertakings' affairs;

(c) those undertakings which have in the undertaking concerned the rights or powers listed in (b);
(d) those undertakings in which an undertaking as referred to in (c) has the rights or powers listed in (b);
(e) those undertakings in which two or more undertakings as referred to in (a) to (d) jointly have the rights or powers listed in (b).

5. Where undertakings concerned by the concentration jointly have the rights or powers listed in paragraph 4(b), in calculating the aggregate turnover of the undertakings concerned for the purposes of Art. 1(2) and (3):
(a) no account shall be taken of the turnover resulting from the sale of products or the provision of services between the joint undertaking and each of the undertakings concerned or any other undertaking connected with any one of them, as set out in paragraph 4(b) to (e);
(b) account shall be taken of the turnover resulting from the sale of products and the provision of services between the joint undertaking and any third undertakings. This turnover shall be apportioned equally amongst the undertakings concerned.

Article 6   Examination of the notification and initiation of proceedings   1. The Commission shall examine the notification as soon as it is received.
(a) Where it concludes that the concentration notified does not fall within the scope of this Regulation, it shall record that finding by means of a decision.
(b) Where it finds that the concentration notified, although falling within the scope of this Regulation, does not raise serious doubts as to its compatibility with the common market, it shall decide not to oppose it and shall declare that it is compatible with the common market.

The decision declaring the concentration compatible shall also cover restrictions directly related and necessary to the implementation of the concentration.

(c) Without prejudice to paragraph 1(a), where the Commission finds that the concentration notified falls within the scope of this Regulation and raises serious doubts as to its compatibility with the common market, it shall decide to initiate proceedings.

1a. Where the Commission finds that, following modification by the undertakings concerned, a notified concentration no longer raises serious doubts within the meaning of paragraph 1(c), it may decide to declare the concentration compatible with the common market pursuant to paragraph 1(b).

The Commission may attach to its decision under paragraph 1(b) conditions and obligations intended to ensure that the undertakings concerned comply with the commitments they have entered into vis-à-vis the Commission with a view to rendering the concentration compatible with the common market.

1b. The Commission may revoke the decision it has taken pursuant to paragraph 1(a) or (b) where:

(a) the decision is based on incorrect information for which one of the undertakings is responsible or where it has been obtained by deceit,

or

(b) the undertakings concerned commit a breach of an obligation attached to the decision.

1c. In the cases referred to in paragraph 1(b), the Commission may take a decision under paragraph 1, without being bound by the deadlines referred to in Article 10(1).

2. The Commission shall notify its decision to the undertakings concerned and the competent authorities of the Member States without delay.

Article 7 Suspension of concentrations 1. A concentration as defined in Article 1 shall not be put into effect either before its notification or until it as been declared compatible with the common market pursuant to a decision under Article 6(1)(b) or Article 8(2) or on the basis of a presumption according to Article 10(6).

[para. 2 repealed]

3. Paragraph 1 shall not prevent the implementation of a public bid which has been notified to the Commission in accordance with Art. 4(1), provided that the acquirer does not exercise the voting rights attached to the securities in question or does so only to maintain the full value of those investments and on the basis of a derogation granted by the Commission under paragraph 4.

4. The Commission may, on request, grant a derogation from the obligations imposed in paragraphs 1 or 3. The request to grant a derogation must be reasoned. In deciding on the request, the Commission shall take into account inter alia the effects of the suspension on one or more undertakings concerned by a concentration or on a third party and the threat to competition posed by the concentration. That derogation may be made subject to conditions and obligations in order to ensure conditions of effective competition. A derogation may be applied for and granted at any time, even before notification or after the transaction.

5. The validity of any transaction carried out in contravention of paragraph 1 shall be dependent on a decision pursuant to Article 6(1)(b) or Article 8(2) or (3) or on a presumption pursuant to Article 10(6).

This Article shall, however, have no effect on the validity of transactions in securities including those convertible into other securities admitted to trading on a market which is regulated and supervised by authorities recognized by public bodies, operates regularly and is accessible directly or indirectly to the public, unless the buyer and seller knew or ought to have known that the transaction was carried out in contravention of paragraph 1.

Article 8   Powers of decision of the Commission   1. Without prejudice to Art. 9, all proceedings initiated pursuant to Art. 6(1)(c) shall be closed by means of a decision as provided for in paragraphs 2 to 5.

2. Where the Commission finds that, following modification by the undertakings concerned if necessary, a notified concentration fulfils the criterion laid down in Article 2(2) and, in the cases referred to in Article 2(4), the criteria laid down in Article 85(3) of the Treaty, it shall issue a decision declaring the concentration compatible with the common market.

It may attach to its decision conditions and obligations intended to ensure that the undertakings concerned comply with the commitments they have entered into vis-à-vis the Commission with a view to rendering the concentration compatible with the common market. The decision declaring the concentration compatible with the common market shall also cover restrictions directly related and necessary to the implementation of the concentration.

3. Where the Commission finds that a concentration fulfils the criterion defined in Article 2(3) or, in the cases referred to in Article 2(4), does not fulfil the criteria laid down in Article 85(3) of the Treaty, it shall issue a decision declaring that the concentration is incompatible with the common market.

4. Where a concentration has already been implemented, the Commission may, in a decision pursuant to paragraph 3 or by separate decision, require the undertakings or assets brought together to be separated or the cessation of joint control or any other action that may be appropriate in order to restore conditions of effective competition.

5. The Commission may revoke the decision it has taken pursuant to paragraph 2 where:
(a) the declaration of compatibility is based on incorrect information for which one of the undertakings is responsible or where it has been obtained by deceit; or
(b) the undertakings concerned commit a breach of an obligation attached to the decision.

6. In the cases referred to in paragraph 5, the Commission may take a decision under paragraph 3, without being bound by the deadline referred to in Art. 10(3).

Article 9   Referral to the competent authorities of the Member States   1. The Commission may, by means of a decision notified without delay to the undertakings concerned and the competent authorities of the other Member States, refer a notified concentration to the competent authorities of the Member State concerned in the following circumstances.

2. Within three weeks of the date of receipt of the copy of the notification a Member State may inform the Commission, which shall inform the undertakings concerned, that:

(a) a concentration threatens to create or to strengthen a dominant position as a result of which effective competition will be significantly impeded on a market within that Member State, which presents all the characteristics of a distinct market, or

(b) a concentration affects competition on a market within that Member State, which presents all the characteristics of a distinct market and which does not constitute a substantial part of the common market.;

3. If the Commission considers that, having regard to the market for the products or services in question and the geographical reference market within the meaning of paragraph 7, there is such a distinct market and that such a threat exists, either:

(a) it shall itself deal with the case in order to maintain or restore effective competition on the market concerned; or

(b) it shall refer the whole or part of the case to the competent authorities of the Member State concerned with a view to the application of that State's national competition law.

If, however, the Commission considers that such a distinct market or threat does not exist it shall adopt a decision to that effect which it shall address to the Member State concerned.

In cases where a Member State informs the Commission that a concentration affects competition in a distinct market within its territory that does not form a substantial part of the common market, the Commission shall refer the whole or part of the case relating to the distinct market concerned, if it considers that such a distinct market is affected.

4. A decision to refer or not to refer pursuant to paragraph 3 shall be taken:

(a) as a general rule within the six-week period provided for in Art. 10(1), second subparagraph, where the Commission, pursuant to Art. 6(1)(b), has not initiated proceedings; or

(b) within three months at most of the notification of the concentration concerned where the Commission has initiated proceedings under Art. 6(1)(c), without taking the preparatory steps in order to adopt the necessary measures under Art. 8(2), second subparagraph, (3) or (4) to maintain or restore effective competition on the market concerned.

5. If within the three months referred to in paragraph 4(b) the Commission, despite a reminder from the Member State concerned, has not taken a decision on referral in accordance with paragraph 3 nor has taken the preparatory steps referred to in paragraph 4(b), it shall be deemed to have taken a decision to refer the case to the Member State concerned in accordance with paragraph 3(b).

6. The publication of any report or the announcement of the findings of the examination of the concentration by the competent authority of the Member State concerned shall be effected not more than four months after the Commission's referral.

7. The geographical reference market shall consist of the area in which the under-takings concerned are involved in the supply and demand of products or services, in which the conditions of competition are sufficiently homogeneous and which can be distinguished from neighbouring areas because, in particular, conditions of competition are appreciably different in those areas. This assessment should take account in particular of the nature and characteristics of the products or services concerned, of the existence of entry barriers or of consumer preferences, of appre-ciable differences of the undertakings' market shares between the area concerned and neighbouring areas or of substantial price differences.

8. In applying the provisions of this Article, the Member State concerned may take only the measures strictly necessary to safeguard or restore effective competition on the market concerned.

9. In accordance with the relevant provisions of the Treaty, any Member State may appeal to the Court of Justice, and in particular request the application of Art. 186, for the purpose of applying its national competition law.

10. This Article may be re-examined at the same time as the thresholds referred to in Article 1.

Article 10   Time limits for initiating proceedings and for decisions   1. The decisions referred to in Art. 6(1) must be taken within one month at most. That period shall begin on the day following that of the receipt of a notification or, if the information to be supplied with the notification is incomplete, on the day following that of the receipt of the complete information.

That period shall be increased to six weeks if the Commission receives a request from a Member State in accordance with Art. 9(2), or where, after notification of a concentration, the undertakings concerned submit commitments pursuant to Article 6(1a), which are intended by the parties to form the basis for a decision pur-suant to Article 6(1)(b).

2. Decisions taken pursuant to Art. 8(2) concerning notified concentrations must be taken as soon as it appears that the serious doubts referred to in Art. 6(1)(c) have been removed, particularly as a result of modifications made by the undertakings concerned, and at the latest by the deadline laid down in paragraph 3.

3. Without prejudice to Art. 8(6), decisions taken pursuant to Art. 8(3) concerning notified concentrations must be taken within not more than four months of the date on which proceedings are initiated.

4. The periods set by paragraphs 1 and 3 shall exceptionally be suspended where, owing to circumstances for which one of the undertakings involved in the concen-tration is responsible, the Commission has had to request information by decision pursuant to Art. 11 or to order an investigation by decision pursuant to Art. 13.

5. Where the Court of Justice gives a Judgement which annuls the whole or part of a Commission decision taken under this Regulation, the periods laid down in this Regulation shall start again from the date of the Judgement.

6. Where the Commission has not taken a decision in accordance with Art. 6(1)(b) or (c) or Art. 8(2) or (3) within the deadlines set in paragraphs 1 and 3 respectively, the concentration shall be deemed to have been declared compatible with the com-mon market, without prejudice to Art. 9.

Article 11   Requests for information   1. In carrying out the duties assigned to it by this Regulation, the Commission may obtain all necessary information from the Governments and competent authorities of the Member States, from the persons referred to in Art. 3(1)(b), and from undertakings and associations of undertakings.

2. When sending a request for information to a person, an undertaking or an association of undertakings, the Commission shall at the same time send a copy of the request to the competent authority of the Member State within the territory of which the residence of the person or the seat of the undertaking or association of undertakings is situated.

3. In its request the Commission shall state the legal basis and the purpose of the request and also the penalties provided for in Art. 14(1)(c) for supplying incorrect information.

4. The information requested shall be provided, in the case of undertakings, by their owners or their representatives and, in the case of legal persons, companies or firms, or of associations having no legal personality, by the persons authorised to represent them by law or by their statutes.

5. Where a person, an undertaking or an association of undertakings does not provide the information requested within the period fixed by the Commission or provides incomplete information, the Commission shall by decision require the information to be provided. The decision shall specify what information is required, fix an appropriate period within which it is to be supplied and state the penalties provided for in Arts. 14(1)(c) and 15(1)(a) and the right to have the decision reviewed by the Court of Justice.

6. The Commission shall at the same time send a copy of its decision to the competent authority of the Member State within the territory of which the residence of the person or the seat of the undertaking or association of undertakings is situated.

Article 12   Investigations by the authorities of the Member States   1. At the request of the Commission, the competent authorities of the Member States shall undertake the investigations which the Commission considers to be necessary under Art. 13(1), or which it has ordered by decision pursuant to Art. 13(3). The officials of the competent authorities of the Member States responsible for conducting those investigations shall exercise their powers upon production of an authorisation in writing issued by the competent authority of the Member State within the territory of which the investigation is to be carried out. Such authorisation shall specify the subject-matter and purpose of the investigation.

2. If so requested by the Commission or by the competent authority of the Member State within the territory of which the investigation is to be carried out, officials of the Commission may assist the officials of that authority in carrying out their duties.

Article 13   Investigative powers of the Commission   1. In carrying out the duties assigned to it by this Regulation, the Commission may undertake all necessary investigations into undertakings and associations of undertakings.
To that end the officials authorised by the Commission shall be empowered:
(a) to examine the books and other business records;
(b) to take or demand copies of or extracts from the books and business records;

(c) to ask for oral explanations on the spot;

(d) to enter any premises, land and means of transport of undertakings.

2. The officials of the Commission authorised to carry out the investigations shall exercise their powers on production of an authorisation in writing specifying the subject-matter and purpose of the investigation and the penalties provided for in Art. 14(1)(d) in cases where production of the required books or other business records is incomplete. In good time before the investigation, the Commission shall inform, in writing, the competent authority of the Member State within the territory of which the investigation is to be carried out of the investigation and of the identities of the authorised officials.

3. Undertakings and associations of undertakings shall submit to investigations ordered by decision of the Commission. The decision shall specify the subject-matter and purpose of the investigation, appoint the date on which it shall begin and state the penalties provided for in Arts. 14(1)(d) and 15(1)(b) and the right to have the decision reviewed by the Court of Justice.

4. The Commission shall in good time and in writing inform the competent authority of the Member State within the territory of which the investigation is to be carried out of its intention of taking a decision pursuant to paragraph 3. It shall hear the competent authority before taking its decision.

5. Officials of the competent authority of the Member State within the territory of which the investigation is to be carried out may, at the request of that authority or of the Commission, assist the officials of the Commission in carrying out their duties.

6. Where an undertaking or association of undertakings opposes an investigation ordered pursuant to this Article, the Member State concerned shall afford the necessary assistance to the officials authorised by the Commission to enable them to carry out their investigation. To this end the Member States shall, after consulting the Commission, take the necessary measures within one year of the entry into force of this Regulation.

Article 14 Fines 1. The Commission may by decision impose on the persons referred to in Art. 3(1)(b), undertakings or associations of undertakings fines of from ECU 1000 to 50000 where intentionally or negligently:

(a) they fail to notify a concentration in accordance with Art. 4;

(b) they supply incorrect or misleading information in a notification pursuant to Art. 4;

(c) they supply incorrect information in response to a request made pursuant to Art. 11 or fail to supply information within the period fixed by a decision taken pursuant to Art. 11;

(d) they produce the required books or other business records in incomplete form during investigations under Arts. 12 or 13, or refuse to submit to an investigation ordered by decision taken pursuant to Art. 13.

2. The Commission may by decision impose fines not exceeding 10% of the aggregate turnover of the undertakings concerned within the meaning of Art. 5 on the persons or undertakings concerned where, either intentionally or negligently, they:

(a) fail to comply with an obligation imposed by decision pursuant to Art. 7(4) or 8(2), second subparagraph;

(b) put into effect a concentration in breach of Art. 7(1) or disregard a decision taken pursuant to Art. 7(2);

(c) put into effect a concentration declared incompatible with the common market by decision pursuant to Art. 8(3) or do not take the measures ordered by decision pursuant to Art. 8(4).

3. In setting the amount of a fine, regard shall be had to the nature and gravity of the infringement.

4. Decisions taken pursuant to paragraphs 1 and 2 shall not be of criminal law nature.

Article 15   Periodic penalty payments   1. The Commission may by decision impose on the persons referred to in Art. 3(1)(b), undertakings or associations of undertakings concerning periodic penalty payments of up to ECU 25000 for each day of delay calculated from the date set in the decision, in order to compel them:

(a) to supply complete and correct information which it has requested by decision pursuant to Art. 11;

(b) to submit to an investigation which it has ordered by decision pursuant to Art. 13.

2. The Commission may by decision impose on the persons referred to in Art. 3(1)(b) or on undertakings periodic penalty payments of up to ECU 100000 for each day of delay calculated from the date set in the decision, in order to compel them:

(a) to comply with an obligation imposed by decision pursuant to Art. 7(4) or Art. 8 (2), second subparagraph, or

(b) to apply the measures ordered by decision pursuant to Art. 8(4).

3. Where the persons referred to in Art. 3(1)(b), undertakings or associations of undertakings have satisfied the obligation which it was the purpose of the periodic penalty payment to enforce, the Commission may set the total amount of the periodic penalty payments at a lower figure than that which would arise under the original decision.

Article 16   Review by the Court of Justice   The Court of Justice shall have unlimited jurisdiction within the meaning of Art. 172 of the Treaty to review decisions whereby the Commission has fixed a fine or periodic penalty payments; it may cancel, reduce or increase the fine or periodic penalty payments imposed.

Article 17   Professional secrecy   1. Information acquired as a result of the application of Arts. 11, 12, 13 and 18 shall be used only for the purposes of the relevant request, investigation or hearing.

2. Without prejudice to Arts. 4(3), 18 and 20, the Commission and the competent authorities of the Member States, their officials and other servants shall not disclose information they have acquired through the application of this Regulation of the kind covered by the obligation of professional secrecy.

3. Paragraphs 1 and 2 shall not prevent publication of general information or of surveys which do not contain information relating to particular undertakings or associations of undertakings.

Article 18   Hearing of the parties and of third persons   1. Before taking any decision provided for in Arts. 7(4), Art. 8(2), second subparagraph, and (3) to (5) and Arts. 14

and 15, the Commission shall give the persons, undertakings and associations of undertakings concerned the opportunity, at every stage of the procedure up to the consultation of the Advisory Committee, of making known their views on the objections against them.

2. By way of derogation from paragraph 1, a decision to grant a derogation from suspension as referred to in Article 7 (4) may be taken provisionally, without the persons, undertakings or associations of undertakings concerned being given the opportunity to make known their views beforehand, provided that the Commission gives them that opportunity as soon as possible after having taken its decision.

3. The Commission shall base its decision only on objections on which the parties have been able to submit their observations. The rights of the defence shall be fully respected in the proceedings. Access to the file shall be open at least to the parties directly involved, subject to the legitimate interest of undertakings in the protection of their business secrets.

4. In so far as the Commission or the competent authorities of the Member States deem it necessary, they may also hear other natural or legal persons. Natural or legal persons showing a sufficient interest and especially members of the administrative or management bodies of the undertakings concerned or the recognised representatives of their employees shall be entitled, upon application, to be heard.

Article 19   Liaison with the authorities of the Member States   1. The Commission shall transmit to the competent authorities of the Member States copies of notifications within three working days and, as soon as possible, copies of the most important documents lodged with or issued by the Commission pursuant to this Regulation. Such documents shall include commitments which are intended by the parties to form the basis for a decision pursuant to Articles 6(1)(b) or 8(2).

2. The Commission shall carry out the procedures set out in this Regulation in close and constant liaison with the competent authorities of the Member States, which may express their views upon those procedures. For the purposes of Art. 9 it shall obtain information from the competent authority of the Member State as referred to in paragraph 2 of that Article and give it the opportunity to make known its views at every stage of the procedure up to the adoption of a decision pursuant to paragraph 3 of that Article; to that end it shall give it access to the file.

3. An Advisory Committee on concentrations shall be consulted before any decision is taken pursuant to Art. 8(2) to (5), 14 or 15, or any provisions are adopted pursuant to Art. 23.

4. The Advisory Committee shall consist of representatives of the authorities of the Member States. Each Member State shall appoint one or two representatives; if unable to attend, they may be replaced by other representatives. At least one of the representatives of a Member State shall be competent in matters of restrictive practices and dominant positions.

5. Consultation shall take place at a joint meeting convened at the invitation of and chaired by the Commission. A summary of the case, together with an indication of the most important documents and a preliminary draft of the decision to be taken for each case considered, shall be sent with the invitation. The meeting shall take place not less than 14 days after the invitation has been sent. The Commission may

in exceptional cases shorten that period as appropriate in order to avoid serious harm to one or more of the undertakings concerned by a concentration.

6. The Advisory Committee shall deliver an opinion on the Commission's draft decision, if necessary by taking a vote. The Advisory Committee may deliver an opinion even if some members are absent and unrepresented. The opinion shall be delivered in writing and appended to the draft decision. The Commission shall take the utmost account of the opinion delivered by the Committee. It shall inform the Committee of the manner in which its opinion has been taken into account.

7. The Advisory Committee may recommend publication of the opinion. The Commission may carry out such publication. The decision to publish shall take due account of the legitimate interest of undertakings in the protection of their business secrets and of the interest of the undertakings concerned in such publication's taking place.

Article 20   Publication of decisions   1. The Commission shall publish the decisions which it takes pursuant to Art. 8(2) to (5) in the *Official Journal of the European Communities*.

2. The publication shall state the names of the parties and the main content of the decision; it shall have regard to the legitimate interest of undertakings in the protection of their business secrets.

Article 21   Jurisdiction   1. Subject to review by the Court of Justice, the Commission shall have sole jurisdiction to take the decisions provided for in this Regulation.

2. No Member State shall apply its national legislation on competition to any consideration that has a Community dimension.

The first subparagraph shall be without prejudice to any Member State's power to carry out any enquiries necessary for the application of Art. 9(2) or after referral, pursuant to Art. 9(3), first subparagraph, indent (b), or (5), to take the measures strictly necessary for the application of Art. 9(8).

3. Notwithstanding paragraphs 1 and 2, Member States may take appropriate measures to protect legitimate interests other than those taken into consideration by this Regulation and compatible with the general principles and other provisions of Community law.

Public security, plurality of the media and prudential rules shall be regarded as legitimate interests within the meaning of the first subparagraph.

Any other public interest must be communicated to the Commission by the Member State concerned and shall be recognised by the Commission after an assessment of its compatibility with the general principles and other provisions of Community law before the measures referred to above may be taken. The Commission shall inform the Member State concerned of its decision within one month of that communication.

Article 22   Application of the Regulation   1. This Regulation alone shall apply to concentrations as defined in Article 3, and Regulations No. 17,[31] (EEC) No. 1017/68,[32] (EEC) No. 4056/86[33] and (EEC) No. 3975/87[34] shall not apply, except in relation to joint ventures that do not have a Community dimension and which have their

[31] OJ Sp. Ed. 1959–62, 87.   [32] OJ 1968 L 175/1.   [33] OJ 1986 L 378/4.
[34] OJ 1987 L 374/1.

object or effect the coordination of the competitive behaviour of undertakings that remain independent.

[para. 2 repealed]

3. If the Commission finds, at the request of a Member State or at the joint request of two or more Member States, that a concentration as defined in Article 3 that has no Community dimension within the meaning of Article 1 creates or strengthens a dominant position as a result of which effective competition would be significantly impeded within the territory of the Member State or States making the joint request, it may, insofar as that concentration affects trade between Member States, adopt the decisions provided for in Article 8(2), second subparagraph, (3) and (4).

4. Articles 2(1)(a) and (b), 5, 6, 8 and 10 to 20 shall apply to a request made pursuant to paragraph 3. Article 7 shall apply to the extent that the concentration has not been put into effect on the date on which the Commission informs the parties that a request has been made.

The period within which proceedings may be initiated pursuant to Article 10(1) shall begin on the day following that of the receipt of the request from the Member State or States concerned. The request must be made within one month at most of the date on which the concentration was made known to the Member State or to all Member States making a joint request or effected. This period shall begin on the date of the first of those events.

5. Pursuant to paragraph 3 the Commission shall take only the measures strictly necessary to maintain or store effective competition within the territory of the Member State or States at the request of which it intervenes.

Article 23   Implementing provisions   The Commission shall have the power to adopt implementing provisions concerning the form, content and other details of notifications pursuant to Art. 4, time limits pursuant to Arts. 7, 9, 10 and 22, and hearings pursuant to Art. 18.

The Commission shall have the power to lay down the procedure and time limits for the submission of commitments pursuant to Articles 6(1a) and 8(2).

Article 24   Relations with non-member countries   1. The Member States shall inform the Commission of any general difficulties encountered by their undertakings with concentrations as defined in Art. 3 in a non-member country.

2. Initially not more than one year after the entry into force of this Regulation and thereafter periodically the Commission shall draw up a report examining the treatment accorded to Community undertakings, in the terms referred to in paragraphs 3 and 4, as regards concentrations in non-member countries. The Commission shall submit those reports to the Council, together with any recommendations.

3. Whenever it appears to the Commission, either on the basis of the reports referred to in paragraph 2 or on the basis of other information, that a non-member country does not grant Community undertakings treatment comparable to that granted by the Community to undertakings from that non-member country, the Commission may submit proposals to the Council for an appropriate mandate for negotiation with a view to obtaining comparable treatment for Community undertakings.

4. Measures taken under this Article shall comply with the obligations of the Community or of the Member States, without prejudice to Art. 234 of the Treaty, under international agreements, whether bilateral or multilateral.

Article 25 Entry into force 1. This Regulation shall enter into force on 21 September 1990.

2. This Regulation shall not apply to any concentration which was the subject of an agreement or announcement or where control was acquired within the meaning of Art. 4(1) before the date of this Regulation's entry into force and it shall not in any circumstances apply to any concentration in respect of which proceedings were initiated before that date by a Member State's authority with responsibility for competition.

3. As regards concentrations to which this regulation applies by virtue of accession, the date of accession shall be substituted for the date of entry into force of this Regulation. The provision of paragraph 2, second alternative, applies in the same way to proceedings initiated by a competition authority of the new Member States or by the EFTA Surveillance Authority.

[final provisions omitted]

Commission Notice of 2 February 1998 on the concept of full-function joint ventures under Council Regulation 4064/89/EEC on the control of concentrations between undertakings[35]

I. INTRODUCTION

[some footnotes omitted]

1. The purpose of this notice is to provide guidance as to how the Commission interprets Article 3 of Council Regulation (EEC) No. 4064/89 as last amended by Regulation (EC) No. 1310/97 (hereinafter referred to as the Merger Regulation) in relation to joint ventures.

2. This Notice replaces the Notice on the distinction between concentrative and cooperative joint ventures. Changes made in this Notice reflect the amendments made to the Merger Regulation as well as the experience gained by the Commission in applying the Merger Regulation since its entry into force on 21 September 1990. The principles set out in this Notice will be followed and further developed by the Commission's practice in individual cases.

3. Under the Community competition rules, joint ventures are undertakings which are jointly controlled by two or more other undertakings. In practice joint ventures encompass a broad range of operations, from merger-like operations to cooperation for particular functions such as R&D, production or distribution.

4. Joint ventures fall within the scope of the Merger Regulation if they meet the requirements of a concentration set out in Article 3 thereof.

---

[35] OJ 1998 C 66.

5. According to recital 23 to Council Regulation (EEC) No. 4064/89 it is appropriate to define the concept of concentration in such a manner as to cover only operations bringing about a lasting change in the structure of the undertakings concerned.

6. The structural changes brought about by concentrations frequently reflect a dynamic process of restructuring in the markets concerned. They are permitted under the Merger Regulation unless they result in serious damage to the structure of competition by creating or strengthening a dominant position.

7. The Merger Regulation deals with the concept of full-function joint ventures in Article 3(2) as follows:
'The creation of a joint venture performing on a lasting basis all the functions of an autonomous economic entity shall constitute a concentration within the meaning of paragraph 1(b).'

II. JOINT VENTURES UNDER ARTICLE 3 OF THE MERGER REGULATION

8. In order to be a concentration within the meaning of Article 3 of the Merger Regulation, an operation must fulfil the following requirements:

1. Joint Control

9. A joint venture may fall within the scope of the Merger Regulation where there is an acquisition of joint control by two or more undertakings, that is, its parent companies (Article 3(1)(b)). The concept of control is set out in Article 3(3). This provides that control is based on the possibility of exercising decisive influence over an undertaking, which is determined by both legal and factual considerations.

10. The principles for determining joint control are set out in detail in the Commission's Notice on the concept of concentration.[36]

2. Structural Change of the Undertakings

11. Article 3(2) provides that the joint venture must perform, on a lasting basis, all the functions of an autonomous economic entity. Joint ventures which satisfy this requirement bring about a lasting change in the structure of the undertakings concerned. They are referred to in this Notice as 'full-function' joint ventures.

12. Essentially this means that a joint venture must operate on a market, performing the functions normally carried out by undertakings operating on the same market. In order to do so the joint venture must have a management dedicated to its day-to-day operations and access to sufficient resources including finance, staff, and assets (tangible and intangible) in order to conduct on a lasting basis its business activities within the area provided for in the joint-venture agreement.[37]

---

[36] Paragraphs 18 to 39.

[37] Case IV/M.527, Thomson CSF/Deutsche Aerospace of 2 December 1994 (para. 10)—intellectual rights; Case IV/M.560 EDS/Lufthansa of 11 May 1995 (para. 11)—outsourcing; Case IV/M.585, Voest Alpine Industrieanlagenbau GmbH/Davy International Ltd of 7 September 1995 (para. 8)—joint venture's right to demand additional expertise and staff from its parent companies; Case IV/M.686, Nokia/Autoliv of 5 February 1996 (para. 7)—joint venture able to terminate 'service agreements' with parent company and to move from site retained by parent company; Case IV/M.791, British Gas Trading Ltd/Group 4 Utility Services Ltd of 7 October 1996 (para. 9)—joint venture's intended assets will be transferred to leasing company and leased by joint venture.

13. A joint venture is not full-function if it only takes over one specific function within the parent companies' business activities without access to the market. This is the case, for example, for joint ventures limited to R&D or production. Such joint ventures are auxiliary to their parent companies' business activities. This is also the case where a joint venture is essentially limited to the distribution or sales of its parent companies' products and, therefore, acts principally as a sales agency. However, the fact that a joint venture makes use of the distribution network or outlet of one or more of its parent companies normally will not disqualify it as 'full-function' as long as the parent companies are acting only as agents of the joint venture.[38]

14. The strong presence of the parent companies in upstream or downstream markets is a factor to be taken into consideration in assessing the full-function character of a joint venture where this presence leads to substantial sales or purchases between the parent companies and the joint venture. The fact that the joint venture relies almost entirely on sales to its parent companies or purchases from them only for an initial start-up period does not normally affect the full-function character of the joint venture. Such a start-up period may be necessary in order to establish the joint venture on a market. It will normally not exceed a period of three years, depending on the specific conditions of the market in question.[39]

Where sales from the joint venture to the parent companies are intended to be made on a lasting basis, the essential question is whether, regardless of these sales, the joint venture is geared to play an active role on the market. In this respect the relative proportion of these sales compared with the total production of the joint venture is an important factor. Another factor is whether sales to the parent companies are made on the basis of normal commercial conditions.[40]

In relation to purchases made by the joint venture from its parent companies, the full-function character of the joint venture is questionable in particular where little value is added to the products or services concerned at the level of the joint venture itself. In such a situation, the joint venture may be closer to a joint sales agency. However, in contrast to this situation where a joint venture is active in a trade market and performs the normal functions of a trading company in such a market, it normally will not be an auxiliary sales agency but a full-function joint venture. A trade market is characterised by the existence of companies which specialise in the selling and distribution of products without being vertically integrated in addition to those which are integrated, and where different sources of supply are available for the products in question. In addition, many trade markets may require operators to invest in specific facilities such as outlets, stockholding, warehouses, depots, transport fleets and sales personnel. In order to constitute a full-function joint venture in a trade market, an undertaking must have the necessary facilities and be

[38] Case IV/M.102, TNT/Canada Post etc. of 2 December 1991 (para. 14).

[39] Case IV/M.560, EDS/Lufthansa of 11 May 1995 (para. 11); Case IV/M.686, Nokia/Autoliv of 5 February 1996 (para. 6); to be contrasted with Case IV/M.904, RSB/Tenex/Fuel Logistics of 2 April 1997 (paras 15-17) and Case IV/M.979, Preussag/Voest-Alpine of 1 October 1997 (paras 9–12). A special case exists where sales by the joint venture to its parent are caused by a legal monopoly downstream of the joint venture (Case IV/M.468, Siemens/Italtel of 17 February 1995 (para. 12), or where the sales to a parent company consist of by-products, which are of minor importance to the joint venture (Case IV/M.550, Union Carbide/Enichem of 13 March 1995 (para. 14).

[40] Case IV/M.556, Zeneca/Vanderhave of 9 April 1996 (para. 8); Case IV/M.751, Bayer/Hüls of 3 July 1996 (para. 10).

likely to obtain a substantial proportion of its supplies not only from its parent companies but also from other competing sources.[41]

15. Furthermore, the joint venture must be intended to operate on a lasting basis. The fact that the parent companies commit to the joint venture the resources described above normally demonstrates that this is the case. In addition, agreements setting up a joint venture often provide for certain contingencies, for example, the failure of the joint venture or fundamental disagreement as between the parent companies.[42] This may be achieved by the incorporation of provisions for the eventual dissolution of the joint venture itself or the possibility for one or more parent companies to withdraw from the joint venture. This kind of provision does not prevent the joint venture from being considered as operating on a lasting basis. The same is normally true where the agreement specifies a period for the duration of the joint venture where this period is sufficiently long in order to bring about a lasting change in the structure of the undertakings concerned,[43] or where the agreement provides for the possible continuation of the joint venture beyond this period. By contrast, the joint venture will not be considered to operate on a lasting basis where it is established for a short finite duration. This would be the case, for example, where a joint venture is established in order to construct a specific project such as a power plant, but it will not be involved in the operation of the plant once its construction has been completed.

III. FINAL

16. The creation of a full-function joint venture constitutes a concentration within the meaning of Article 3 of the Merger Regulation. Restrictions accepted by the parent companies of the joint venture that are directly related and necessary for the implementation of the concentration ('ancillary restrictions'), will be assessed together with the concentration itself.[44]

Further, the creation of a full-function joint venture may as a direct consequence lead to the coordination of the competitive behaviour of undertakings that remain independent. In such cases Article 2(4) of the Merger Regulation provides that those cooperative effects will be assessed within the same procedure as the concentration. This assessment will be made in accordance with the criteria of Article 85(1) and (3) of the Treaty with a view to establishing whether or not the operation is compatible with the common market.

The applicability of Article 85 of the Treaty to other restrictions of competition, that are neither ancillary to the concentration, nor a direct consequence of the creation of the joint venture, will normally have to be examined by means of Regulation No. 17.

17. The Commission's interpretation of Article 3 of the Merger Regulation with respect to joint ventures is without prejudice to the interpretation which may be given by the Court of Justice or the Court of First Instance of the European Communities.

---

[41] Case IV/M.788, AgrEVO/Marubeni of 3 September 1996 (paras 9 and 10).
[42] Case IV/M.891, Deutsche Bank/Commerzbank/J.M. Voith of 23 April 1997 (para. 7).
[43] Case IV/M.791, British Gas Trading Ltd/Group 4 Utility Services Ltd of 7 October 1996 (para. 10); to be contrasted with Case IV/M.722, Teneo/Merill Lynch/Bankers Trust of 15 April 1996 (para. 15).
[44] See Commission Notice regarding restrictions ancillary to concentrations, OJ 1990 C 203/5.

Consumer Protection

Council Directive of 25 July 1985 on the approximation of the laws, regulations and administrative provisions of the Member States concerning liability for defective products (85/374/EEC)[1]

The Council of the European Communities,

HAVING REGARD to the Treaty establishing the European Economic Community, and in particular Art. 100 thereof,

[recitals omitted]

Whereas approximation of the laws of the Member States concerning the liability of the producer for damage caused by the defectiveness of his products is necessary because the existing divergences may distort competition and affect the movement of goods within the common market and entail a differing degree of protection of the consumer against damage caused by a defective product to his health or property;

Whereas liability without fault on the part of the producer is the sole means of adequately solving the problem, peculiar to our age of increasing technicality, of a fair apportionment of the risks inherent in modern technological production;

Whereas liability without fault should apply only to movables which have been industrially produced; whereas, as a result, it is appropriate to exclude liability for agricultural products and game, except where they have undergone a processing of an industrial nature which could cause a defect in these products; whereas the liability provided for in this Directive should also apply to movables which are used in the construction of immovables or are installed in immovables;

Whereas protection of the consumer requires that all producers involved in the production process should be made liable, in so far as their finished product, component part or any raw material supplied by them was defective; whereas, for the same reason, liability should extend to importers of products into the Community and to persons who present themselves as producers by affixing their name, trade mark or other distinguishing feature or who supply a product the producer of which cannot be identified;

Whereas, in situations where several persons are liable for the same damage, the protection of the consumer requires that the injured person should be able to claim full compensation for the damage from any one of them;

Whereas, to protect the physical well-being and property of the consumer, the defectiveness of the product should be determined by reference not to its fitness for use but to the lack of the safety which the public at large is entitled to expect; whereas the safety is assessed by excluding any misuse of the product not reasonable under the circumstances;

[1] OJ 1985 L 210/29.

Whereas a fair apportionment of risk between the injured person and the producer implies that the producer should be able to free himself from liability if he furnishes proof as to the existence of certain exonerating circumstances;

Whereas the protection of the consumer requires that the liability of the producer remains unaffected by acts or omissions of other persons having contributed to cause the damage; whereas, however, the contributory negligence of the injured person may be taken into account to reduce or disallow such liability;

Whereas the protection of the consumer requires compensation for death and personal injury as well as compensation for damage to property; whereas the latter should nevertheless be limited to goods for private use or consumption and be subject to a deduction of a lower threshold of a fixed amount in order to avoid litigation in an excessive number of cases; whereas this Directive should not prejudice compensation for pain and suffering and other non-material damages payable, where appropriate, under the law applicable to the case;

Whereas a uniform period of limitation for the bringing of action for compensation is in the interests both of the injured person and of the producer;

Whereas products age in the course of time, higher safety standards are developed and the state of science and technology progresses; whereas, therefore, it would not be reasonable to make the producer liable for an unlimited period for the defectiveness of his product; whereas, therefore, liability should expire after a reasonable length of time, without prejudice to claims pending at law;

Whereas, to achieve effective protection of consumers, no contractual derogation should be permitted as regards the liability of the producer in relation to the injured person;

Whereas under the legal systems of the Member States an injured party may have a claim for damages based on grounds of contractual liability or on grounds of non-contractual liability other than that provided for in this Directive; in so far as these provisions also serve to attain the objective of effective protection of consumers, they should remain unaffected by this Directive; whereas, in so far as effective protection of consumers in the sector of pharmaceutical products is already also attained in a Member State under a special liability system, claims based on this system should similarly remain possible;

Whereas, to the extent that liability for nuclear injury or damage is already covered in all Member States by adequate special rules, it has been possible to exclude damage of this type from the scope of this Directive;

Whereas, since the exclusion of primary agricultural products and game from the scope of this Directive may be felt, in certain Member States, in view of what is expected for the protection of consumers, to restrict unduly such protection, it should be possible for a Member State to extend liability to such products;

Whereas, for similar reasons, the possibility offered to a producer to free himself from liability if he proves that the state of scientific and technical knowledge at the time when he put the product into circulation was not such as to enable the existence of a defect to be discovered may be felt in certain Member States to restrict unduly the protection of the consumer; whereas it should therefore be possible for a Member State to maintain in its legislation or to provide by new legislation that this exonerating circumstance is not admitted; whereas, in the case of new legislation, making use of this derogation should, however, be subject to a Community stand-still procedure, in order to raise, if possible, the level of protection in a uniform manner throughout the Community;

Whereas, taking into account the legal traditions in most of the Member States, it is inappropriate to set any financial ceiling on the producer's liability without fault; whereas, in so far as there are, however, differing traditions, it seems possible to admit that a Member State may derogate from the principle of unlimited liability by providing a limit for the total liability of the producer for damage resulting from a death or personal injury and caused by identical items with the same defect, provided that this limit is established at a level sufficiently high to guarantee adequate protection of the consumer and the correct functioning of the common market;

Whereas the harmonisation resulting from this cannot be total at the present stage, but opens the way towards greater harmonisation; whereas it is therefore necessary that the Council receive at regular intervals, reports from the Commission on the application of this Directive, accompanied, as the case may be, by appropriate proposals;

Whereas it is particularly important in this respect that a re-examination be carried out of those parts of the Directive relating to the derogations open to the Member States, at the expiry of a period of sufficient length to gather practical experience on the effects of these derogations on the protection of consumers and on the functioning of the common market,

HAS ADOPTED this Directive:

Article 1   The producer shall be liable for damage caused by a defect in his product.

Article 2   For the purpose of this Directive 'product' means all movables, with the exception of primary agricultural products and game, even though incorporated into another movable or into an immovable. 'Primary agricultural products' means the products of the soil, of stock-farming and of fisheries, excluding products which have undergone initial processing. 'Product' includes electricity.

Article 3   1. 'Producer' means the manufacturer of a finished product, the producer of any raw material or the manufacturer of a component part and any person who, by putting his name, trade mark or other distinguishing feature on the product presents himself as its producer.

2. Without prejudice to the liability of the producer, any person who imports into the Community a product for sale, hire, leasing or any form of distribution in the course of his business shall be deemed to be a producer within the meaning of this Directive and shall be responsible as a producer.

3. Where the producer of the product cannot be identified, each supplier of the product shall be treated as its producer unless he informs the injured person, within a reasonable time, of the identity of the producer or of the person who supplied him with the product. The same shall apply, in the case of an imported product, if this product does not indicate the identity of the importer referred to in paragraph 2, even if the name of the producer is indicated.

Article 4 The injured person shall be required to prove the damage, the defect and the causal relationship between defect and damage.

Article 5 Where, as a result of the provisions of this Directive, two or more persons are liable for the same damage, they shall be liable jointly and severally, without prejudice to the provisions of national law concerning the rights of contribution or recourse.

Article 6 1. A product is defective when it does not provide the safety which a person is entitled to expect, taking all circumstances into account, including:
(a) the presentation of the product;
(b) the use to which it could reasonably be expected that the product would be put;
(c) the time when the product was put into circulation.

2. A product shall not be considered defective for the sole reason that a better product is subsequently put into circulation.

Article 7 The producer shall not be liable as a result of this Directive if he proves:
(a) that he did not put the product into circulation; or
(b) that, having regard to the circumstances, it is probable that the defect which caused the damage did not exist at the time when the product was put into circulation by him or that this defect came into being afterwards; or
(c) that the product was neither manufactured by him for sale or any form of distribution for economic purpose nor manufactured or distributed by him in the course of his business; or
(d) that the defect is due to compliance of the product with mandatory regulations issued by the public authorities; or
(e) that the state of scientific and technical knowledge at the time when he put the product into circulation was not such as to enable the existence of the defect to be discovered; or
(f) in the case of a manufacturer of a component, that the defect is attributable to the design of the product in which the component has been fitted or to the instructions given by the manufacturer of the product.

Article 8 1. Without prejudice to the provisions of national law concerning the right of contribution or recourse, the liability of the producer shall not be reduced when the damage is caused both by a defect in product and by the act or omission of a third party.

2. The liability of the producer may be reduced or disallowed when, having regard to all the circumstances, the damage is caused both by a defect in the product and by the fault of the injured person or any person for whom the injured person is responsible.

Article 9 For the purpose of Art. 1, 'damage' means:
(a) damage caused by death or by personal injuries;
(b) damage to, or destruction of, any item of property other than the defective product itself, with a lower threshold of 500 ECU, provided that the item of property:
  (i) is of a type ordinarily intended for private use or consumption, and
  (ii) was used by the injured person mainly for his own private use or consumption.

   This Article shall be without prejudice to national provisions relating to non-material damage.

Article 10   1. Member States shall provide in their legislation that a limitation period of three years shall apply to proceedings for the recovery of damages as provided for in this Directive. The limitation period shall begin to run from the day on which the plaintiff became aware, or should reasonably have become aware, of the damage, the defect and the identity of the producer.

2. The laws of Member States regulating suspension or interruption of the limitation period shall not be affected by this Directive.

Article 11   Member States shall provide in their legislation that the rights conferred upon the injured person pursuant to this Directive shall be extinguished upon the expiry of a period of 10 years from the date on which the producer put into circulation the actual product which caused the damage, unless the injured person has in the meantime instituted proceedings against the producer.

Article 12   The liability of the producer arising from this Directive may not, in relation to the injured person, be limited or excluded by a provision limiting his liability or exempting him from liability.

Article 13   This Directive shall not affect any rights which an injured person may have according to the rules of the law of contractual or non-contractual liability or a special liability system existing at the moment when this Directive is notified.

Article 14   This Directive shall not apply to injury or damage arising from nuclear accidents and covered by international conventions ratified by the Member States.

Article 15   1. Each Member State may:
(a) by way of derogation from Art. 2, provide in its legislation that within the meaning of Art. 1 of this Directive 'product' also means primary agricultural products and game;
(b) by way of derogation from Art. 7(e), maintain or, subject to the procedure set out in paragraph 2 of this Article, provide in this legislation that the producer shall be liable even if he proves that the state of scientific and technical knowledge at the time when he put the product into circulation was not such as to enable the existence of a defect to be discovered.

2. A Member State wishing to introduce the measure specified in paragraph 1 (b) shall communicate the text of the proposed measure to the Commission. The Commission shall inform the other Member States thereof.

   The Member State concerned shall hold the proposed measure in abeyance for nine months after the Commission is informed and provided that in the meantime the Commission has not submitted to the Council a proposal amending this Directive on the relevant matter. However, if within three months of receiving the said information, the Commission does not advise the Member State concerned that it intends submitting such a proposal to the Council, the Member State may take the proposed measure immediately.

   If the Commission does submit to the Council such a proposal amending this Directive within the aforementioned nine months, the Member State concerned shall hold the proposed measure in abeyance for a further period of 18 months from the date on which the proposal is submitted.

3. Ten years after the date of notification of this Directive, the Commission shall submit to the Council a report on the effect that rulings by the courts as to the application of Art. 7(e) and of paragraph 1(b) of this Article have on consumer protection and the functioning of the common market. In the light of this report the Council, acting on a proposal from the Commission and pursuant to the terms of Art. 100 of the Treaty, shall decide whether to repeal Art. 7(e).

Article 16   1. Any Member State may provide that a producer's total liability for damage resulting from a death or personal injury and caused by identical items with the same defect shall be limited to an amount which may not be less than 70 million ECU.

2. Ten years after the date of notification of this Directive, the Commission shall submit to the Council a report on the effect on consumer protection and the functioning of the common market of the implementation of the financial limit on liability by those Member States which have used the option provided for in paragraph 1. In the light of this report the Council, acting on a proposal from the Commission and pursuant to the terms of Art. 100 of the Treaty, shall decide whether to repeal paragraph 1.

Article 17   This Directive shall not apply to products put into circulation before the date on which the provisions referred to in Art. 19 enter into force.

Article 18   1. For the purposes of this Directive, the ECU shall be that defined by Regulation (EEC) No. 3180/78,[2] as amended by Regulation (EEC) No. 2626/84.[3] The equivalent in national currency shall initially be calculated at the rate obtaining on the date of adoption of this Directive.

2. Every five years the Council, acting on a proposal from the Commission, shall examine and, if need be, revise the amounts in this Directive, in the light of economic and monetary trends in the Community.

Article 19   1. Member States shall bring into force, not later than three years from the date of notification of this Directive, the laws, regulations and administrative provisions necessary to comply with this Directive. They shall forthwith inform the Commission thereof.[4]

2. The procedure set out in Art. 15(2) shall apply from the date of notification of this Directive.

Article 20   Member States shall communicate to the Commission the texts of the main provisions of national law which they subsequently adopt in the field governed by this Directive.

Article 21   Every five years the Commission shall present a report to the Council on the application of this Directive and, if necessary, shall submit appropriate proposals to it.

Article 22   This Directive is addressed to the Member States.

[*final provisions omitted*]

---

[2] OJ 1978 L 379/1.   [3] OJ 1984 L 247/1.
[4] This Directive was notified to the Member States on 30 July 1985.

Council Directive of 5 April 1993 on unfair terms in consumer contracts (93/13/EEC)[5]

The Council of the European Communities,

HAVING REGARD to the treaty establishing the European Economic Community, and in particular Article 100 A thereof,

HAVING REGARD to the proposal from the Commission,

IN COOPERATION with the European Parliament,

HAVING REGARD to the opinion of the Economic and Social Committee,

Whereas it is necessary to adopt measures with the aim of progressively establishing the internal market before 31 December 1992; whereas the internal market comprises an area without internal frontiers in which goods, persons, services and capital move freely;

Whereas the laws of Member States relating to the terms of contract between the seller of goods or supplier of services, on the one hand, and the consumer of them, on the other hand, show many disparities, with the result that the national markets for the sale of goods and services to consumers differ from each other and that distortions of competition may arise amongst the sellers and suppliers, notably when they sell and supply in other Member States;

Whereas, in particular, the laws of Member States relating to unfair terms in consumer contracts show marked divergences;

Whereas it is the responsibility of the Member States to ensure that contracts concluded with consumers do not contain unfair terms;

Whereas, generally speaking, consumers do not know the rules of law which, in Member States other than their own, govern contracts for the sale of goods or services; whereas this lack of awareness may deter them from direct transactions for the purchase of goods or services in another Member State;

Whereas, in order to facilitate the establishment of the internal market and to safeguard the citizen in his role as consumer when acquiring goods and services under contracts which are governed by the laws of Member States other than his own, it is essential to remove unfair terms from those contracts;

Whereas sellers of goods and suppliers of services will thereby be helped in their task of selling goods and supplying services, both at home and throughout the internal market; whereas competition will thus be stimulated, so contributing to increased choice for Community citizens as consumers;

Whereas the two Community programmes for a consumer protection and information policy underlined the importance of safeguarding consumers in the matter of unfair terms of contract; whereas this protection ought to be provided by laws and regulations which are either harmonized at Community level or adopted directly at that level;

Whereas in accordance with the principle laid down under the heading 'Protection of the economic interests of the consumers', as stated in those programmes:

---

[5] OJ 1993 L 95/29.

'acquirers of goods and services should be protected against the abuse of power by the seller or supplier, in particular against one-sided standard contracts and the unfair exclusion of essential rights in contracts';

Whereas more effective protection of the consumer can be achieved by adopting uniform rules of law in the matter of unfair terms; whereas those rules should apply to all contracts concluded between sellers or suppliers and consumers; whereas as a result *inter alia* contracts relating to employment, contracts relating to succession rights, contracts relating to rights under family law and contracts relating to the incorporation and organization of companies or partnership agreements must be excluded from this Directive;

Whereas the consumer must receive equal protection under contracts concluded by word of mouth and written contracts regardless, in the latter case, of whether the terms of the contract are contained in one or more documents;

Whereas, however, as they now stand, national laws allow only partial harmonization to be envisaged; whereas, in particular, only contractual terms which have not been individually negotiated are covered by this Directive; whereas Member States should have the option, with due regard for the Treaty, to afford consumers a higher level of protection through national provisions that are more stringent than those of this Directive;

Whereas the statutory or regulatory provisions of the Member States which directly or indirectly determine the terms of consumer contracts are presumed not to contain unfair terms; whereas, therefore, it does not appear to be necessary to subject the terms which reflect mandatory statutory or regulatory provisions and the principles or provisions of international conventions to which the Member States or the Community are party; whereas in that respect the wording 'mandatory statutory or regulatory provisions' in Article 1(2) also covers rules which, according to the law, shall apply between the contracting parties provided that no other arrangements have been established;

Whereas Member States must, however, ensure that unfair terms are not included, particularly because this Directive also applies to trades, business or professions of a public nature;

Whereas it is necessary to fix in a general way the criteria for assessing the unfair character of contract terms;

Whereas the assessment, according to the general criteria chosen, of the unfair character of terms, in particular in sale or supply activities of a public nature providing collective services which take account of solidarity among users, must be supplemented by a means of making an overall evaluation of the different interests involved; whereas this constitutes the requirement of good faith, whereas, in making an assessment of good faith, particular regard shall be had to the strength of the bargaining positions of the parties, whether the consumer had an inducement to agree to the term and whether the goods or services were sold or supplied to the special order of the consumer; whereas the requirement of good faith may be satisfied by the seller or supplier where he deals fairly and equitably with the other party whose legitimate interests he has to take into account;

Whereas, for the purposes of this Directive, the annexed list of terms can be of indicative value only and, because of the cause of the minimal character of the

Directive, the scope of these terms may be the subject of amplification or more restrictive editing by the Member States in their national laws;

Whereas the nature of goods or services should have an influence on assessing the unfairness of contractual terms;

Whereas, for the purposes of this Directive, assessment of unfair character shall not be made of terms which describe the main subject matter of the contract nor the quality/price ratio of the goods or services supplied; whereas the main subject matter of the contract and the price/quality ratio may nevertheless be taken into account in assessing the fairness of other terms; whereas it follows, *inter alia*, that in insurance contracts, the terms which clearly define or circumscribe the insured risk and the insurer's liability shall not be subject to such assessment since these restrictions are taken into account in calculating the premium paid by the consumer;

Whereas contracts should be drafted in plain, intelligible language, the consumer should actually be given an opportunity to examine all the terms and, if in doubt, the interpretation most favourable to the consumer should prevail;

Whereas Member States should ensure that unfair terms are not used in contracts concluded with consumers by a seller or supplier and that if, nevertheless, such terms are so used, they will not bind the consumer, and the contract will continue to bind the parties upon those terms if it is capable of continuing in existence without the unfair provisions;

Whereas there is a risk that, in certain cases, the consumer may be deprived of protection under this Directive by designating the law of a non-Member country as the law applicable to the contract; whereas provisions should therefore be included in this Directive designed to avert this risk;

Whereas persons or organizations, if regarded under the law of a Member State as having a legitimate interest in the matter, must have facilities for initiating proceedings concerning terms of contract drawn up for general use in contracts concluded with consumers, and in particular unfair terms, either before a court or before an administrative authority competent to decide upon complaints or to initiate appropriate legal proceedings; whereas this possibility does not, however, entail prior verification of the general conditions obtaining in individual economic sectors;

Whereas the courts or administrative authorities of the Member States must have at their disposal adequate and effective means of preventing the continued application of unfair terms in consumer contracts,

HAS ADOPTED this Directive:

Article 1   1. The purpose of this Directive is to approximate the laws, regulations and administrative provisions of the Member States relating to unfair terms in contracts concluded between a seller or supplier and a consumer.

2. The contractual terms which reflect mandatory statutory or regulatory provisions and the provisions or principles of international conventions to which the Member States or the Community are party, particularly in the transport area, shall not be subject to the provisions of this Directive.

Article 2   For the purposes of this Directive:

(a) 'unfair terms' means the contractual terms defined in Article 3;

(b) 'consumer' means any natural person who, in contracts covered by this Directive, is acting for purposes which are outside his trade, business or profession;

(c) 'seller or supplier' means any natural or legal person who, in contracts covered by this Directive, is acting for purposes relating to his trade, business or profession, whether publicly owned or privately owned.

Article 3   1. A contractual term which has not been individually negotiated shall be regarded as unfair if, contrary to the requirement of good faith, it causes a significant imbalance in the parties' rights and obligations arising under the contract, to the detriment of the consumer.

2. A term shall always be regarded as not individually negotiated where it has been drafted in advance and the consumer has therefore not been able to influence the substance of the term, particularly in the context of a pre-formulated standard contract.

The fact that certain aspects of a term or one specific term have been individually negotiated shall not exclude the application of this Article to the rest of a contract if an overall assessment of the contract indicates that it is nevertheless a pre-formulated standard contract.

Where any seller or supplier claims that a standard term has been individually negotiated, the burden of proof in this respect shall be incumbent on him.

Where any seller or supplier claims that a standard term has been individually negotiated, the burden of proof in this respect shall be incumbent on him.

3. The Annex shall contain an indicative and non-exhaustive list of the terms which may be regarded as unfair.

Article 4   1. Without prejudice to Article 7, the unfairness of a contractual term shall be assessed, taking into account the nature of the goods or services for which the contract was concluded and by referring, at the time of conclusion of the contract, to all the circumstances attending the conclusion of the contract and to all the other terms of the contract or of another contract on which it is dependent.

2. Assessment of the unfair nature of the terms shall relate neither to the definition of the main subject matter of the contract nor to the adequacy of the price and remuneration, on the one hand, as against the services or goods supplies in exchange, on the other, in so far as these terms are in plain intelligible language.

Article 5   In the case of contracts where all of certain terms offered to the consumer are in writing, these terms must always be drafted in plain, intelligible language. Where there is doubt about the meaning of a term, the interpretation most favourable to the consumer shall prevail. This rule on interpretation shall not apply in the context of the procedures laid down in Article 7(2).

Article 6   1. Member States shall lay down that unfair terms used in a contract concluded with a consumer by a seller or supplier shall, as provided for under their national law, not be binding on the consumer and that the contract shall continue to bind the parties upon those terms if it is capable of continuing in existence without the unfair terms.

2. Member States shall take the necessary measures to ensure that the consumer does not lose the protection granted by this Directive by virtue of the choice of the law of a non-Member country as the law applicable to the contract if the latter has a close connection with the territory of the Member States.

Article 7   1. Member States shall ensure that, in the interests of consumers and of competitions, adequate and effective means exist to prevent the continued use of unfair terms in contracts concluded with consumers by sellers or suppliers.

2. The means referred to in paragraph 1 shall include provisions whereby persons or organizations, having a legitimate interest under national law in protecting consumers, may take action according to the national law concerned before the courts or before competent administrative bodies for a decision as to whether contractual terms drawn up for general use are unfair, so that they can apply appropriate and effective means to prevent the continued use of such terms.

3. With due regard for national laws, the legal remedies referred to in paragraph 2 may be directed separately or jointly against a number of sellers or suppliers from the same economic sector or their associations which use or recommend the use of the same general contractual terms or similar terms.

Article 8   Member States may adopt or retain the most stringent provisions compatible with the Treaty in the area covered by this Directive, to ensure a maximum degree of protection for the consumer.

Article 9   The Commission shall present a report to the European Parliament and to the Council concerning the application of this Directive five years at the latest after the date in Article 10 91).

[final provisions omitted]

ANNEX: TERMS REFERRED TO IN ARTICLE 3(3)

1. Terms which have the object or effect of:
 (a) excluding or limiting the legal liability of a seller or supplier in the event of the death of a consumer or personal injury to the latter resulting from an act or omission of that seller or supplier;
 (b) inappropriately excluding or limiting the legal rights of the consumer *vis-á-vis* the seller or supplier or another party in the event of total or partial non-performance or inadequate performance by the seller or supplier of any of the contractual obligations, including the option of offsetting a debt owed to the seller or supplier against any claim which the consumer may have against him;
 (c) making an agreement binding on the consumer whereas provision of services by the seller or supplier is subject to a condition whose realization depends on his own will alone;
 (d) permitting the seller or supplier to retain sums paid by the consumer where the latter decides not to conclude or perform the contract, without providing for the consumer to receive compensation of an equivalent amount from the seller or supplier where the latter is the party cancelling the contract;
 (e) requiring any consumer who fails to fulfil his obligation to pay a disproportionately high sum in compensation;

(f) authorizing the seller or supplier to dissolve the contract on a discretionary basis where the same facility is not granted to the consumer, or permitting the seller or supplier to retain the sums paid for services not yet supplied by him where it is the seller or supplier himself who dissolves the contract;

(g) enabling the seller or supplier to terminate a contract of indeterminate duration without reasonable notice except where there are serious grounds for doing so;

(h) automatically extending a contract of fixed duration where the consumer does not indicate otherwise, when the deadline fixed for the consumer to express this desire not to extend the contract is unreasonably early;

(i) irrevocably binding the consumer to terms with which he had no real opportunity of becoming acquainted before the conclusion of the contract;

(j) enabling the seller or supplier to alter the terms of the contract unilaterally without a valid reason which is specified in the contract;

(k) enabling the seller or supplier to alter unilaterally without a valid reason any characteristics of the product or service to be provided;

(l) providing for the price of goods to be determined at the time of delivery or allowing a seller of goods or supplier of services to increase their price without in both cases giving the consumer the corresponding right to cancel the contract if the final price is too high in relation to the price agreed when the contract was concluded;

(m) giving the seller or supplier the right to determine whether the goods or services supplied are in conformity with the contract, or giving him the exclusive right to interpret any term of the contract;

(n) limiting the seller's or supplier's obligation to respect commitments undertaken by his agents or making his commitments subject to compliance with a particular formality;

(o) obliging the consumer to fulfil all his obligations where the seller or supplier does not perform his;

(p) giving the seller or supplier the possibility of transferring his rights and obligations under the contract, where this may serve to reduce the guarantees for the consumer, without the latter's agreement;

(q) excluding or hindering the consumer's right to take legal action or exercise any other legal remedy, particularly by requiring the consumer to take disputes exclusively to arbitration not covered by legal provisions, unduly restricting the evidence available to him or imposing on him a burden of proof which, according to the applicable law, should lie with another party to the contract.

2. Scope of subparagraphs (g), (j) and (l)

(a) Subparagraph (g) is without hindrance to terms by which a supplier of financial services reserves the right to terminate unilaterally a contract of indeterminate duration without notice where there is a valid reason, provided that the supplier is required to inform the other contracting party or parties thereof immediately.

(b) Subparagraph (j) is without hindrance to terms under which a supplier of financial services reserves the right to alter the rate of interest payable by the consumer or due to the latter, or the amount of other charges for financial services without notice where there is a valid reason, provided that the supplier is required to inform the other contracting party or parties thereof at the earliest opportunity and that the latter are free to dissolve the contract immediately.

Subparagraph (j) is also without hindrance to terms under which a seller or supplier reserves the right to alter unilaterally the conditions of a contract of indeterminate duration, provided that he is required to inform the consumer with reasonable notice and that the consumer is free to dissolve the contract.

(c) Subparagraphs (g), (j) and (l) do not apply to:

— transactions in transferable securities, financial instruments and other products or services where the price is linked to fluctuations in a stock exchange quotation or index or a financial market rate that the seller or supplier does not control;

— contracts for the purchase or sale of foreign currency, traveller's cheques or international money orders denominated in foreign currency;

(d) Subparagraph (l) is without hindrance to price-indexation clauses, where lawful, provided that the method by which prices vary is explicitly described.

Environmental Law

Council Directive of 15 July 1975 on waste
(75/442/EEC)[1]

The Council of the European Communities,

HAVING REGARD to the Treaty establishing the European Economic Community, and in particular Articles 100 and 235 thereof;

Whereas any disparity between the provisions on waste disposal already applicable or in preparation in the various Member States may create unequal conditions of competition and thus directly affect the functioning of the common market; whereas it is therefore necessary to approximate laws in this field, as provided for in Article 100 of the Treaty;

Whereas the essential objective of all provisions relating to waste disposal must be the protection of human health and the environment against harmful effects caused by the collection, transport, treatment, storage and tipping of waste;

Whereas the recovery of waste and the use of recovered materials should be encouraged in order to conserve natural resources;

Whereas the programme of action of the European Communities on the environment, stresses the need for Community action, including the harmonization of legislation;

Whereas effective and consistent regulations on waste disposal which neither obstruct intra-Community trade nor affect conditions of competition should be applied to movable property which the owner disposes of or is required to dispose of under the provisions of national law in force, with the exception of radioactive, mining and agricultural waste, animal carcasses, waste waters, gaseous effluents and waste covered by specific Community rules;

Whereas, in order to ensure the protection of the environment, provision should be made for a system of permits for undertakings which treat, store or tip waste on behalf of third parties, for a supervisory system for undertakings which dispose of their own waste and for those which collect the waste of others, and for a plan embracing the essential factors to be taken into consideration in respect of the various waste disposal operations;

Whereas that proportion of the costs not covered by the proceeds of treating the waste must be defrayed in accordance with the 'polluter pays' principle,

HAS ADOPTED this Directive:

Article 1   For the purposes of this Directive:
(a) 'waste' shall mean any substance or object in the categories set out in Annex I which the holder discards or intends or is required to discard.

The Commission, acting in accordance with the procedure laid down in Article 18, will draw up, not later than 1 April 1993, a list of wastes belonging to the

---

[1] OJ 1975 L 194/47, as amended by Directive 91/156/EEC, OJ 1991 L 78/32, and by Commission Decision 96/350/EC, OJ 1996 L 135/32.

categories listed in Annex I. This list will be periodically reviewed and, if necessary, revised by the same procedure;
(b) 'producer' shall mean anyone whose activities produce waste ('original producer') and/or anyone who carries out pre-processing, mixing or other operations resulting in a change in the nature or composition of this waste;
(c) 'holder' shall mean the producer of the waste or the natural or legal person who is in possession of it;
(d) 'management' shall mean the collection, transport, recovery and disposal of waste, including the supervision of such operations and after-care of disposal sites;
(e) 'disposal' shall mean any of the operations provided for in Annex II, A;
(f) 'recovery' shall mean any of the operations provided for in Annex II, B;
(g) 'collection' shall mean the gathering, sorting and/or mixing of waste for the purpose of transport.

Article 2 1. The following shall be excluded from the scope of this Directive:
(a) gaseous effluents emitted into the atmosphere;
(b) where they are already covered by other legislation:

    (i) radioactive waste;
    (ii) waste resulting from prospecting, extraction, treatment and storage of mineral resources and the working of quarries;
    (iii) animal carcasses and the following agricultural waste: faecal matter and other natural, non-dangerous substances used in farming;
    (iv) waste wasters, with the exception of waste in liquid form;
    (v) decommissioned explosives.

2. Specific rules for particular instances or supplementing those of this Directive on the management of particular categories of waste may be laid down by means of individual Directives.

Article 3[2] 1. Member States shall take appropriate measures to encourage:
(a) firstly, the prevention or reduction of waste production and its harmfulness, in particular by:

    — the development of clean technologies more sparing in their use of natural resources,
    — the technical development and marketing of products designed so as to make no contribution or to make the smallest possible contribution, by the nature of their manufacture, use or final disposal, to increasing the amount or harmfulness of waste and pollution hazards,
    — the development of appropriate techniques for the final disposal of dangerous substances contained in waste destined for recovery;

(b) secondly:

    (i) the recovery of waste by means of recycling, re-use or reclamation or any other process with a view to extracting secondary raw materials, or
    (ii) the use of waste as a source of energy.

---

[2] Directive 96/59/EC, OJ 1996 L 243/31, Article 5(1), provides: 'By way of derogation from Article 3 of Directive 75/442/EEC Member States shall prohibit the separation of PCBs from other substances for the purpose of reusing the PCBs'.

2. Except where Council Directive 83/189/EEC of 28 March 1983 laying down a procedure for the provision of information in the field of technical standards and regulations[3] applies, Member States shall inform the Commission of any measures they intend to take to achieve the aims set out in paragraph 1. The Commission shall inform the other Member States and the committee referred to in Article 18 of such measures.

Article 4   Member States shall take the necessary measures to ensure that waste is recovered or disposed of without endangering human health and without using processes or methods which could harm the environment, and in particular:
- without risk to water, air, soil and plants and animals,
- without causing a nuisance through noise or odours,
- without adversely affecting the countryside or places of special interest.

   Member States shall also take the necessary measures to prohibit the abandonment, dumping or uncontrolled disposal of waste.

Article 5   1. Member States shall take appropriate measures, in cooperation with other Member States where this is necessary or advisable, to establish an integrated and adequate network of disposal installations, taking account of the best available technology not involving excessive costs. The network must enable the Community as a whole to become self-sufficient in waste disposal and the Member States to move towards that aim individually, taking into account geographical circumstances or the need for specialized installations for certain types of waste.

2. The network must also enable waste to be disposed of in one of the nearest appropriate installations, by means of the most appropriate methods and technologies in order to ensure a high level of protection for the environment and public health.

Article 6   Member States shall establish or designate the competent authority or authorities to be responsible for the implementation of this Directive.

Article 7   1. In order to attain the objectives referred to in Article 3, 4 and 5, the competent authority or authorities referred to in Article 6 shall be required to draw up as soon as possible one or more waste management plans. Such plans shall relate in particular to:
- the type, quantity and origin of waste to be recovered or disposed of,
- general technical requirements,
- any special arrangements for particular wastes,
- suitable disposal sites or installations.
Such plans may, for example, cover:
- the natural or legal persons empowered to carry out the management of waste,
- the estimated costs of the recovery and disposal operations,
- appropriate measures to encourage rationalization of the collection, sorting and treatment of waste.

2. Member States shall collaborate as appropriate with the other Member States concerned and the Commission to draw up such plans. They shall notify the Commission thereof.

[3] OJ 1983 L 109/8.

3. Member States may take the measures necessary to prevent movements of waste which are not in accordance with their waste management plans. They shall inform the Commission and the Member States of any such measures.

Article 8   Member States shall take the necessary measures to ensure that any holder of waste:

— has it handled by a private or public waste collector or by an undertaking which carries out the operations listed in Annex II A or B, or
— recovers or disposes of it himself in accordance with the provisions of this Directive.

Article 9   1. For the purposes of implementing Articles 4, 5 and 7, any establishment or undertaking which carries out the operations specified in Annex II A must obtain a permit from the competent authority referred to in Article 6.
Such permit shall cover:

— the types and quantities of waste,
— the technical requirements,
— the security precautions to be taken,
— the disposal site,
— the treatment method.

2. Permits may be granted for a specified period, they may be renewable, they may be subject to conditions and obligations, or, notably, if the intended method of disposal is unacceptable from the point of view of environmental protection, they may be refused.

Article 10   For the purposes of implementing Article 4, any establishment or undertaking which carries out the operations referred to in Annex II B must obtain a permit.

Article 11   1. Without prejudice to Council Directive 78/319/EEC of 20 March 1978 on toxic and dangerous waste,[4] as last amended by the Act of Accession of Spain and Portugal, the following may be exempted from the permit requirement imposed in Article 9 or Article 10:

(a) establishments or undertakings carrying out their own waste disposal at the place of production;
    and
(b) establishments or undertakings that carry out waste recovery.

   This exemption may apply only:

— if the competent authorities have adopted general rules for each type of activity laying down the types and quantities of waste and the conditions under which the activity in question may be exempted from the permit requirements,

and
— if the types or quantities of waste and methods of disposal or recovery are such that the conditions imposed in Article 4 are complied with.

2. The establishments or undertakings are referred to in paragraph 1 shall be registered with the competent authorities.

---

4 OJ 1978 L 84/43.

3. Member States shall inform the Commission of the general rules adopted pursuant to paragraph 1.

Article 12   Establishments or undertakings which collect or transport waste on a professional basis or which arrange for the disposal or recovery of waste on behalf of others (dealers or brokers), where not subject to authorization, shall be registered with the competent authorities.

Article 13   Establishments or undertakings which carry out the operations referred to in Articles 9 to 12 shall be subject to appropriate periodic inspections by the competent authorities.

Article 14   All establishments or undertakings referred to in Articles 9 and 10 shall:
— keep a record of the quantity, nature, origin, and, where relevant, the destination, frequency of collection, mode of transport and treatment method in respect of the waste referred to in Annex I and the operations referred to in Annex II A or B,
— make this information available, on request, to the competent authorities referred to in Article 6.
Member States may also require producers to comply with the provisions of this Article.

Article 15   In accordance with the 'polluter pays' principle, the cost of disposing of waste must be borne by:
— the holder who has waste handled by a waste collector or by an undertaking as referred to in Article 9,
and/or
— the previous holders or the producer of the product from which the waste came.

Article 16   1. Every three years, and for the first time on 1 April 1995, Member States shall send the Commission a report on the measures taken to implement this Directive. This report shall be based on a questionnaire, drawn up in accordance with the procedure referred to in Article 18, which the Commission shall send to the Member States six months before the above date.

2. On the basis of the reports referred to in paragraph 1, the Commission shall publish a consolidated report every three years, and for the first time on 1 April 1996.

Article 17   The amendments necessary for adapting the Annexes to this Directive to scientific and technical progress shall be adopted in accordance with the procedure laid down in Article 18.

Article 18   The Commission shall be assisted by a committee composed of the representatives of the Member States and chaired by the representative of the Commission.

The representative of the Commission shall submit to the committee a draft of the measures to be taken.

The committee shall deliver its opinion on the draft within a time limit which the chairman may lay down according to the urgency of the matter. The opinion shall be delivered by the majority laid down in Article 148 (2) of the EEC Treaty in the case of decisions which the Council is required to adopt on a proposal form the Commission. The votes of the representatives of the Member States within the Committee shall be weighted in the manner set out in that Article. The chairman shall not vote.

The Commission shall adopt the measures envisaged if they are in accordance with the opinion of the committee.

If the measures envisaged are not in accordance with the opinion of the committee, or if no opinion is delivered, the Commission shall, without delay, submit to the Council a proposal relating to the measures to be taken. The Council shall act by a qualified majority.

If, on the expiry of a period of three months from the date of referral to the Council, the Council has not acted, the proposed measures shall be adopted by the Commission.

[provisions omitted]

ANNEX I. CATEGORIES OF WASTE

Q1   Production or consumption residues not otherwise specified below
Q2   Off-specification products
Q3   Products whose date for appropriate use has expired
Q4   Materials spilled, lost or having undergone other mishap, including any materials, equipment, etc., contaminated as a result of the mishap
Q5   Materials contaminated or soiled as a result of planned actions (e.g. residues from cleaning operations, packing materials, containers, etc.)
Q6   Unusable parts (e.g. reject batteries, exhausted catalysts, etc.)
Q7   Substances which no longer perform satisfactorily (e.g. contaminated acids, contaminated solvents, exhausted tempering salts, etc.)
Q8   Residues of industrial processes (e.g. slags, still bottoms, etc.)
Q9   Residues from pollution abatement processes (e.g. scrubber sludges, baghouse dusts, spent filters, etc.)
Q10 Machining/finishing residues (e.g. lathe turnings, mill scales, etc.)
Q11 Residues from raw materials extraction and processing (e.g. mining residues, oil field slops, etc.)
Q12 Adulterated materials (e.g. oils contaminated with PCBs, etc.)
Q13 Any materials, substances or products whose use has been banned by law
Q14 Products for which the holder has no further use (e.g. agricultural, household, office, commercial and shop discards, etc.)
Q15 Contaminated materials, substances or products resulting from remedial action with respect to land
Q16 Any materials, substances or products which are not contained in the above categories.

ANNEX IIA. DISPOSAL OPERATIONS

NB: This Annex is intended to list disposal operations such as they occur in practice. In accordance with Article 4 waste must be disposed of without endangering human health and without the use of processes or methods likely to harm the environment.

D1 Deposit into or onto land (e.g. landfill, etc.)

D2 Land treatment (e.g. biodegradation of liquid or sludgy discards in soils, etc.)

D3 Deep injection (e.g. injection of pumpable discards into wells, salt domes or naturally occurring repositories, etc.)

D4 Surface impoundment (e.g. placement of liquid or sludgy discards into pits, ponds or lagoons, etc.)

D5 Specially engineered landfill (e.g. placement into lined discrete cells which are capped and isolated from one another and the environment, etc.)

D6 Release into a water body except seas/oceans

D7 Release into seas/oceans including sea-bed insertion

D8 Biological treatment not specified elsewhere in this Annex which results in final compounds or mixtures which are discarded by means of any of the operations numbered D1 to D12

D9 Physico-chemical treatment not specified elsewhere in this Annex which results in final compounds or mixtures which are discarded by means of any of the operations numbered D1 to D12 (e.g. evaporation, drying, calcination, etc.)

D10 Incineration on land

D11 Incineration at sea

D12 Permanent storage (e.g. emplacement of containers in a mine, etc.)

D13 Blending or mixing prior to submission to any of the operations numbered D1 to D12

D14 Repackaging prior to submission to any of the operations numbered D1 to D13

D15 Storage pending any of the operations numbered D1 to D14 (excluding temporary storage, pending collection, on the site where it is produced)

ANNEX II B. RECOVERY OPERATIONS

NB: This Annex is intended to list recovery operations as they occur in practice. In accordance with Article 4 waste must be recovered without endangering human health and without the use of processes or methods likely to harm the environment.

R1 Use principally as a fuel or other means to generate energy

R2 Solvent reclamation/regeneration

R3 Recycling/reclamation of organic substances which are not used as solvents (including composting and other biological transformation processes)

R4 Recycling/reclamation of metals and metal compounds

R5 Recycling/reclamation of other inorganic materials

R6 Regeneration of acids or bases

R7 Recovery of components used for pollution abatement

R8 Recovery of components from catalysts

R9 Oil re-refining or other reuses of oil

R10 Land treatment resulting in benefit to agriculture or ecological improvement

R11 Use of wastes obtained from any of the operations numbered R1 to R10

R12 Exchange of wastes for submission to any of the operations numbered R1 to R11

R13 Storage of wastes pending any of the operations numbered R1 to R12 (excluding temporary storage, pending collection, on the site where it is produced)

Council Directive of 27 June 1985 on the assessment of the effects of certain public and private projects on the environment (85/337/EEC)[5]

The Council of the European Communities

HAVING REGARD to the Treaty establishing the European Economic Community, and in particular Articles 100 and 235 thereof,

[recitals omitted]

Whereas the 1973 and 1977 action programmes of the European Communities on the environment, as well as the 1983 action programme, the main outlines of which have been approved by the Council of the European Communities and the representatives of the Governments of the Member States, stress that the best environmental policy consists in preventing the creation of pollution or nuisances at source, rather than subsequently trying to counteract their effects; whereas they affirm the need to take effects on the environment into account at the earliest possible stage in all the technical planning and decision-making processes; whereas to that end, they provide for the implementation of procedures to evaluate such effects;

Whereas the disparities between the laws in force in the various Member States with regard to the assessment of the environmental effects of public and private projects may create unfavourable competitive conditions and thereby directly affect the functioning of the common market; whereas, therefore, it is necessary to approximate national laws in this field pursuant to Article 100 of the Treaty;

Whereas, in addition, it is necessary to achieve one of the Community's objectives in the sphere of the protection of the environment and the quality of life;

Whereas, since the Treaty has not provided the powers required for this end, recourse should be had to Article 235 of the Treaty;

Whereas general principles for the assessment of environmental effects should be introduced with a view to supplementing and coordinating development consent procedures governing public and private projects likely to have a major effect on the environment;

Whereas development consent for public and private projects which are likely to have significant effects on the environment should be granted only after prior assessment of the likely significant environmental effects of these projects has been carried out; whereas this assessment must be conducted on the basis of the appropriate information supplied by the developer, which may be supplemented by the authorities and by the people who may be concerned by the project in question;

Whereas the principles of the assessment of environmental effects should be harmonized, in particular with reference to the projects which should be subject to assessment, the main obligations of the developers and the content of the assessment;

---

[5] OJ 1985 L 175/40, as amended by Directive 97/11/EC, OJ 1997 L 73/5.

Whereas projects belonging to certain types have significant effects on the environment and these projects must as a rule be subject to systematic assessment;

Whereas projects of other types may not have significant effects on the environment in every case and whereas these projects should be assessed where the Member States consider that their characteristics so require;

Whereas, for projects which are subject to assessment, a certain minimal amount of information must be supplied, concerning the project and its effects;

Whereas the effects of a project on the environment must be assessed in order to take account of concerns to protect human health, to contribute by means of a better environment to the quality of life, to ensure maintenance of the diversity of species and to maintain the reproductive capacity of the ecosystem as a basic resource for life;

Whereas, however, this Directive should not be applied to projects the details of which are adopted by a specific act of national legislation, since the objectives of this Directive, including that of supplying information, are achieved through the legislative process;

Whereas, furthermore, it may be appropriate in exceptional cases to exempt a specific project from the assessment procedures laid down by this Directive, subject to appropriate information being supplied to the Commission,

HAS ADOPTED this Directive:

Article 1　1. This Directive shall apply to the assessment of the environmental effects of those public and private projects which are likely to have significant effects on the environment.

2. For the purposes of this Directive:
'project' means:
— the execution of construction works or of other installations or schemes,
— other interventions in the natural surroundings and landscape including those involving the extraction of mineral resources;
'developer' means:
the applicant for authorization for a private project or the public authority which initiates a project;
'development consent' means:
the decision of the competent authority or authorities which entitles the developer to proceed with the project.

3. The competent authority or authorities shall be that or those which the Member States designate as responsible for performing the duties arising from this Directive.

4. Projects serving national defence purposes are not covered by this Directive.

5. This Directive shall not apply to projects the details of which are adopted by a specific act of national legislation, since the objectives of this Directive, including that of supplying information, are achieved through the legislative process.

Article 2　1. Member States shall adopt all measures necessary to ensure that, before consent is given, projects likely to have significant effects on the environment by virtue, inter alia, of their nature, size or location are made subject to a requirement for development consent and an assessment with regard to their effects. These projects are defined in Article 4.

2. The environmental impact assessment may be integrated into the existing procedures for consent to projects in the Member States, or, failing this, into other procedures or into procedures to be established to comply with the aims of this Directive.

2a. Member States may provide for a single procedure in order to fulfil the requirements of this Directive and the requirements of Council Directive 96/61/EC of 24 September 1996 on integrated pollution prevention and control.[6]

3. Without prejudice to Article 7, Member States may, in exceptional cases, exempt a specific project in whole or in part from the provisions laid down in this Directive;
   In this event, the Member States shall:
(a) consider whether another form of assessment would be appropriate and whether the information thus collected should be made available to the public;
(b) make available to the public concerned the information relating to the exemption and the reasons for granting it;
(c) inform the Commission, prior to granting consent, of the reasons justifying the exemption granted, and provide it with the information made available, where applicable, to their own nationals.

   The Commission shall immediately forward the documents received to the other Member States.

   The Commission shall report annually to the Council on the application of this paragraph.

Article 3   The environmental impact assessment shall identify, describe and assess in an appropriate manner, in the light of each individual case and in accordance with Articles 4 to 11, the direct and indirect effects of a project on the following factors:

— human beings, fauna and flora;
— soil, water, air, climate and the landscape;
— material assets and the cultural heritage;
— the interaction between the factors mentioned in the first, second and third indents.

Article 4   1. Subject to Article 2(3), projects listed in Annex I shall be made subject to an assessment in accordance with Articles 5 to 10.

2. Subject to Article 2(3), for projects listed in Annex II, the Member States shall determine through:
(a) a case-by-case examination,
or
(b) thresholds or criteria set by the Member State

whether the project shall be made subject to an assessment in accordance with Articles 5 to 10.

   Member States may decide to apply both procedures referred to in (a) and (b).

---

[6] OJ 1996 L 257/26.

3. When a case-by-case examination is carried out or thresholds or criteria are set for the purpose of paragraph 2, the relevant selection criteria set out in Annex III shall be taken into account.

4. Member States shall ensure that the determination made by the competent authorities under paragraph 2 is made available to the public.

Article 5   1. In the case of projects which, pursuant to Article 4, must be subjected to an environmental impact assessment in accordance with Articles 5 to 10, Member States shall adopt the necessary measures to ensure that the developer supplies in an appropriate form the information specified in Annex IV inasmuch as:
(a) the Member States consider that the information is relevant to a given stage of the consent procedure and to the specific characteristics of a particular project or type of project and of the environmental features likely to be affected;
(b) the Member States consider that a developer may reasonably be required to compile this information having regard inter alia to current knowledge and methods of assessment.

2. Member States shall take the necessary measures to ensure that, if the developer so requests before submitting an application for development consent, the competent authority shall give an opinion on the information to be supplied by the developer in accordance with paragraph 1. The competent authority shall consult the developer and authorities referred to in Article 6(1) before it gives its opinion. The fact that the authority has given an opinion under this paragraph shall not preclude it from subsequently requiring the developer to submit further information.

   Member States may require the competent authorities to give such an opinion, irrespective of whether the developer so requests.

3. The information to be provided by the developer in accordance with paragraph 1 shall include at least:

— a description of the project comprising information on the site, design and size of the project,
— a description of the measures envisaged in order to avoid, reduce and, if possible, remedy significant adverse effects,
— the data required to identify and assess the main effects which the project is likely to have on the environment,
— an outline of the main alternatives studied by the developer and an indication of the main reasons for his choice, taking into account the environmental effects,
— a non-technical summary of the information mentioned in the previous indents.

4. Member States shall, if necessary, ensure that any authorities holding relevant information, with particular reference to Article 3, shall make this information available to the developer.

Article 6   1. Member States shall take the measures necessary to ensure that the authorities likely to be concerned by the project by reason of their specific environmental responsibilities are given an opportunity to express their opinion on the information supplied by the developer and on the request for development consent. To this end, Member States shall designate the authorities to be consulted, either in general terms or on a case-by-case basis. The information gathered pursuant to Article 5 shall be forwarded to those authorities. Detailed arrangements for consultation shall be laid down by the Member States.

2. Member States shall ensure that any request for development consent and any information gathered pursuant to Article 5 are made available to the public within a reasonable time in order to give the public concerned the opportunity to express an opinion before the development consent is granted.

3. The detailed arrangements for such information and consultation shall be determined by the Member States, which may in particular, depending on the particular characteristics of the projects or sites concerned:

— determine the public concerned,
— specify the places where the information can be consulted,
— specify the way in which the public may be informed, for example by bill-posting within a certain radius, publication in local newspapers, organization of exhibitions with plans, drawings, tables, graphs, models,
— determine the manner in which the public is to be consulted, for example, by written submissions, by public enquiry,
— fix appropriate time limits for the various stages of the procedure in order to ensure that a decision is taken within a reasonable period.

Article 7   1. Where a Member State is aware that a project is likely to have significant effects on the environment in another Member State or where a Member State likely to be significantly affected so requests, the Member State in whose territory the project is intended to be carried out shall send to the affected Member State as soon as possible and no later than when informing its own public, inter alia:

(a) a description of the project, together with any available information on its possible transboundary impact;
(b) information on the nature of the decision which may be taken,

and shall give the other Member State a reasonable time in which to indicate whether it wishes to participate in the Environmental Impact Assessment procedure, and may include the information referred to in paragraph 2.

2. If a Member State which receives information pursuant to paragraph 1 indicates that it intends to participate in the Environmental Impact Assessment procedure, the Member State in whose territory the project is intended to be carried out shall, if it has not already done so, send to the affected Member State the information gathered pursuant to Article 5 and relevant information regarding the said procedure, including the request for development consent.

3. The Member States concerned, each insofar as it is concerned, shall also:

(a) arrange for the information referred to in paragraphs 1 and 2 to be made available, within a reasonable time, to the authorities referred to in Article 6(1) and the public concerned in the territory of the Member State likely to be significantly affected; and
(b) ensure that those authorities and the public concerned are given an opportunity, before development consent for the project is granted, to forward their opinion within a reasonable time on the information supplied to the competent

authority in the Member State in whose territory the project is intended to be carried out.

4. The Member States concerned shall enter into consultations regarding, inter alia, the potential transboundary effects of the project and the measures envisaged to reduce or eliminate such effects and shall agree on a reasonable time frame for the duration of the consultation period.

5. The detailed arrangements for implementing the provisions of this Article may be determined by the Member States concerned.

Article 8 The results of consultations and the information gathered pursuant to Articles 5, 6 and 7 must be taken into consideration in the development consent procedure.

Article 9 1. When a decision to grant or refuse development consent has been taken, the competent authority or authorities shall inform the public thereof in accordance with the appropriate procedures and shall make available to the public the following information:

— the content of the decision and any conditions attached thereto,
— the main reasons and considerations on which the decision is based,
— a description, where necessary, of the main measures to avoid, reduce and, if possible, offset the major adverse effects.

2. The competent authority or authorities shall inform any Member State which has been consulted pursuant to Article 7, forwarding to it the information referred to in paragraph 1.

Article 10 The provisions of this Directive shall not affect the obligation on the competent authorities to respect the limitations imposed by national regulations and administrative provisions and accepted legal practices with regard to commercial and industrial confidentiality, including intellectual property, and the safeguarding of the public interest.

Where Article 7 applies, the transmission of information to another Member State and the receipt of information by another Member State shall be subject to the limitations in force in the Member State in which the project is proposed.

Article 11 1. The Member States and the Commission shall exchange information on the experience gained in applying this Directive.

2. In particular, Member States shall inform the Commission of any criteria and/or thresholds adopted for the selection of the projects in question, in accordance with Article 4(2).

3. Five years after notification of this Directive, the Commission shall send the European Parliament and the Council a report on its application and effectiveness. The report shall be based on the aforementioned exchange of information.

4. On the basis of this exchange of information, the Commission shall submit to the Council additional proposals, should this be necessary, with a view to this Directive's being applied in a sufficiently coordinated manner.

Article 12 1. Member States shall take the measures necessary to comply with this Directive within three years of its notification.

2. Member States shall communicate to the Commission the texts of the provisions of the national law which they adopt in the field covered by this Directive.

[final provisions omitted]

ANNEX I. PROJECTS SUBJECT TO ARTICLE 4 (1)

1. Crude-oil refineries (excluding undertakings manufacturing only lubricants from crude oil) and installations for the gasification and liquefaction of 500 tonnes or more of coal or bituminous shale per day.

2. — Thermal power stations and other combustion installations with a heat output of 300 megawatts or more, and
   — nuclear power stations and other nuclear reactors including the dismantling or decommissioning of such power stations or reactors[7] (except research installations for the production and conversion of fissionable and fertile materials, whose maximum power does not exceed 1 kilowatt continuous thermal load).

3. (a) Installations for the reprocessing of irradiated nuclear fuel.
   (b) Installations designed:
      — for the production or enrichment of nuclear fuel,
      — for the processing of irradiated nuclear fuel or high-level radioactive waste,
      — for the final disposal of irradiated nuclear fuel,
      — solely for the final disposal of radioactive waste,
      — solely for the storage (planned for more than 10 years) of irradiated nuclear fuels or radioactive waste in a different site than the production site.

4. — Integrated works for the initial smelting of cast-iron and steel;
   — Installations for the production of non-ferrous crude metals from ore, concentrates or secondary raw materials by metallurgical, chemical or electrolytic processes.

5. Installations for the extraction of asbestos and for the processing and transformation of asbestos and products containing asbestos: for asbestos-cement products, with an annual production of more than 20,000 tonnes of finished products, for friction material, with an annual production of more than 50 tonnes of finished products, and for other uses of asbestos, utilization of more than 200 tonnes per year.

6. Integrated chemical installations, i.e. those installations for the manufacture on an industrial scale of substances using chemical conversion processes, in which several units are juxtaposed and are functionally linked to one another and which are:
   (i) for the production of basic organic chemicals;
   (ii) for the production of basic inorganic chemicals;
   (iii) for the production of phosphorous-, nitrogen- or potassium-based fertilizers (simple or compound fertilizers);

---

[7] Nuclear power stations and other nuclear reactors cease to be such an installation when all nuclear fuel and other radioactively contaminated elements have been removed permanently from the installation site.

(iv) for the production of basic plant health products and of biocides;
(v) for the production of basic pharmaceutical products using a chemical or biological process;
(vi) for the production of explosives.

7. (a) Construction of lines for long-distance railway traffic and of airports[8] with a
basic runway length of 2 100 m or more;
(b) Construction of motorways and express roads;[9]
(c) Construction of a new road of four or more lanes, or realignment and/or
widening of an existing road of two lanes or less so as to provide four or more
lanes, where such new road, or realigned and/or widened section of road
would be 10 km or more in a continuous length.

8. (a) Inland waterways and ports for inland-waterway traffic which permit the
passage of vessels of over 1,350 tonnes;
(b) Trading ports, piers for loading and unloading connected to land and outside
ports (excluding ferry piers) which can take vessels of over 1 350 tonnes.

9. Waste disposal installations for the incineration, chemical treatment as defined
in Annex IIA to Directive 75/442/EEC under heading D9, or landfill of hazardous
waste (i.e. waste to which Directive 91/689/EEC[10] applies).

10. Waste disposal installations for the incineration or chemical treatment as
defined in Annex IIA to Directive 75/442/EEC under heading D9 of non-hazardous
waste with a capacity exceeding 100 tonnes per day.

11. Groundwater abstraction or artificial groundwater recharge schemes where the
annual volume of water abstracted or recharged is equivalent to or exceeds 10 million cubic metres.

12. (a) Works for the transfer of water resources between river basins where this
transfer aims at preventing possible shortages of water and where the
amount of water transferred exceeds 100 million cubic metres/year;
(b) In all other cases, works for the transfer of water resources between river
basins where the multi-annual average flow of the basin of abstraction
exceeds 2,000 million cubic metres/year and where the amount of water
transferred exceeds 5 % of this flow.

In both cases transfers of piped drinking water are excluded.

13. Waste water treatment plants with a capacity exceeding 150,000 population
equivalent as defined in Article 2 point (6) of Directive 91/271/EEC.[11]

14. Extraction of petroleum and natural gas for commercial purposes where the
amount extracted exceeds 500 tonnes/day in the case of petroleum and 500,000
m³/day in the case of gas.

15. Dams and other installations designed for the holding back or permanent storage of water, where a new or additional amount of water held back or stored
exceeds 10 million cubic metres.

---

[8] For the purposes of this Directive, 'airport' means airports which comply with the definition in the
1944 Chicago Convention setting up the International Civil Aviation Organization (Annex 14).
[9] For the purposes of the Directive, 'express road' means a road which complies with the definition in
the European Agreement on Main International Traffic Arteries of 15 November 1975.
[10] OJ 1991 L 377/20, as last amended by Directive 94/31/EC, OJ 1994 L 168/28.
[11] OJ 1991 L 135/40, as last amended by the 1994 Act of Accession.

16. Pipelines for the transport of gas, oil or chemicals with a diameter of more than 800 mm and a length of more than 40 km.

17. Installations for the intensive rearing of poultry or pigs with more than:
(a) 85,000 places for broilers, 60,000 places for hens;
(b) 3,000 places for production pigs (over 30 kg); or
(c) 900 places for sows.

18. Industrial plants for the
(a) production of pulp from timber or similar fibrous materials;
(b) production of paper and board with a production capacity exceeding 200 tonnes per day.

19. Quarries and open-cast mining where the surface of the site exceeds 25 hectares, or peat extraction, where the surface of the site exceeds 150 hectares.

20. Construction of overhead electrical power lines with a voltage of 220 kV or more and a length of more than 15 km.

21. Installations for storage of petroleum, petrochemical, or chemical products with a capacity of 200,000 tonnes or more.

ANNEX II. PROJECTS SUBJECT TO ARTICLE 4(2)

1. Agriculture, silviculture and aquaculture
(a) Projects for the restructuring of rural land holdings;
(b) Projects for the use of uncultivated land or semi-natural areas for intensive agricultural purposes;
(c) Water management projects for agriculture, including irrigation and land drainage projects;
(d) Initial afforestation and deforestation for the purposes of conversion to another type of land use;
(e) Intensive livestock installations (projects not included in Annex I);
(f) Intensive fish farming;
(g) Reclamation of land from the sea.

2. Extractive industry
(a) Quarries, open-cast mining and peat extraction (projects not included in Annex I);
(b) Underground mining;
(c) Extraction of minerals by marine or fluvial dredging;
(d) Deep drillings, in particular:

— geothermal drilling,
— drilling for the storage of nuclear waste material,
— drilling for water supplies,

with the exception of drillings for investigating the stability of the soil;
(e) Surface industrial installations for the extraction of coal, petroleum, natural gas and ores, as well as bituminous shale.

3. Energy industry
(a) Industrial installations for the production of electricity, steam and hot water (projects not included in Annex I);

(b) Industrial installations for carrying gas, steam and hot water; transmission of electrical energy by overhead cables (projects not included in Annex I);
(c) Surface storage of natural gas;
(d) Underground storage of combustible gases;
(e) Surface storage of fossil fuels;
(f) Industrial briquetting of coal and lignite;
(g) Installations for the processing and storage of radioactive waste (unless included in Annex I);
(h) Installations for hydroelectric energy production;
(i) Installations for the harnessing of wind power for energy production (wind farms).

4. Production and processing of metals
(a) Installations for the production of pig iron or steel (primary or secondary fusion) including continuous casting;
(b) Installations for the processing of ferrous metals:

   (i) hot-rolling mills;
   (ii) smitheries with hammers;
   (iii) application of protective fused metal coats;

(c) Ferrous metal foundries;
(d) Installations for the smelting, including the alloyage, of non-ferrous metals, excluding precious metals, including recovered products (refining, foundry casting, etc.);
(e) Installations for surface treatment of metals and plastic materials using an electrolytic or chemical process;
(f) Manufacture and assembly of motor vehicles and manufacture of motor-vehicle engines;
(g) Shipyards;
(h) Installations for the construction and repair of aircraft;
(i) Manufacture of railway equipment;
(j) Swaging by explosives;
(k) Installations for the roasting and sintering of metallic ores.

5. Mineral industry
(a) Coke ovens (dry coal distillation);
(b) Installations for the manufacture of cement;
(c) Installations for the production of asbestos and the manufacture of asbestos-products (projects not included in Annex I);
(d) Installations for the manufacture of glass including glass fibre;
(e) Installations for smelting mineral substances including the production of mineral fibres;
(f) Manufacture of ceramic products by burning, in particular roofing tiles, bricks, refractory bricks, tiles, stoneware or porcelain.

6. Chemical industry (Projects not included in Annex I)

(a) Treatment of intermediate products and production of chemicals;
(b) Production of pesticides and pharmaceutical products, paint and varnishes, elastomers and peroxides;
(c) Storage facilities for petroleum, petrochemical and chemical products.

7. Food industry
(a)   Manufacture of vegetable and animal oils and fats;
(b) Packing and canning of animal and vegetable products;
(c) Manufacture of dairy products;
(d) Brewing and malting;
(e) Confectionery and syrup manufacture;
(f) Installations for the slaughter of animals;
(g) Industrial starch manufacturing installations;
(h) Fish-meal and fish-oil factories;
(i) Sugar factories.

8. Textile, leather, wood and paper industries
(a)   Industrial plants for the production of paper and board (projects not included in Annex I);
(b) Plants for the pretreatment (operations such as washing, bleaching, mercerization) or dyeing of fibres or textiles;
(c) Plants for the tanning of hides and skins;
(d) Cellulose-processing and production installations.

9. Rubber industry
Manufacture and treatment of elastomer-based products.

10. Infrastructure projects
(a)   Industrial estate development projects;
(b)   Urban development projects, including the construction of shopping centres and car parks;
(c)   Construction of railways and intermodal transshipment facilities, and of intermodal terminals (projects not included in Annex I);
(d)   Construction of airfields (projects not included in Annex I);
(e)   Construction of roads, harbours and port installations, including fishing harbours (projects not included in Annex I);
(f)   Inland-waterway construction not included in Annex I, canalization and flood-relief works;
(g)   Dams and other installations designed to hold water or store it on a long-term basis (projects not included in Annex I);
(h)   Tramways, elevated and underground railways, suspended lines or similar lines of a particular type, used exclusively or mainly for passenger transport;
(i)   Oil and gas pipeline installations (projects not included in Annex I);
(j)   Installations of long-distance aqueducts;
(k)   Coastal work to combat erosion and maritime works capable of altering the coast through the construction, for example, of dykes, moles, jetties and other sea defence works, excluding the maintenance and reconstruction of such works;
(l)   Groundwater abstraction and artificial groundwater recharge schemes not included in Annex I;
(m) Works for the transfer of water resources between river basins not included in Annex I.

11. Other projects
(a)   Permanent racing and test tracks for motorized vehicles;
(b) Installations for the disposal of waste (projects not included in Annex I);

(c) Waste-water treatment plants (projects not included in Annex I);
(d) Sludge-deposition sites;
(e) Storage of scrap iron, including scrap vehicles;
(f) Test benches for engines, turbines or reactors;
(g) Installations for the manufacture of artificial mineral fibres;
(h) Installations for the recovery or destruction of explosive substances;
(i) Knackers' yards.

12. Tourism and leisure
(a) Ski-runs, ski-lifts and cable-cars and associated developments;
(b) Marinas;
(c) Holiday villages and hotel complexes outside urban areas and associated developments;
(d) Permanent camp sites and caravan sites;
(e) Theme parks.

13. — Any change or extension of projects listed in Annex I or Annex II, already authorized, executed or in the process of being executed, which may have significant adverse effects on the environment;
   — Projects in Annex I, undertaken exclusively or mainly for the development and testing of new methods or products and not used for more than two years.

ANNEX III. SELECTION CRITERIA REFERRED TO IN ARTICLE 4(3)

1. Characteristics of projects
The characteristics of projects must be considered having regard, in particular, to:
— the size of the project,
— the cumulation with other projects,
— the use of natural resources,
— the production of waste,
— pollution and nuisances,
— the risk of accidents, having regard in particular to substances or technologies used.

2. Location of projects
The environmental sensitivity of geographical areas likely to be affected by projects must be considered, having regard, in particular, to:
— the existing land use,
— the relative abundance, quality and regenerative capacity of natural resources in the area,
— the absorption capacity of the natural environment, paying particular attention to the following areas:
   (a) wetlands;
   (b) coastal zones;
   (c) mountain and forest areas;
   (d) nature reserves and parks;
   (e) areas classified or protected under Member States' legislation; special

protection areas designated by Member States pursuant to Directive 79/409/EEC and 92/43/EEC;

(f) areas in which the environmental quality standards laid down in Community legislation have already been exceeded;

(g) densely populated areas;

(h) landscapes of historical, cultural or archaeological significance.

3. Characteristics of the potential impact

The potential significant effects of projects must be considered in relation to criteria set out under 1 and 2 above, and having regard in particular to:

— the extent of the impact (geographical area and size of the affected population),
— the transfrontier nature of the impact,
— the magnitude and complexity of the impact,
— the probability of the impact,
— the duration, frequency and reversibility of the impact.

ANNEX IV. INFORMATION REFERRED TO IN ARTICLE 5(1)

1. Description of the project, including in particular:

— a description of the physical characteristics of the whole project and the land-use requirements during the construction and operational phases,
— a description of the main characteristics of the production processes, for instance, nature and quantity of the materials used,
— an estimate, by type and quantity, of expected residues and emissions (water, air and soil pollution, noise, vibration, light, heat, radiation, etc.) resulting from the operation of the proposed project.

2. An outline of the main alternatives studied by the developer and an indication of the main reasons for this choice, taking into account the environmental effects.

3. A description of the aspects of the environment likely to be significantly affected by the proposed project, including, in particular, population, fauna, flora, soil, water, air, climatic factors, material assets, including the architectural and archaeological heritage, landscape and the inter-relationship between the above factors.

4. A description (1) of the likely significant effects of the proposed project on the environment resulting from:

— the existence of the project,
— the use of natural resources,
— the emission of pollutants, the creation of nuisances and the elimination of waste,
  and the description by the developer of the forecasting methods used to assess the effects on the environment.

5. A description of the measures envisaged to prevent, reduce and where possible offset any significant adverse effects on the environment.

6. A non-technical summary of the information provided under the above headings.

7. An indication of any difficulties (technical deficiencies or lack of know-how) encountered by the developer in compiling the required information. This descrip-

tion should cover the direct effects and any indirect, secondary, cumulative, short, medium and long-term, permanent and temporary, positive and negative effects of the project.'

Social Policy

Council Directive of 10 February 1975 on the approximation of the laws of the Member States relating to the application of the principle of equal pay for men and women (75/117/EEC)[1]

The Council of the European Communities,

HAVING REGARD to the Treaty establishing the European Economic Community, and in particular Art. 100 thereof;

HAVING REGARD to the proposal from the Commission;

HAVING REGARD to the Opinion of the European Parliament;

HAVING REGARD to the Opinion of the Economic and Social Committee;

Whereas implementation of the principle that men and women should receive equal pay contained in Art. 119 of the Treaty is an integral part of the establishment and functioning of the common market;

Whereas it is primarily the responsibility of the Member States to ensure the application of this principle by means of appropriate laws, regulations and administrative provisions;

Whereas the Council resolution of 21 January 1974 concerning a social action programme aimed at making it possible to harmonise living and working conditions while the improvement is being maintained and at achieving a balanced social and economic development of the Community, recognised that priority should be given to action taken on behalf of women as regards access to employment and vocational training and advancement, and as regards working conditions, including pay;

Whereas it is desirable to reinforce the basic laws by standards aimed at facilitating the practical application of the principle of equality in such a way that all employees in the Community can be protected in these matters;

Whereas differences continue to exist in the various Member States despite the efforts made to apply the resolution of the conference of the Member States of 30 December 1961 on equal pay for men and women and whereas, therefore, the national provisions should be approximated as regards application of the principle of equal pay,

HAVING REGARD this Directive:

Article 1 The principle of equal pay for men and women outlined in Art. 119 of the Treaty, hereinafter called 'principle of equal pay', means, for the same work or for work to which equal value is attributed, the elimination of all discrimination on grounds of sex with regard to all aspects and conditions of remuneration.

In particular, where a job classification system is used for determining pay, it must be based on the same criteria for both men and women and so drawn up as to exclude any discrimination on grounds of sex.

[1] OJ 1975 L 45/19.

Article 2   Member States shall introduce into their national legal systems such measures as are necessary to enable all employees who consider themselves wronged by failure to apply the principle of equal pay to pursue their claims by judicial process after possible recourse to other competent authorities.

Article 3   Member States shall abolish all discrimination between men and women arising from laws, regulations or administrative provisions which is contrary to the principle of equal pay.

Article 4   Member States shall take the necessary measures to ensure that provisions appearing in collective agreements, wage scales, wage agreements or individual contracts of employment which are contrary to the principle of equal pay shall be, or may be declared, null and void or may be amended.

Article 5   Member States shall take the necessary measures to protect employees against dismissal by the employer as a reaction to a complaint within the undertaking or to any legal proceedings aimed at enforcing compliance with the principle of equal pay.

Article 6   Member States shall, in accordance with their national circumstances and legal systems, take the measures necessary to ensure that the principle of equal pay is applied. They shall see that effective means are available to take care that this principle is observed.

Article 7   Member States shall take care that the provisions adopted pursuant to this Directive, together with the relevant provisions already in force, are brought to the attention of employees by all appropriate means, for example at their place of employment.

[*final provisions omitted*]

Council Directive of 9 February 1976 on the implementation of the principle of equal treatment for men and women as regards access to employment, vocational training and promotion, and working conditions (76/207/EEC)[2]

The Council of the European Communities,

HAVING REGARD to the Treaty establishing the European Economic Community, and in particular Art. 235 thereof,

HAVING REGARD to the proposal from the Commission,

HAVING REGARD to the opinion of the European Parliament,

HAVING REGARD to the opinion of the Economic and Social Committee,

Whereas the Council, in its resolution of 21 January 1974 concerning a social action programme, included among the priorities action for the purpose of achieving equality between men and women as regards access to employment and vocational training and promotion and as regards working conditions, including pay;

---

[2] OJ 1976 L 39/40.

Whereas, with regard to pay, the Council adopted on 10 February 1975 Directive 75/117/EEC on the approximation of the laws of the Member States relating to the application of the principle of equal pay for men and women;

Whereas Community action to achieve the principle of equal treatment for men and women in respect of access to employment and vocational training and promotion and in respect of other working conditions also appears to be necessary; whereas equal treatment for male and female workers constitutes one of the objectives of the Community, in so far as the harmonisation of living and working conditions while maintaining their improvement are *inter alia* to be furthered; whereas the Treaty does not confer the necessary specific powers for this purpose;

Whereas the definition and progressive implementation of the principle of equal treatment in matters of social security should be ensured by means of subsequent instruments,

Has adopted this Directive:

Article 1   1. The purpose of this Directive is to put into effect in the Member States the principle of equal treatment for men and women as regards access to employment, including promotion, and to vocational training and as regards working conditions and, on the conditions referred to in paragraph 2, social security. This principle is hereinafter referred to as 'the principle of equal treatment'.

2. With a view to ensuring the progressive implementation of the principle of equal treatment in matters of social security, the Council, acting on a proposal from the Commission, will adopt provisions defining its substance, its scope and the arrangements for its application.

Article 2   1. For the purposes of the following provisions, the principle of equal treatment shall mean that there shall be no discrimination whatsoever on grounds of sex either directly or indirectly by reference in particular to marital or family status.

2. This Directive shall be without prejudice to the right of Member States to exclude from its field of application those occupational activities and, where appropriate, the training leading thereto, for which, by reason of their nature or the context in which they are carried out, the sex of the worker constitutes a determining factor.

3. This Directive shall be without prejudice to provisions concerning the protection of women, particularly as regards pregnancy and maternity.

4. This Directive shall be without prejudice to measures to promote equal opportunity for men and women, in particular by removing existing inequalities which affect women's opportunities in the areas referred to in Art. 1(1).

Article 3   1. Application of the principle of equal treatment means that there shall be no discrimination whatsoever on grounds of sex in the conditions, including selection criteria, for access to all jobs or posts, whatever the sector or branch of activity, and to all levels of the occupational hierarchy.

2. To this end, Member States shall take the measures necessary to ensure that:
(a) any laws, regulations and administrative provisions contrary to the principle of equal treatment shall be abolished;

(b) any provisions contrary to the principle of equal treatment which are included in collective agreements, individual contracts of employment, internal rules of undertakings or in rules governing the independent occupations and professions shall be, or may be declared, null and void or may be amended;

(c) those laws, regulations and administrative provisions contrary to the principle of equal treatment when the concern for protection which originally inspired them is no longer well founded shall be revised; and that where similar provisions are included in collective agreements labour and management shall be requested to undertake the desired revision.

Article 4   Application of the principle of equal treatment with regard to access to all types and to all levels, of vocational guidance, vocational training, advanced vocational training and retraining, means that Member States shall take all necessary measures to ensure that:

(a) any laws, regulations and administrative provisions contrary to the principle of equal treatment shall be abolished;

(b) any provisions contrary to the principle of equal treatment which are included in collective agreements, individual contracts of employment, internal rules of undertakings or in rules governing the independent occupations and professions shall be, or may be declared, null and void or may be amended;

(c) without prejudice to the freedom granted in certain Member States to certain private training establishments, vocational guidance, vocational training, advanced vocational training and retraining shall be accessible on the basis of the same criteria and at the same levels without any discrimination on grounds of sex.

Article 5[3]   1. Application of the principle of equal treatment with regard to working conditions, including the conditions governing dismissal, means that men and women shall be guaranteed the same conditions without discrimination on grounds of sex.

2. To this end, Member States shall take the measures necessary to ensure that:

(a) any laws, regulations and administrative provisions contrary to the principle of equal treatment shall be abolished;

(b) any provisions contrary to the principle of equal treatment which are included in collective agreements, individual contracts of employment, internal rules of undertakings or in rules governing the independent occupations and professions shall be, or may be declared, null and void or may be amended;

(c) those laws, regulations and administrative provisions contrary to the principle of equal treatment when the concern for protection which originally inspired them is no longer well founded shall be revised; and that where similar provisions are included in collective agreements labour and management shall be requested to undertake the desired revision.

Article 6   Member States shall introduce into their national legal systems such measures as are necessary to enable all persons who consider themselves wronged by failure to apply to them the principle of equal treatment within the meaning of

---

[3] Article 5 of the Directive shall not apply to Austria in respect of night work for women until 31 December 2001. See Treaty of Accession 1994 Annex XV.V.

Arts. 3, 4 and 5 to pursue their claims by judicial process after possible recourse to other competent authorities.

Article 7   Member States shall take the necessary measures to protect employees against dismissal by the employer as a reaction to a complaint within the undertaking or to any legal proceedings aimed at enforcing compliance with the principle of equal treatment.

Article 8   Member States shall take care that the provisions adopted pursuant to this Directive, together with the relevant provisions already in force, are brought to the attention of employees by all appropriate means, for example at their place of employment.

Article 9   1. Member States shall put into force the laws, regulations and administrative provisions necessary in order to comply with this Directive within 30 months of its notification and shall immediately inform the Commission thereof.

However, as regards the first part of Art. 3(2)(c) and the first part of Art. 5(2)(c), Member States shall carry out a first examination and if necessary a first revision of the laws, regulations and administrative provisions referred to therein within four years of notification of this Directive.

2. Member States shall periodically assess the occupational activities referred to in Art. 2(2) in order to decide, in the light of social developments, whether there is justification for maintaining the exclusions concerned. They shall notify the Commission of the results of this assessment.

3. Member States shall also communicate to the Commission the texts of laws, regulations and administrative provisions which they adopt in the field covered by this Directive.

[final provisions omitted]

Council Directive of 19 December 1978 on the progressive implementation of the principle of equal treatment for men and women in matters of social security (79/7/EEC)[4]

The Council of the European Communities,

HAVING REGARD to the Treaty establishing the European Economic Community, and in particular Art. 235 thereof,

HAVING REGARD to the proposal from the Commission,

HAVING REGARD to the opinion of the European Parliament,

HAVING REGARD to the opinion of the Economic and Social Committee,

Whereas Art. 1(2) of Council Directive 76/207/EEC of 9 February 1976 on the implementation of the principle of equal treatment for men and women as regards access to employment, vocational training and promotion, and working conditions provides that, with a view to ensuring the progressive implementation of the principle of equal treatment in matters of social security, the Council, acting

---

[4] OJ 1979 L 6/24.

on a proposal from the Commission, will adopt provisions defining its substance, its scope and the arrangements for its application; whereas the Treaty does not confer the specific powers required for this purpose;

Whereas the principle of equal treatment in matters of social security should be implemented in the first place in the statutory schemes which provide protection against the risks of sickness, invalidity, old age, accidents at work, occupational diseases and unemployment, and in social assistance in so far as it is intended to supplement or replace the above-mentioned schemes;

Whereas the implementation of the principle of equal treatment in matters of social security does not prejudice the provisions relating to the protection of women on the ground of maternity; whereas, in this respect, Member States may adopt specific provisions for women to remove existing instances of unequal treatment,

HAS ADOPTED this Directive:

Article 1   The purpose of this Directive is the progressive implementation, in the field of social security and other elements of social protection provided for in Art. 3, of the principle of equal treatment for men and women in matters of social security, hereinafter referred to as 'the principle of equal treatment'.

Article 2   This Directive shall apply to the working population—including self-employed persons, workers and self-employed persons whose activity is interrupted by illness, accident or involuntary unemployment and persons seeking employment—and to retired or invalided workers and self-employed persons.

Article 3   1. This Directive shall apply to:
(a) statutory schemes which provide protection against the following risks:
  — sickness,
  — invalidity,
  — old age,
  — accidents at work and occupational diseases,
  — unemployment;
(b) social assistance, in so far as it is intended to supplement or replace the schemes referred to in (a).

2. This Directive shall not apply to the provisions concerning survivors' benefits nor to those concerning family benefits, except in the case of family benefits granted by way of increases of benefits due in respect of the risks referred to in paragraph 1(a).

3. With a view to ensuring implementation of the principle of equal treatment in occupational schemes, the Council, acting on a proposal from the Commission, will adopt provisions defining its substance, its scope and the arrangements for its application.

Article 4   1. The principle of equal treatment means that there shall be no discrimination whatsoever on ground of sex either directly, or indirectly by reference in particular to marital or family status, in particular as concerns:
  — the scope of the schemes and the conditions of access thereto,

— the obligation to contribute and the calculation of contributions,
— the calculation of benefits including increases due in respect of a spouse and for dependants and the conditions governing the duration and retention of entitlement to benefits.

2. The principle of equal treatment shall be without prejudice to the provisions relating to the protection of women on the grounds of maternity.

Article 5   Member States shall take the measures necessary to ensure that any laws, regulations and administrative provisions contrary to the principle of equal treatment are abolished.

Article 6   Member States shall introduce into their national legal systems such measures as are necessary to enable all persons who consider themselves wronged by failure to apply the principle of equal treatment to pursue their claims by judicial process, possibly after recourse to other competent authorities.

Article 7   1. This Directive shall be without prejudice to the right of Member States to exclude from its scope:
(a) the determination of pensionable age for the purposes of granting old-age and retirement pensions and the possible consequences thereof for other benefits;
(b) advantages in respect of old-age pension schemes granted to persons who have brought up children; the acquisition of benefit entitlements following periods of interruption of employment due to the bringing up of children;
(c) the granting of old-age or invalidity benefit entitlements by virtue of the derived entitlements of a wife;
(d) the granting of increases of long-term invalidity, old-age, accidents at work and occupational disease benefits for a dependent wife;
(e) the consequences of the exercise, before the adoption of this Directive, of a right of option not to acquire rights or incur obligations under a statutory scheme.

2. Member States shall periodically examine matters excluded under paragraph 1 in order to ascertain, in the light of social developments in the matter concerned, whether there is justification for maintaining the exclusions concerned.

Article 8   1. Member States shall bring into force the laws, regulations and administrative provisions necessary to comply with this Directive within six years of its notification. They shall immediately inform the Commission thereof.

2. Member States shall communicate to the Commission the text of laws, regulations and administrative provisions which they adopt in the field covered by this Directive, including measures adopted pursuant to Art. 7(2).

They shall inform the Commission of their reasons for maintaining any existing provisions on the matters referred to in Art. 7(1) and of the possibilities for reviewing them at a later date.

Article 9   Within seven years of notification of this Directive, Member States shall forward all information necessary to the Commission to enable it to draw up a report on the application of this Directive for submission to the Council and to propose such further measures as may be required for the implementation of the principle of equal treatment.

[final provisions omitted]

Council Directive of 24 July 1986 on the implementation of the principle of equal treatment for men and women in occupational social security schemes (86/378/EEC)[5]

The Council of the European Communities,

HAVING REGARD to the Treaty establishing the European Economic Community, and in particular Arts. 100 and 235 thereof,

[recitals omitted]

Whereas the Treaty provides that each Member State shall ensure the application of the principle that men and women should receive equal pay for equal work; whereas 'pay' should be taken to mean the ordinary basic or minimum wage or salary and any other consideration, whether in cash or in kind, which the worker receives, directly or indirectly, from his employer in respect of his employment;

Whereas, although the principle of equal pay does indeed apply directly in cases where discrimination can be determined solely on the basis of the criteria of equal treatment and equal pay, there are also situations in which implementation of this principle implies the adoption of additional measures which more clearly define its scope;

Whereas Art. 1(2) of Council Directive 76/207/EEC of 9 February 1976 on the implementation of the principle of equal treatment for men and women as regards access to employment, vocational training and promotion, and working conditions provides that, with a view to ensuring the progressive implementation of the principle of equal treatment in matters of social security, the Council, acting on a proposal from the Commission, will adopt provisions defining its substance, its scope and the arrangements for its application; whereas the Council adopted to this end Directive 79/7/EEC of 19 December 1978 on the progressive implementation of the principle of equal treatment for men and women in matters of social security;

---

[5] OJ 1986 L 225/40, as amended by Directive 96/97/EC, OJ 1997 L 46/20. Article 2 of the latter directive provides: '1. Any measure implementing this Directive, as regards paid workers, must cover all benefits derived from periods of employment subsequent to 17 May 1990 and shall apply retroactively to that date, without prejudice to workers or those claiming under them who have, before that date, initiated legal proceedings or raised an equivalent claim under national law. In that event, the implementation measures must apply retroactively to 8 April 1976 and must cover all the benefits derived from periods of employment after that date. For Member States which acceded to the Community after 8 April 1976, that date shall be replaced by the date on which Article 119 of the Treaty became applicable on their territory. 2. The second sentence of paragraph 1 shall not prevent national rules relating to time limits for bringing actions under national law from being relied on against workers or those claiming under them who initiated legal proceedings or raise an equivalent claim under national law before 17 May 1990, provided that they are not less favourable for that type of action than for similar actions of a domestic nature and that they do not render the exercise of Community law impossible in practice. 3. For Member States whose accession took place after 17 May 1990 and who were on 1 January 1994 Contracting Parties to the Agreement on the European Economic Area, the date of 17 May 1990 in paragraph 1 and 2 of this Directive is replaced by 1 January 1994'.

Whereas Art. 3(3) of Directive 79/7/EEC provides that, with a view to ensuring implementation of the principle of equal treatment in occupational schemes, the Council, acting on a proposal from the Commission, will adopt provisions defining its substance, its scope and the arrangements for its application;

Whereas the principle of equal treatment should be implemented in occupational social security schemes which provide protection against the risks specified in Art. 3(1) of Directive 79/7/EEC as well as those which provide employees with any other consideration in cash or in kind within the meaning of the Treaty;

Whereas implementation of the principle of equal treatment does not prejudice the provisions relating to the protection of women by reason of maternity,

HAS ADOPTED this Directive:

Article 1   The object of this Directive is to implement, in occupational social security schemes, the principle of equal treatment for men and women, hereinafter referred to as 'the principle of equal treatment'.

Article 2   1. 'Occupational social security schemes' means schemes not governed by Directive 79/7/EEC whose purpose is to provide workers, whether employees or self-employed, in an undertaking or group of undertakings, area of economic activity, occupational sector or group of sectors with benefits intended to supplement the benefits provided by statutory social security schemes or to replace them, whether membership of such schemes is compulsory or optional.

2. This Directive does not apply to:
(a) individual contracts for self-employed workers;
(b) schemes for self-employed workers having only one member;
(c) insurance contracts to which the employer is not a party, in the case of salaried workers;
(d) optional provisions of occupational schemes offered to participants individually to guarantee them:
  — either additional benefits, or
  — a choice of date on which the normal benefits for self-employed workers will start, or a choice between several benefits;

(e) occupational schemes in so far as benefits are financed by contributions paid by workers on a voluntary basis.

3. This Directive does not preclude an employer granting to persons who have already reached the retirement age for the purposes of granting a pension by virtue of an occupational scheme, but who have not yet reached the retirement age for the purposes of granting a statutory retirement pension, a pension supplement, the aim of which is to make equal or more nearly equal the overall amount of benefit paid to these persons in relation to the amount paid to persons of the other sex in the same situation who have already reached the statutory retirement age, until the persons benefiting from the supplement reach the statutory retirement age.'

Article 3   This Directive shall apply to members of the working population, including self-employed persons, persons whose activity is interrupted by illness, maternity, accident or involuntary unemployment and persons seeking employment, to retired and disabled workers and to those claiming under them, in accordance with national law and/or practice.

Article 4   This Directive shall apply to:

(a) occupational schemes which provide protection against the following risks:

—   sickness,
—   invalidity,
—   old age, including early retirement,
—   industrial accidents and occupational diseases,
—   unemployment;

(b) occupational schemes which provide for other social benefits, in cash or in kind, and in particular survivors' benefits and family allowances, if such benefits are accorded to employed persons and thus constitute a consideration paid by the employer to the worker by reason of the latter's employment.

Article 5   1. Under the conditions laid down in the following provisions, the principle of equal treatment implies that there shall be no discrimination on the basis of sex, either directly or indirectly, by reference in particular to marital or family status, especially as regards:

—   the scope of the schemes and the conditions of access to them;
—   the obligation to contribute and the calculation of contributions;
—   the calculation of benefits, including supplementary benefits due in respect of a spouse or dependants, and the conditions governing the duration and retention of entitlement to benefits.

2. The principle of equal treatment shall not prejudice the provisions relating to the protection of women by reason of maternity.

Article 6   1. Provisions contrary to the principle of equal treatment shall include those based on sex, either directly or indirectly, in particular by reference to marital or family status, for:

(a) determining the persons who may participate in an occupational scheme;
(b) fixing the compulsory or optional nature of participation in an occupational scheme;
(c) laying down different rules as regards the age of entry into the scheme or the minimum period of employment or membership of the scheme required to obtain the benefits thereof;
(d) laying down different rules, except as provided for in points (h) and (i), for the reimbursement of contributions when a worker leaves a scheme without having fulfilled the conditions guaranteeing a deferred right to long-term benefits;
(e) setting different conditions for the granting of benefits or restricting such benefits to workers of one or other of the sexes;
(f) fixing different retirement ages;
(g) suspending the retention or acquisition of rights during periods of maternity leave or leave for family reasons which are granted by law or agreement and are paid by the employer;
(h) setting different levels of benefit, except in so far as may be necessary to take account of actuarial calculation factors which differ according to sex in the case of defined-contribution schemes.

In the case of funded defined-benefit schemes, certain elements (examples of which are annexed) may be unequal where the inequality of the amounts results from the effects of the use of actuarial factors differing according to sex at the time when the scheme's funding is implemented;

(i) setting different levels for workers' contributions;

setting different levels for employers' contributions, except:

— in the case of defined-contribution schemes if the aim is to equalize the amount of the final benefits or to make them more nearly equal for both sexes,

— in the case of funded defined-benefit schemes where the employer's contributions are intended to ensure the adequacy of the funds necessary to cover the cost of the benefits defined,

(j) laying down different standards or standards applicable only to workers of a specified sex, except as provided for in points (h) and (i), as regards the guarantee or retention of entitlement to deferred benefits when a worker leaves a scheme.

2. Where the granting of benefits within the scope of this Directive is left to the discretion of the scheme's management bodies, the latter must comply with the principle of equal treatment

Article 7   Member States shall take all necessary steps to ensure that:

(a) provisions contrary to the principle of equal treatment in legally compulsory collective agreements, staff rules of undertakings or any other arrangements relating to occupational schemes are null and void, or may be declared null and void or amended;

(b) schemes containing such provisions may not be approved or extended by administrative measures.

Article 8   1. Member States shall take the necessary steps to ensure that the provisions of occupational schemes for self-employed workers contrary to the principle of equal treatment are revised with effect from 1 January 1993 at the latest.

2. This Directive shall not preclude rights and obligations relating to a period of membership of an occupational scheme for self-employed workers prior to revision of that scheme from remaining subject to the provisions of the scheme in force during that period.

Article 9   As regards schemes for self-employed workers, Member States may defer compulsory application of the principle of equal treatment with regard to:

(a) determination of pensionable age for the granting of old-age or retirement pensions, and the possible implications for other benefits:

— either until the date on which such equality is achieved in statutory schemes,

— or, at the latest, until such equality is prescribed by a directive;

(b) survivors' pensions until Community law establishes the principle of equal treatment in statutory social security schemes in that regard;

(c) the application of the first subparagraph of point (i) of Article 6(1) to take account of the different actuarial calculation factors, at the latest until 1 January 1999

Article 9a   Where men and women may claim a flexible pensionable age under the same conditions, this shall not be deemed to be incompatible with this Directive.

Article 10   Member States shall introduce into their national legal systems such measures as are necessary to enable all persons who consider themselves injured by failure to apply the principle of equal treatment to pursue their claims before the courts, possibly after bringing the matters before other competent authorities.

Article 11   Member States shall take all the necessary steps to protect workers against dismissal where this constitutes a response on the part of the employer to a complaint made at undertaking level or to the institution of legal proceedings aimed at enforcing compliance with the principle of equal treatment.

[final provisions omitted]

ANNEX

Examples of elements which may be unequal, in respect of funded defined-benefit schemes, as referred to in Article 6(h):
— conversion into a capital sum of part of a periodic pension,
— transfer of pension rights,
— a reversionary pension payable to a dependant in return for the surrender of part of a pension,
— a reduced pension where the worker opts to take early retirement.

Council Directive of 11 December 1986 on the application of the principle of equal treatment between men and women engaged in an activity, including agriculture, in a self-employed capacity, and on the protection of self-employed women during pregnancy and motherhood (86/613/EEC)[6]

The Council of the European Communities,

HAVING REGARD to the Treaty establishing the European Economic Community, and in particular Arts. 100 and 235 thereof,

[recitals omitted]

HAS ADOPTED this Directive:

SECTION I. AIMS AND SCOPE

Article 1   The purpose of this Directive is to ensure, in accordance with the following provisions, application in the Member States of the principle of equal treatment as between men and women engaged in an activity in a self-employed capacity, or contributing to the pursuit of such an activity, as regards those aspects not covered by Directives 76/207/EEC and 79/7/EEC.

---

[6] OJ 1986 L 359/56.

Article 2   This Directive covers:

(a) self-employed workers, i.e. all persons pursuing a gainful activity for their own account, under the conditions laid down by national law, including farmers and members of the liberal professions;

(b) their spouses, not being employees or partners, where they habitually, under the conditions laid down by national law, participate in the activities of the self-employed worker and perform the same tasks or ancillary tasks.

Article 3   For the purposes of this Directive the principle of equal treatment implies the absence of all discrimination on grounds of sex, either directly or indirectly, by reference in particular to marital or family status.

SECTION II. EQUAL TREATMENT BETWEEN SELF-EMPLOYED MALE AND FEMALE WORKERS—POSITION OF THE SPOUSES WITHOUT PROFESSIONAL STATUS OF SELF-EMPLOYED WORKERS—PROTECTION OF SELF-EMPLOYED WORKERS OR WIVES OF SELF-EMPLOYED WORKERS DURING PREGNANCY AND MOTHERHOOD

Article 4   As regards self-employed persons, Member States shall take the measures necessary to ensure the elimination of all provisions which are contrary to the principle of equal treatment as defined in Directive 76/207/EEC, especially in respect of the establishment, equipment or extension of a business or the launching or extension of any other form of self-employed activity including financial facilities.

Article 5   Without prejudice to the specific conditions for access to certain activities which apply equally to both sexes, Member States shall take the measures necessary to ensure that the conditions for the formation of a company between spouses are not more restrictive than the conditions for the formation of a company between unmarried persons.

Article 6   Where a contributory social security system for self-employed workers exists in a Member State, that Member State shall take the necessary measures to enable the spouses referred to in Art. 2(b) who are not protected under the self-employed worker's social security scheme to join a contributory social security scheme voluntarily.

Article 7   Member States shall undertake to examine under what conditions recognition of the work of the spouses referred to in Art. 2(b) may be encouraged and, in the light of such examination, consider any appropriate steps for encouraging such recognition.

Article 8   Member States shall undertake to examine whether, and under what conditions, female self-employed workers and the wives of self-employed workers may, during interruptions in their occupational activity owing to pregnancy or motherhood,

— have access to services supplying temporary replacements or existing national social services, or

— be entitled to cash benefits under a social security scheme or under any other public social protection system.

Section III. General and Final Provisions

Article 9 Member States shall introduce into their national legal systems such measures as are necessary to enable all persons who consider themselves wronged by failure to apply the principle of equal treatment in self-employed activities to pursue their claims by judicial process, possibly after recourse to other competent authorities.

Article 10 Member States shall ensure that the measures adopted pursuant to this Directive, together with the relevant provisions already in force, are brought to the attention of bodies representing self-employed workers and vocational training centres.

Article 11 The Council shall review this Directive, on a proposal from the Commission, before 1 July 1993.

[final provisions omitted]

Council Directive of 15 December 1997 on the burden of proof in cases of discrimination based on sex (97/80/EC)[7]

The Council of the European Union,

[recitals omitted]

(1) Whereas, on the basis of the Protocol on social policy annexed to the Treaty, the Member States, with the exception of the United Kingdom of Great Britain and Northern Ireland (hereinafter called 'the Member States'), wishing to implement the 1989 Social Charter, have concluded an Agreement on social policy;

(2) Whereas the Community Charter of the Fundamental Social Rights of Workers recognizes the importance of combating every form of discrimination, including discrimination on grounds of sex, colour, race, opinions and beliefs;

(3) Whereas paragraph 16 of the Community Charter of the Fundamental Social Rights of Workers on equal treatment for men and women, provides, inter alia, that 'action should be intensified to ensure the implementation of the principle of equality for men and women as regards, in particular, access to employment, remuneration, working conditions, social protection, education, vocational training and career development';

(4) Whereas, in accordance with Article 3(2) of the Agreement on social policy, the Commission has consulted management and labour at Community level on the possible direction of Community action on the burden of proof in cases of discrimination based on sex;

(5) Whereas the Commission, considering Community action advisable after such consultation, once again consulted management and labour on the content of the proposal contemplated in accordance with Article 3(3) of the same Agreement; whereas the latter have sent their opinions to the Commission;

---

[7] Extended to the United Kingdom, and amended, by Directive 98/52/EC, OJ 1998 L 205/66. The latter directive is based on Article 100 EC.

(6) Whereas, after the second round of consultation, neither management nor labour have informed the Commission of their wish to initiate the process—possibly leading to an agreement—provided for in Article 4 of the same Agreement;

(7) Whereas, in accordance with Article 1 of the Agreement, the Community and the Member States have set themselves the objective, inter alia, of improving living and working conditions; whereas effective implementation of the principle of equal treatment for men and women would contribute to the achievement of that aim;

(8) Whereas the principle of equal treatment was stated in Article 119 of the Treaty, in Council Directive 75/117/EEC of 10 February 1975 on the approximation of the laws of the Member States relating to the application of the principle of equal pay for men and women and in Council Directive 76/207/EEC of 9 February 1976 on the implementation of the principle of equal treatment for men and women as regards access to employment, vocational training and promotion and working conditions;

(9) Whereas Council Directive 92/85/EEC of 19 October 1992 on the introduction of measures to encourage improvements in the safety and health at work of pregnant workers and workers who have recently given birth or are breastfeeding[8] also contributes to the effective implementation of the principle of equal treatment for men and women; whereas that Directive should not work to the detriment of the aforementioned Directives on equal treatment; whereas, therefore, female workers covered by that Directive should likewise benefit from the adaptation of the rules on the burden of proof;

(10) Whereas Council Directive 96/34/EC of 3 June 1996 on the framework agreement on parental leave concluded by UNICE, CEEP and the ETUC,[9] is also based on the principle of equal treatment for men and women;

(11) Whereas the references to 'judicial process' and 'court' cover mechanisms by means of which disputes may be submitted for examination and decision to independent bodies which may hand down decisions that are binding on the parties to those disputes;

(12) Whereas the expression 'out-of-court procedures' means in particular procedures such as conciliation and mediation;

(13) Whereas the appreciation of the facts from which it may be presumed that there has been direct or indirect discrimination is a matter for national judicial or other competent bodies, in accordance with national law or practice;

(14) Whereas it is for the Member States to introduce, at any appropriate stage of the proceedings, rules of evidence which are more favourable to plaintiffs;

(15) Whereas it is necessary to take account of the specific features of certain Member States' legal systems, inter alia where an inference of discrimination is drawn if the respondent fails to produce evidence that satisfies the court or other competent authority that there has been no breach of the principle of equal treatment;

(16) Whereas Member States need not apply the rules on the burden of proof to proceedings in which it is for the court or other competent body to investigate the facts of the case; whereas the procedures thus referred to are those in which the

[8] OJ 1992 L 348/1.   [9] OJ 1996 L 145/4.

plaintiff is not required to prove the facts, which it is for the court or competent body to investigate;

(17) Whereas plaintiffs could be deprived of any effective means of enforcing the principle of equal treatment before the national courts if the effect of introducing evidence of an apparent discrimination were not to impose upon the respondent the burden of proving that his practice is not in fact discriminatory;

(18) Whereas the Court of Justice of the European Communities has therefore held that the rules on the burden of proof must be adapted when there is a prima facie case of discrimination and that, for the principle of equal treatment to be applied effectively, the burden of proof must shift back to the respondent when evidence of such discrimination is brought;

(19) Whereas it is all the more difficult to prove discrimination when it is indirect; whereas it is therefore important to define indirect discrimination;

(20) Whereas the aim of adequately adapting the rules on the burden of proof has not been achieved satisfactorily in all Member States and, in accordance with the principle of subsidiarity stated in Article 3b of the Treaty and with that of proportionality, that aim must be attained at Community level; whereas this Directive confines itself to the minimum action required and does not go beyond what is necessary for that purpose,

HAS ADOPTED this Directive:

Article 1 Aim The aim of this Directive shall be to ensure that the measures taken by the Member States to implement the principle of equal treatment are made more effective, in order to enable all persons who consider themselves wronged because the principle of equal treatment has not been applied to them to have their rights asserted by judicial process after possible recourse to other competent bodies.

Article 2 Definitions 1. For the purposes of this Directive, the principle of equal treatment shall mean that there shall be no discrimination whatsoever based on sex, either directly or indirectly.

2. For purposes of the principle of equal treatment referred to in paragraph 1, indirect discrimination shall exist where an apparently neutral provision, criterion or practice disadvantages a substantially higher proportion of the members of one sex unless that provision, criterion or practice is appropriate and necessary and can be justified by objective factors unrelated to sex.

Article 3 Scope 1. This Directive shall apply to:
(a) the situations covered by Article 119 of the Treaty and by Directives 75/117/EEC, 76/207/EEC and, insofar as discrimination based on sex is concerned, 92/85/EEC and 96/34/EC;
(b) any civil or administrative procedure concerning the public or private sector which provides for means of redress under national law pursuant to the measures referred to in (a) with the exception of out-of-court procedures of a voluntary nature or provided for in national law.

2. This Directive shall not apply to criminal procedures, unless otherwise provided by the Member States.

Article 4   Burden of proof   1. Member States shall take such measures as are necessary, in accordance with their national judicial systems, to ensure that, when persons who consider themselves wronged because the principle of equal treatment has not been applied to them establish, before a court or other competent authority, facts from which it may be presumed that there has been direct or indirect discrimination, it shall be for the respondent to prove that there has been no breach of the principle of equal treatment.

2. This Directive shall not prevent Member States from introducing rules of evidence which are more favourable to plaintiffs.

3. Member States need not apply paragraph 1 to proceedings in which it is for the court or competent body to investigate the facts of the case.

Article 5   Information   Member States shall ensure that measures taken pursuant to this Directive, together with the provisions already in force, are brought to the attention of all the persons concerned by all appropriate means.

Article 6   Non-regression   Implementation of this Directive shall under no circumstances be sufficient grounds for a reduction in the general level of protection of workers in the areas to which it applies, without prejudice to the Member States' right to respond to changes in the situation by introducing laws, regulations and administrative provisions which differ from those in force on the notification of this Directive, provided that the minimum requirements of this Directive are complied with.

Article 7   Implementation   The Member States shall bring into force the laws, regulations and administrative provisions necessary for them to comply with this Directive by 1 January 2001. They shall immediately inform the Commission thereof.

As regards the United Kingdom of Great Britain and Northern Ireland, the date of 1 January 2001 in paragraph 1 shall be replaced by 22 July 2001.

When the Member States adopt those measures they shall contain a reference to this Directive or shall be accompanied by such a reference on the occasion of their official publication. The methods of making such references shall be laid down by the Member States.

The Member States shall communicate to the Commission, within two years of the entry into force of this Directive, all the information necessary for the Commission to draw up a report to the European Parliament and the Council on the application of this Directive.

[final provisions omitted]

Council Directive of 14 February 1977 on the approximation of the laws of the Member States relating to the safeguarding of employees' rights in the event of transfers of undertakings, businesses or parts of undertakings or businesses (77/187/EEC)[10]

The Council of the European Communities,

HAVING REGARD to the Treaty establishing the European Economic Community, and in particular Art. 100 thereof,

[recitals omitted]

Whereas economic trends are bringing in their wake, at both national and Community level, changes in the structure of undertakings, through transfers of undertakings, businesses or parts of businesses to other employers as a result of legal transfers or mergers;

Whereas it is necessary to provide for the protection of employees in the event of a change of employer, in particular, to ensure that their rights are safeguarded;

Whereas differences still remain in the Member States as regards the extent of the protection of employees in this respect and these differences should be reduced;

Whereas these differences can have a direct effect on the functioning of the common market;

Whereas it is therefore necessary to promote the approximation of laws in this field while maintaining the improvement described in Art. 117 of the Treaty,

HAS ADOPTED this Directive:

SECTION I. SCOPE AND DEFINITIONS

Article 1   1. (a) This Directive shall apply to any transfer of an undertaking, business, or part of an undertaking or business to another employer as a result of a legal transfer or merger.
(b) Subject to subparagraph (a) and the following provisions of this Article, there is a transfer within the meaning of this Directive where there is a transfer of an economic entity which retains its identity, meaning an organised grouping of resources which has the objective of pursuing an economic activity, whether or not that activity is central or ancillary.
(c) This Directive shall apply to public and private undertakings engaged in economic activities whether or not they are operating for gain. An administrative reorganisation of public administrative authorities, or the transfer of administrative functions between public administrative authorities, is not a transfer within the meaning of this Directive.

2. This Directive shall apply where and insofar as the undertaking, business or part of the undertaking or business to be transferred is situated within the territorial scope of the Treaty.

---

[10] OJ 1977 L 61/26, as amended by Directive 98/50/EC, OJ 1998 L 201/88. Text as amended to be implemented in the Member States by 17 July 2001. For unamended text see *Basic Community Laws*, 6th edition, p. 631 et seq.

3. This Directive shall not apply to sea-going vessels.

Article 2   1. For the purposes of this Directive:
(a) 'transferor' shall mean any natural or legal person who, by reason of a transfer within the meaning of Article 1(1), ceases to be the employer in respect of the undertaking, business or part of the undertaking or business;
(b) 'transferee' shall mean any natural or legal person who, by reason of a transfer within the meaning of Article 1(1), becomes the employer in respect of the undertaking, business or part of the undertaking or business;
(c) 'representatives of employees' and related expressions shall mean the representatives of the employees provided for by the laws or practices of the Member States;
(d) 'employee' shall mean any person who, in the Member State concerned, is protected as an employee under national employment law.

2. This Directive shall be without prejudice to national law as regards the definition of contract of employment or employment relationship.

However, Member States shall not exclude from the scope of this Directive contracts of employment or employment relationships solely because:
(a) of the number of working hours performed or to be performed;
(b) they are employment relationships governed by a fixed-duration contract of employment within the meaning of Article 1(1) of Council Directive 91/383/EEC of 25 June 1991 supplementing the measures to encourage improvements in the safety and health at work of workers with a fixed-duration employment relationship or a temporary employment relationship;[11] or
(c) they are temporary employment relationships within the meaning of Article 1(2) of Directive 91/383/EEC, and the undertaking, business or part of the undertaking or business transferred is, or is part of, the temporary employment business which is the employer.

Section II. Safeguarding of Employees' Rights

Article 3   1. The transferor's rights and obligations arising from a contract of employment or from an employment relationship existing on the date of a transfer shall, by reason of such transfer, be transferred to the transferee.

Member States may provide that, after the date of transfer, the transferor and the transferee shall be jointly and severally liable in respect of obligations which arose before the date of transfer from a contract of employment or an employment relationship existing on the date of the transfer.

2. Member States may adopt appropriate measures to ensure that the transferor notifies the transferee of all the rights and obligations which will be transferred to the transferee under this Article, so far as those rights and obligations are or ought to have been known to the transferor at the time of the transfer. A failure by the transferor to notify the transferee of any such right or obligation shall not affect the transfer of that right or obligation and the rights of any employees against the transferee and/or transferor in respect of that right or obligation.

---

[11] OJ 1991 L 206/19.

3. Following the transfer, the transferee shall continue to observe the terms and conditions agreed in any collective agreement on the same terms applicable to the transferor under that agreement, until the date of termination or expiry of the collective agreement or the entry into force or application of another collective agreement.

Member States may limit the period for observing such terms and conditions with the proviso that it shall not be less than one year.

4. (a) Unless Member States provide otherwise, paragraphs 1 and 3 shall not apply in relation to employees' rights to old-age, invalidity or survivors' benefits under supplementary company or inter-company pension schemes outside the statutory social security schemes in Member States.

    (b) Even where they do not provide in accordance with subparagraph (a) that paragraphs 1 and 3 apply in relation to such rights, Member States shall adopt the measures necessary to protect the interests of employees and of persons no longer employed in the transferor's business at the time of the transfer in respect of rights conferring on them immediate or prospective entitlement to old age benefits, including survivors' benefits, under supplementary schemes referred to in subparagraph (a).

Article 4   1. The transfer of the undertaking, business or part of the undertaking or business shall not in itself constitute grounds for dismissal by the transferor or the transferee. This provision shall not stand in the way of dismissals that may take place for economic, technical or organisational reasons entailing changes in the workforce.

Member States may provide that the first subparagraph shall not apply to certain specific categories of employees who are not covered by the laws or practice of the Member States in respect of protection against dismissal.

2. If the contract of employment or the employment relationship is terminated because the transfer involves a substantial change in working conditions to the detriment of the employee, the employer shall be regarded as having been responsible for termination of the contract of employment or of the employment relationship.

Article 4a   1. Unless Member States provide otherwise, Articles 3 and 4 shall not apply to any transfer of an undertaking, business or part of an undertaking or business where the transferor is the subject of bankruptcy proceedings or any analogous insolvency proceedings which have been instituted with a view to the liquidation of the assets of the transferor and are under the supervision of a competent public authority (which may be an insolvency practitioner authorised by a competent public authority).

2. Where Articles 3 and 4 apply to a transfer during insolvency proceedings which have been opened in relation to a transferor (whether or not those proceedings have been instituted with a view to the liquidation of the assets of the transferor) and provided that such proceedings are under the supervision of a competent public authority (which may be an insolvency practitioner determined by national law) a Member State may provide that:

(a) notwithstanding Article 3(1), the transferor's debts arising from any contracts of employment or employment relationships and payable before the transfer or before the opening of the insolvency proceedings shall not be transferred to the transferee, provided that such proceedings give rise, under the law of that Member State, to protection at least equivalent to that provided for in situations covered by Council Directive 80/987/EEC of 20 October 1980 on the approximation of the laws of the Member States relating to the protection of employees in the event of the insolvency of their employer,[12]

and, or alternatively, that

(b) the transferee, transferor, or person or persons exercising the transferor's functions, on the one hand, and the representatives of the employees on the other hand may agree alterations, insofar as current law or practice permits, to the employees' terms and conditions of employment designed to safeguard employment opportunities by ensuring the survival of the undertaking, business or part of the undertaking or business.

3. A Member State may apply paragraph 2(b) to any transfers where the transferor is in a situation of serious economic crisis, as defined by national law, provided that the situation is declared by a competent public authority and open to judicial supervision, on condition that such provisions already exist in national law by 17 July 1998.

The Commission shall present a report on the effects of this provision before 17 July 2003 and shall submit any appropriate proposals to the Council.

4. Member States shall take appropriate measures with a view to preventing misuse of insolvency proceedings in such a way as to deprive employees of the rights provided for in this Directive.

Article 5   1. If the undertaking, business or part of an undertaking or business preserves its autonomy, the status and function of the representatives or of the representation of the employees affected by the transfer shall be preserved on the same terms and subject to the same conditions as existed before the date of the transfer by virtue of law, regulation, administrative provision or agreement, provided that the conditions necessary for the constitution of the employees' representation are fulfilled.

The first subparagraph shall not apply if, under the laws, regulations, administrative provisions or practice in the Member States, or by agreement with the representatives of the employees, the conditions necessary for the reappointment of the representatives of the employees or for the reconstitution of the representation of the employees are fulfilled.

Where the transferor is the subject of bankruptcy proceedings or any analogous insolvency proceedings which have been instituted with a view to the liquidation of the assets of the transferor and are under the supervision of a competent public authority (which may be an insolvency practitioner authorised by a competent public authority), Member States may take the necessary measures to ensure that the transferred employees are properly represented until the new election or designation of representatives of the employees.

If the undertaking, business or part of an undertaking or business does not preserve its autonomy, the Member States shall take the necessary measures to ensure that the employees transferred who were represented before the transfer continue

---

[12] OJ 1980 L 280/23, as last amended by Directive 87/164/EEC, OJ 1987 L 66/11.

to be properly represented during the period necessary for the reconstitution or reappointment of the representation of employees in accordance with national law or practice.

2. If the term of office of the representatives of the employees affected by the transfer expires as a result of the transfer, the representatives shall continue to enjoy the protection provided by the laws, regulations, administrative provisions or practice of the Member States.

Section III. Information and consultation

Article 6   1. The transferor and transferee shall be required to inform the representatives of their respective employees affected by the transfer of the following:

— the date or proposed date of the transfer,
— the reasons for the transfer,
— the legal, economic and social implications of the transfer for the employees,
— any measures envisaged in relation to the employees.

The transferor must give such information to the representatives of his employees in good time before the transfer is carried out.

The transferee must give such information to the representatives of his employees in good time, and in any event before his employees are directly affected by the transfer as regards their conditions of work and employment.

2. Where the transferor or the transferee envisages measures in relation to his employees, he shall consult the representatives of his employees in good time on such measures with a view to reaching an agreement.

3. Member States whose laws, regulations or administrative provisions provide that representatives of the employees may have recourse to an arbitration board to obtain a decision on the measures to be taken in relation to employees may limit the obligations laid down in paragraphs 1 and 2 to cases where the transfer carried out gives rise to a change in the business likely to entail serious disadvantages for a considerable number of the employees.

The information and consultations shall cover at least the measures envisaged in relation to the employees.

The information must be provided and consultations taken place in good time before the change in the business as referred to in the first subparagraph is effected.

4. The obligations laid down in this Article shall apply irrespective of whether the decision resulting in the transfer is taken by the employer or an undertaking controlling the employer.

In considering alleged breaches of the information and consultation requirements laid down by this Directive, the argument that such a breach occurred because the information was not provided by an undertaking controlling the employer shall not be accepted as an excuse.

5. Member States may limit the obligations laid down in paragraphs 1, 2 and 3 to undertakings or businesses which, in terms of the number of employees, meet the conditions for the election or nomination of a collegiate body representing the employees.

6. Member States shall provide that, where there are no representatives of the employees in an undertaking or business through no fault of their own, the employees concerned must be informed in advance of:

— the date or proposed date of the transfer,
— the reason for the transfer,
— the legal, economic and social implications of the transfer for the employees,
— any measures envisaged in relation to the employees.

Section IV. Final provisions

Article 7   This Directive shall not affect the right of Member States to apply or introduce laws, regulations or administrative provisions which are more favourable to employees or to promote or permit collective agreements or agreements between social partners more favourable to employees.

Article 7a   Member States shall introduce into their national legal systems such measures as are necessary to enable all employees and representatives of employees who consider themselves wronged by failure to comply with the obligations arising from this Directive to pursue their claims by judicial process after possible recourse to other competent authorities.

Article 7b   The Commission shall submit to the Council an analysis of the effects of the provisions of this Directive before 17 July 2006. It shall propose any amendment which may seem necessary.

[final provisions omitted]

Council Directive of 23 November 1993 concerning certain aspects of the organization of working time (93/104/EEC)[13]

The Council of the European Communities,

[recitals omitted]

Whereas Article 118a of the Treaty provides that the Council shall adopt, by means of directives, minimum requirements for encouraging improvements, especially in the working environment, to ensure a better level of protection of the safety and health of workers;

[recitals omitted]

Whereas the Community Charter of the Fundamental Social Rights of Workers, adopted at the meeting of the European Council held at Strasbourg on 9 December 1989 by the Heads of State or of Government of 11 Member States, and in particular points 7, first subparagraph, 8 and 19, first subparagraph, thereof, declared that:

'7. The completion of the internal market must lead to an improvement in the living and working conditions of workers in the European Community. This process must result from an approximation of these conditions while the

---
[13] OJ 1993 L 307/18.

improvement is being maintained, as regards in particular the duration and organization of working time and forms of employment other than open-ended contracts, such as fixed-term contracts, part-time working, temporary work and seasonal work.

8. Every worker in the European Community shall have a right to a weekly rest period and to annual paid leave, the duration of which must be progressively harmonized in accordance with national practices.

19. Every worker must enjoy satisfactory health and safety conditions in his working environment. Appropriate measures must be taken in order to achieve further harmonization of conditions in this area while maintaining the improvements made.';

Whereas the improvement of workers' safety, hygiene and health at work is an objective which should not be subordinated to purely economic considerations;

Whereas this Directive is a practical contribution towards creating the social dimension of the internal market;

Whereas laying down minimum requirements with regard to the organization of working time is likely to improve the working conditions of workers in the Community;

Whereas, in order to ensure the safety and health of Community workers, the latter must be granted minimum daily, weekly and annual periods of rest and adequate breaks; whereas it is also necessary in this context to place a maximum limit on weekly working hours;

Whereas account should be taken of the principles of the International Labour Organization with regard to the organization of working time, including those relating to night work;

Whereas, with respect to the weekly rest period, due account should be taken of the diversity of cultural, ethnic, religious and other factors in the Member States; whereas, in particular, it is ultimately for each Member State to decide whether Sunday should be included in the weekly rest period, and if so to what extent;

Whereas research has shown that the human body is more sensitive at night to environmental disturbances and also to certain burdensome forms of work organization and that long periods of night work can be detrimental to the health of workers and can endanger safety at the workplace;

Whereas there is a need to limit the duration of periods of night work, including overtime, and to provide for employers who regularly use night workers to bring this information to the attention of the competent authorities if they so request;

Whereas it is important that night workers should be entitled to a free health assessment prior to their assignment and thereafter at regular intervals and that whenever possible they should be transferred to day work for which they are suited if they suffer from health problems;

Whereas the situation of night and shift workers requires that the level of safety and health protection should be adapted to the nature of their work and that the organization and functioning of protection and prevention services and resources should be efficient;

Whereas specific working conditions may have detrimental effects on the safety and health of workers; whereas the organization of work according to a certain pattern must take account of the general principle of adapting work to the worker;

Whereas, given the specific nature of the work concerned, it may be necessary to adopt separate measures with regard to the organization of working time in certain sectors or activities which are excluded from the scope of this Directive;

Whereas, in view of the question likely to be raised by the organization of working time within an undertaking, it appears desirable to provide for flexibility in the application of certain provisions of this Directive, whilst ensuring compliance with the principles of protecting the safety and health of workers;

Whereas it is necessary to provide that certain provisions may be subject to derogations implemented, according to the case, by the Member States or the two sides of industry; whereas, as a general rule, in the event of a derogation, the workers concerned must be given equivalent compensatory rest periods,

HAS ADOPTED this Directive:

SECTION I. SCOPE AND DEFINITIONS

Article 1 Purpose and scope 1. This Directive lays down minimum safety and health requirements for the organization of working time.

2. This Directive applies to:

(a) minimum periods of daily rest, weekly rest and annual leave, to breaks and maximum weekly working time; and

(b) certain aspects of night work, shift work and patterns of work.

3. This Directive shall apply to all sectors of activity, both public and private, within the meaning of Article 2 of Directive 89/391/EEC,[14] without prejudice to Article 17 of this Directive, with the exception of air, rail, road, sea, inland waterway and lake transport, sea fishing, other work at sea and the activities of doctors in training.

4. The provisions of Directive 89/391/EEC are fully applicable to the matters referred to in paragraph 2, without prejudice to more stringent and/or specific provisions contained in this Directive.

Article 2 Definitions For the purposes of this Directive, the following definitions shall apply:

1. working time shall mean any period during which the worker is working, at the employer's disposal and carrying out his activity or duties, in accordance with national laws and/or practice;

2. rest period shall mean any period which is not working time;

3. night time shall mean any period of not less than seven hours, as defined by national law, and which must include in any case the period between midnight and 5 a.m.;

[14] OJ 1989 L 183/1.

4. night worker shall mean:

(a) on the one hand, any worker, who, during the night time, works at least three hours of his daily working time as a normal course; and

(b) on the other hand, any worker who is likely during night time to work a certain proportion of his annual working time, as defined at the choice of the Member State concerned:

   (i) by national legislation, following consultation with the two sides of industry; or

   (ii) by collective agreements or agreements concluded between the two sides of industry at national or regional level;

5. shift work shall mean any method of organizing work in shifts whereby workers succeed each other at the same work stations according to a certain pattern, including a rotating pattern, and which may be continuous or discontinuous, entailing the need for workers to work at different times over a given period of days or weeks;

6. shift worker shall mean any worker whose work schedule is part of shift work.

SECTION II. MINIMUM REST PERIODS—OTHER ASPECTS OF THE ORGANIZATION OF WORKING TIME

Article 3   Daily rest   Member States shall take the measures necessary to ensure that every worker is entitled to a minimum daily rest period of 11 consecutive hours per 24-hour period.

Article 4   Breaks   Member States shall take the measures necessary to ensure that, where the working day is longer than six hours, every worker is entitled to a rest break, the details of which, including duration and the terms on which it is granted, shall be laid down in collective agreements or agreements between the two sides of industry or, failing that, by national legislation.

Article 5   Weekly rest period   Member States shall take the measures necessary to ensure that, per each seven-day period, every worker is entitled to a minimum uninterrupted rest period of 24 hours plus the 11 hours' daily rest referred to in Article 3.

   The minimum rest period referred to in the first subparagraph shall in principle include Sunday.

   If objective, technical or work organization conditions so justify, a minimum rest period of 24 hours may be applied.

Article 6   Maximum weekly working time   Member States shall take the measures necessary to ensure that, in keeping with the need to protect the safety and health of workers:

1. the period of weekly working time is limited by means of laws, regulations or administrative provisions or by collective agreements or agreements between the two sides of industry;

2. the average working time for each seven-day period, including overtime, does not exceed 48 hours.

Article 7   Annual leave   1. Member States shall take the measures necessary to ensure that every worker is entitled to paid annual leave of at least four weeks in accordance with the conditions for entitlement to, and granting of, such leave laid down by national legislation and/or practice.

2. The minimum period of paid annual leave may not be replaced by an allowance in lieu, except where the employment relationship is terminated.

SECTION III. NIGHT WORK—SHIFT WORK—PATTERNS OF WORK

Article 8   Length of night work   Member States shall take the measures necessary to ensure that:

1. normal hours of work for night workers do not exceed an average of eight hours in any 24-hour period;

2. night workers whose work involves special hazards or heavy physical or mental strain do not work more than eight hours in any period of 24 hours during which they perform night work.

   For the purposes of the aforementioned, working involving special hazards or heavy physical or mental strain shall be defined by national legislation and/or practice or by collective agreements or agreements concluded between the two sides of industry, taking account of the specific effects and hazards of night work.

Article 9   Health assessment and transfer of night workers to day work   1. Member States shall take the measures necessary to ensure that:
(a) night workers are entitled to a free health assessment before their assignment and thereafter at regular intervals;
(b) night workers suffering from health problems recognized as being connected with the fact that they perform night work are transferred whenever possible to day work to which they are suited.

2. The free health assessment referred to in paragraph 1(a) must comply with medical confidentiality.

3. The free health assessment referred to in paragraph 1(a) may be conducted within the national health system.

Article 10   Guarantees for night-time working   Member States may make the work of certain categories of night workers subject to certain guarantees, under conditions laid down by national legislation and/or practice, in the case of workers who incur risks to their safety or health linked to night-time working.

Article 11   Notification of regular use of night workers   Member States shall take the measures necessary to ensure that an employer who regularly uses night workers brings this information to the attention of the competent authorities if they so request.

Article 12   Safety and health protection   Member States shall take the measures necessary to ensure that:

1. night workers and shift workers have safety and health protection appropriate to the nature of their work;

2. appropriate protection and prevention services or facilities with regard to the safety and health of night workers and shift workers are equivalent to those applicable to other workers and are available at all times.

Article 13 Pattern of work Member States shall take the measures necessary to ensure that an employer who intends to organize work according to a certain pattern takes account of the general principle of adapting work to the worker, with a view, in particular, to alleviating monotonous work and work at a predetermined work-rate, depending on the type of activity, and of safety and health requirements, especially as regards breaks during working time.

SECTION IV. MISCELLANEOUS PROVISIONS

Article 14 More specific Community provisions The provisions of this Directive shall not apply where other Community instruments contain more specific requirements concerning certain occupations or occupational activities.

Article 15 More favourable provisions This Directive shall not affect Member States' right to apply or introduce laws, regulations or administrative provisions more favourable to the protection of the safety and health of workers or to facilitate or permit the application of collective agreements or agreements concluded between the two sides of industry which are more favourable to the protection of the safety and health of workers.

Article 16 Reference periods Member States may lay down:

1. for the application of Article 5 (weekly rest period), a reference period not exceeding 14 days;

2. for the application of Article 6 (maximum weekly working time), a reference period not exceeding four months.

   The periods of paid annual leave, granted in accordance with Article 7, and the periods of sick leave shall not be included or shall be neutral in the calculation of the average;

3. for the application of Article 8 (length of night work), a reference period defined after consultation of the two sides of industry or by collective agreements or agreements concluded between the two sides of industry at national or regional level.

   If the minimum weekly rest period of 24 hours required by Article 5 falls within that reference period, it shall not be included in the calculation of the average.

Article 17 Derogations 1. With due regard for the general principles of the protection of the safety and health of workers, Member States may derogate from Article 3, 4, 5, 6, 8 or 16 when, on account of the specific characteristics of the activity concerned, the duration of the working time is not measured and/or predetermined or can be determined by the workers themselves, and particularly in the case of:
(a) managing executives or other persons with autonomous decision-taking powers;
(b) family workers; or
(c) workers officiating at religious ceremonies in churches and religious communities.

2. Derogations may be adopted by means of laws, regulations or administrative provisions or by means of collective agreements or agreements between the two sides of industry provided that the workers concerned are afforded equivalent periods of compensatory rest or that, in exceptional cases in which it is not possible, for

objective reasons, to grant such equivalent periods of compensatory rest, the workers concerned are afforded appropriate protection:

2.1. from Articles 3, 4, 5, 8 and 16;

(a) in the case of activities where the worker's place of work and his place of residence are distant from one another or where the worker's different places of work are distant from one another;

(b) in the case of security and surveillance activities requiring a permanent presence in order to protect property and persons, particularly security guards and caretakers or security firms;

(c) in the case of activities involving the need for continuity of service or production, particularly:

(i) services relating to the reception, treatment and/or care provided by hospitals or similar establishments, residential institutions and prisons;

(ii) dock or airport workers;

(iii) press, radio, television, cinematographic production, postal and telecommunications services, ambulance, fire and civil protection services;

(iv) gas, water and electricity production, transmission and distribution, household refuse collection and incineration plants;

(v) industries in which work cannot be interrupted on technical grounds;

(vi) research and development activities;

(vii) agriculture;

(d) where there is a foreseeable surge of activity, particularly in:

(i) agriculture;

(ii) tourism;

(iii) postal services;

2.2. from Articles 3, 4, 5, 8 and 16;

(a) in the circumstances described in Article 5(4) of Directive 89/391/EEC;

(b) in cases of accident or imminent risk of accident;

2.3. from Articles 3 and 5:

(a) in the case of shift work activities, each time the worker changes shift and cannot take daily and/or weekly rest periods between the end of one shift and the start of the next one;

(b) in the case of activities involving periods of work split up over the day, particularly those of cleaning staff.

3. Derogations may be made from Articles 3, 4, 5, 8 and 16 by means of collective agreements or agreements concluded between the two sides of industry at national or regional level or, in conformity with the rules laid down by them, by means of collective agreements or agreements concluded between the two sides of industry at a lower level.

Member States in which there is no statutory system ensuring the conclusion of collective agreements or agreements concluded between the two sides of industry at national or regional level, on the matters covered by this Directive, or those Member States in which there is a specific legislative framework for this purpose and within the limits thereof, may, in accordance with national legislation and/or practice, allow derogations from Articles 3, 4, 5, 8 and 16 by way of collective agreements or agreements concluded between the two sides of industry at the appropriate collective level.

The derogations provided for in the first and second subparagraphs shall be allowed on condition that equivalent compensating rest periods are granted to the workers concerned or, in exceptional cases where it is not possible for objective reasons to grant such periods, the workers concerned are afforded appropriate protection.

Member States may lay down rules:

— for the application of this paragraph by the two sides of industry, and
— for the extension of the provisions of collective agreements or agreements concluded in conformity with this paragraph to other workers in accordance with national legislation and/or practice.

4. The option to derogate from point 2 of Article 16, provided in paragraph 2, points 2.1. and 2.2. and in paragraph 3 of this Article, may not result in the establishment of a reference period exceeding six months.

However, Member States shall have the option, subject to compliance with the general principles relating to the protection of the safety and health of workers, of allowing, for objective or technical reasons or reasons concerning the organization of work, collective agreements or agreements concluded between the two sides of industry to set reference periods in no event exceeding 12 months.

Before the expiry of a period of seven years from the date referred to in Article 18(1)(a), the Council shall, on the basis of a Commission proposal accompanied by an appraisal report, re-examine the provisions of this paragraph and decide what action to take.

Article 18 *Final provisions* 1. (a) Member States shall adopt the laws, regulations and administrative provisions necessary to comply with this Directive by 23 November 1996, or shall ensure by that date that the two sides of industry establish the necessary measures by agreement, with Member States being obliged to take any necessary steps to enable them to guarantee at all times that the provisions laid down by this Directive are fulfilled.

(b) (i) However, a Member State shall have the option not to apply Article 6, while respecting the general principles of the protection of the safety and health of workers, and provided it takes the necessary measures to ensure that:

— no employer requires a worker to work more than 48 hours over a seven-day period, calculated as an average for the reference period referred to in point 2 of Article 16, unless he has first obtained the worker's agreement to perform such work,

— no worker is subjected to any detriment by his employer because he is not willing to give his agreement to perform such work,

— the employer keeps up-to-date records of all workers who carry out such work,

— the records are placed at the disposal of the competent authorities, which may, for reasons connected with the safety and/or health of workers, prohibit or restrict the possibility of exceeding the maximum weekly working hours,

— the employer provides the competent authorities at their request with information on cases in which agreement has been given by workers to perform work exceeding 48 hours over a period of seven days, calculated as an average for the reference period referred to in point 2 of Article 16.

Before the expiry of a period of seven years from the date referred to in (a), the Council shall, on the basis of a Commission proposal accompanied by an appraisal report, re-examine the provisions of this point (i) and decide on what action to take.

(ii) Similarly, Member States shall have the option, as regards the application of Article 7, of making use of a transitional period of not more than three years from the date referred to in (a), provided that during that transitional period:

— every worker receives three weeks' paid annual leave in accordance with the conditions for the entitlement to, and granting of, such leave laid down by national legislation and/or practice, and

— the three-week period of paid annual leave may not be replaced by an allowance in lieu, except where the employment relationship is terminated.

(c) Member states shall forthwith inform the Commission thereof.

2. When Member States adopt the measures referred to in paragraph 1, they shall contain a reference to this Directive or shall be accompanied by such reference on the occasion of their official publication. The methods of making such a reference shall be laid down by the Member states.

3. Without prejudice to the right of Member States to develop, in the light of changing circumstances, different legislative, regulatory or contractual provisions in the field of working time, as long as the minimum requirements provided for in this Directive are complied with, implementation of this Directive shall not constitute valid grounds for reducing the general level of protection afforded to workers.

4. Member States shall communicate to the Commission the texts of the provisions of national law already adopted or being adopted in the field governed by this Directive.

5. Member States shall report to the Commission every five years on the practical implementation of the provisions of this Directive, indicating the viewpoints of the two sides of industry.

The Commission shall inform the European Parliament, the Council, the Economic and Social Committee and the Advisory Committee on Safety, Hygiene and Health Protection at Work thereof.

[*final provisions omitted*]

Community Charter of the Fundamental Social Rights of Workers adopted by the Heads of State or Government of the Member States of the European Community meeting at Strasbourg on 9 December 1989[15]

Whereas, under the terms of Art. 117 of the EEC Treaty, the Member States have agreed on the need to promote improved living and working conditions for workers so as to make possible their harmonisation while the improvement is being maintained;

Whereas following on from the conclusions of the European Councils of Hanover and Rhodes the European Council of Madrid considered that, in the context of the establishment of the single European market, the same importance must be attached to the social aspects as to the economic aspects and whereas, therefore, they must be developed in a balanced manner;

HAVING REGARD to the Resolutions of the European Parliament of 15 March 1989, 14 September 1989 and 22 November 1989, and to the Opinion of the Economic and Social Committee of 22 February 1989;

Whereas the completion of the internal market is the most effective means of creating employment and ensuring maximum well-being in the Community; whereas employment development and creation must be given first priority in the completion of the internal market; whereas it is for the Community to take up the challenges of the future with regard to economic competitiveness, taking into account, in particular, regional imbalances;

Whereas the social consensus contributes to the strengthening of the competitiveness of undertakings, of the economy as a whole and to the creation of employment; whereas in this respect it is an essential condition for ensuring sustained economic development;

Whereas the completion of the internal market must favour the approximation of improvements in living and working conditions, as well as economic and social cohesion within the European Community while avoiding distortions of competition;

Whereas the completion of the internal market must offer improvements in the social field for workers of the European Community, especially in terms of freedom of movement, living and working conditions, health and safety at work, social protection, education and training;

Whereas, in order to ensure equal treatment, it is important to combat every form of discrimination, including discrimination on grounds of sex, colour, race, opinions and beliefs, and whereas, in a spirit of solidarity, it is important to combat social exclusion;

Whereas it is for Member States to guarantee that workers from non-member countries and members of their families who are legally resident in a Member State of the European Community are able to enjoy, as regards their living and working conditions, treatment comparable to that enjoyed by workers who are nationals of the Member State concerned;

[15] Text adopted by the Heads of State or Government of 11 Member States.

Whereas inspiration should be drawn from the Conventions of the International Labour Organisation and from the European Social Charter of the Council of Europe;

Whereas the Treaty, as amended by the Single European Act, contains provisions laying down the powers of the Community relating *inter alia* to the freedom of movement of workers (Arts. 7, 48 to 51), the right of establishment (Arts. 52 to 58), the social field under the conditions laid down in Arts. 117 to 122—in particular as regards the improvement of health and safety in the working environment (Art. 118a), the development of the dialogue between management and labour at European level (Art. 118b), equal pay for men and women for equal work (Art. 119)—the general principles for implementing a common vocational training policy (Art. 128), economic and social cohesion (Art. 130a to 130e) and, more generally, the approximation of legislation (Arts. 100, 100a and 235); whereas the implementation of the Charter must not entail an extension of the Community's powers as defined by the Treaties;

Whereas the aim of the present Charter is on the one hand to consolidate the progress made in the social field, through action by the Member States, the two sides of industry and the Community;

Whereas its aim is on the other hand to declare solemnly that the implementation of the Single European Act must take full account of the social dimension of the Community and that it is necessary in this context to ensure at appropriate levels the development of the social rights of workers of the European Community, especially employed workers and self-employed persons;

Whereas, in accordance with the conclusions of the Madrid European Council, the respective roles of Community rules, national legislation and collective agreements must be clearly established;

Whereas, by virtue of the principle of subsidiarity, responsibility for the initiatives to be taken with regard to the implementation of these social rights lies with the Member States or their constituent parts and, within the limits of its powers, with the European Community; whereas such implementation may take the form of laws, collective agreements or existing practices at the various appropriate levels and whereas it requires in many spheres the active involvement of the two sides of industry;

Whereas the solemn proclamation of fundamental social rights at European Community level may not, when implemented, provide grounds for any retrogression compared with the situation currently existing in each Member State,

HAVE ADOPTED the following declaration constituting the 'Community charter of the fundamental social rights of workers':

TITLE I. FUNDAMENTAL SOCIAL RIGHTS OF WORKERS

Freedom of movement

1. Every worker of the European Community shall have the right to freedom of movement throughout the territory of the Community, subject to restrictions justified on grounds of public order, public safety or public health.

2. The right to freedom of movement shall enable any worker to engage in any occupation or profession in the Community in accordance with the principles of equal treatment as regards access to employment, working conditions and social protection in the host country.

3. The right of freedom of movement shall also imply:

— harmonisation of conditions of residence in all Member States, particularly those concerning family reunification;
— elimination of obstacles arising from the non-recognition of diplomas or equivalent occupational qualifications;
— improvement of the living and working conditions of frontier workers.

Employment and remuneration

4. Every individual shall be free to choose and engage in an occupation according to the regulations governing each occupation.

5. All employment shall be fairly remunerated.
   To this end, in accordance with arrangements applying in each country:

— workers shall be assured of an equitable wage, i.e. a wage sufficient to enable them to have a decent standard of living;
— workers subject to terms of employment other than an open-ended full-time contract shall benefit from an equitable reference wage;
— wages may be withheld, seized or transferred only in accordance with national law; such provisions should entail measures enabling the worker concerned to continue to enjoy the necessary means of subsistence for him or herself and his or her family.

6. Every individual must be able to have access to public placement services free of charge.

Improvement of living and working conditions

7. The completion of the internal market must lead to an improvement in the living and working conditions of workers in the European Community. This process must result from an approximation of these conditions while the improvement is being maintained, as regards in particular the duration and organisation of working time and forms of employment other than open-ended contracts, such as fixed-term contracts, part-time working, temporary work and seasonal work.
   The improvement must cover, where necessary, the development of certain aspects of employment regulations such as procedures for collective redundancies and those regarding bankruptcies.

8. Every worker of the European Community shall have a right to a weekly rest period and to annual paid leave, the duration of which must be progressively harmonised in accordance with national practices.

9. The conditions of employment of every worker of the European Community shall be stipulated in laws, a collective agreement or a contract of employment, according to arrangements applying in each country.

Social protection

According to the arrangements applying in each country:

10. Every worker of the European Community shall have a right to adequate social protection and shall, whatever his status and whatever the size of the undertaking in which he is employed, enjoy an adequate level of social security benefits.

Persons who have been unable either to enter or re-enter the labour market and have no means of subsistence must be able to receive sufficient resources and social assistance in keeping with their particular situation.

Freedom of association and collective bargaining

11. Employers and workers of the European Community shall have the right of association in order to constitute professional organisations or trade unions of their choice for the defence of their economic and social interests.

Every employer and every worker shall have the freedom to join or not to join such organisations without any personal or occupational damage being thereby suffered by him.

12. Employers or employers' organisations, on the one hand, and workers' organisations, on the other, shall have the right to negotiate and conclude collective agreements under the conditions laid down by national legislation and practice.

The dialogue between the two sides of industry at European level which must be developed, may, if the parties deem it desirable, result in contractual relations in particular at inter-occupational and sectoral level.

13. The right to resort to collective action in the event of a conflict of interests shall include the right to strike, subject to the obligations arising under national regulations and collective agreements.

In order to facilitate the settlement of industrial disputes the establishment and utilization at the appropriate levels of conciliation, mediation and arbitration procedures should be encouraged in accordance with national practice.

14. The internal legal order of the Member States shall determine under which conditions and to what extent the rights provided for in Articles 11 to 13 apply to the armed forces, the police and the civil service.

Vocational training

15. Every worker of the European Community must be able to have access to vocational training and to benefit therefrom throughout his working life. In the conditions governing access to such training there may be no discrimination on grounds of nationality.

The competent public authorities, undertakings or the two sides of industry, each within their own sphere of competence, should set up continuing and permanent training systems enabling every person to undergo retraining more especially through leave for training purposes, to improve his skills or to acquire new skills, particularly in the light of technical developments.

Equal treatment for men and women

16. Equal treatment for men and women must be assured. Equal opportunities for men and women must be developed.

To this end, action should be intensified to ensure the implementation of the principle of equality between men and women as regards in particular access to employment, remuneration, working conditions, social protection, education, vocational training and career development.

Measures should also be developed enabling men and women to reconcile their occupational and family obligations.

Information, consultation and participation for workers

17. Information, consultation and participation for workers must be developed along appropriate lines, taking account of the practices in force in the various Member States.

This shall apply especially in companies or groups of companies having establishments or companies in two or more Member States of the European Community.

18. Such information, consultation and participation must be implemented in due time, particularly in the following cases:

— when technological changes which, from the point of view of working conditions and work organisation, have major implications for the work-force, are introduced into undertakings;
— in connection with restructuring operations in undertakings or in cases of mergers having an impact on the employment of workers;
— in cases of collective redundancy procedures;
— when transfrontier workers in particular are affected by employment policies pursued by the undertaking where they are employed.

Health protection and safety at the workplace

19. Every worker must enjoy satisfactory health and safety conditions in his working environment. Appropriate measures must be taken in order to achieve further harmonisation of conditions in this area while maintaining the improvements made.

These measures shall take account, in particular, of the need for the training, information, consultation and balanced participation of workers as regards the risks incurred and the steps taken to eliminate or reduce them.

The provisions regarding implementation of the internal market shall help to ensure such protection.

Protection of children and adolescents

20. Without prejudice to such rules as may be more favourable to young people, in particular those ensuring their preparation for work through vocational training, and subject to derogations limited to certain light work, the minimum employment age must not be lower than the minimum school-leaving age and, in any case, not lower than 15 years.

21. Young people who are in gainful employment must receive equitable remuneration in accordance with national practice.

22. Appropriate measures must be taken to adjust labour regulations applicable to young workers so that their specific development and vocational training and access to employment needs are met.

   The duration of work must, in particular, be limited—without it being possible to circumvent this limitation through recourse to overtime—and night work prohibited in the case of workers of under 18 years of age, save in the case of certain jobs laid down in national legislation or regulations.

23. Following the end of compulsory education, young people must be entitled to receive initial vocational training of a sufficient duration to enable them to adapt to the requirements of their future working life; for young workers, such training should take place during working hours.

Elderly persons

According to the arrangements applying in each country:

24. Every worker of the European Community must, at the time of retirement, be able to enjoy resources affording him or her a decent standard of living.

25. Any person who has reached retirement age but who is not entitled to a pension or who does not have other means of subsistence, must be entitled to sufficient resources and to medical and social assistance specifically suited to his needs.

Disabled persons

26. All disabled persons, whatever the origin and nature of their disablement, must be entitled to additional concrete measures aimed at improving their social and professional integration.

   These measures must concern, in particular, according to the capacities of the beneficiaries, vocational training, ergonomics, accessibility, mobility, means of transport and housing.

TITLE II. IMPLEMENTATION OF THE CHARTER

27. It is more particularly the responsibility of the Member States, in accordance with national practices, notably through legislative measures or collective agreements, to guarantee the fundamental social rights in this Charter and to implement the social measures indispensable to the smooth operation of the internal market as part of a strategy of economic and social cohesion.

28. The European Council invites the Commission to submit as soon as possible initiatives which fall within its powers, as provided for in the Treaties, with a view to the adoption of legal instruments for the effective implementation, as and when the internal market is completed, of those rights which come within the Community's area of competence.

29. The Commission shall establish each year, during the last three months, a report on the application of the Charter by the Member States and by the European Community.

30. The report of the Commission shall be forwarded to the European Council, the European Parliament and the Economic and Social Committee.

PART III

UNITED KINGDOM SOURCES

European Communities Act 1972 (as Amended) (Extracts)

An Act to make provision in connection with the enlargement of the European Communities to include the United Kingdom, together with (for certain purposes) the Channel Islands, the Isle of Man and Gibraltar.
Be it enacted [*text omitted*] as follows:

PART I. GENERAL PROVISIONS

1 Short title and interpretation

(1) This Act may be cited as the European Communities Act 1972.

(2) In this Act 'the Communities' means the European Economic Community, the European Coal and Steel Community and the European Atomic Energy Community;
'the Treaties' or 'the Community Treaties' means [*list of relevant instruments omitted*]

2 General implementation of Treaties

(1) All such rights, powers, liabilities, obligations and restrictions from time to time created or arising by or under the Treaties, and all such remedies and procedures from time to time provided for by or under the Treaties, as in accordance with the Treaties are without further enactment to be given legal effect or used in the United Kingdom shall be recognised and available in law, and be enforced, allowed and followed accordingly; and the expression 'enforceable Community right' and similar expressions shall be read as referring to one to which this subsection applies.

(2) Subject to Schedule 2 of this Act, at any time after its passing Her Majesty may by Order in Council, and any designated Minister or department may by regulations, make provision:

(a) for the purpose of implementing any Community obligation of the United Kingdom, or of enabling any rights enjoyed or to be enjoyed by the United Kingdom under or by virtue of the Treaties to be exercised; or

(b) for the purpose of dealing with matters arising out of or related to any such obligation or rights or the coming into force, or the operation from time to time, of subsection (1) above;

and in the exercise of any statutory power or duty, including any power to give directions or to legislate by means of orders, rules, regulations or other subordinate instrument, the person entrusted with the power or duty may have regard to the objects of the Communities and to any such obligation or rights as aforesaid.

In this subsection 'designated Minister or department' means such Minister of the Crown or government department as may from time to time be designated by Order in Council in relation to any matter or for any purpose, but subject to such restrictions or conditions (if any) as may be specified by the Order in Council.

(3) There shall be charged on and issued out of the Consolidated Fund or, if so determined by the Treasury, the National Loans Fund the amounts required to meet any Community obligation to make payments to any of the Communities or Member States, or any Community obligation in respect of contributions to the

capital or reserves of the European Investment Bank or in respect of loans to the Bank, or to redeem any notes or obligations issued or created in respect of any such Community obligation; and, except as otherwise provided by or under any enactment:

(a) any other expenses incurred under or by virtue of the Treaties or this Act by any Minister of the Crown or government department may be paid out of moneys provided by Parliament; and

(b) any sums received under or by virtue of the Treaties or this Act by any Minister of the Crown or government department, save for such sums as may be required for disbursements permitted by any other enactment, shall be paid into the Consolidated Fund or, if so determined by the Treasury, the National Loans Fund.

(4) The provision that may be made under subsection (2) above includes, subject to Schedule 2 to this Act, any such provision (of any such extent) as might be made by Act of Parliament, and any enactment passed or to be passed, other than one contained in this Part of this Act, shall be construed and have effect subject to the foregoing provisions of this section; but, except as may be provided by any Act passed after this Act, Schedule 2 shall have effect in connection with the powers conferred by this and the following sections of this Act to make Orders in Council and regulations.

(5) And the references in that subsection to a Minister of the Crown or government department and to a statutory power or duty shall include a Minister or department of the Government of Northern Ireland and a power or duty arising under or by virtue of an Act of the Parliament of Northern Ireland.

(6) A law passed by the legislature of any of the Channel Islands or of the Isle of Man, or a colonial law (within the meaning of the Colonial Laws Validity Act 1865) passed or made for Gibraltar, if expressed to be passed or made in the implementation of the Treaties and of the obligations of the United Kingdom thereunder, shall not be void or inoperative by reason of any inconsistency with or repugnancy to an Act of Parliament, passed or to be passed, that extends to the Island or Gibraltar or any provision having the force and effect of an Act there (but not including this section), nor by reason of its having some operation outside the Island or Gibraltar; and any such Act or provision that extends to the Island or Gibraltar shall be construed and have effect subject to the provisions of any such law.

3 *Decisions on, and proof of, Treaties and Community instruments etc.*

(1) For the purposes of all legal proceedings any question as to the meaning or effect of any of the Treaties, or as to the validity, meaning or effect of any Community instrument, shall be treated as a question of law (and, if not referred to the European Court, be for determination as such in accordance with the principles laid down by and any relevant decision of the European Court or any court attached thereto).

(2) Judicial notice shall be taken of the Treaties, of the *Official Journal of the Communities* and of any decision of, or expression of opinion by, the European Court or any court attached thereto on any such question as aforesaid; and the *Official Journal* shall be admissible as evidence of any instrument or other act thereby communicated of any of the Communities or of any Community institution.

[*section 3(3)–(5), sections 4–12, and schedules 1, 3, and 4 omitted*]

SCHEDULE 2. PROVISIONS AS TO SUBORDINATE LEGISLATION

1 (1) The powers conferred by section 2(2) of this Act to make provision for the purposes mentioned in section 2(2)(a) and (b) shall not include power:
(a) to make any provision imposing or increasing taxation; or
(b) to make any provision taking effect from a date earlier than that of the making of the instrument containing the provision; or
(c) to confer any power to legislate by means of orders, rules, regulations or other subordinate instrument, other than rules of procedure for any court or tribunal; or
(d) to create any new criminal offence punishable with imprisonment for more than two years or punishable on summary conviction with imprisonment for more than three months or with a fine of more than level 5 on the standard scale (if not calculated on a daily basis) or with a fine of more than £100 a day.

(2) Subparagraph (1)(c) above shall not be taken to preclude the modification of a power to legislate conferred otherwise than under section 2(2), or the extension of any such power to purposes of the like nature as those for which it was conferred; and a power to give directions as to matters of administration is not to be regarded as a power to legislate within the meaning of subparagraph (1)(c).

2 (1) Subject to paragraph 3 below, where a provision contained in any section of this Act confers power to make regulations (otherwise than by modification or extension of an existing power), the power shall be exercisable by statutory instrument.

(2) Any statutory instrument containing an Order in Council or regulations made in the exercise of a power so conferred, if made without a draft having been approved by resolution of each House of Parliament, shall be subject to annulment in pursuance of a resolution of either House.

3 Nothing in paragraph 2 above shall apply to any Order in Council made by the Governor of Northern Ireland or to any regulations made by a Minister or department of the Government of Northern Ireland; but where a provision contained in any section of this Act confers power to make such an Order in Council or regulations, then any Order in Council or regulations made in the exercise of that power, if made without a draft having been approved by resolution of each House of the Parliament of Northern Ireland, shall be subject to negative resolution within the meaning of section 41 (6) of the Interpretation Act (Northern Ireland) 1954 as if the Order or regulations were a statutory instrument within the meaning of that Act.

European Parliamentary Elections Act 1978 (as Amended) (Extracts)

Be it enacted [*text omitted*] as follows:

1 *Election of MEPs*
This Act makes provision for the election in the United Kingdom of Members of the European Parliament ('MEPs').

2   *Electoral regions and number of MEPs*

(1) The United Kingdom shall be divided into electoral regions.

(2) England shall be divided into nine electoral regions.

(3) Scotland, Wales and Northern Ireland shall each constitute a single electoral region.

(4) The number of MEPs elected in the United Kingdom shall be 87, of whom
(a) 71 shall be elected for electoral regions in England,
(b) 8 shall be elected for Scotland,
(c) 5 shall be elected for Wales, and
(d) 3 shall be elected for Northern Ireland.

(5) Schedule 2 (which sets out the electoral regions in England, and makes provision for the number of MEPs to be elected for each region) shall have effect.

3   *Electoral system in Great Britain*

(1) The system of election in an electoral region in Great Britain shall be a regional list system [*details omitted*].

3A   *Electoral system in Northern Ireland*
The system of election in Northern Ireland shall be a single transferable vote system [*details omitted*].

[*sections 3B–D, 4 and 5 omitted*]

6   *Parliamentary approval of Treaties increasing Parliament's powers*

(1) No treaty which provides for any increase in the powers of the Parliament shall be ratified by the United Kingdom unless it has been approved by an Act of Parliament.

(2) In this section 'treaty' includes any international agreement, and any protocol or annex to a treaty or international agreement.

[*sections 7–9 and the Schedules omitted*]

European Communities Amendment Act 1993 (as Amended) (Extracts)[1]

Be it enacted [*text omitted*] as follows:

[*section 1 omitted*]

2   *Economic and monetary union*
No notification shall be given to the Council of the European Communities that the United Kingdom intends to move to the third stage of economic and monetary union (in accordance with the Protocol on certain provisions relating to the United Kingdom adopted at Maastricht on 7th February 1992) unless a draft of the notification has first been approved by Act of Parliament and unless Her Majesty's Government has reported to Parliament on its proposals for the co-ordination of economic policies, its role in the European Council of Finance Ministers (ECOFIN) in

---

[1] New Treaty numbers are added in square brackets.

pursuit of the objectives of Article 2 [2] of the Treaty establishing the European Community as provided for in Articles 103 [99] and 102a [100], and the work of the European Monetary Institute in preparation for economic and monetary union.

3   Annual Report by Bank of England
In implementing Article 108 [109] of the Treaty establishing the European Community, and ensuring compatibility of the statutes of the national central bank, Her Majesty's Government shall, by order, make provision for the Governor of the Bank of England to make an annual report to Parliament, which shall be subject to approval by a Resolution of each House of Parliament.

4   Information for the Commission
In implementing the provisions of Article 103(3) [99(3)] of the Treaty establishing the European Community, information shall be submitted to the Commission from the United Kingdom indicating performance on economic growth, industrial investment, employment and balance of trade, together with comparisons with those items of performance from other Member States.

5   Convergence criteria
Before submitting the information required in implementing Article 103(3) [99(3)] of the Treaty establishing the European Community, Her Majesty's Government shall report to Parliament for its approval an assessment of the medium term economic and budgetary position in relation to public investment expenditure and to the social, economic and environmental goals set out in Article 2, which report shall form the basis of any submission to the Council and Commission in pursuit of their responsibilities under Articles 103 [99] and 104c [104].

6   Committee of the Regions
A person may be proposed as a member or alternate member for the United Kingdom of the Committee of the Regions constituted under Article 198a [263] of the Treaty establishing the European Community only if, at the time of the proposal, he is an elected member of a local authority.

[sections 7 and 8 omitted]

Rules of the Supreme Court, Order 114[2]

REFERENCES TO THE EUROPEAN COURT

1   Interpretation
In this Order:
'the Court' means the court by which an order is made and includes the Court of Appeal;
'the European Court' means the Court of Justice of the European Communities; and
'order' means an order referring a question to the European Court for a preliminary ruling under Art. 177 [234] of the Treaty establishing the European Community, Art. 150 of the Treaty establishing the European Atomic Energy Community or Art. 41 of the Treaty establishing the European Coal and Steel Community or for a ruling on the interpretation of any of the instruments referred to in s. 1(1) of the Civil

---

[2] New Treaty numbers are added in square brakcets.

Jurisdiction and Judgments Act 1982 or in s. 1 of the Contracts (Applicable Law Act) 1990.

2   Making of order

(1) An order may be made by the Court of its own motion at any stage in a cause or matter, or on application by a party before or at the trial or hearing thereof.

(2) Where an application is made before the trial or hearing, it shall be made by motion.

(3) In the High Court no order shall be made except by a judge in person.

3   Schedule to order to set out request for ruling
An order shall set out in a schedule the request for the preliminary ruling of the European Court, and the Court may give directions as to the manner and form in which the schedule is to be prepared.

4   Stay of proceedings pending ruling
The proceedings in which an order is made shall, unless the Court otherwise orders, be stayed until the European Court has given a preliminary ruling on the question referred to it.

5   Transmission of order to the European Court
When an order has been made, the Senior Master shall send a copy thereof to the Registrar of the European Court; but in the case of an order made by the High Court, he shall not do so, unless the Court otherwise orders, until the time for appealing against the order has expired or, if an appeal is entered within that time, until the appeal has been determined or otherwise disposed of.

6   Appeals from orders made by High Court
An order made by the High Court shall be deemed to be a final decision, and accordingly an appeal against it shall lie to the Court of Appeal without leave; but the period within which a notice of appeal must be served under O. 59, r. 4(1), shall be 14 days.